William Mitchell Fawcett

A Compendium of the Law of Landlord and Tenant

William Mitchell Fawcett

A Compendium of the Law of Landlord and Tenant

ISBN/EAN: 9783337232795

Printed in Europe, USA, Canada, Australia, Japan

Cover: Foto ©Suzi / pixelio.de

More available books at **www.hansebooks.com**

A COMPENDIUM

OF

The Law

OF

LANDLORD AND TENANT.

BY

WILLIAM MITCHELL FAWCETT,
OF LINCOLN'S INN, ESQ., BARRISTER-AT-LAW.

LONDON:
BUTTERWORTHS, 7, FLEET STREET,
Law Publishers to the Queen's most excellent Majesty.

DUBLIN: HODGES, FOSTER & CO.   EDINBURGH: T. & T. CLARK; BELL & BRADFUTE.
CALCUTTA: THACKER, SPINK & CO.   BOMBAY: THACKER, VINING & CO.
MELBOURNE: GEORGE ROBERTSON.

1871.

LONDON:
PRINTED BY C. ROWORTH AND SONS,
NEWTON STREET, W.C.

PREFACE.

THE aim of this Volume is to present in a small compass a practical view of the existing Law of Landlord and Tenant. Matters of merely historical interest, and topics collateral to the special subject, have been systematically excluded. It has been deemed unnecessary to treat of the details of judicial procedure, or to insert a large number of precedents of leases, since the professional reader has already on his shelves works on these topics of the highest authority and value. A few simple forms of leases are, however, appended, and forms of notices, &c., will be found in the foot notes, under the respective subjects to which they relate.

The plan of the Author has been, as far as possible, to state the law in the language of the authorities by whom it was established. Hence, principles laid down by judges are generally given in their own words, and the essential words of statutes are quoted. A concise summary of the effect of each enactment is attempted in the marginal notes attached to it.

The references to Bacon's Abridgment, not mentioning any title of that work, are to the title "Leases," written by Lord Chief Baron Gilbert.

CONTENTS.

	PAGE
INDEX OF CASES CITED	ix
INDEX OF STATUTES	xxv
EXPLANATION OF ABBREVIATIONS USED	xxx
ERRATA ET ADDENDA	xxxiv

CHAP. I.

REQUISITES TO THE EXPRESS CREATION OF THE RELATION OF LANDLORD AND TENANT.

SECT. I. Property capable of being let 1
    II. Persons capable of making and taking leases 2
        (1) Restrictions arising from disability 2
        (2) Restrictions arising from limited interest 26
        (3) Restrictions arising from confidential relations .. 43
    III. An actual letting 44
    IV. Of the exclusive possession of the premises 47

CHAP. II.

THE DIFFERENT KINDS OF TENANCY.

SECT. I. Tenancy by sufferance 49
    II. Tenancy at will 50
    III. Tenancy from year to year 53
    IV. Tenancy for years 57
    V. Tenancy for life 59

CHAP. III.

THE CONTRACT OF TENANCY.

SECT. I. Agreements for leases 60
        (1) Statutory requisites 61
        (2) In what cases parol agreements are enforceable .. 62
        (3) Rights of intended lessee 64
        (4) Remedies for breach of agreement 65
        (5) Stamps 66

CONTENTS.

	PAGE
SECT. II. Leases	67
(1) Statutory requisites	67
(2) In what cases extrinsic evidence is admissible	69
(3) Form and construction of lease	71
(4) Stamps	93
(5) Counterparts and duplicates	102
(6) Matters relating to completion of lease	102

CHAP. IV.
TERMS OF TENANCY.

SECT. I. Rent	109
(1) What may be reserved as rent	109
(2) Payments which are not rent	110
(3) When rent is payable	112
(4) Where payable	115
(5) To whom payable	115
(6) Amount payable	117
(7) Apportionment	126
(8) Payment and remittance	128
(9) Effect of payment	129
(10) Remedies for recovery of rent	130
(a) Distress	131
(b) On execution against tenant	181
(c) On bankruptcy of tenant	185
(d) Action	187
II. Repairs	189
(1) Where there is no express agreement	189
(2) Where there is an express agreement	191
III. Waste	198
(1) Voluntary	198
(2) Permissive	199
(3) Remedies for	200
IV. Mode of using premises	200
(1) Where there is no express agreement	200
(2) Where there is an express agreement	202
V. Cultivation of land	207
(1) Where there is no express agreement	207
(2) Where there is an express agreement	209
VI. Fences	214
(1) Liability to repair where there is no express agreement	214
(2) Ownership of	215
VII. Trees	217
(1) Where there is no express agreement	217
(2) Where there is an express agreement	218
VIII. Insurance	220

CONTENTS.

	PAGE
SECT. IX. Taxes	223
(1) Where there is no express agreement	223
(2) Where there is an express agreement	225
X. Quiet enjoyment	229
(1) Where there is no express agreement	229
(2) Where there is an express agreement	232
XI. Underleases	235
(1) Right to underlet	235
(2) What constitutes an underlease	236
(3) Rights and liabilities of underlessee	237
XII. Assignments	239
(1) Voluntary	239
(a) Right to assign	240
(b) Mode of making assignment	244
(c) Rights and liabilities of assignee	245
(d) Grant by landlord of his reversion	252
(2) Involuntary	253
(a) On death	253
(b) On bankruptcy of lessee	256
(c) On conviction of lessee for treason or felony	258
XIII. Live stock	258
XIV. Game	259

CHAP. V.

DETERMINATION OF THE TENANCY.

SECT. I. Modes applicable to particular kinds of tenancy	262
(1) Determination of tenancy at sufferance	262
(2) Determination of tenancy at will	263
(3) Determination of tenancy from year to year	265
(a) When determinable	265
(b) Notice to quit	265
(c) Verbal disclaimer	274
(4) Determination of tenancies for optional terms of years	275
(5) Determination of tenancies for life	275
II. Modes generally applicable	277
(1) Merger	277
(2) Surrender	278
(3) Forfeiture	283
(a) Where there is no express proviso for re-entry	283
(b) Where there is an express proviso	284
(c) Waiver of forfeiture	286
(d) Relief against forfeiture	288

CHAP. VI.

TERMS OF QUITTING.

		PAGE
SECT. I. Fixtures		292
(1) What articles are fixtures		292
(2) Ownership of fixtures where there is no express agreement		293
(3) Ownership under express agreements		297
II. Emblements		298
(1) In what cases they may be claimed		298
(2) Provision as to tenants of landlords entitled for uncertain interests		299
III. Away-going crops		300
IV. Compensation for tillages, &c.		300
V. Delivery of possession		301
(1) Tenant's obligation to give possession		301
(2) Landlord's remedies for recovering possession		302
(a) Indirect		302
(b) Direct		305

APPENDIX.

FORMS OF LEASES.

I. Short statutory form	317
II. Lease in the statutory form	324
III. Lease of a house	325
IV. Lease of a farm	328
INDEX	333

INDEX OF CASES CITED.

—— v. Cooper, 112.
Abbey v. Petch, 171.
Absolom v. Knight, 119.
Adams v. Gamble, 9.
—— v. Gibney, 229.
—— v. Grane, 139.
Alchorne v. Gomme, 116, 133.
Aldenburgh v. Peaple, 150.
Alderman v. Neate, 46.
Aldridge v. Howard, 212.
Alford v. Vickery, 111, 272.
Allen v. Flicker, 167.
Amfield v. White, 226.
Anderson v. Martindale, 87.
—— v. Midland Ry. Co., 47, 52, 145.
Andrew v. Hancock, 119, 120, 121.
Andrew's Case, 230.
Andrews v. Dixon, 183.
—— v. Russell, 168.
Anon., 5.
Appleton v. Campbell, 201.
—— v. Doily, 135.
Archbold v. Scully, 151.
Arden v. Pullen, 190.
—— v. Sullivan, 56.
Arnitt v. Garnett, 183.
Arnsby v. Woodward, 284, 286.
Ashfield v. Ashfield, 5.
Attack v. Bramwell, 155, 175, 179.
Attersol v. Stevens, 199.
Att.-Gen. v. Brentwood School, 2.
—— v. Fullerton, 217.
—— v. Stephens, 217.
—— v. Great Yarmouth, 22.
Aubrey v. Fisher, 217.
Augustien v. Challis, 184.
Auriol v. Mills, 250.
Auworth v. Johnson, 189.
Aveline v. Whisson, 103.
Avenell v. Croker, 157, 168.
Avery v. Cheslyn, 294.
Aylet v. Dodd, 118.
Aylett v. Ashton, 9.
Aylward v. Kearney, 44.

BACH v. Meats, 148, 149.
Bachelour v. Gage, 250.
Baggallay v. Pettit, 87.
Bagge v. Mawby, 158.
Bagshawe v. Goward, 162.
Baker v. Davis, 120.
—— v. Gostling, 237.
—— v. Greenhill, 226.
—— v. Holtpzaffel, 124.
—— v. Meryweather, 106.
Ball v. Cullimore, 51, 264.
Bamford v. Creasy, 291.
Bandy v. Cartwright, 229.
Bannister v. Hyde, 155, 163.
Barber v. Brown, 117.
—— v. Whiteley, 215.
Bargent v. Thompson, 290.
Barker v. Barker, 197.
Barlow v. Rhodes, 76.
Barnard v. Godscall, 250.
Barnfather v. Jordan, 249.
Barrow v. Ashburnham, 260.
Barrs v. Lea, 110, 112.
Barry v. Goodman, 97.
—— v. Stanton, 241.
Barwick's Case, 82.
Barwick v. Foster, 113.
—— v. Thompson, 42.
Baston v. Carew, 310.
Bastow & Co., In re, 143.
Baylis v. Dinely, 5.
—— v. Le Gros, 194.
Bayliss v. Fisher, 157.
Bateman v. Allen, 11.
Baumann v. James, 62.
Baxter v. Browne, 46.
—— v. Portsmouth, 9.
Bayly, Ex parte, 186.
Bayley v. Bradley, 49.
Baylye v. Offord, 247.
Bayne v. Walker, 190.
Baynes v. Smith, 141.
Beale v. Sanders, 54.
Bealey v. Stuart, 206.
Beardmore v. Wilson, 237.

INDEX OF CASES CITED.

Beaty v. Gibbons, 214.
Beaudeley v. Brook, 69.
Beaufort v. Bates, 196.
Beavan v. Delahay, 150.
―― v. M'Donnell, 9.
Beck v. Rebow, 294.
Belasyse v. Burbridge, 138.
Belcher v. M'Intosh, 193.
Belfour v. Weston, 124.
Bennett v. Bayes, 154.
―― v. Ireland, 53, 56, 125.
―― v. Robins, 134.
―― v. Womack, 84, 86.
Benson v. Gibson, 118.
Berney v. Moore, 237.
Berrey v. Lindley, 57, 268.
Berriman v. Peacock, 217, 218.
Bertie v. Beaumont, 48.
Bethell v. Blencowe, 270.
Bettisworth's Case, 76.
Bicknell v. Hood, 45.
Biggins v. Goode, 180, 181.
Bignell v. Clarke, 162.
Birch v. Dawson, 294.
―― v. Stephenson, 118, 212.
―― v. Wright, 235, 264.
Bird v. Defonvielle, 231, 269.
―― v. Elwes, 192.
―― v. Higginson, 69.
Birkbeck v. Paget, 260.
Bishop of Bath's Case, 81.
―――― Salisbury's Case, 18.
Bishop v. Bryant, 167.
―― v. Elliott, 294, 298.
―― v. Goodwin, 123.
―― v. Howard, 54.
Bisset v. Caldwell, 141.
Blades v. Arundale, 141.
Blake v. Foster, 135.
Blatchford v. Cole, 304.
―― v. Plymouth, 232.
Bleakley v. Smith, 61.
Bliss v. Collins, 128.
Blount v. Pearman, 97.
Blunden's Case, 113.
Blyth v. Dennett, 273, 274.
Boardman v. Mostyn, 63.
Boase v. Jackson, 97.
Bolton v. Tomlin, 53, 54.
Bond v. Rosling, 68.
Boodle v. Cambell, 122, 126.
Boone v. Eyre, 87.
―― v. Mitchell, 96.
Booth v. Macfarlane, 305.
Boraston v. Green, 150.
Boroughes' Case, 115.
Boulton v. Reynolds, 166.
Bowen v. Owen, 167.

Bowers v. Cator, 63.
―― v. Nixon, 118.
Bowes v. Croll, 56, 57.
Boyce v. Tamlyn, 215.
Boyd v. Profaze, 155.
Bradburne v. Botfield, 87.
Bradbury v. Wright, 84.
Braddyl v. Ball, 178.
Bramston v. Robins, 120, 122.
Brandon v. Brandon, 134.
Branscombe v. Bridges, 154, 157.
Brashier v. Jackson, 45.
Braythwayte v. Hitchcock, 51, 53, 55.
Brecknock Co. v. Pritchard, 192.
Brett v. Cumberland, 250.
Brewster v. Kitchel, 226.
Bridges v. Potts, 57, 265, 266.
Briggs v. Sowry, 186.
Brocklehurst v. Lawe, 186.
Brocklington v. Saunders, 57, 301.
Bromley v. Holden, 147.
Brooke v. Noakes, 147.
Brown v. Arundell, 139.
―― v. Burtinshaw, 280.
―― v. Crump, 207, 208.
―― v. Glenn, 155.
―― v. Quilter, 191.
―― v. Shevill, 139.
―― v. Storey, 41.
―― v. Trumper, 58, 196.
Browne v. Joddrell, 8.
―― v. Powell, 115, 166.
―― v. Raban, 86.
―― v. Warner, 45.
Browning v. Dann, 155.
Brudnell's Case, 82.
Bryan v. Weatherhead, 76.
Buck v. Nurton, 76.
Buckland v. Butterfield, 293, 294.
―― v. Papillon, 59, 86, 257.
Buckley v. Taylor, 112, 132.
Buckworth v. Simpson, 255.
Bullen v. Denning, 77, 78.
Bullock v. Dommitt, 192.
Bulwer v. Bulwer, 298.
Burdett v. Withers, 193.
Burling v. Read, 306.
Burnett v. Lynch, 229, 251.
Burrows v. Gradin, 116, 133.
Burt v. Haslett, 297.
Burton v. Barclay, 79, 245, 277.
Buszard v. Capel, 144.
Bute v. Thompson, 123.
Butler v. Mulvihill, 44.
―― v. Swinnerton, 232.
Buxton v. Lister, 65, 66.

CADBY v. Martinez, 275.
Cadle v. Moody, 281.
Caldecott v. Smythies, 300, 301.
Calvert v. Sebright, 232.
Calvin's Case, 2.
Camden v. Batterbury, 47.
Campbell v. Hooper, 9.
——— v. Lewis, 247.
——— v. Wenlock, 202.
Cannan v. Hartley, 280.
Cannock v. Jones, 84, 195.
Canterbury v. Reg., 190.
Capel v. Buszard, 144.
Carden v. Tuck, 75.
Cardigan v. Armitage, 77, 79.
Carew v. Cooper, 2.
Carpenter v. Colins, 240, 264.
——— v. Cresswell, 87.
Carter v. Carter, 121.
——— v. Cummins, 125.
Cartwright v. Smith, 146.
Castleman v. Hicks, 160.
Cattley v. Arnold, 53.
Chadwick v. Clarke, 66.
——— v. Marsden, 77.
Chancellor v. Poole, 249.
Chandler v. Doulton, 157.
Chandos v. Talbot, 217.
Channon v. Patch, 218.
Chapman v. Beecham, 80.
——— v. Bluck, 46, 72.
——— v. Towner, 45, 53.
Chappell v. Gregory, 190.
Cheetham v. Hampson, 215.
Child v. Chamberlain, 174.
Christ's Hospital v. Harrild, 226.
Christy v. Tancred, 302.
Church v. Brown, 86, 88, 236, 240.
Churchill v. Evans, 215.
Claridge v. Mackenzie, 130.
Clark, In re, 2.
——— v. Calvert, 138.
——— v. Gaskarth, 138.
——— v. Glasgow Ass. Co., 192.
Clarke v. Fuller, 44, 61.
——— v. Holford, 113, 132.
——— v. Roystone, 208, 301.
——— v. Westrope, 213.
Clayton's Case, 80.
Clayton v. Blakey, 53, 68.
——— v. Burtenshaw, 44, 45.
——— v. Gregson, 71.
——— v. Illingworth, 66.
Clegg v. Rowland, 199.
Clements v. Lambert, 76.
——— v. Welles, 238.
Clennel v. Read, 120.
Clifton v. Walmesley, 124.

Climie v. Wood, 295.
Clinan v. Cooke, 62.
Close v. Wilberforce, 245.
Clun's Case, 113, 114.
Cobb v. Stokes, 81, 303, 304.
Cocker v. Musgrove, 184.
Cockson v. Cock, 247.
Codd v. Brown, 301.
Coe v. Clay, 229, 230.
Coker v. Guy, 70.
Colbron v. Travers, 225.
Cole v. Forth, 199.
——— v. Green, 199.
——— v. West London, &c. Ry. Co., 75.
Coleman v. Foster, 47.
Coles v. Trecothick, 31.
Collen v. Gardiner, 31.
Collett v. Curling, 112, 266.
Colley v. Streeton, 239.
Collins and Harding's Case, 126, 127.
——— v. Harding, 110.
——— v. Crouch, 255.
Collison v. Lettsom, 249.
Colton v. Lingham, 58.
Colyer v. Speer, 182, 183.
Congham v. King, 246.
Cooke v. Cholmondeley, 75.
——— v. Claynorth, 44.
——— v. Yates, 75.
Coomber v. Howard, 112.
Coombes v. Dutton, 93.
Cooper, Ex parte, 32.
——— v. Blandy, 42.
——— v. Twibill, 205.
Copeland v. Stephens, 107.
Corder v. Drakeford, 97.
Cornish v. Cleife, 194.
——— v. Searrell, 43, 129.
——— v. Stubbs, 47, 54.
Cosser v. Collinge, 238.
Coster v. Cowling, 97.
Cotesworth v. Spokes, 285.
Cotton's Case, 15.
Couch v. Goodman, 103.
Counter v. Macpherson, 195.
Coupland v. Maynard, 149.
Courtown v. Ward, 218.
Cowan v. Milbourn, 201.
Coward v. Gregory, 193, 194, 195.
Cowper v. Fletcher, 30.
Cox v. Bent, 52, 53.
——— v. Bishop, 245.
——— v. Knight, 129.
——— v. Painter, 159.
——— v. Slater, 62.
Cramer v. Mott, 137, 156.
Creak v. Justices of Brighton, 310.

Crisp v. Churchill, 201.
Crocker v. Fothergill, 315.
Croft v. Lumley, 89, 90, 287.
Cromwell v. Andrews, 114.
Crosier v. Tomkinson, 140.
Cross v. Eglin, 77.
—— v. Jordan, 286.
Crossfield v. Morrison, 251.
Crowley v. Vitty, 118.
Crowther v. Ramsbottom, 165.
Crusoe v. Bugby, 236, 241.
Cubitt v. Porter, 216.
Culling v. Tuffnall, 293, 295.
Cumberland v. Bowes, 213.
—— v. Glamis, 54.
Cumming v. Bedborough, 120.
Curtis v. Hubbard, 154.
—— v. Spitty, 246.
—— v. Wheeler, 136.
Cuthbertson v. Irving, 42, 43.
Cutting v. Derby, 114, 303.

DAKIN v. Cope, 284.
Dalby v. Hirst, 208, 301.
Dallman v. King, 124.
Dancer v. Hastings, 134.
Dane v. Kirkwall, 8.
Daniel v. Gracie, 83, 110, 131, 132.
Daniels v. Davison, 62, 264.
Dann v. Spurrier, 29, 63, 275.
Darby v. Harris, 138.
Darcy v. Askwith, 199.
Davies v. Powell, 140.
Davis v. Eyton, 88, 298.
—— v. Gyde, 129.
—— v. Jones, 295.
—— v. Shepherd, 77.
Davison v. Gent, 281.
—— v. Stanley, 280.
—— v. Wilson, 306.
Dawson v. Cropp, 158.
—— v. Dyer, 234.
—— v. Massey, 44.
De Medina v. Polson, 54.
Dean v. Allalley, 293.
Dean and Chapter of Bristol v. Jones, 195.
—————— —————— Windsor's Case, 247.
Delaney v. Fox, 42.
Denby v. Moore, 119, 120.
Dendy v. Nicholl, 286.
Denn v. Cartwright, 81, 265.
—— v. Fearnside, 51.
Denton v. Richmond, 118.
Descarlett v. Dennett, 291.
Descharmes, *Ex parte*, 186.

Dibble v. Bowater, 114, 132, 149.
Digby v. Atkinson, 54, 55, 192, 193.
Dinsdale v. Iles, 263.
Dixon v. Geldard, 218.
—— v. Harrison, 135.
Dobbyn v. Somers, 69, 76.
Dod v. Monger, 156, 164.
Dodd v. Acklom, 115, 279, 280.
Doe v. Abel, 93.
—— v. Adams, 42.
—— v. Allen, 286.
—— v. Amey, 53, 54, 56, 57.
—— v. Archer, 28, 269.
—— v. Ashburner, 45, 46.
—— v. Austin, 42, 102.
—— v. Bancks, 284.
—— v. Batten, 273, 304.
—— v. Baytup, 42.
—— v. Bell, 53, 54, 68, 267, 268.
—— v. Benham, 110.
—— v. Benjamin, 46.
—— v. Benson, 71, 113.
—— v. Bevan, 241, 257.
—— v. Biggs, 267.
—— v. Birch, 284, 287.
—— v. Bird, 194, 197, 203, 220.
—— v. Bond, 91.
—— v. Bonsfield, 29.
—— v. Bridges, 17.
—— v. Browne, 270.
—— v. Burt, 70, 76.
—— v. Butcher, 28.
—— v. Butler, 269.
—— v. Calvert, 273.
—— v. Carew, 89.
—— v. Carter, 235, 241.
—— v. Cartwright, 44.
—— v. Cawdor, 274.
—— v. Chamberlain, 51.
—— v. Clare, 45.
—— v. Clarke, 45, 58, 129.
—— v. Collinge, 17, 53.
—— v. Collins, 75.
—— v. Cooper, 274.
—— v. Courtenay, 280.
—— v. Cox, 50, 52.
—— d. Cox, 269.
—— v. Crago, 55.
—— v. Crick, 269, 272.
—— v. Crouch, 219.
—— v. David, 90.
—— v. Davies, 52, 88.
—— v. Davis, 298.
—— v. Day, 80, 108.
—— v. Derry, 48.
—— v. Dixon, 275.
—— v. Dobell, 267.
—— v. Dodd, 59, 72, 82.

INDEX OF CASES CITED. xiii

Doe v. Donovan, 266.
— v. Dyson, 286.
— v. Edwards, 42.
— v. Elsam, 89, 203, 205.
— v. Evans, 274.
— v. Eykins, 287.
— v. Eyre, 9.
— v. Forster, 267.
— v. Forwood, 271.
— v. Foster, 47, 53, 269.
— v. Francis, 55.
— v. Frowd, 274.
— v. Fuller, 42.
— v. Galloway, 74.
— v. Gardiner, 52.
— v. Geekie, 55.
— v. Gladwin, 221, 222.
— v. Godwin, 89.
— v. Goldwin, 269, 270.
— v. Gower, 274.
— v. Grafton, 266.
— v. Greathed, 74.
— v. Green, 81, 265.
— v. Groves, 51.
— v. Grubb, 274.
— v. Guest, 205.
— v. Hall, 272.
— v. Hayes, 30.
— v. Hazell, 266.
— v. Hiscocks, 70.
— v. Hobson, 96.
— v. Houghton, 104.
— v. Howard, 268.
— v. Hughes, 268, 271.
— v. Hulme, 271.
— v. Humphreys, 273.
— v. Ingleby, 90.
— v. Jackson, 51, 194.
— v. Jenkins, 28.
— v. Jepson, 91.
— v. Jersey, 74.
— v. Johnson, 268.
— v. Jones, 50, 91, 194, 263, 287.
— v. Keeling, 203.
— v. Kennard, 93.
— v. Kneller, 83, 91.
— v. Lambley, 267.
— v. Laming, 220, 236, 241.
— v. Lawder, 49, 262.
— v. Lawrence, 88.
— v. Lea, 71.
— v. Lewis, 96, 194.
— v. Lines, 268.
— v. Long, 274.
— v. Lucas, 272.
— v. Mainby, 265.
— v. Maisey, 262.
— v. Marchetti, 89.

Doe v. Martin, 76.
— v. Masters, 284.
— v. Matthews, 268.
— v. Meylor, 126.
— v. Miles, 48.
— v. Miller, 51.
— v. Mills, 42.
— v. Milward, 273.
— v. M'Kaeg, 50.
— v. Moffatt, 53, 54.
— v. Morse, 54, 110.
— v. Murrell, 262.
— v. Ongley, 42, 271.
— v. Palmer, 273.
— v. Parker, 283.
— v. Pasquali, 274.
— v. Paul, 285.
— v. Peck, 220, 286.
— v. Phillips, 93.
— v. Poole, 280.
— v. Porter, 254.
— v. Powell, 45, 46, 242.
— v. Price, 219, 263.
— v. Pritchard, 88, 90, 286.
— v. Pyke, 282.
— v. Quigley, 49, 51.
— v. Raffan, 55, 266.
— v. Ramsbotham, 42.
— v. Read, 271.
— v. Rees, 88, 286.
— v. Reid, 205.
— v. Rhodes, 268.
— v. Ries, 46.
— v. Roberts, 5.
— v. Rock, 51, 264.
— v. Roe, 106, 245, 285.
— v. Rollings, 274.
— v. Rowe, 221.
— v. Rowlands, 197.
— v. Samuel, 268.
— v. Sandham, 86.
— v. Shewin, 220, 221.
— v. Slight, 106.
— v. Smaridge, 265.
— v. Smith, 45, 53, 92, 241, 257, 269.
— v. Snowdon, 265, 268.
— v. Somerton, 272.
— v. Spence, 268.
— v. Spiller, 269.
— v. Spry, 203, 205.
— v. Stagg, 279.
— v. Stanion, 274.
— v. Stapleton, 268.
— v. Steel, 269, 273.
— v. Stennett, 52.
— v. Stevens, 87, 89.
— v. Steward, 58.

INDEX OF CASES CITED.

Doe v. Stratton, 54.
— v. Summersett, 271.
— v. Sutton, 193.
— v. Taniere, 18, 53.
— v. Thomas, 264, 281.
— v. Thompson, 41, 274.
— v. Timothy, 269.
— v. Tressider, 29.
— v. Turford, 272.
— v. Turner, 262, 264.
— v. Ulph, 220.
— v. Walker, 107, 278.
— v. Walters, 270.
— v. Watkins, 268, 272.
— v. Watson, 42.
— v. Watt, 88, 284.
— v. Watts, 28, 52, 53, 54.
— v. Weller, 12, 112, 267.
— v. Wells, 283.
— v. Whittick, 274.
— v. Wilkinson, 130, 269.
— v. Williams, 86.
— v. Wood, 52, 53, 55, 72.
— v. Woodbridge, 203, 287.
— v. Woodman, 272.
— v. Worsley, 236.
— v. Wrightman, 267, 269, 271.
— v. Yarborough, 18.
Dollen v. Batt, 253.
Donellan v. Read, 111.
Doughty v. Bowman, 247, 248.
Dowell v. Dew, 64.
Dowse v. Earle, 194.
Drake v. Mitchell, 129.
— v. Munday, 72, 83, 84.
Drant v. Brown, 66.
Draper v. Crofts, 302.
— v. Thompson, 153.
Drury v. Macnamara, 230.
— v. Molins, 211.
Duck v. Braddyll, 96, 139.
Dudley v. Folliott, 233.
— v. Warde, 294.
Dumergue v. Rumsey, 297.
Dunk v. Hunter, 45, 111, 131.
Duppa v. Mayo, 114.
Dyer v. Bowley, 121.
Dyne v. Nutley, 74.

EAGLETON v. Gutteridge, 97, 137, 155.
Easterby v. Sampson, 84.
Ecclesiastical Commissioners v. Merral, 14.
Eccleston v. Clipsham, 87.
Edge v. Strafford, 61, 68, 108, 188.
Edmondson v. Nuttall, 179.

Edwards v. Rees, 122.
Eldridge v. Stacey, 154, 155, 168.
Elliott v. Johnson, 246.
Elwes v. Maw, 295.
Elworthy v. Sandford, 105.
Empson v. Soden, 294.
England v. Slade, 42.
Enys v. Donnithorne, 79.
Etherton v. Popplewell, 159, 165.
Evans, In re, 3.
——— v. Elliot, 41, 133, 166.
——— v. Roberts, 61, 298.
——— v. Vaughan, 233.
——— v. Wright, 170.
Ewart v. Graham, 261.
Ewer v. Moyle, 126.
Exhall Coal Co., In re, 143.

FABIAN v. Winston, 285.
Farewell v. Dickinson, 110.
Farrall v. Hilditch, 84.
Farrance v. Elkington, 305.
Farrant v. Olmius, 118.
Farrell v. Davenport, 63.
Faviell v. Gaskoin, 301.
Fenner v. Duplock, 180.
Fenny v. Child, 45, 72.
Fenton v. Logan, 143.
Feret v. Hill, 201.
Ferguson v. ———, 189, 190.
——— v. Cornish, 58.
Festing v. Taylor, 225.
Few v. Perkins, 195.
Field v. Adams, 140.
——— v. Mitchell, 157.
Fielden v. Tattersall, 213.
Filliter v. Phippard, 190.
Finch v. Miller, 54, 112, 167.
Findon v. M'Laren, 139.
Finlay v. Bristol and Exeter Ry. Co., 14, 55.
Fisher v. Algar, 172.
——— v. Dixon, 294.
Fitzmaurice v. Bayley, 52, 62.
Fleming v. Snook, 210.
Fletcher v. Marillier, 148.
——— v. Saunders, 167.
Flight v. Barton, 238.
Foley v. Addenbrooke, 88, 206, 297.
Foquet v. Moor, 111, 280.
Ford v. Tiley, 65.
Fordham v. Ackers, 177.
Forster v. Cookson, 181.
——— v. Rowland, 61, 65.
Foulger v. Taylor, 148.
Fowell v. Tranter, 275.
Fowkes v. Joyce, 140.

Fowle v. Freeman, 61.
—— v. Welsh, 233.
Frame v. Dawson, 63, 64.
Francis v. Wigzell, 9.
—— v. Wyatt, 140.
Franklin v. Carter, 119.
Franklinski v. Ball, 41.
Freeman v. Rosher, 153.
—— v. West, 82.
French v. Phillips, 152.
Frosel v. Welsh, 29.
Frusher v. Lee, 171.
Fuller v. Abbot, 119, 225.
Fulmerstone v. Steward, 280.
Furneaux v. Fotherby and Clark, 149.

GABELL v. Shevell, 119.
Gale v. Bates, 212.
Gandy v. Jubber, 191, 215.
Gange v. Lockwood, 194.
Gardiner v. Colyer, 261.
—— v. Williamson, 69, 110.
Garrard v. Frankel, 69.
Gas Light Co. v. Turner, 201.
Gaskell v. King, 225.
Gauntlett v. King, 153.
Gawler v. Chaplin, 183.
Gerrard v. Clifton, 124.
Gethin v. Wilks, 185.
Gibson v. Holland, 61.
—— v. Ireson, 139.
Giddens v. Dodd, 275.
Gilbertson v. Richards, 112.
Giles v. Spencer, 151.
Gilham v. Arkwright, 148.
Gillingham v. Gwyer, 144.
Gilman v. Elton, 139.
Gingell v. Purkins, 73.
Girardy v. Richardson, 201.
Gisbourn v. Hurst, 140.
Gladman v. Plumer, 137.
Glynn v. Thomas, 151, 152.
Goddard's Case, 73.
Goodland v. Blewitt, 115.
Goodright v. Cordwent, 273.
—— v. Richardson, 58, 81.
—— v. Vivian, 199.
Goodtitle v. Herbert, 51.
Goodwin v. Longhurst, 29.
Goodwyn v. Cheveley, 144.
Gore v. Lloyd, 45.
Gorely, *Ex parte*, 222, 223.
Gorton v. Falkner, 137, 138, 143.
Gott v. Gandy, 190.
Gough v. Howard, 208.
Gould v. Bradstock, 154.

Gower v. Hunt, 119.
Grace, *Ex parte*, 44.
Graham v. Allsopp, 122.
—— v. Wade, 228.
—— v. Whichelo, 280.
Granger v. Collins, 208, 229.
Grant v. Ellis, 150, 187.
Graves v. Weld, 298.
Gray v. Bompas, 273.
—— v. Friar, 58.
Great Ship Co., *In re*, 143.
Green v. Eales, 196.
—— v. Jenkins, 17.
Green's Settled Estates, *Re*, 35.
Greenaway v. Adams, 236.
Greenslade v. Tapscott, 236.
Greenwood v. Tyber, 82.
Gregg v. Coates, 192.
Gregory v. Doidge, 130.
—— v. Mighell, 63.
—— v. Wilson, 291.
Griffenhoofe v. Daubuz, 120.
Griffin v. Scott, 172.
Griffith v. Hodges, 231.
Griffiths v. Rigby, 206.
Grimman v. Legge, 279, 280.
Grissell v. Robinson, 106.
Grosvenor v. Hampstead Junction Ry. Co., 75.
Grove, *Ex parte*, 186.
Grute v. Locroft, 12.
Grymes v. Boweren, 294.
—— v. Peacock, 76.
Gudgen v. Besset, 103.
Gunter v. Halsey, 64.
Gutteridge v. Munyard, 192, 204.
Guy v. West, 216.
Gwillim v. Stone, 64.
Gwinnet v. Phillips, 165.
Gwynne v. Maynstone, 81.

HABERDASHERS' CO. v. Isaac, 88, 236.
Haines v. Burnett, 86.
—— v. Welch, 299.
Haldane v. Johnson, 115.
Hall v. Ball, 105.
—— v. Burgess, 188, 231.
—— v. Chandless, 105.
—— v. City of London Brewery Co., 229.
—— v. Denbigh, 73.
—— v. Lund, 71.
—— v. Sebright, 72.
Hallifax v. Chambers, 207.
Hamerton v. Stead, 51, 281.

Hamilton v. Clanricarde, 31.
Hammond v. Mather, 286.
Hancock v. Austin, 47, 111, 154, 155.
——— v. Caffyn, 46, 47, 230.
Harding v. Crethorn, 281, 302.
——— v. Wilson, 76, 77.
Hare v. Groves, 85, 124.
Harley v. King, 251.
Harnett v. Maitland, 190, 200.
Harper v. Taswell, 169.
Harrington v. Wise, 83, 284.
Harris v. Davis, 3.
——— v. Jones, 191.
——— v. Shipway, 129.
Harrison v. Barnby, 117.
——— v. Barry, 132, 172.
——— v. Blackburn, 107, 108.
——— v. Jackson, 31.
——— v. North, 125.
Hart v. Leach, 175.
——— v. Windsor, 125, 202.
Hartshorne v. Watson, 284.
Harvey v. Bridges, 306.
——— v. Pocock, 179.
Harvy v. Thomas, 12.
Haseler v. Lemoyne, 153.
Hatch v. Hale, 154, 166.
Havens v. Middleton, 221.
Hawkins v. Rutt, 129.
——— v. Sherman, 245.
Hayling v. Okey, 299.
Hayne v. Cummings, 68, 88.
Hayward v. Haswell, 46.
——— v. Parke, 238.
Heald v. Hay, 2.
Heap v. Barton, 297.
Hearn v. Allen, 76.
——— v. Tomlin, 51.
Heckman v. Isaac, 220.
Hegan v. Johnson, 111.
Hegarty v. Milne, 66.
Hellawell v. Eastwood, 139, 293.
Hellier v. Casbard, 83.
Hemingway v. Fernandes, 248.
Hemming v. Brabazon, 15.
Henderson v. Hay, 86.
——— v. Mears, 231.
——— v. Squire, 302.
Henson v. Cooper, 70.
Herlakenden's Case, 218.
Herne v. Benbow, 199.
Hersey v. Giblett, 59.
Hewitt v. Isham, 78.
Hewson v. South Western Ry. Co., 75.
Hey v. Wyche, 221.
Heywood v. Cope, 65.

Hickman v. Isaacs, 204.
Hickman v. Machin, 116.
Hicks v. Downing, 237.
Hill v. Barclay, 291.
——— v. Grange, 113.
——— v. Ramm, 97.
——— v. Saunders, 135.
Hillary v. Gay, 305.
Hills v. Rowland, 211.
Hilton v. Goodhind, 118.
——— v. Green, 260.
Hinchcliffe v. Kinnoul, 76.
Hinde v. Gray, 203.
Hindle v. Pollitt, 214.
Hirst v. Horn, 303.
Hitchcock v. Coker, 203.
Hitchings v. Thompson, 130.
Hoby v. Roebuck, 111.
Hodgson v. Gascoigne, 182.
Holcombe v. Hewson, 205.
Holder v. Coates, 218.
Holding v. Pigott, 300.
Holland v. Bird, 154, 166.
——— v. Cole, 241.
——— v. Palser, 83.
Hollis v. Carr, 84.
Holmes v. Blogg, 5.
Holtzapffel v. Baker, 124.
Hood v. Kendall, 211.
Hooper, Ex parte, 63.
——— v. Clark, 246, 248.
Hopkins v. Helmore, 114.
Hopwood v. Whaley, 255.
Horner v. Graves, 203.
Hornidge v. Wilson, 255.
Horsefall v. Davy, 147.
——— v. Mather, 189, 190.
——— v. Testar, 194, 195.
Horseford v. Webster, 151.
Hoskins v. Knight, 182.
Houghton v. Kœnig, 102.
House v. Laxton, 73.
How v. Greek, 104.
——— v. Kennett, 188.
Howard v. Shaw, 51.
——— v. Wood, 2.
Howe v. Scarrott, 135.
Huffell v. Armitstead, 266.
Hughes v. Clark, 102.
——— v. Richman, 211.
Huguenin v. Basely, 44.
Humble v. Langston, 250, 251.
Humphreys v. Franks, 267.
Hunt v. Allgood, 274.
Hunter v. Hunt, 239.
——— v. Miller, 211.
Hurleston v. Woodroffe, 76.
Hurst v. Hurst, 226, 229.

INDEX OF CASES CITED. xvii

Hutchins v. Chambers, 158.
——— v. Scott, 114, 156.
Hutton v. Warren, 200, 208, 301.
Hyatt v. Griffiths, 54, 57.
Hyde v. Hill, 120, 228.

IBBETT v. De La Salle, 153.
Ibbs v. Richardson, 302.
Iggulden v. May, 83, 86, 229.
Inman v. Stamp, 61.
Ive v. Sams, 78, 280.
Izon v. Gorton, 124.

JACKSON v. Oglander, 62.
Jacob v. King, 176.
Jacomb v. Harwood, 30.
James v. Dean, 254, 264.
——— v. Emery, 87.
——— v. Jenkins, 28.
Jeffryes v. Evans, 79, 232, 260, 261.
Jenkins v. Church, 28.
——— v. Gething, 293.
——— v. Green, 77, 78.
Jenner v. Clegg, 111, 273.
——— v. Yolland, 144, 170.
Jenney v. Brook, 78.
Jennings v. Major, 106.
——— v. Throgmorton, 201.
Jervis v. Tomkinson, 80, 123.
Jesus Coll. v. Gibbs, 15.
Jinks v. Edwards, 280.
John v. Jenkins, 45, 148.
Johnson v. Edgware, Highgate and London Ry. Co., 92.
——— v. Jones, 116, 121.
——— v. Upham, 158, 166.
Johnstone v. Hudlestone, 304.
Jolly v. Arbuthnot, 43, 134.
Jones v. Bone, 205.
——— v. Carter, 267.
——— v. Davies, 278.
——— v. Green, 118.
——— v. Hamp, 171.
——— v. Jones, 135.
——— v. Marsh, 271.
——— v. Mills, 266, 274.
——— v. Nixon, 58, 265.
——— v. Phipps, 270, 271.
——— v. Reynolds, 45, 47, 72.
——— v. Shears, 206, 273.
——— v. Thorne, 204.
Joule v. Jackson, 140.
Jourdain v. Wilson, 247.

F.

KEATES v. Cadogan, 202.
Keech v. Hall, 41, 64.
Keen v. Priest, 143, 144, 176, 179.
Keightley v. Watson, 87.
Kelly v. Coote, 5.
Kemp v. Derrett, 266.
——— v. Sober, 203.
Kendall v. Hill, 86.
Kenney v. May, 168.
Kerby v. Harding, 163, 164.
Kerslake v. White, 76.
Ketsey's Case, 4, 5.
Kine v. Balfe, 63.
King v. England, 171, 172.
Kingdon v. Nottle, 254.
Kingsbury v. Collins, 298, 299.
Kintrea v. Perston, 252.
Kirtland v. Pounsett, 51.
Kirton v. Elliott, 5.
Knight v. Benett, 53, 131, 150.
——— v. Egerton, 180, 181.
——— v. Mory, 241.
Knotts v. Curtis, 180.
Kooystra v. Lucas, 77.

LACEY v. Lear, 305.
Ladd v. Thomas, 166.
Laing's Trust, In re, 35.
Lambert v. Norris, 111.
Lancaster v. De Trafford, 62.
Langford v. Selmes, 112.
Lant v. Norris, 84.
Lanyon v. Carne, 110.
Latham v. Attwood, 298.
Lawrance v. Faux, 281.
Lawton v. Lawton, 294.
——— v. Salmon, 294.
Lay v. Mottram, 85.
Laycock v. Tuffnell, 119.
Laythoarp v. Bryant, 61.
Leach v. Thomas, 189, 190, 294.
Leader v. Homewood, 296.
Lear v. Caldicott, 158.
Leather Cloth Co. v. Lorsont, 203.
Lee v. Cooke, 158.
——— v. Smith, 53, 54, 57, 132.
Leeds v. Cheetham, 124, 191.
Legh v. Heald, 78.
——— v. Hewitt, 207, 208.
——— v. Lillie, 118, 213.
Lehmann v. M'Arthur, 242.
Leigh v. Shepherd, 136.
Le Keux v. Nash, 249.
Lester v. Foxcroft, 62.
Lewes v. Ridge, 246.
Lewis v. Read, 153.
Liebenrood v. Vines, 211.

b

Liford's Case, 78.
Line v. Stephenson, 230.
Lingham v. Warren, 158.
Lloyd v. Cheetham, 2.
—— v. Crisp, 243.
—— v. Rosbec, 302.
Loader v. Kemp, 197.
Lock v. Furze, 235.
Locke v. Matthews, 263.
Lockier v. Paterson, 175.
Lofft v. Dennis, 124, 191.
London v. Greyme, 199.
—— v. Southwell, 78.
London and N. W. Ry. Co. v. Garnett, 204.
London and N. W. Ry. Co. v. West, 42.
London Cotton Co., In re, 143.
Loring v. Warburton, 166.
Love v. Pares, 219.
Lovelock v. Franklyn, 72, 97.
Lowe v. Griffith, 6.
—— v. Ross, 108, 188.
Lowndes v. Fountain, 213.
Lucas v. Comerford, 245.
—— v. Tarleton, 172, 180, 181.
Ludford v. Barber, 28.
Luxmore v. Robson, 193.
Lyde v. Russell, 296.
Lyon v. Reed, 280.
—— v. Tomkies, 169.
—— v. Weldon, 168.
Lyster v. Brown, 147.

MACHER v. Foundling Hospital, 204.
Maddon v. White, 4.
Maitland v. Mackinnon, 76.
Makin v. Watkinson, 197.
Mallam v. Arden, 113.
Mallory's Case, 113.
Malpas v. Ackland, 30.
Mann v. Lovejoy, 53, 54.
Manning v. Fitzgerald, 74.
—— v. Lunn, 226.
Mansfield v. Blackburn, 297.
Marson v. London, Chatham and Dover Ry. Co., 75.
Martin v. Gilham, 189.
Martyn v. Clue, 247.
—— v. Williams, 246.
Martyr v. Bradley, 297.
—— v. Lawrence, 74.
Mason v. Corder, 243.
Massey v. Goodall, 212.
Mather v. Fraser, 293.
Matthias v. Mesnard, 139.

Matts v. Hawkins, 216.
Matures v. Westwood, 247.
Mayfield v. Robinson, 69.
Mayhew v. Suttle, 48.
Mayho v. Buckhurst, 248.
Mayor of Congleton v. Pattison, 247, 248.
Mayor of Thetford v. Tyler, 55, 189.
M'Donnell v. Pope, 280, 281.
Medwin v. Sandham, 86.
Melling v. Leak, 52.
Merrill v. Frame, 230.
Messenger v. Armstrong, 81, 303.
Messent v. Reynolds, 229.
Micklethwait v. Winter, 79.
Mildmay v. Shirley, 55.
Miller v. Maynwaring, 12, 80.
Minshall v. Lloyd, 296.
Minshull v. Oakes, 247.
Mitcalfe v. Westaway, 77.
Mitchell v. Reynolds, 203.
Molton v. Camroux, 9.
Monk v. Cooper, 124.
—— v. Noyes, 194.
Moodie v. Garnance, 126.
Moore v. Clark, 197.
—— v. Drinkwater, 153.
—— v. Plymouth, 261.
Moores v. Choat, 245.
Morgan v. Bissell, 45, 46.
Morley v. Pincombe, 141.
Morphett v. Jones, 62, 63.
Morrice v. Antrobus, 112.
Morris v. Edgington, 76.
Morrison v. Chadwick, 126.
Mortal v. Lyons, 62.
Morton v. Woods, 43, 104, 133, 264.
Moss v. Barton, 59.
—— v. Gallimore, 41, 116, 133.
Mountney v. Collier, 42.
Mule v. Garrett, 251.
Mundy v. Jolliffe, 63.
Muspratt v. Gregory, 137, 140.

NARGETT v. Nias, 143.
Nash v. Gray, 114.
—— v. Lucas, 154.
—— v. Palmer, 233.
Naylor v. Arnitt, 30.
—— v. Collinge, 297.
Neale v. Mackenzie, 66, 127.
—— v. Parkin, 77.
—— v. Ratcliffe, 195.
Neave v. Moss, 42.
Newman v. Anderton, 110.
Newson v. Smythies, 210, 301.
Newton v. Harland, 306.

INDEX OF CASES CITED.

Newton v. Wilmot, 232, 261.
Niblet v. Smith, 176.
Nickells v. Atherstone, 281.
Nixon v. Freeman, 154.
Noke v. Awder, 247.
North Western Ry. Co. v. M'Michael, 5.
Norton v. Herron, 103.
Norval v. Pascoe, 247.
Noye v. Reed, 216.
Nunn v. Fabian, 62, 63.
Nuttall v. Staunton, 149, 150.

OAKAPPLE v. Copons, 267.
Oakley v. Monck, 56.
Oates v. Frith, 112.
Odell v. Wake, 249.
Ogilvie v. Foljambe, 62.
Ognel's Case, 135.
Omerod v. Hardman, 69.
Onslow v. ———, 207, 208.
——— v. Corrie, 249.
Opperman v. Smith, 145, 148.
Orgill v. Kemshead, 250.
Orme v. Broughton, 65.
Osborn v. Wise, 70, 71.
Owen v. De Beauvoir, 150.
——— v. Legh, 173.
Oxley v. James, 136, 235.

PACKER v. Gibbins, 124.
Page v. More, 303.
Paget v. Foley, 187.
Pain v. Coombs, 63.
Palmer v. Earith, 226.
——— v. Edwards, 237.
Papillon v. Brunton, 272.
Paradine v. Jane, 125.
Parish v. Sleeman, 228.
Parker v. Taswell, 65, 68.
——— v. Webb, 247.
Parmenter v. Webber, 112, 237.
Parrot v. Anderson, 129.
Parry v. Deere, 97.
——— v. Duncan, 148.
——— v. Hindle, 12.
——— v. House, 42.
Parsons v. Gingell, 140.
Patten v. Reid, 255.
Paul v. Nurse, 240, 249.
Paull v. Best, 186.
Payne v. Burridge, 227.
——— v. Haine, 193.
Pearce v. Cheslyn, 46.
Pearse v. Boulter, 272.
Pease v. Chaytor, 176.

Pease v. Coates, 204.
Peirse v. Shaw, 54.
Pembroke v. Berkeley, 284.
Penfold v. Abbot, 229.
Penley v. Watts, 239.
Penniall v. Harborne, 221.
Pennington v. Cardale, 18.
Penry v. Brown, 195, 297.
Penton v. Robart, 295, 296.
Perring v. Brook, 45.
Peter v. Kendal, 281.
Phené v. Popplewell, 279.
Phillips v. Berryman, 176.
——— v. Edwards, 62.
——— v. Hartley, 44.
——— v. Jones, 206.
——— v. Whitsed, 165.
Pigot's Case, 105.
Pigott v. Birtles, 144, 157.
Pike v. Eyre, 235.
Pilkington v. Dalton, 113.
——— v. Hastings, 166.
Pilling v. Armitage, 29.
Pilton, Ex parte, 310.
Pincomb v. Thomas, 78.
Pinero v. Judson, 47, 57.
Pinhorn v. Souster, 240, 264.
Pitman v. Woodbury, 103.
Pitt v. Shew, 172.
——— v. Smith, 44.
——— v. Snowden, 134.
Plant v. James, 76.
Pleasant v. Benson, 271, 282.
Pluck v. Digges, 237.
Plummer, Ex parte, 186.
Pocock v. Eustace, 120.
Pollen v. Brewer, 263, 306.
Pollitt v. Forest, 132.
Pollock v. Stacy, 237.
Poole's Case, 294, 296.
Poole v. Bentley, 46.
——— v. Longueville, 144.
Pope v. Biggs, 116.
Pordage v. Cole, 87.
Porter v. Shepherd, 87.
——— v. Swetnam, 83.
Portman v. Mill, 75.
Portmore v. Goring, 106.
Postman v. Harrell, 148.
Potts v. Smith, 232.
Poulteney v. Holmes, 112, 237.
Powis v. Smith, 117.
Powley v. Walker, 207, 208.
Pownall v. Moores, 214.
Poynter v. Buckley, 170.
Pratt v. Keith, 119.
Preece v. Corrie, 112, 237.
Prescott v. Boucher, 135.

INDEX OF CASES CITED.

Preston v. Mercean, 70.
Price v. Dyer, 275.
—— v. Worwood, 220, 287.
Progress Assurance, *In re*, 143.
Propert v. Parker, 61, 65, 86.
Prosser v. Phillips, 93.
Proud v. Bates, 79.
Proudlove v. Twemlow, 173.
Pugh v. Arton, 297.
—— v. Griffith, 155.
—— v. Leeds, 80.
Pullen v. Palmer, 136.
Pulteney v. Shelton, 271.
Purvis v. Rayer, 64, 252.
Pyle v. Partridge, 152.
Pym v. Blackburn, 64.

QUARRINGTON v. Arthur, 206.
Quincey, *Ex parte*, 294.

RAND v. Vaughan, 149.
Randall v. Lynch, 84.
Randle v. Lory, 92.
Rankin v. Lay, 211.
Rawlings v. Morgan, 198.
Rawlin's Estate, *In re*, 36.
Rawlins v. Turner, 68.
Rawson v. Eicke, 45.
Raymond v. Fitch, 220, 253.
Readshaw v. Balders, 225.
Redpath v. Roberts, 231.
Rees v. Davies, 308.
—— v. King, 91.
Reeve v. Bird, 281.
Reg. v. Aylesbury, 227.
—— v. Chawton, 81, 265.
—— v. Everist, 110.
—— v. Hockworthy, 69, 97.
—— v. Raines, 177.
—— v. Recorder of Richmond, 272.
—— v. Slawstone, 272.
—— v. Westbrook, 110.
Regnart v. Porter, 51, 111, 131.
Rex v. Banbury, 281.
—— v. Cheshunt, 48.
—— v. Chipping Norton, 14.
—— v. Collett, 51.
—— v. Cotton, 171.
—— v. Duffield North, 14.
—— v. Jobling, 51.
—— v. Kelstern, 48.
—— v. Londonthorpe, 293.
—— v. Osbourne, 209.
—— v. Otley, 293.
—— v. Topping, 90.
Reynel's Case, 2

Reynolds v. Barford, 182.
—— v. Waring, 62.
Rhodes v. Bullard, 87.
Rich v. Basterfield, 191.
—— v. Jackson, 70.
—— v. Woolley, 164.
Richardson v. Ardley, 184.
—— v. Evans, 242.
—— v. Gifford, 53, 54, 56, 68.
—— v. Langridge, 50, 52, 55.
Ricketts v. Weaver, 253.
Ridgway v. Sneyd, 123.
—— v. Stafford, 171.
—— v. Wharton, 65.
Right v. Bawden, 55.
—— v. Beard, 51.
—— v. Darby, 81.
Riseley v. Ryle, 182, 183.
Robbins v. Jones, 101.
Roberts v. Barker, 57, 208.
—— v. Brett, 87.
—— v. Davey, 284.
—— v. Hayward, 269.
Robinson v. Hoffman, 116, 136.
—— v. Learoyd, 303.
—— v. Macdonnell, 96.
—— v. Rosher, 245.
—— v. Waddington, 169.
Rockingham v. Penrice, 114.
Roden v. Eyton, 167, 171.
Rodgers v. Parker, 172, 173, 181.
Roe v. Archbishop of York, 281.
—— v. Charnock, 265.
—— v. Galliers, 88.
—— v. Harrison, 241, 242.
—— v. Hayley, 275.
—— v. Lees, 52.
—— v. Paine, 194.
—— v. Pierce, 269.
—— v. Summerset, 30.
—— v. Sales, 236.
—— v. Ward, 267.
—— v. Wilkinson, 265.
Roffey v. Henderson, 297.
Rogers v. Humphreys, 41, 116, 133.
—— v. Pitcher, 129.
Rolfe v. Peterson, 118.
Rollason v. Leon, 68.
Rolls v. Rock, 78.
Roper v. Coombes, 64.
Rosse v. Wainman, 79.
Roulston v. Clarke, 132.
Rowles v. Mason, 15.
Rubery v. Stevens, 254, 255.
Russell v. Rider, 163.
——, *Ex parte*, 140.
Ryall v. Rich, 304.
Ryan v. Shilcock, 154.

INDEX OF CASES CITED. xxi

Ryan v. Thompson, 122.
Ryley v. Hicks, 68.

SACHEVERELL v. Froggatt, 84.
Saffyn's Case, 107.
Sainter v. Ferguson, 65.
Salmon v. Matthews, 110.
Saltoun v. Houstoun, 84.
Sampson v. Easterby, 84, 248.
Sanders v. Karnell, 56.
Sapsford v. Fletcher, 121.
Saunders v. Merryweather, 89.
——— v. Oliffe, 76.
——— v. Wakefield, 62.
Saunderson v. Hanson, 120, 121.
Saward v. Leggatt, 192.
Say v. Barwick, 44.
——— v. Smith, 81.
Scales v. Lawrence, 194.
Scott v. Buckley, 154.
Seers v. Hind, 241.
Selby v. Greaves, 111.
——— v. Selby, 61.
Semayne's Case, 155.
Senior v. Armytage, 301.
Seton v. Slade, 61.
Sharp v. Milligan, 86.
Shaw v. Kay, 80, 195.
——— v. Stenton, 233.
Shillibeer v. Jarvis, 63.
Shippey v. Derrison, 61.
Shopland v. Ryoler, 236.
Simmons v. Norton, 199, 218.
Simons v. Farren, 204.
Simpkin v. Ashhurst, 49.
Simpson v. Hartopp, 138, 139, 141.
——— v. Scottish Union Insurance Co., 222.
——— v. Titterell, 284.
Sims v. Thomas, 187.
Six Carpenters' Case, 166.
Skerry v. Preston, 129.
Skull v. Glenister, 69, 76.
Slack v. Crewe, 31.
Slator v. Brady, 4, 5.
——— v. Trimble, 4.
Sleap v. Newman, 255.
Slingsby's Case, 87.
Slipper v. Tottenham and Hampstead Junction Ry. Co., 241.
Smallman v. Pollard, 183.
Smith v. Ashforth, 157, 159.
——— v. Chance, 212.
——— v. Clark, 272.
——— v. Eldridge, 188.
——— v. Goodwin, 158, 166.
——— v. Humble, 120, 228.

Smith v. Low, 5, 42, 43.
——— v. Malings, 126.
——— v. Mapleback, 112, 237, 279.
——— v. Marrable, 202.
——— v. Peat, 197.
——— v. Ridgway, 76.
——— v. Russell, 141, 183.
——— v. Twoart, 188.
——— v. White, 201.
——— v. Wilson, 71.
——— v. Wright, 162.
Snell v. Snell, 219.
Solme v. Bullock, 76.
Somerset v. Fogwell, 69.
Sorsbie v. Park, 87.
Soulsby v. Neving, 302, 304.
Souter v. Drake, 252.
Southwark (St. Saviour's) v. Smith, 245.
Spencer v. Marriott, 234, 238.
Spencer's Case, 110, 247, 248, 259.
Spenser's Estates, In re, 2.
Spice v. Webb, 156.
St. Alban's v. Ellis, 84, 85.
——— v. Shore, 87.
St. Saviour's (Southwark) v. Smith, 245.
Staines v. Morris, 250, 251.
Standen v. Christmas, 252.
Staniforth v. Fox, 46.
Stanley v. Hayes, 232.
——— v. Wharton, 145, 147.
Stansfield v. Mayor of Portsmouth, 297.
Staveley v. Allcock, 136.
Steele v. Mart, 73, 80.
——— v. Midland Ry. Co., 75.
Steer v. Crowley, 96.
Steeven's Hospital v. Dyas, 15.
Stevens v. Copp, 249.
Steiglitz v. Egginton, 31.
Stevenson v. Lambard, 126, 246, 247.
——— v. Newnham, 152.
Stevenson's Case, 84.
Stiles v. Cowper, 29.
Stokes v. Moore, 61.
Stone v. Whiting, 281.
Storey v. Robinson, 140.
Story v. Johnson, 5.
Stranks v. St. John, 64.
Stroud, In re, 52, 70.
Stubbs v. Parsons, 120.
Sturgeon v. Wingfield, 42.
Sturgess v. Farringdon, 121.
Styles v. Wardle, 80.
Sucksmith v. Wilson, 301.
Sullivan v. Bishop, 111, 304.

Sumner v. Bromilow, 297, 298.
Surcome v. Pinniger, 63.
Surplice v. Farnsworth, 126.
Sutherland v. Briggs, 63.
Sutton v. Temple, 125, 202.
Swaine v. Holman, 13.
Swann v. Falmouth, 156, 163.
Swatman v. Ambler, 103.
Sweet v. Senger, 227.
Swinfen v. Bacon, 302.
Swire v. Leach, 139, 140.

TANCRED v. Christy, 302.
—— v. Leyland, 151, 152.
Tanner v. Christian, 103.
Tarte v. Derby, 46.
Tatem v. Chaplin, 247.
Taunton v. Costar, 305.
Taylerson v. Peters, 149.
Tayleur v. Wildin, 274.
Taylor v. Caldwell, 47.
—— v. Jackson, 44.
—— v. Lanyon, 181.
—— v. Meads, 9.
—— v. Needham, 42.
—— v. Portington, 65.
—— v. Shum, 249, 255.
—— v. Zamira, 121, 122.
Tempest v. Rawling, 45.
Temple v. Brown, 64.
Tennant v. Field, 156, 159, 165, 166.
Tew v. Jones, 51.
Theed v. Starkey, 226.
Thetford v. Tyler, 55, 189.
Thomas v. Cook, 281.
—— v. Harries, 156, 160.
—— v. Hayward, 247, 248, 249.
—— v. Packer, 57.
—— v. Thomas, 267.
Thompson v. Hakewill, 88.
—— v. Lapworth, 227.
—— v. Maberly, 265.
—— v. Mashiter, 140.
Thorn v. Woolcombe, 237.
Thornton v. Adams, 148.
—— v. Sherratt, 206.
Thresher v. E. London Waterworks Co., 295.
Thunder v. Belcher, 41, 236.
Thynne v. Glengall, 62, 65.
Tidey v. Mollett, 68.
Tidswell v. Whitworth, 228.
Timmins v. Rowlison, 304.
Tinckler v. Prentice, 119, 225.
Toler v. Slater, 12, 104.
Tomlinson v. Day, 126.

Tooker v. Smith, 57.
Toplis v. Grane, 152.
Torriano v. Young, 189, 200.
Towne v. D'Heinriche, 108, 188.
Townrow v. Benson, 119.
Trappes v. Harter, 293, 295.
Tremeere v. Morrison, 255.
Trent v. Hunt, 116, 134, 165.
Tress v. Savage, 53, 54.
Turner v. Allday, 112.
—— v. Barnes, 149.
—— v. Cameron, 139, 293.
—— v. Camerons, &c. Co., 107.
—— v. Ford, 171.
—— v. Hutchinson, 31.
—— v. Meymott, 305.
—— v. Power, 66, 94.
Tutton v. Darke, 150.

UPTON v. Fergusson, 280.
—— v. Townend, 230, 231.

VALLIANT v. Dodemede, 249, 250.
Van v. Corpe, 86, 238.
Vasper v. Eddows, 163.
Venning v. Bray, 115.
Vere v. Loveden, 86.
Vernon v. Smith, 247.
Vertue v. Beasley, 166.
Vivian v. Blomberg, 20.
Vonhollen v. Knowles, 74.
Vowles v. Miller, 216.
Vyvyan v. Arthur, 247.

WADDILOVE v. Barnett, 116.
Wadham v. Marlowe, 250, 257.
Wagstaff v. Clack, 141.
Wain v. Warlters, 62.
Wakefield v. Brown, 247.
Wakeman v. Lindsey, 164.
Walker v. Giles, 72.
—— v. Godè, 56, 267.
—— v. Hatton, 192, 238, 239.
—— v. Richardson, 281.
Walker's Case, 127.
Wallace v. King, 169, 180.
—— v. M'Laren, 116.
Waller v. Andrews, 120, 122.
Wallis v. Delmar, 263.
Walls v. Atcheson, 231.
Walmsley v. Milne, 293.
Walsall v. Heath, 12.
Walter v. Rumbal, 165, 170.
*Walters v. Northern Coal Mining Co., 66.

Wankford v. Wankford, 30.
Wansbrough v. Maton, 293.
Ward v. Andrews, 217.
—— v. Byrne, 203.
—— v. Const, 228.
—— v. Day, 47, 286, 287.
—— v. Hartpole, 44.
—— v. Lumley, 281.
—— v. Shew, 134.
Wardell v. Usher, 295.
Warman v. Faithfull, 46.
Warner v. Willington, 62.
Warwicke v. Noakes, 129.
Washborn v. Black, 158, 159.
Watherell v. Howells, 198.
Watkins v. Gravesend and Milton Union, 47.
Watson v. Atkins, 228.
—— v. Home, 228.
—— v. Main, 149.
—— v. Waud, 83.
Weakly v. Bucknell, 54.
Weatherall v. Geering, 241.
Weaver v. Sessions, 205.
Webb v. Austin, 42.
—— v. Plummer, 208, 301.
—— v. Rorke, 44.
—— v. Russell, 252.
Weeton v. Woodcock, 296.
Weigall v. Waters, 119, 191.
Wells v. Moody, 156, 157.
Welsh v. Rose, 151.
West v. Dobb, 242, 248.
—— v. Fritch, 104.
—— v. Nibbs, 166.
Westwood v. Cowne, 168.
Whalley v. Tompson, 76.
Wharton v. Naylor, 141.
Wheeler v. Branscombe, 116.
—— v. Montefiore, 107.
—— v. Stevenson, 231.
Whistler v. Pasloe, 78.
Whitchurch v. Bevis, 64.
White v. Binstead, 184.
—— v. Foljambe, 42.
—— v. Wakley, 196.
Whiteacre v. Symonds, 274.
Whitehead v. Bennett, 295.
—— v. Clifford, 279.
—— v. Taylor, 136.
Whitfield v. Brandwood, 120, 228.
—— v. Weedon, 215.
Whitley v. Roberts, 137.
Whitlock v. Horton, 72.
Whitlock's Case, 84.
Whitmore v. Walker, 116, 121, 122.
Whittaker v. Barker, 301.
Whitty v. Dillon, 217.

Whitworth v. Maden, 181.
Wickenden v. Webster, 203.
Wickham v. Hawker, 261.
—— v. Lee, 304.
Wigglesworth v. Dallison, 300, 301.
Wildbor v. Rainforth, 305.
Wilde v. Waters, 298.
Wilder v. Speer, 162.
Wilkinson v. Colley, 271.
—— v. Ibbett, 170.
—— v. Rogers, 205, 247.
—— v. Terry, 152.
Willcox v. Marshall, 62.
Williams v. Bartholomew, 117.
—— v. Bosanquet, 245, 247.
—— v. Burrell, 234.
—— v. Earle, 248.
—— v. Evans, 245.
—— v. Hayward, 237.
—— v. Holmes, 132, 139.
—— v. Lake, 61, 62.
—— v. Lewsey, 182.
—— v. Roberts, 146, 147.
Willoughby v. Backhouse, 156.
Wills v. Strudling, 63.
Willson v. Davenport, 119.
Wilmot v. Rose, 210.
Wilson v. Chisholm, 46.
—— v. Hart, 238.
—— v. Nightingale, 164.
—— v. Whateley, 297.
—— v. Wilson, 220.
Wilton v. Dunn, 116.
Wiltshear v. Cottrell, 293.
Winn v. Ingleby, 294.
—— v. White, 196.
Winterbottom v. Ingham, 51.
Winterbourne v. Morgan, 172.
Wiscot's Case, 11.
Withers v. Bircham, 87.
Witton v. Bye, 112.
Witty v. Williams, 132.
Wollaston v. Hakewill, 237, 246, 254, 255.
—— v. Stafford, 158.
Wolveridge v. Steward, 250, 251.
Wood v. Clarke, 139.
—— v. Leadbitter, 47, 69.
—— v. Manley, 47.
—— v. Nunn, 148, 156.
—— v. Tate, 14.
Woodcock v. Worthington, 106.
Woodhouse v. Jenkins, 234.
Woods v. Durrant, 159.
—— v. Pope, 198.
Woodward v. Gyles, 118.
Woolcock v. Dew, 193.
Woollam v. Hearn, 69.

Wootley v. Gregory, 165.
Worthington v. Gimson, 76.
—— v. Warrington, 97.
Wotton v. Hele, 233.
Wright v. Colls, 65.
—— v. Smith, 302.
—— v. Stavert, 61.
Wyburd v. Tuck, 80.
Wyndham v. Way, 78, 294.

YATES v. Ratledge, 182, 183.
—— v. Tearle, 175.
Yaw v. Leman, 228.
Yellowly v. Gower, 31, 190, 200.
Yeoman v. Ellison, 137.

ZOUCH v. Parsons, 4, 5.
—— v. Willingale, 273.

INDEX OF STATUTES CITED.

*** The letter *t.* indicates that the reference to the Statute is contained in the text. The letter *n.* refers to the foot note containing the reference to the Statute. Where neither of these letters is appended to the number of the page, the reference to the Statute may be found in the margin; and, generally, in that case, the essential words of the Statute are quoted.

	PAGE
51 Hen. 3, stat. 4	143
52 Hen. 3, c. 4	157
52 Hen. 3, c. 15	144
3 Edw. 1, c. 16	145 *n.* (h), 161 *n.* (d)
7 Edw. 1, stat. 2, c. 1	15 *n.* (x)
32 Hen. 8, c. 28, ss. 1, 2, 4	15
32 Hen. 8, c. 34, ss. 1, 2	252
32 Hen. 8, c. 37, ss. 1, 3	135
5 & 6 Edw. 6, c. 16, ss. 2, 3	2 *n.* (c)
1 & 2 Ph. & M. c. 12, s. 1	160
—————— s. 2	174
1 Eliz. c. 19, s. 5	18
13 Eliz. c. 10, s. 3	18
14 Eliz. c. 11, ss. 17, 19	18
14 Eliz. c. 14	18 *n.* (k)
18 Eliz. c. 11, s. 2	20
39 Eliz. c. 5, s. 2	18 *n.* (k)
15 Car. 2, c. 17, s. 8	105
19 Car. 2, c. 6	276 *n.* (c)
29 Car. 2, c. 3, ss. 1, 2	67
—————— s. 3	244, 279
—————— s. 4	61
2 Will. & M. sess. 1, c. 5	159 *t.*
—————— s. 2	160 *t.*, 164, *n.* (s), 167, 169
—————— s. 3	137, 160, 171
—————— s. 4	163
—————— s. 5	179
1 Anne, stat. 1, c. 7, ss. 5, 6	22
2 & 3 Anne, c. 4	105
4 Anne, c. 16, s. 9	117, 253
—————— s. 10	116 *n.* (a), 117, 253
5 Anne, c. 18	105
6 Anne, c. 18, s. 1	276
—————— s. 2	276 *n.* (f)
—————— ss. 3, 5	277
6 Anne, c. 35	105

INDEX OF STATUTES CITED.

	PAGE
7 Anne, c. 12, s. 3	143 n. (u)
7 Anne, c. 20	105
8 Anne, c. 14	158 t.
———— s. 1	181, 184 t.
———— s. 2	146 n. (n)
———— ss. 6, 7	149
2 Geo. 2, c. 22, s. 13	119 n. (t)
4 Geo. 2, c. 28	159 t.
———— s. 1	302
———— s. 6	282
8 Geo. 2, c. 6	105
8 Geo. 2, c. 24, ss. 4, 5	119 n. (t)
9 Geo. 2, c. 36, s. 1	22, 23 nn. (n), (y), 24 n. (c), 25 n. (o)
———— s. 3	22, 23, n. (u)
11 Geo. 2, c. 19	164 t.
———— s. 1	145
———— s. 2	146
———— ss. 3, 4	147
———— s. 7	146
———— s. 8	138, 145, 160, 168 t., 173 n. (s)
———— s. 9	160, 164 n. (t), 166
———— s. 10	158
———— s. 14	188
———— s. 16	310
———— s. 17	310 t.
———— s. 18	304
———— s. 19	180
———— s. 20	181
5 Geo. 3, c. 17, s 1	15
13 Geo. 3, c. 81, s. 15	29
14 Geo. 3, c. 78	247 t.
———— s. 83	222
———— s. 86	190
38 Geo. 3, c. 5, s. 17	120 n. (c)
39 & 40 Geo. 3, c. 41	18 n. (m)
47 Geo. 3, sess. 2, c. 25, s. 4	2 n. (c)
48 Geo. 3, c. 73	22 t.
48 Geo. 3, c. 149, ss. 22 – 25	73 n. (r)
52 Geo. 3, c. 161	22 t.
55 Geo. 3, c. 184, s. 8	73 n. (r), 96 t.
56 Geo. 3, c. 50, ss. 1, 2, 3	209
———— s. 5	209 t.
———— s. 6	142
———— s. 7	208
———— s. 11	210
57 Geo. 3, c. 52	310 n. (a)
57 Geo. 3, c. 93, s. 1	173
———— s. 2	174
———— s. 6	175
———— sched.	167 n. (i), 174
3 Geo. 4, c. 126, s. 57	69 n. (i)
10 Geo. 4, c. 50, ss. 22 – 24, 26 – 33	22
———— s. 92	93 t.
11 Geo. 4 & 1 Will. 4, c. 65, s. 12	6, 12
———— s. 15	6
———— s. 16	6, 12
———— s. 17	3
1 & 2 Will. 4, c. 32, ss. 8, 11	259

INDEX OF STATUTES CITED.

	PAGE
1 & 2 Will. 4, c. 32, s. 12	260
3 & 4 Will. 4, c. 27, s. 2	150
——— s. 42	151, 188
3 & 4 Will. 4, c. 42, s. 3	187
——— ss. 4, 5	188 n. (g)
——— s. 37	135
——— s. 38	136
3 & 4 Will. 4, c. 74, ss. 15, 34	26
——— s. 40	26, 27
——— s. 41	27
——— ss. 77, 79	9
5 & 6 Will. 4, c. 76, ss. 94, 95, 96	21
6 & 7 Will. 4, c. 20, s. 1	20
——— s. 4	21
6 & 7 Will. 4, c. 64	20 n. (r)
6 & 7 Will. 4, c. 71, s. 70	120 n. (h)
6 & 7 Will. 4, c. 104, s. 2	21
1 & 2 Vict. c. 74, s. 1	306
——— s. 2	308
——— s. 3	309
——— s. 4	309 t.
1 & 2 Vict. c. 106, s. 28	21
——— s. 59	19
2 & 3 Vict. c. 71, s. 39	179
5 & 6 Vict. c. 27	16, 20 t.
——— s. 15	16 n. (b)
5 & 6 Vict. c. 35, s. 60	223 n. (c)
——— s. 73	225
——— s. 103	119 n. (z), 225
5 & 6 Vict. c. 97, s. 2	164 n. (n), 310 t.
5 & 6 Vict. c. 108	19 t., 20 t.
——— ss. 1—9, 18, 20—32	16
6 & 7 Vict. c. 40, ss. 1, 2	142 t.
——— ss. 18, 19	142
7 & 8 Vict. c. 66, s. 5	13
7 & 8 Vict. c. 96, s. 67	182
8 & 9 Vict. c. 106, s. 2	72, 82 n. (m)
——— s. 3	67, 244, 279
——— s. 9	282
8 & 9 Vict. c. 124, ss. 1, 2, 3	317
——— ss. 4—8	318
12 & 13 Vict. c. 26, ss. 2, 4	32
——— s. 5	32 n. (o)
——— s. 7	33
12 & 13 Vict. c. 92, ss. 5, 6	161
13 Vict. c. 17, s. 2	34
——— s. 3	33
14 & 15 Vict. c. 25, s. 1	299
——— s. 2	141, 142 n. (t), 184
——— s. 3	295
——— s. 4	225
14 & 15 Vict. c. 99, s. 6	106 t.
14 & 15 Vict. c. 104, s. 11	19
15 & 16 Vict. c. 76, s. 209	315
——— s. 210	284 n. (o), 285, 288 n. (o)
——— s. 211	288
——— s. 212	289
——— s. 213	313

xxviii INDEX OF STATUTES CITED.

	PAGE
15 & 16 Vict. c. 76, s. 214	314
——— s. 218	315
15 & 16 Vict. c. 80	3 n. (i)
16 & 17 Vict. c. 70, ss. 113, 114, 115	8
——— s. 127	240 n. (q)
——— ss. 129, 130—134	7
17 & 18 Vict. c. 60, s. 1	162
17 & 18 Vict. c. 125, ss. 79—82	200 n. (s)
19 & 20 Vict. c. 108, ss. 50, 52	311
——— ss. 63, 64	176
——— ss. 65, 66	177
——— s. 70	177 t.
——— s. 71	178
——— s. 75	184
19 & 20 Vict. c. 120, ss. 2—10	4, 8, 11
——— s. 2	35
——— s. 3	37 t.
——— s. 4	35 t.
——— s. 5	40
——— s. 6	35 t.
——— s. 7	39
——— s. 8	37
——— s. 9	39
——— s. 10	39
——— s. 16	11, 37
——— ss. 17, 18	37
——— ss. 19, 20	38
——— s. 26	38
——— s. 27	35 t.
——— ss. 28, 29	40
——— s. 32	28
——— s. 33	11
——— s. 34	10, 36 t.
——— s. 36	4, 8
——— ss. 37, 38, 39	11
——— s. 40	38
——— s. 43	40
——— s. 44	10 t., 35 n. (r)
21 & 22 Vict. c. 27, s. 2	66
21 & 22 Vict. c. 44	22 t.
21 & 22 Vict. c. 57	20 t.
——— s. 1	16
——— s. 9	19
21 & 22 Vict. c. 77, s. 1	35 n. (r)
——— s. 2	35 n. (s)
——— s. 3	29
——— s. 4	35 n. (t)
——— s. 5	40 n. (y)
——— s. 8	11 n. (g)
22 & 23 Vict. c. 35	290 t.
——— ss. 1, 2	243
——— s. 3	253
——— ss. 4, 5, 6	289
——— s. 7	222
——— s. 9	222 t.
——— s. 12	34
——— s. 21	245
——— s. 27	255

INDEX OF STATUTES CITED.

	PAGE
23 & 24 Vict. c. 38, s. 6	287
23 & 24 Vict. c. 59, s. 3	22 *t.*
23 & 24 Vict. c. 124, s. 8	19
23 & 24 Vict. c. 126, ss. 1, 2, 3	290
———————— ss. 4—11	290 *t.*
24 Vict. c. 9	26 *n.* (c)
———————— s. 1	23 *n.* (x)
24 & 25 Vict. c. 21, s. 2	205 *t.*
24 & 25 Vict. c. 105	20
24 & 25 Vict. c. 133, s. 38	120 *n.* (g)
25 & 26 Vict. c. 52	20
25 & 26 Vict. c. 89, s. 84	143 *t.*
———————— s. 163	143
26 & 27 Vict. c. 49, ss. 21—26	22 *t.*
26 & 27 Vict. c. 106	24 *n.* (d)
27 & 28 Vict. c. 45, s. 1	39 *n.* (x)
———————— s. 3	35 *n.* (r)
28 & 29 Vict. c. 96, s. 2	169 *n.* (s)
28 & 29 Vict. c. 99, s. 1	62 *n.* (o)
29 & 30 Vict. c. 57, s. 2	24 *n.* (b)
29 & 30 Vict. c. 81	16 *n.* (a)
30 & 31 Vict. c. 142, s. 11	315
31 & 32 Vict. c. 44	23 *n.* (t)
32 & 33 Vict. c. 41, ss. 1, 2	224
———————— s. 3	224 *n.* (h)
———————— s. 4	224 *n.* (i)
———————— s. 8	224
32 & 33 Vict. c. 70, s. 89	224 *n.* (g)
32 & 33 Vict. c. 71, s. 11	186 *n.* (c)
———————— s. 15	256 *n.* (u)
———————— s. 17	256
———————— ss. 23, 24	257
———————— s. 34	152 *n.* (y), 186
———————— s. 35	187
———————— s. 125 (7)	187
———————— s. 125 (9)	187 *n.* (e)
33 Vict. c. 14, s. 2	13
33 & 34 Vict. c. 23, ss. 6, 8	14
———————— s. 10	258
———————— s. 12	14, 258
———————— s. 14	258
33 & 34 Vict. c. 35, ss. 2, 3, 4	127
———————— s. 5	127 *n.* (y)
———————— s. 7	128
33 & 34 Vict. c. 93	9 *n.* (e)
33 & 34 Vict. c. 97	98
———————— s. 8	97
———————— s. 10	96
———————— ss. 15, 16	94
———————— s. 17	95
———————— s. 93	102
———————— s. 96	66
———————— s. 97	99
———————— s. 98	100
———————— ss. 99, 100	101
———————— sched.	67, 96 *n.* (r), 102, 168, 279 *n.* (m)
33 & 34 Vict. c. 99	73 *n.* (r)

ABBREVIATIONS

USED IN THE CITATION OF CASES AND TEXT BOOKS.

A. & E.	Adolphus & Ellis's Reports.
Aleyn	Aleyn's Reports.
Ambl.	Ambler's Reports.
Anstr.	Anstruther's Reports.
Atk.	Atkyn's Reports.
Bac. Abr.	Bacon's Abridgment, tit. *Leases* (5th Edit. by Gwillim).
Ball & B.	Ball & Beatty's Reports.
Barnes	Barnes's Notes of Cases.
B. & A.	Barnewall & Alderson's Reports.
B. & Ad.	Barnewall & Adolphus's Reports.
B. & C.	Barnewall & Cresswell's Reports.
B. & S.	Best & Smith's Reports.
Beav.	Beavan's Reports.
Bing.	Bingham's Reports.
Bing. N. C.	Bingham's New Cases.
Black. Com.	Blackstone's Commentaries.
H. Bl.	Henry Blackstone's Reports.
W. Bl.	Sir William Blackstone's Reports.
Bli.	Bligh's House of Lords' Reports.
Bli., N. S.	Bligh's Reports, New Series.
B. & P.	Bosanquet & Puller's Reports.
B. & P. N. R.	Bosanquet & Puller's New Reports.
O. Bridg. Rep.	Sir Orlando Bridgman's Reports, by Bannister.
B. & B.	Broderip & Bingham's Reports.
Bro. C. C.	Brown's Chancery Cases.
Bro. P. C.	Brown's Parliamentary Cases.
Bullen & Leake's Pleadings	Bullen & Leake's Precedents of Pleadings.
Bull. N. P.	Buller's Nisi Prius.
Bulstr.	Bulstrode's Reports.
Burr.	Burrow's Reports.
Camp.	Campbell's Reports.
Car. & M.	Carrington & Marshman's Reports.
C. & K.	Carrington & Kirwan's Reports.
C. & P.	Carrington & Payne's Reports.
C. B.	Common Bench Reports.
C. B., N. S.	Common Bench Reports, New Series.

Ch. Cas.	.. ..	.. Cases in Chancery.
Chit.	.. ..	.. Chitty's Reports.
Ch. Pl.	.. ..	.. Chitty on Pleading (7th Edit.).
Co. Lit.	.. ..	.. Coke on Littleton (Hargrave & Butler's Edit.).
Co. R.	.. ..	.. Coke's Reports.
Coll. P. C.	.. ..	.. Colles's Parliamentary Cases.
Com. Dig.	.. ..	.. Comyn's Digest.
Cowp.	.. ..	.. Cowper's Reports.
Cox	.. ..	.. Cox's Reports.
Cro. Eliz.	.. ..	.. Croke's Reports, Part 1.
Cro. Jac.	.. ..	.. Croke's Reports, Part 2.
Cro. Car.	.. ..	.. Croke's Reports, Part 3.
Cr. & J.	.. ..	.. Crompton & Jervis's Reports.
Cr. & M.	.. ..	.. Crompton & Meeson's Reports.
Cr., M. & R.	.. ..	.. Crompton, Meeson & Roscoe's Reports.
D. & L.	.. ..	.. Dowling & Lowndes's Reports.
D. & R.	.. ..	.. Dowling & Ryland's Reports.
Dart V. & P.	.. ..	.. Dart on Vendors and Purchasers (4th Edit.).
De G., F. & J.	.. ..	.. De Gex, Fisher & Jones's Reports.
De G. & J.	.. ..	.. De Gex & Jones's Reports.
De G. & S.	.. ..	.. De Gex & Smales's Reports.
De G., J. & S.	.. ..	.. De Gex, Jones & Smith's Reports.
De G., M. & G.	.. ..	.. De Gex, Macnaghten & Gordon's Reports.
Dougl.	.. ..	.. Douglas's Reports.
Dow	.. ..	.. Dow's Parliamentary Cases.
Drew.	.. ..	.. Drewry's Reports.
E. & B.	.. ..	.. Ellis & Blackburn's Reports.
E. & E.	.. ..	.. Ellis & Ellis's Reports.
East..	.. ..	.. East's Reports.
E., B. & E.	.. ..	.. Ellis, Blackburn & Ellis's Reports.
Esp.	.. ..	.. Espinasse's Reports.
Ex.	.. ..	.. Exchequer Reports.
F. & F.	.. ..	.. Foster & Finlason's Reports.
Forrest	.. ..	.. Forrest's Reports.
G. & D.	.. ..	.. Gale & Davison's Reports.
Giff.	.. ..	.. Giffard's Reports.
Godb.	.. ..	.. Godbolt's Reports.
Gow	.. ..	.. Gow's Reports.
H. & C.	.. ..	.. Hurlstone & Coltman's Reports.
H. & N.	.. ..	.. Hurlstone & Norman's Reports.
Hardr.	.. ..	.. Hardres's Reports.
Hare	.. ..	.. Hare's Reports.
Hem. & M.	.. ..	.. Hemming & Miller's Reports.
Hill's Rep.	.. ..	.. Hill's Reports (New York).
H. L. C.	.. ..	.. House of Lords Cases.
Hob.	.. ..	.. Hobart's Reports.
Holt, N. P.	.. ..	.. Holt's Nisi Prius Cases.

Ir. C. L. R.	Irish Common Law Reports.
Ir. Ch. R.	Irish Chancery Reports.
J. & H.	Johnson & Hemming's Reports.
Jarm. Conv.	Jarman's Conveyancing, by Swee.
W. Jones	Sir William Jones's Reports.
Jur.	Jurist (New Series).
Jur., O. S.	Jurist (Old Series).
K. & J.	Kay & Johnson's Reports.
Keen	Keen's Reports.
Ld. Ken.	Lord Kenyon's Reports.
Leon.	Leonard's Reports.
Lev.	Levinz's Reports.
Lit.	Littleton's Tenures.
L. J.	Law Journal, New Series.
L. R.	The Law Reports.
L. T., N. S.	Law Times, New Series.
Lutw.	Lutwyche's Reports.
M. & Gr.	Manning & Granger's Reports.
M. & M.	Moody & Malkin's Reports.
M. & P.	Moore & Payne's Reports.
M. & S.	Maule & Selwyn's Reports.
M. & Sc.	Moore & Scott's Reports.
M. & W.	Meeson & Welsby's Reports.
M'Clel.	M'Cleland's Reports.
M'Clel. & Y.	M'Cleland & Younge's Reports.
Mac. & G.	Macnaghten & Gordon's Reports.
Macqueen	Macqueen's House of Lords Cas
Madd.	Maddock's Reports.
Man. & Ry.	Manning & Ryland's Reports.
Marsh.	Marshall's Reports.
Mer.	Merivale's Reports.
Mod.	Modern Reports.
Moo.	J. B. Moore's Reports.
Moo. & R.	Moody & Robinson's Reports.
Moo. & Sc.	Moore & Scott's Reports.
Moore, P. C. C.	Moore's Privy Council Cases.
My. & Cr.	Mylne & Craig's Reports.
My. & K.	Mylne & Keen's Reports.
N. & P.	Nevile & Perry's Reports.
P. & D.	Perry & Davison's Reports.
Parker	Parker's Reports.
Peake, N. P. C.	Peake's Nisi Prius Cases.
Peake's Add. Cas.	Peake's Additional Cases.
Phil.	Phillip's Reports.
Plowd.	Plowden's Commentaries.
Poph.	Popham's Reports.
Price	Price's Reports.

P. W.	Peere Williams's Reports.
Q. B.	Queen's Bench Reports.
R. & R. C. C.	Russell & Ryan's Crown Cases.
Ld. Raym.	Lord Raymond's Reports.
Ridg. P. C.	Ridgeway's Parliamentary Cases.
Rol. Abr.	Rolle's Abridgment.
Russ.	Russell's Reports.
Russ. & M.	Russell & Mylne's Reports.
Ry. & M.	Ryan & Moody's Reports.
Salk.	Salkeld's Reports.
Saund.	Saunder's Reports.
Sc. N. R.	Scott's New Reports.
Sch. & Lef.	Schoales & Lefroy's Reports.
Scott	Scott's Reports.
Selw. N. P.	Selwyn's Nisi Prius (13th Edit.).
Shep. Touch.	Sheppard's Touchstone.
Sid.	Siderfin's Reports.
Sim.	Simon's Reports.
Sim. N. S.	Simon's Reports, New Series.
Sm. & G.	Smale & Giffard's Reports.
Smith, L. C.	Smith's Leading Cases (6th Edit.).
Smith, L. & T.	Smith on Landlord and Tenant.
Stark.	Starkie's Reports.
Stra.	Strange's Reports.
Styles	Styles's Reports.
Sug. V. & P.	Sugden on Vendors and Purchasers.
Swanst.	Swanston's Reports.
Taunt.	Taunton's Reports.
T. R.	Durnford & East's Term Reports.
Tyr.	Tyrwhitt's Reports.
Tyr. & Gr.	Tyrwhitt & Granger's Reports.
V. & B.	Vesey & Beames's Reports.
Vaugh.	Vaughan's Reports.
Ventr.	Ventris's Reports.
Vern.	Vernon's Reports
Ves.	Vesey junior's Reports.
Wh. & Tud. L. C. Eq.	White & Tudor's Leading Cases in Equity.
Willes	Willes's Reports.
Williams on Exors.	Williams on Executors.
Wils.	Wilson's Reports.
Wms. Saund.	Saunders's Reports, by Williams.
Woodfall, L. & T.	Woodfall's Landlord and Tenant.
Y. & C. C. C.	Younge & Collyer's Chancery Cases.
Y. & C. Ex.	Younge & Collyer's Exchequer Cases.
Y. & J.	Younge & Jervis's Reports.
Yelv.	Yelverton's Reports.
Yo.	Younge's Reports.

ERRATA.

Page 30, note (*d*), *for* "*Doe* v. *Hayes*" *read* "*Doe* v. *Sturges*" (the marginal headings to this case in Taunton's Reports are wrong).

„ 164, last line of text, *for* "tenant" *read* "landlord."

THE

Law of Landlord and Tenant.

CHAP. I.
REQUISITES TO THE EXPRESS CREATION OF THE RELATION OF LANDLORD AND TENANT.

	PAGE
SECT. I. PROPERTY CAPABLE OF BEING LET	1
II. PERSONS CAPABLE OF MAKING AND TAKING LEASES	2
(1) Restrictions arising from disability	2
Infants	2
Lunatics	7
Married women	9
Aliens	13
Convicts	14
Corporations	14
Ecclesiastical	15
Municipal	21
The crown	22
Trustees for charitable uses	22
(2) Restrictions arising from limited interest	26
Tenants in tail	26
Tenants for life	28
Copyholders	29
Joint tenants	30
Trustees	30
Executors and administrators	30
Agents	31
Leases under powers	31
Leases of settled estates	34
Mortgagor and mortgagee	41
Leases by estoppel	42
(3) Restrictions arising from confidential relations	43
III. AN ACTUAL LETTING	44
Agreements distinguished from leases	44
IV. OF THE EXCLUSIVE POSSESSION OF THE PREMISES	47
Licences distinguished from leases	47
Occupation as servant or agent	47

SECT. I.—*Property capable of being let.*

IN accordance with the rule that whatever may be granted for ever may be granted for a time, leases may General rule. be made of all kinds of interests and possessions; not only of lands and houses, but also of goods and chattels, live stock and incorporeal hereditaments (*a*).

Exceptions. But offices to which a trust is annexed (*b*), or which concern the administration of justice, cannot be absolutely leased for years (*c*).

Dignities and honours cannot be granted for years (*d*).

Assignments of pensions granted by the crown for military services are void (*e*).

SECT. II.—*Persons capable of making and taking Leases.*

Alien enemies. Alien enemies, since they are disabled from maintaining any action or getting anything within the realm (*f*), can neither make nor take leases of any kind of property.

But in other cases leases for limited terms, and subject to the observance of conditions and restrictions, may be granted or accepted by, or on behalf of, persons ordinarily unable to contract, or possessing only a limited interest in the demised premises.

(1) *Restrictions arising from Disability.*

Infants. Where any person under the age of twenty-one years shall be seised or possessed of (*g*), or entitled to

---

(*a*) See Bac. Abr. (A.) 7.

(*b*) It would seem that the patronage of a grammar-school, granted by letters-patent to the founder and his heirs, is capable of being leased. See *Att.-Gen.* v. *Brentwood School*, 3 B. & Ad. 59.

(*c*) Bac. Abr. (A.) 8—10; *Reynel's Case*, 9 Co. R., at p. 96 b; *Howard* v. *Wood*, 2 Lev. 245; see also Stat. 5 & 6 Edw. 6, c. 16, ss. 2, 3.

(*d*) Bac. Abr. (A.) 10; Co. Lit. 16 b; 9 Co. R. 97 b.

(*e*) Stat. 47 Geo. 3, sess. 2, c. 25, s. 4; *Lloyd* v. *Cheetham*, 3 Giff. 171; 30 L. J., Ch. 640. See *Heald* v. *Hay*, 3 Giff. 467; 31 L. J., Ch. 311; *Carew* v. *Cooper*, 4 Giff. 619; 33 L. J., Ch. 289; 13 W. R. 586.

(*f*) See *Calvin's Case*, 7 Co. R., at p. 17.

(*g*) See *In re Clark*, 35 L. J., Ch. 314; L. R., 1 Ch. 292; *In re Spenser's Estates*, 37 L. J.,

any land in fee or in tail, or to any leasehold land for an absolute interest, and it shall appear to the Court of Chancery to be for the benefit of such person that a lease or underlease should be made of such estates for terms of years, for encouraging the erection of buildings thereon, or for repairing buildings actually being thereon, or the working of mines, or otherwise improving the same, or for farming or other purposes, it shall be lawful for such infant, or his guardian in the name of such infant, by the direction of the Court of Chancery, to be signified by an order to be made in a summary way upon the petition of such infant or his guardian, to make such lease of the land, or any part thereof, according to his interest therein, and to the nature of the tenure of such estates, for such term of years and subject to such rents and covenants as the said court shall direct (*h*).

Stat. 11 Geo. 4 & 1 Will. 4, c. 65, s. 17.

Leases may be made by direction of Court of Chancery.

But in no such case shall any fine be taken, and in every such case the best rent that can be obtained, regard being had to the nature of the lease, shall be reserved, and the lease shall be settled and approved of by a master of the said Court (*i*); and a counterpart of every such lease shall be executed by the lessee, and deposited in the master's office (*j*) till such infant shall attain twenty-one.

Requisites.

Provided that no lease be made of the capital mansion-house and the park and grounds respectively held therewith for any period exceeding the minority of any such infant.

Ch. 18; *In re Evans*, 2 My. & K. 318.
(*h*) See *Harris* v. *Davis*, 9 Jur. 1084.
(*i*) Now in the chambers of a Vice-Chancellor or the Master of the Rolls. See Stat. 15 & 16 Vict. c. 80.
(*j*) Now in the Record and Writ Clerks' Office. Ord. 42, r. 3.

Leases of the whole or any parts of settled estates to which infants are entitled, or of any rights or privileges affecting such estates, may be authorized by the Court of Chancery, upon the application of guardians on behalf of infants, for the terms of years and subject to the provisions and restrictions contained in the Settled Estates Acts (*k*). But in the cases of infant tenants in tail no application to the Court, or consent to any application, may be made or given by any guardian without the special direction of the Court.

A lease reserving rent, granted by an infant otherwise than under the provisions of these statutes, may be avoided by him on attaining his majority (*l*), or by his heir if he dies before that event (*m*). It has been doubted whether a lease reserving no rent, or a nominal rent merely, is not absolutely void, because then, as it is said, there is no semblance of benefit to the infant. But there is no authority for the proposition that the rent reserved in an infant's lease must be the best, in order to prevent it from being void (*n*). An infant cannot avoid a lease reserving rent until he comes of age (*o*), and if the lessee is then in possession the lessor who desires to disaffirm the lease must manifest his intention to do so by some act of notoriety, as ejectment, entry, demand of possession, or the like; or must

---

(*k*) See *post*, p. 34.

(*l*) *Zouch* v. *Parsons*, 3 Burr. at p. 1806; *Slator* v. *Brady*, 14 Ir. C. L. R., Ex. 61; *Slator* v. *Trimble*, 14 Ir. C. L. R., Q. B. 342, 351; Bac. Abr. (B.) 11. It has been said, however, that an infant cannot avoid a lease which is for his benefit. Per Buller, J., in *Maddon* v. *White*, 2 T. R., at p. 161. See *Ketsey's Case*, Cro. Jac. 320.

(*m*) Co. Lit. 45 b.

(*n*) Judgment in *Slator* v. *Brady*, 14 Ir. C. L. R., Ex., at p. 65. See also judgment of Hayes, J., in *Slator* v. *Trimble*, *Id.*, at p. 356.

(*o*) Bac. Abr. (B.) 11; *Slator* v. *Trimble*, 14 Ir. C. L. R., Q. B., 342, 352, 356. But see remarks of Parke, B., 5 Ex. 124.

at the least give notice (*p*). The execution by him of a new lease of the same premises to another person will not divest the estate created by the former demise(*q*).

If the lessor, after attaining his majority, accepts rent due after that event, or otherwise, either verbally or by deed, recognizes the lease as subsisting, he cannot subsequently avoid it (*r*).

The lease of an infant, to be good, must be his own personal act. If he appoints a person to make a lease it does not bind the infant, nor is the infant's ratification of such lease binding (*s*).

The lessee can in no case avoid the lease on account of the infancy of the lessor (*t*).

Leases granted to infants may be avoided by them when they come of age; and if at that period the lessee disaffirms the lease, he is not liable for rent (*u*). If, however, he continues to occupy the demised premises, and does not signify his intention to avoid the lease within a reasonable time after attaining his majority, he becomes liable to pay the rent (including arrears accrued during his minority (*x*)), and to perform all the other obligations attached to the estate (*y*). If the premises comprised in the lease come within the

Leases to infants.

(*p*) See judgment in *Slator* v. *Brady*, 14 Ir. C. L. R., Ex., at p. 66.
(*q*) *Slator* v. *Brady*, 14 Ir. C. L. R., Ex. 61.
(*r*) *Ashfield* v. *Ashfield*, W. Jones, 157; *Smith* v. *Low*, 1 Atk. 489; *Story* v. *Johnson*, 2 Y. & C., Ex. 586; *Anon.*, 4 Leon. 4. See *Baylis* v. *Dinely*, 3 M. & S., at p. 481.
(*s*) Per Parke, B., in *Doe* v. *Roberts*, 16 M. & W., at p. 781.
(*t*) Per Lord Mansfield, C. J.,

in *Zouch* v. *Parsons*, 3 Burr., at p. 1806.
(*u*) *Ketsey's Case*, Cro. Jac. 320; S. C., nom. *Kirton* v. *Elliott*, 2 Bulst. 69. See 7 Burr. 719.
(*x*) Bac. Abr. (B.) 12; *Ketsey's Case*, Cro. Jac. 320.
(*y*) *North Western Ry. Co.* v. *M'Michael*, 5 Ex. 114, 124; 20 L. J., Ex. 97; *Holmes* v. *Blogg*, 8 Taunt. 35, 39. See *Kelly* v. *Coote*, 5 Ir. C. L. R. 469.

designation of *necessaries*, the infant lessee is liable for the rent (z).

Stat. 11 Geo. 4 & 1 Will. 4, c. 65, s. 12.

Where any person under the age of twenty-one years, or a *feme covert*, is entitled to any lease for life or years, it shall be lawful for such person, or his guardian or other person on his behalf, and for such *feme covert* or any person on her behalf, to apply to the Court of Chancery in England, the Courts of Equity of the Counties Palatine of Lancaster and Durham, respectively, as to land within their respective jurisdiction, by petition or motion; and by the order and direction of the said Courts respectively such infant or *feme covert*, or his guardian, or any person appointed in the place of such infant or *feme covert* by the said Courts respectively, may from time to time by deed surrender such lease and accept in the place, and for the benefit of such person under the age of twenty-one years, or *feme covert*, one or more new lease or leases of the premises comprised in such lease surrendered, for such number of lives, or for such term or terms of years determinable upon such number of lives, or for such term or terms of years absolute, as was or were mentioned in the lease so surrendered at the making thereof, or otherwise as the said Courts shall respectively direct.

By order of the Court of Chancery leases to which infants or married women are entitled may be surrendered and renewed.

Sect. 15. Renewed lease to be to same uses, &c. as surrendered lease.

Every lease to be renewed as aforesaid shall operate to the same uses, and be liable to the same trusts, charges and conditions, as the lease surrendered would have been subject to in case such surrender had not been made.

Sect. 16. By order of the Court of Chancery infants may accept of sur-

Where any person under the age of twenty-one years, or a *feme covert*, might, in pursuance of any covenant or agreement, if not under disability, be compelled to renew any lease, it shall be lawful for such

(z) See *Lowe* v. *Griffith*, 1 Scott, 458.

infant, or his guardian in the name of such infant, or such *feme covert*, by the direction of the Court of Chancery, to be signified by an order to be made in a summary way upon the petition of such infant or his guardian, or of such *feme covert*, or of any person entitled to such renewal, from time to time to accept of a surrender of such lease, and to make a new lease of the premises comprised in such lease, for such number of lives, or for such term or terms determinable upon such number of lives, or for such term or terms of years absolute, as was or were mentioned in the lease so surrendered at the making thereof, or otherwise as the Court by such order shall direct.

<small>renders of leases and make new leases.</small>

Where a lunatic is entitled to land in fee or in tail, or to leasehold land for an absolute interest, and it appears to the Lord Chancellor to be for his benefit that a lease or underlease should be made thereof for terms of years, for encouraging the erection of buildings thereon, or for repairing buildings actually being thereon, or otherwise improving the same, or for farming or other purposes, the committee of the estate may, in the name and on behalf of the lunatic, under order of the Lord Chancellor, make such lease of the land or any part thereof, according to the lunatic's estate and interest therein, and to the nature of the tenure thereof, for such term or terms of years, and subject to such rents and covenants as the Lord Chancellor shall order. Under the same order, leases may be made of mines either already opened, or unopened where necessary for the maintenance of the lunatic or expedient; leasing powers vested in lunatics exercised; and surrenders of leases accepted, and new leases made, subject to certain conditions.

<small>Lunatics.
Stat. 16 & 17 Vict. c. 70, s. 129.
Leases may be made by committee under order of Lord Chancellor.
Sects. 130—132.
Sect. 133.
Sect. 134.</small>

Stat. 19 & 20 Vict. c. 120, ss. 2—10. Leases of lunatics' settled estates may be authorized by the Court of Chancery.	Leases of the whole or any parts of settled estates to which lunatics are entitled, or of any rights or privileges affecting such estates, may be authorized by the Court of Chancery, upon the application of committees on behalf of lunatics, for the terms of years, and subject to the provisions and restrictions contained in the Settled Estates Acts (*a*). But in the cases of
Sect. 36.	lunatic tenants in tail, no application to the Court, or consent to any application, may be made or given by any committee without the special direction of the Court.
Stat. 16 & 17 Vict. c. 70, s. 113. Committee, under order of Lord Chancellor, may surrender and renew leases to which lunatic is entitled.	Where a lunatic is entitled to a lease for life or years, the committee of his estate may, in his name and on his behalf, under an order of the Lord Chancellor, by deed surrender the lease, and in the name and on behalf of the lunatic accept a new lease of the premises comprised in the lease surrendered, for such number of lives or for such term of years as was mentioned in the lease surrendered at the making thereof, or otherwise as the Lord Chancellor shall order.
Sect. 114. Expenses of renewal to be charged on estate.	Every fine upon renewal, and all reasonable charges incident thereto, may be paid out of the lunatic's estate, or may, with interest, be a charge upon the leasehold premises, as the Lord Chancellor shall order.
Sect. 115. Renewed lease to be to same uses, &c. as surrendered ease.	Every lease renewed shall operate to the same uses, and be liable to the same trusts, charges and conditions as the lease surrendered would have been subject to if the surrender had not been made.
Leases by lunatic personally.	A lease granted by or to a lunatic *personally* is void if it appears that the other contracting party knew of his state of mind, and took advantage of it (*b*). But if this is not proved, and especially if the contract, having been entered into by the other party fairly and in good

(*a*) See *post*, p. 34.   P. 679. See *Browne* v. *Joddrell*,
(*b*) *Dane* v. *Kirkwall*, 8 C. &   M. & M. 105.

faith, has also been executed and completed, and the property forming the subject-matter of the contract has been paid for and fully enjoyed, such contract cannot afterwards be set aside either by the lunatic or those who represent him (*c*).

Where by settlements or wills married women are expressly empowered to demise, they may do so without the concurrence of their husbands (*d*). A married woman who has property settled to her separate use, without restraint on alienation, may, generally speaking, dispose of it as a *feme sole* (*e*). Leases of such property need not be acknowledged under the Fines and Recoveries Act (*f*).

Married women. When they may demise alone.

It shall be lawful for every married woman, in every case except that of being tenant in tail, for which provision is made by this act (*g*), by deed to dispose of lands of any tenure as fully and effectually as she could do if she were a *feme sole*, except that no such disposition shall be valid unless the husband concur in the deed by which the same shall be effected, nor unless the deed be acknowledged by her, upon her executing the same or afterwards, as her act and deed, before a judge of one of the superior courts at Westminster, or before two perpetual or two special commissioners.

Stat. 3 & 4 Will. 4, c. 74, ss. 77, 79.

With concurrence of husband may demise by deed acknowledged.

It shall be lawful for any person entitled to the possession or to the receipt of the rents and profits of any

Stat. 19 & 20 Vict. c. 120, s. 32.

(*c*) *Molton* v. *Camroux*, 2 Ex. 487, 503; 4 Ex. 17; 18 L. J., Ex. 68, 356; *Bearan* v. *M'Donnell*, 9 Ex. 309; 10 Ex. 184; 23 L. J., Ex. 94, 336. See *Campbell* v. *Hooper*, 3 Sm. & G. 153; 24 L. J., Ch. 644; *Baxter* v. *Portsmouth*, 5 B. & C. 170.

(*d*) 3 Atk. 711. See *Doe* v. *Eyre*, 3 C. B. 557; 5 C. B. 713.

(*e*) Per Plumer, V.-C., in *Francis* v. *Wigzell*, 1 Madd., at p. 261; *Aylett* v. *Ashton*, 1 My. & Cr. 105. See stat. 33 & 34 Vict. c. 93.

(*f*) *Taylor* v. *Meads*, 34 L. J., Ch. 203; *Adams* v. *Gamble*, 12 Ir. Ch. Rep. 102.

(*g*) See *post*, p. 27.

Husband entitled to settled estates in right of his wife;	settled estates for an estate for life, or for a term of years determinable with his life, or for any greater estate, either in his own right or in right of his wife *under a settlement made since November 1st, 1856* (*sect.* 44), unless the settlement shall contain an express declaration that it shall not be lawful for such person to make such demise; and also for any person
or to unsettled estates in right of wife seised in fee; also tenant by the curtesy, or in dower, may make leases not exceeding twenty-one years.	entitled to the possession or to the receipt of the rents and profits of any unsettled estates as tenant by the curtesy, or in dower, or in right of a wife who is seised in fee, without any application to the Court, to demise the same or any part thereof, except the principal mansion-house and the demesnes thereof, and other lands usually occupied therewith, from time to time, for any term not exceeding twenty-one years to take effect in possession.
Requisites.	Provided, that every such demise be made by deed, and the best rent that can reasonably be obtained be thereby reserved, without any fine, which rent shall be incident to the immediate reversion; that such demise be not made without impeachment of waste, and do contain a covenant for payment of the rent, and such other usual and proper covenants as the lessor shall think fit, and also a condition of re-entry on nonpayment, for a period not less than twenty-eight days, of the rent thereby reserved, and on non-observance of any of the covenants or conditions therein contained; and provided a counterpart of every deed of lease be executed by the lessee.
Sect. 34. Evidence of execution of counterpart.	The execution of any lease by the lessor or lessors shall be deemed sufficient evidence that a counterpart of such lease has been duly executed by the lessee as required by this act.

PERSONS CAPABLE OF MAKING AND TAKING LEASES. 11

Every demise authorized by the preceding section shall be valid against the person granting the same, and all other persons entitled to estates subsequent to the estate of such person under the same settlement, if the estates be settled, and in the case of unsettled estates against all persons claiming through or under the wife or husband (as the case may be) of the person granting the same (and also against the wife of any husband making such demise of estates to which he is entitled in right of such wife (*g*)). Sect. 33.
Against whom demises are valid.

Leases of settled estates, in which married women have limited interests, may be granted under the authority of the Court of Chancery (*h*). Sects. 2—10, 16—18.
Leases of married women's settled estates

Where a married woman shall apply to the Court, or consent to an application to the Court, under the Settled Estates Act, she shall first be examined by the Court, or some solicitor duly appointed by the Court for that purpose, apart from her husband touching her knowledge of the nature and effect of the application, and it shall be ascertained that she freely desires to make or consent to such application. may be authorized by the Court of Chancery.
Sects. 37, 38.
Separate examination.

Subject to such examination, married women may make or consent to any applications, whether they be of full age or infants. Sect. 39.

Leases of the freehold property of the wife, made either by husband and wife or by the husband alone, not authorized by the above-mentioned statutes or by an express power, are valid, to the extent of the term, during the joint lives of husband and wife (*i*). If not by deed, such leases on the death of the husband become Leases of wife's freeholds not in pursuance of statutes.

(*g*) Stat. 21 & 22 Vict. c. 77, s. 8.
(*h*) See *post*, p. 34.
(*i*) *Bateman* v. *Allen*, Cro. Eliz. 437; *Wiscot's Case*, 2 Co. R., at p. 61 b.

void as against the wife surviving and persons claiming under her (*k*). If made by deed, they are voidable on the death of the husband by the widow, but if, after her husband's decease, she accepts rent due after that event, or otherwise recognizes the leases as subsisting, they will become good and unavoidable (*l*). If the widow does no act to disaffirm the lease, but allows the tenant to continue in possession during her lifetime, the lease will be good and subsisting up to her death; and the rent which accrued due during her lifetime is recoverable by her executors (*m*). If the husband survives, and (having had issue by his wife born alive, that might by possibility inherit the estate as her heir) becomes tenant by the curtesy, the lease will be good for the whole term, provided the husband lives so long, but upon his death will absolutely determine (*n*).

Leases of wife's leaseholds.

Underleases of the leasehold property of the wife may be made by the husband in his own name, to commence either during his life or after his decease, and such underleases will be valid, though the wife should survive (*o*).

Stat. 11 Geo. 4 & 1 Will. 4, c. 65, ss. 12, 16. Renewal of leases to which married women are entitled.

Leases to which married women are entitled may be surrendered and renewed by direction of the Court of Chancery (*p*), and married women may also, in certain cases, under the same direction, accept surrenders and make renewals of leases (*p*).

Leases to married women.

A lease granted to a married woman may be disaffirmed by her husband, but vests in her until he

(*k*) *Walsall* v. *Heath*, Cro. Eliz. 656; *Harvy* v. *Thomas*, Cro. Eliz. 216; judgment in *Parry* v. *Hindle*, 2 Taunt., at p. 181.

(*l*) *Doe* v. *Weller*, 7 T. R. 478. See *Toler* v. *Slater*, 37 L. J., Q. B. 33; L. R., 3 Q. B. 42; Bac. Abr. (C.) 17.

(*m*) See *Toler* v. *Slater*, L. R., 3 Q. B., at p. 46.

(*n*) *Miller* v. *Maynwaring*, Cro. Car. 397.

(*o*) *Grute* v. *Locroft*, Cro. Eliz. 287; Bac. Abr. (C.) 16.

(*p*) See *ante*, p. 6.

expresses his dissent (*q*). After his death, however, the wife or her heirs may avoid the lease, unless after the decease of her husband she has assented to it (*r*).

Real and personal property of every description may be taken, acquired, held and disposed of by an alien in the same manner in all respects as by a natural-born British subject; and a title to real and personal property of every description may be derived through, from, or in succession to an alien, in the same manner in all respects as through, from, or in succession to a natural-born British subject: Provided— Aliens. Stat. 33 Vict. c. 14, s. 2. May take and dispose of real and personal property.

(1.) That this section shall not confer any right on an alien to hold real property situate out of the United Kingdom, and shall not qualify an alien for any office, or for any municipal, parliamentary or other franchise:

(2.) That this section shall not entitle an alien to any right or privilege as a British subject, except such rights and privileges in respect of property as are hereby expressly given to him:

(3.) That this section shall not affect any estate or interest in real or personal property to which any person has or may become entitled, either mediately or immediately, in possession or expectancy, in pursuance of any disposition made before the passing of this Act, or in pursuance of any devolution by law on the death of any person dying before the passing of this Act (12 May, 1870) (*s*).

(*q*) See end of judgment in *Swaine* v. *Holman*, Hob. 204; Co. Lit. 3 a.
(*r*) Co. Lit. 3 a.
(*s*) Before this act aliens might take lands, houses, &c. for the purpose of occupation or of trade for any term not exceeding twenty-one years. Stat. 7 & 8 Vict. c. 66, s. 5.

Convicts.
Stat. 33 & 34 Vict. c. 23, ss. 6, 8.

No action at law or suit in equity for the recovery of any property, debt, or damage whatsoever shall be brought by any convict [*i.e.* any person against whom judgment of death or penal servitude has been, after 4th July, 1870, pronounced or recorded by any Court of competent jurisdiction in England, Wales or Ireland, upon any charge of treason or felony] against any person during the time while he shall be subject to the operation of this Act; and every such convict shall be incapable, during such time as aforesaid, of alienating or charging any property, or of making any contract, save as hereinafter provided.

Are incapable of alienating property or making contract.

Sect. 12. Administrator may let property.

The administrator (*s*) shall have absolute power to let any part of the property of the convict as to him shall seem fit.

Corporations.

Since, as a general rule, corporations can only contract under seal, leases by or to them must be made by deed, sealed with their common seal (*t*). But although leases by corporations not so made are void, yet if the tenant has actually occupied and paid rent under the void instrument, and the corporation has received such rent, an implied tenancy from year to year may exist upon such of the terms of the void instrument as are applicable to that kind of tenancy, and an action may be maintained by the corporation for a breach of such terms (*u*). If there has been part performance of a contract for a lease by a corporation not under the

---

(*s*) Appointed under the provisions of the act. See *post*, Chap. IV., Sect. 12, (2).

(*t*) *Finlay* v. *Bristol and Exeter Ry. Co.*, 7 Ex. 409; 21 L. J., Ex. 117. See *Rex* v. *Inhabitants of Chipping Norton*, 5 East, 239;

Rex v. *Inhabitants of North Duffield*, 3 M. & S. 247.

(*u*) *Wood* v. *Tate*, 2 B. & P. (N. R.) 247; *Ecclesiastical Commissioners* v. *Merral*, 38 L. J., Ex. 93; L. R., 4 Ex. 162.

corporate seal, a court of equity will decree specific performance of such contract (*v*). Corporations may take leases of tenements or hereditaments of moderate and usual length, such as a husbandry lease for twenty-one years (*w*). But a lease for a term of unusual duration may incur the penalty of forfeiture imposed on land brought into mortmain under colour of a lease (*x*). There would seem to be no decision as to what length of term will have this effect; but it has been said that leases for one hundred years (*y*), or for eighty-one years (*z*), are within the Mortmain Acts.

Ecclesiastical corporations are either aggregate, consisting of several persons, as the dean and chapter of a cathedral; or sole, consisting of one person, as a bishop. Ecclesiastical.

The legislative provisions relating to leases by these bodies are very numerous, but the substance of the enactments may be stated as follows:—

Persons having any estate of inheritance in right of their churches, (including prebendaries and chancellors, treasurers and precentors of cathedral churches (*a*), but) excepting parsons and vicars, may make leases by indenture, good and effectual against the lessors and their successors, of lands, tenements or hereditaments commonly let for twenty years next before such leases, and also of tithes, tolls and other incorporeal hereditaments, for terms not exceeding twenty-one years or three lives 1. *Enabling statutes.*
Stats. 32 Hen. 8, c. 28, ss. 1, 2, 4; 5 Geo. 3, c. 17, s. 1.
Corporations sole (except parsons and vicars) may lease lands, &c. for twenty-one years, or three lives.

(*v*) *Steeven's Hospital* v. *Dyas*, 15 Ir. Ch. Rep. 405.
(*w*) See *Jesus Coll.* v. *Gibbs*, 1 Y. & C., Ex. 145, 147.
(*x*) Stat. 7 Edw. 1, stat. 2, c. 1.
(*y*) *Howles* v. *Mason*, 2 Brownlow, at p. 197. Per Tanfield, C.B.,

in *Cotton's Case*, Godb., at p. 192.
(*z*) Per Bridgman, C. J., in *Hemming* v. *Brabazon*, O. Bridg. Rep. (by Bannister), at p. 7. See 1 Platt on Leases, 541.
(*a*) Bac. Abr. (E.) 49.

from the making thereof; subject to the observance of certain conditions.

<small>Stat. 5 & 6 Vict. c. 108, ss. 1—9, 18, 20—32.</small>

Any ecclesiastical corporation, aggregate or sole, except any college or corporation of vicars choral, priest vicars, senior vicars, custos and vicars, or minor canons and any ecclesiastical hospital or the master thereof, with the consent of the Ecclesiastical Commissioners; and in the case of a lease made by any incumbent of a benefice, with the consent of the patron thereof, and in the case of certain copyholds with the consent of the lord of the manor, testified in each case as in the act is mentioned (ss. 21—27), may by deed grant building, repairing or improving leases for any term not exceeding ninety-nine years, and leases of mines or quarries, running water, way-leaves and other like easements, for any term not exceeding sixty years; subject to the observance of the conditions and restrictions mentioned in the act.

<small>With certain consents any ecclesiastical corporation may grant building leases for ninety-nine years; leases of running water, easements or mines for sixty years.</small>

<small>Stat. 21 & 22 Vict. c. 57, s. 1. Or may lease in such manner as the Ecclesiastical Commissioners shall direct.</small>

In any case in which the Ecclesiastical Commissioners are satisfied that the property of any ecclesiastical corporation, by the last-mentioned act authorized to be leased, might, to the permanent advantage of the estate, be leased in any manner, any ecclesiastical corporation (except the corporations excepted in the said act), with such consents as in the said act are mentioned, and with the approval of the Commissioners, to be testified by deed under their common seal, may lease all or any part of their lands, houses, mines, minerals or other property, either in consideration of premiums or not, and generally in such manner as the commissioners may think proper (a).

<small>Stat. 5 & 6 Vict. c. 27.</small>

The incumbent of any benefice (b), with the consent

(a) This act and the previous act do not apply to the Isle of Man. Stat. 29 & 30 Vict. c. 81.
(b) See sect. 15.

of the patron and bishop, and, where the lands are copyhold, and a lease cannot be made without his licence, with the consent of the lord of the manor, such consents being testified in the manner mentioned in the act, may lease by deed any part of the glebe lands, or other lands belonging to such benefice (except the parsonage house, &c., and at least ten acres of glebe, where the glebe is within five miles from the parsonage house), for any term not exceeding fourteen years, or twenty years if the lessee is to execute improvements; subject to the observance of certain conditions. *Incumbents, with consent of patron and bishop, may lease glebe for fourteen or twenty years.*

Leases granted by a spiritual corporation sole not under the provisions of these statutes and without confirmation, are valid during the life or tenure of office of the lessor. Upon his death or other avoidance they become either voidable or absolutely void, according as the lessor has the whole or only a qualified fee simple (c). In the latter case the acceptance of rent by the successor will not set up such lease, but may create a tenancy from year to year (d). Where a lease by a bishop, which has been granted in consideration of the surrender of a prior lease by deed-poll, has been avoided by the successor, the first lease is not revived by such avoidance (e). But with the confirmation required by law, i.e., in the case of a bishop, with the confirmation of his dean and chapter, and in the case of a parson or vicar, with the confirmation of his patron and bishop, these corporations may grant leases which will bind their successors (f). *Leases by spiritual corporations sole not in pursuance of statutes.*

(c) Bac. Abr. (II.) 120. A bishop has the whole fee, a vicar a qualified fee.

(d) *Doe* v. *Collinge*, 7 C. B. 939; 18 L. J., C. P. 305, *post*, p. 53.

(e) *Doe* v. *Bridges*, 1 B. & Ad. 847.

(f) Bac. Abr. (G. 2) 99. See *Green* v. *Jenkins*, 28 Beav. 87; 1 De G., F. & J. 454; 29 L. J., Ch. 505.

A patron may confirm explicitly by deed or writing, or by consequence of law; as, for instance, where a parson makes a lease for years to the patron, who grants or assigns it over to another (*g*). It is not material whether the confirmation be before or after the making of the lease, provided it be made in the lifetime of the parties to the lease (*h*).

<small>Leases by spiritual corporations aggregate.</small>

Spiritual corporations aggregate, without any confirmation, may grant leases binding on their successors (*i*).

<small>2. *Restraining statutes.*
Stats. 1 Eliz. c. 19, s. 5;
13 Eliz. c. 10, s. 3.
Leases by spiritual corporations must not exceed twenty-one years and must observe certain conditions.</small>

But leases made by any archbishop or bishop, master and fellows of any college, dean and chapter of any cathedral or collegiate church, master or guardians of any hospital (*k*), parson, vicar, or any other having any spiritual or ecclesiastical living, of any hereditaments belonging to their spiritual promotion, exceeding twenty-one years, or three lives from the time at which they are made (*l*), or not reserving the accustomed yearly rent (*m*), or more, payable yearly during the term, though valid during the life of the corporation sole (*n*), or of the head of the corporation aggregate (*o*), by whom they were granted, are voidable by his successor (*p*), but may be confirmed by his acceptance of rent from the lessee (*p*). This restriction does not extend to leases for terms not exceeding forty years of houses not the capital or dwelling houses of the lessors, or grounds to such houses appertaining, not exceeding

<small>Stat. 14 Eliz. c. 11, ss. 17, 19.
Except leases not exceeding forty years of houses in towns, &c.</small>

(*g*) Bac. Abr. (G. 2) 109.
(*h*) Bac. Abr. (G. 4) 114.
(*i*) Bac. Abr. (G. 1) 99.
(*k*) See stats. 14 Eliz. c. 14; 39 Eliz. c. 5, s. 2.
(*l*) In 1 Eliz. c. 19, "from such time as any such lease shall begin."
(*m*) See *Doe* v. *Yarborough*, 7 Moore, 258; 1 Bing. 24; stat. 39 & 40 Geo. 3, c. 41.

(*n*) 2 Shep. Touch. 283; *Bishop of Salisbury's Case*, 10 Co. R. 58 b, 60 b.
(*o*) Co. Lit. 45 a.
(*p*) *Pennington* v. *Cardale*, 3 H. & N. 656, 666; 27 L. J., Ex. 438. See per Holroyd, J., in 4 B. & A. 217; *Doe* v. *Taniere*, 12 Q. B. 998; 18 L. J., Q. B. 49.

ten acres, situate in any city, borough, town corporate or market town, or the suburbs of any of them; provided such leases are made subject to certain conditions specified in the statute.

Any agreement for letting the house of residence, or the buildings, gardens, &c., necessary for the convenient occupation of the same, belonging to any benefice, to which house any spiritual person may be required by order of the bishop to proceed and to reside therein, or which may be assigned as a residence to any curate by the bishop, shall be made in writing, and shall contain a condition for avoiding the same, upon a copy of such order, assignment, or appointment being served upon the occupier thereof or left at the house, and otherwise shall be null and void. Stat. 1 & 2 Vict. c. 106, s. 59. Agreements for letting houses, &c. to contain condition.

No lease of lands acquired by an ecclesiastical corporation under this act can be granted by such corporation otherwise than from year to year, or for a term of years in possession not exceeding fourteen years, and subject to the conditions mentioned in the statute. But such corporation, with the approval of the Church Estates Commissioners, may grant mining or building leases upon such terms as the commissioners may think fit. Stat. 14 & 15 Vict. c. 104, s. 11. Lands acquired under may be leased for fourteen years.

No lease of lands acquired by any ecclesiastical corporation under this act can (except under stat. 5 & 6 Vict. c. 108, or this act) be granted otherwise than from year to year, or for a term not exceeding fourteen years, subject to certain conditions. Stat. 21 & 22 Vict. c. 57, s. 9. Lands acquired under may be leased for fourteen years.

No lands assigned as the endowment of any see under this act can be leased otherwise than from year to year or for a term not exceeding twenty-one years, subject to certain conditions. But with the approval of the Estates Committee of the Ecclesiastical Commissioners Stat. 23 & 24 Vict. c. 124, s. 8. Lands assigned as endowment of see may be leased for twenty-one years.

mining or building or other leases may be granted upon such terms as they may think fit.

Stats. 24 & 25 Vict. c. 105; 25 & 26 Vict. c. 52. No lease by any future prebendary, rector, &c. to be valid unless made in pursuance of certain acts.

It shall not be lawful for a prebendary of any prebend, not being a prebend of any cathedral or collegiate church, rector, vicar, perpetual curate or incumbent, who, after the passing of this act (6th August, 1861), may become possessed of, or entitled to any manors, lands, tenements or hereditaments belonging to any ecclesiastical benefice in England, to make any grant by copy of court-roll or lease of any such manors, lands, &c., in consideration of any fine, premium or foregift, or in any other way than under the provisions of the statutes 5 & 6 Vict. c. 27; 5 & 6 Vict. c. 108; or 21 & 22 Vict. c. 57.

Stat. 18 Eliz. c. 11, s. 2. Concurrent leases restrained.

Leases made by the ecclesiastical, spiritual or collegiate persons mentioned in stat. 13 Eliz. c. 10, of any of their ecclesiastical, spiritual or collegiate lands, tenements or hereditaments, whereof any former lease for years is in being not to be expired, surrendered or ended within three years next after the making of any such new lease, are void (*q*).

Stat. 6 & 7 Will. 4, c. 20, s. 1 (r). Renewal of leases only to be granted after certain time.

No ecclesiastical corporation, sole or aggregate, can grant any new lease, by way of renewal of any lease which has been previously granted for two or more lives, until one or more of the persons for whose lives such lease has been made shall die, and then only for the surviving lives or life, and for such new life or lives as, together with the life or lives of such survivor or survivors, shall make up the number of lives, not exceeding three in the whole, for which such lease has been originally made. Leases originally granted for forty years may be renewed after fourteen years have

(*q*) See *Vivian* v. *Blomberg*, 3 Bing., N. C. 311.

(*r*) Explained by stat. 6 & 7 Will. 4, c. 64.

expired; leases for thirty years, after ten years; and
leases for twenty-one years, after seven years. But
where it is certified that for ten years past such has
been the usual practice, leases may be renewed at
shorter periods. Leases granted for terms of years
cannot be renewed for lives. *Sect. 4.*

Any spiritual person, holding any cathedral prefer‑
ment or benefice, or any curacy or lectureship, or licensed
or otherwise allowed to perform the duties of any eccle‑
siastical office whatever, is prohibited from taking to
farm for occupation by himself, by lease or otherwise,
for term of life, or years, or at will, any lands exceeding
eighty acres in the whole, for the purpose of using,
occupying or cultivating the same, without the permis‑
sion in writing of the bishop of the diocese specially
given for that purpose under his hand; and every such
permission must specify the number of years, not ex‑
ceeding seven, for which such permission is given;
under a penalty of 40*s.* per annum for each acre of land
above eighty acres which such spiritual person occupies
contrary to the provision aforesaid. *Leases to ecclesiastical persons. Stat. 1 & 2 Vict. c. 106, s. 28. Beneficed clergy not to occupy more than eighty acres of land without permission of bishop.*

Municipal corporations may grant leases of certain
buildings and of ground for building on, or for making
gardens, &c., for terms not exceeding seventy-five years,
either at a reserved rent or a fine, or both; but they
cannot otherwise lease their lands, tenements, or here‑
ditaments for any term exceeding thirty-one years,
without the approbation of the Lords Commissioners of
the Treasury, or any three of them. *Municipal corporations. Stats. 5 & 6 Will. 4, c. 76, ss. 94, 96; 6 & 7 Will. 4, c. 104, s. 2. May grant building leases for seventy-five years and other leases for thirty-one years.*

These corporations, however, may renew leases in
cases in which, on the 5th June, 1835, they were bound by
covenant or agreement, or enjoined by any deed, will or
other document, or sanctioned by ancient usage to make
renewal; and also in all cases in which they had there‑ *Sect. 95.*

tofore ordinarily made renewal of any lease they may renew such lease as they might have done in case this act had not been passed (*s*).

The crown may lease manors, messuages, lands, tenements or hereditaments belonging thereto (advowsons and vicarages excepted) for any term not exceeding thirty-one years, or three lives, or some term of years determinable upon one, two or three lives; and subject to the observance of certain conditions. Leases for the purposes of rebuilding or repairing may be granted for terms not exceeding fifty years, or three lives; subject also to the fulfilment of certain conditions.

Lands belonging to the crown vested in the Commissioners of Woods and Forests may be leased by the commissioners for any term not exceeding thirty-one years, or for building and certain other purposes for any term not exceeding ninety-nine years; subject to the observance of certain conditions.

As to leases of lands belonging to the Duchy of Lancaster, see stats. 48 Geo. 3, c. 73; 52 Geo. 3, c. 161.

As to leases of lands belonging to the Duchy of Cornwall, see stat. 26 & 27 Vict. c. 49, ss. 21—26.

As to leases by the Universities of Oxford, Cambridge and Durham, and the colleges of Winchester and Eton, see stats. 21 & 22 Vict. c. 44; 23 & 24 Vict. c. 59, s. 3.

Leases of lands, tenements or hereditaments to any person or body corporate, in trust or for the benefit of any charitable uses (except leases of land for the erection thereon of buildings for religious or educational purposes, not exceeding two acres in extent in each

(*s*) See *Att.-Gen.* v. *Great Yarmouth*, 21 Beav. 625.

case, and *bonâ fide* made for a full and valuable consideration (*t*)) will be absolutely void, unless the following requisites are observed:—

(1.) The lease must be made by deed, sealed and delivered in the presence of two or more credible witnesses (*u*), but the deed need not be indented (*x*).

(2.) Unless made *bonâ fide* for a full and valuable consideration, actually paid at or before the making such lease, without fraud or collusion, the deed must be made twelve calendar months at least before the death of the lessor (including the days of execution and death (*y*)). Such consideration may consist wholly or in part of a rent, rent-charge, or other annual payment reserved or made payable to the lessor or to any other person (*x*).

(3.) The deed must be enrolled in Chancery within six calendar months next after the execution thereof (*y*). But upon the application by summons in a summary way of any person interested in any charitable trust the Court of Chancery, if satisfied, by affidavit or otherwise, that the deed or other instrument conveying the hereditaments for charitable uses was made really and *bonâ fide* for full and valuable consideration, actually paid at or before the making or perfecting thereof, or reserved by way of rent-charge or other annual payment, or partly paid at or before the making or per-

Requisites.

(*t*) See stat. 31 & 32 Vict. c. 44. For a list of the institutions excepted from the act of Geo. 2, see Tudor on Charitable Uses, p. 93.
(*u*) Stat. 9 Geo. 2, c. 36, ss. 1, 3.
(*x*) Stat. 24 Vict. c. 9, s. 1.
(*y*) Stat. 9 Geo. 2, c. 36, s. 1.

fecting of such deed or other instrument, and partly reserved as aforesaid, without fraud or collusion, and that at the time of the application to the Court possession or enjoyment is held under such deed or instrument, and that the omission to enrol the same in proper time has arisen from mere ignorance or inadvertence, or from the destruction thereof by time or accident, may make an order authorizing the enrolment in the Court of the deed or instrument to which the application relates, and the same shall thereupon be enrolled accordingly at any time within six calendar months from the date of the order, and no acknowledgment shall be necessary prior to enrolment (*b*).

(4.) The deed must be made to take effect in possession for the charitable use intended immediately from the making thereof (*c*). But every deed or assurance by which any land shall have been demised for any term of years for any charitable use shall be deemed to have been made to take effect for the charitable use thereby intended immediately from the making thereof, if the term for which such land shall have been thereby demised was thereby made to commence and take effect in possession at any time within one year from the date of such deed or assurance (*d*).

(5.) The deed must be without any power of revocation, reservation, trust, condition, limitation, clause or agreement whatsoever, for the benefit

---

(*b*) Stat. 29 & 30 Vict. c. 57, s. 2.

(*c*) Stat. 9 Geo. 2, c. 36, s. 1.

(*d*) Stat. 26 & 27 Vict. c. 106.

of the donor or grantor, or of any person or persons claiming under him (*e*). But no deed made after 17th May, 1861, shall be deemed to be null and void by reason of such deed or assurance, or any deed forming part of the same transaction, containing any grant or reservation of any peppercorn or other nominal rent, or of any mines or minerals, or easement, or any covenants or provisions as to the erection, repair, position or description of buildings, the formation or repair of streets or roads, drainage or nuisances, or any covenants or provisions of the like nature, for the use and enjoyment as well of the hereditaments comprised in such deed or assurance as of any other adjacent or neighbouring hereditaments, or any right of entry on nonpayment of any such rent, or on breach of any such covenant or provision, or any stipulations of the like nature for the benefit of the donor or grantor, or of any person or persons claiming under him, nor (in the case of any such assurance of hereditaments of copyhold or customary tenure or of any estate or interest therein) by reason of the same not being made by deed, nor (in the case of such assurances made *bonâ fide* on a sale for a full and valuable consideration) by reason of such consideration consisting wholly or partly of a rent, rent-charge, or other annual payment reserved or made payable to the vendor, or to any other person, with or without a right of re-entry for nonpayment thereof: provided always that in all reserva-

(*e*) Stat. 9 Geo. 2, c. 36, s. 1.

tions authorized by this act the donor, grantor or vendor shall reserve the same benefits for his representatives as for himself (*e*).

(2) *Restrictions arising from Limited Interest.*

Tenants in tail. Stat. 3 & 4 Will. 4, c. 74, ss. 15, 40. Tenants in tail may dispose of lands entailed for estate in fee simple or any less estate.

Every actual tenant in tail shall have full power to dispose of for an estate in fee simple absolute, *or for any less estate,* the lands entailed, as against all persons claiming the lands entailed by force of any estate tail which shall be vested in or might be claimed by, or which but for some previous act would have been vested in or might have been claimed by, the person making the disposition, at the time of his making the same, and also as against all persons whose estates are to take effect after the determination or in defeasance of any such estate tail; saving always the rights of all persons in respect of estates prior to the estate tail, and the rights of all other persons, except those against whom such disposition is by this act authorized to be made.

Sect. 34. Where there is protector his consent is necessary to make lease valid against remaindermen and reversioners.

If at the time when any person, actual tenant in tail of lands under a settlement, but not entitled to the remainder or reversion in fee immediately expectant on the determination of his estate tail, shall be desirous of making under this act a disposition of the lands entailed, there shall be a protector of such settlement, the consent of such protector shall be requisite to enable such actual tenant in tail to dispose of the lands entailed to the full extent to which he is hereinbefore authorized to dispose of the same; but such actual tenant in tail may, without such consent, make a disposition under this act of the lands entailed, which shall be good against all persons who, by force of any estate tail which

(*e*) Stat. 24 Vict. c. 9.

shall be vested in or might be claimed by, or which but for some previous act or default would have been vested in or might have been claimed by, the person making the disposition at the time of his making the same, shall claim the lands entailed.

Every disposition of lands under this act by a tenant in tail thereof shall be effected by some one of the assurances (not being a will) by which such tenant in tail could have made the disposition if his estate were an estate at law in fee simple absolute. Provided, nevertheless, that no disposition by a tenant in tail shall be of any force either at law or in equity, under this act, unless made or evidenced by deed; and that no disposition by a tenant in tail resting only on contract, either express or implied, or otherwise, and whether supported by a valuable or meritorious consideration or not, shall be of any force at law or in equity under this act, notwithstanding such disposition shall be made or evidenced by deed; and if the tenant in tail making the disposition shall be a married woman, the concurrence of her husband shall be necessary to give effect to the same; and any deed which may be executed by her for effecting the disposition shall be acknowledged by her as hereinafter directed (*f*). Sect. 40.

Lease must be by deed.

When tenant in tail is married woman, husband's concurrence necessary.

No assurance by which any disposition of lands shall be effected under this act by a tenant in tail thereof (except a lease for any term not exceeding twenty-one years, to commence from the date of such lease, or from any time not exceeding twelve calendar months from the date of such lease, where a rent shall be thereby reserved, which, at the time of granting such lease, shall be a rack-rent, or not less than five-sixth parts of a rack-rent), shall have any operation under this act, unless it Sect. 41.

Lease for term exceeding twenty-one years or commencing more than a year from the date or reserving a rent less than five-sixths of a rack-rent must be enrolled in chancery.

(*f*) See *ante*, p. 9.

be enrolled in chancery within six calendar months after the execution thereof.

<small>Stat. 19 & 20 Vict. c. 120, s. 32.
Tenants in tail, or for life of settled estates may demise for twenty-one years.</small>

Persons entitled to settled estates for life, or for years determinable with life, or for any greater estate, under a settlement made since November 1st, 1856, may demise the settled estates for terms not exceeding twenty-one years, subject to the observance of the restrictions and conditions contained in the statute (*i*).

<small>Leases by tenants in tail not in pursuance of statutes.</small>

A lease for years by a tenant in tail not authorized by the above-mentioned statutes, or by a power to lease, is not absolutely determined by his death, but the issue in tail is at liberty either to affirm or avoid it as he may think fit (*k*). His affirmance may be either expressed, or implied from acceptance of rent (*l*), or bringing an action for recovery thereof, or an action of waste (*m*). But to operate as an affirmance of the lease the rent must be accepted by the issue in tail from the tenant, and not from a person to whom he has underlet the land (*m*).

<small>Leases by tenants for life not in pursuance of statutes.</small>

Leases by a tenant for life, not in pursuance of these statutes or of any express power, are valid during the life of the lessor, but on his decease become absolutely void (*n*), and incapable of confirmation by the succeeding owner (*o*). But a new tenancy from year to year may be created by his acceptance of rent from the tenant (*p*), and where the succeeding owner has knowingly permitted or encouraged the tenant to expend

---

(*i*) See *ante*, p. 9.
(*k*) Bac. Abr. (D.) 18.
(*l*) *Doe* v. *Jenkins*, 5 Bing. 469, 476; 3 M. & P. 59.
(*m*) Bac. Abr. (D.) 19.
(*n*) *Doe* v. *Butcher*, 1 Dougl. 50; *Doe* v. *Archer*, 1 B. & P. 531.

(*o*) *Ludford* v. *Barber*, 1 T. R. 86; *James* v. *Jenkins*, Bull. N. P. 96 b; *Doe* v. *Butcher*, 1 Dougl. 50; *Jenkins* v. *Church*, Cowp. 482; *Doe* v. *Watts*, 7 T. R. 83.
(*p*) See *post*, Chap. II., Sect. 3.

money in improvements on the premises, the Court of Chancery will not allow the lease to be invalidated (*q*).

As to leases by tenants for terms of years, see *Underleases, post,* Chap. IV., Sect. 11.

If a copyholder makes a lease not warranted by the custom of the manor, and without the lord's licence, this is a forfeiture of his copyhold; but the lease is good against everybody but the lord (*r*), and even as between parties to the lease and the lord, the demise against custom is only a ground of forfeiture which the lord may waive (*s*). It seems that a lease for a year may be made by a copyholder without the lord's licence or any special custom (*t*). *Copyholders.*

All the powers to authorize and grant leases contained in the Settled Estates Act, 1856 (*u*) and this act shall be deemed to include powers to the lords of settled manors to give licences to their copyhold or customary tenants to grant leases of lands held by them of such manors to the same extent and for the same purposes as leases may be authorized or granted of freehold hereditaments under the said act and this act. Stat. 21 & 22 Vict. c. 77, s. 3.
Lords of settled manors may grant licences to lease.

It shall be lawful for the lord of any manor, with the consent of three-fourths of the persons having right of common upon the wastes and commons within his manor, at a meeting to be held after fourteen days' notice, such notice to be given in the manner directed in the statute, at any time to demise for any term, not Stat. 13 Geo. 3, c. 81, s. 15.
Lord, with consent of three-fourths of commoners, may lease twelfth part of wastes.

(*q*) *Stiles* v. *Cowper,* 3 Atk. 692. See *Dann* v. *Spurrier,* 7 Ves. 231, 235; *Pilling* v. *Armitage,* 12 Ves. 78, 88.

(*r*) Bac. Abr. (I. 6) 132; *Goodwin* v. *Longhurst,* Cro. Eliz. 535;

Doe v. *Tressider,* 1 Q. B. 416; 10 L. J., Q. B. 160.

(*s*) *Doe* v. *Bousfield,* 6 Q. B. 492; 14 L. J., Q. B. 42.

(*t*) See *Frosel* v. *Welsh,* Cro. Jac. 403.

(*u*) See *post,* p. 34.

exceeding four years, any part of such wastes and commons not exceeding a twelfth part thereof, for the best and most improved yearly rent that can by public auction be got for the same; the clear net rents reserved to the lord by any lease to be granted as aforesaid shall be applied in draining, fencing, or otherwise improving the residue of such wastes and commons.

Joint tenants. One joint tenant may demise his share to another, so as to create the relationship of landlord and tenant between them, with a right to distrain in respect of rent in arrear (x).

Trustees. It has been held that a trustee of lands may grant a lease of reasonable duration, such as a lease for ten years (y). But if the trust is a simple one, and the *cestui que trust* is in possession, the trustee cannot make any lease without his concurrence (z).

Executors and administrators. Executors and administrators, as they may dispose absolutely of terms for years vested in them in right of their testators or intestates, so may they lease the same for any fewer number of years, and the rents reserved on such leases shall be assets in their hands, and go in a course of administration (a). An administrator cannot make a lease until letters of administration have been granted to him (b). An executor, on the other hand, may demise before probate (c). A lease by one of several executors (d) or administrators (e) is good.

(x) *Cowper* v. *Fletcher*, 6 B. & S. 464; 34 L. J., Q. B. 187; Co. Lit. 186 a.

(y) See *Naylor* v. *Arnitt*, 1 Russ. & M. 501; Lewin on Trusts, 388.

(z) Lewin on Trusts, 388. See *Malpas* v. *Ackland*, 3 Russ. 273.

(a) Bac. Abr. (I. 7) 136.

(b) See *Wankford* v. *Wankford*, 1 Salk., at p. 301.

(c) *Roe* v. *Summerset*, 2 W. Bl. 692, 694.

(d) *Doe* v. *Hayes*, 7 Taunt., at p. 222.

(e) See *Jacomb* v. *Harwood*, 2 Ves. sen. 267.

An agreement for a lease made with an agent who **Agents.** acts under a power of attorney, and a lease executed by such agent in pursuance of the agreement, effectually bind the principal (*f*). An agent to execute a lease by deed must be appointed by deed (*g*), but if the lease to be made by the agent is not under seal he need not be authorized in writing (*h*). A steward has no general authority to enter into contracts for granting leases of farms for terms of years (*i*). A farm bailiff accustomed to let from year to year upon the ordinary terms and to receive rents, has no authority in law to let upon unusual terms unknown to the owner (*k*).

It is doubtful whether an agent employed to let a house has an implied general authority to let persons into possession, but slight evidence will be sufficient to show an express authority (*l*).

Settlements and wills often expressly empower tenants **Leases under** in tail or for life, or trustees, to grant leases. To **powers.** powers of leasing there are usually attached conditions and restrictions which must be carefully observed by the person exercising the power, or the lease made under it will be void as against persons entitled in remainder or reversion, except in the cases provided for by the statutes mentioned hereafter (*m*). Such leases, however, are good, as between the parties to them, by way of estoppel (*n*).

(*f*) *Hamilton* v. *Clanricarde*, 1 Bro. P. C. 341.

(*g*) *Steiglitz* v. *Egginton*, Holt, N. P. 141; *Harrison* v. *Jackson*, 7 T. R. 207.

(*h*) *Coles* v. *Trecothick*, 9 Ves., at p. 250.

(*i*) *Collen* v. *Gardiner*, 21 Beav. 540.

(*k*) *Turner* v. *Hutchinson*, 2 F. & F. 185.

(*l*) *Slack* v. *Crewe*, 2 F. & F. 59.

(*m*) For the construction of powers to lease, see Sugden on Powers, Chap. XVII.

(*n*) *Yellowly* v. *Gower*, 11 Ex. 274; 24 L. J., Ex. 289. See *post*, p. 42.

Relief on defective execution of powers of leasing.
Stat. 12 & 13 Vict. c. 26, s. 2.
Invalid lease made *bonâ fide* and under which lessee has entered, to be considered as contract for grant of valid lease.

Where in the intended exercise of a valid power of leasing a lease has been granted (*o*), which is, by reason of the non-observance or omission of some condition or restriction, or by reason of any other deviation from the terms of such power (*p*), invalid, such lease, in case the same have been made *bonâ fide*, and the lessee named therein, his heirs, executors, administrators or assigns (as the case may require), have entered thereunder, shall be considered in equity as a contract for a grant, at the request of the lessee, his heirs, executors, administrators or assigns (as the case may require), of a valid lease under such power, to the like purport and effect as such invalid lease as aforesaid, save so far as any variation may be necessary in order to comply with the terms of such power; and all persons who would have been bound by a lease lawfully granted under such power shall be bound in equity by such contract. But no lessee under any such invalid lease as aforesaid, his heirs, executors, administrators or assigns, shall be entitled by virtue of any such equitable contract as aforesaid to obtain any variation of such lease, where the persons who would have been bound by such contract are willing to confirm such lease without variation.

Lease not to be varied if persons bound by equitable contract are willing to confirm lease without variation.

Sect. 4.
Where estate of lessor continues after time when lease might have been lawfully granted by him, lease will be valid.

Where a lease granted in the intended exercise of a valid power of leasing is invalid by reason that at the time of the granting thereof the person granting the same could not lawfully grant such lease, but the estate of such person in the hereditaments comprised in such lease shall have continued after the time when such

(*o*) When a valid power of leasing is vested in a person granting a lease, and such lease cannot have effect and continuance, according to the terms thereof, independently of such power, such lease shall be deemed to be granted in the intended exercise of such power, although such power be not referred to in such lease (sect. 5).

(*p*) *Ex parte Cooper*, 34 L. J., Ch. 373.

lease might have been granted by him in the lawful exercise of such power, such lease shall take effect, and be as valid as if the same had been granted at such last-mentioned time.

But this act shall not extend to any lease by an ecclesiastical corporation or spiritual person, or to any lease of the possessions of any college, hospital or charitable foundation, or to any lease where, before the passing of this act (26th June, 1849), the hereditaments comprised in such lease have been surrendered or relinquished, or recovered adversely by reason of the invalidity thereof, or there has been any judgment or decree in any action or suit concerning the validity of such lease. *Sect. 7. Except in case of leases by ecclesiastical corporations, &c., or where (before 26 June, 1849) the demised premises have been surrendered or recovered adversely.*

Where during the continuance of the possession taken under any such invalid lease as in the above act mentioned, the person for the time being entitled (subject to such possession as aforesaid) to the hereditaments comprised in such lease, or to the possession or the receipt of the rents and profits thereof, is able to confirm such lease without variation, the lessee, his heirs, executors or administrators (as the case may require), or any person who would have been bound by the lease if the same had been valid, shall, upon the request of the person so able to confirm the same, be bound to accept a confirmation accordingly; and such confirmation may be by memorandum or note in writing, signed by the persons confirming and accepting respectively, or by some other persons by them respectively thereunto lawfully authorized; and after confirmation and acceptance of confirmation such lease shall be valid, and shall be deemed to have had from the granting thereof the same effect as if the same had been originally valid. *Stat. 13 Vict. c. 17, s. 3. Where reversioner is able to confirm invalid lease without variation, lessee at his request is bound to accept such confirmation.*

Sect. 2. Where note confirming lease is signed by person accepting rent, such acceptance to be deemed confirmation.	Where, upon or before the acceptance of rent under any such invalid lease, any receipt, memorandum or note in writing, confirming such lease, is signed by the person accepting such rent, or some other person by him thereunto lawfully authorized, such acceptance (*q*) shall, as against the person so accepting such rent, be deemed a confirmation of such lease.
Stat. 22 & 23 Vict. c. 35, s. 12. Deed attested by two witnesses to be valid execution, as regards execution and attestation, of power of appointment by deed or writing.	A deed executed (after 13th August, 1859), in the presence of, and attested by two or more witnesses in the manner in which deeds are ordinarily executed and attested, shall, so far as respects the execution and attestation thereof, be a valid execution of a power of appointment by deed or by any instrument in writing not testamentary, notwithstanding it shall have been expressly required that a deed or instrument in writing made in exercise of such power should be executed or attested with some additional or other form of execution or attestation or solemnity. But this provision shall not operate to defeat any direction in the instrument creating the power that the consent of any particular person shall be necessary to a valid execution, or that any act shall be performed in order to give validity to any appointment, having no relation to the mode of
Donee of power may execute it conformably to power.	executing and attesting the instrument; or prevent the donee of a power from executing it conformably to the power by writing or otherwise than by an instrument executed and attested as an ordinary deed, and to any such execution of a power this provision shall not extend.
Leases of settled estates.	It shall be lawful for the Court of Chancery, if it shall deem it proper and consistent with a due regard

(*q*) See 34 L. J., Ch. 378.

for the interests of all parties entitled under the settlement, and subject to the provisions and restrictions in this act contained, from time to time (sect. 4) to authorize leases, or preliminary contracts for leases (see sect. 6), either of the whole or any parts (sect. 4) of any settled estates (*r*), or of any rights or privileges over or affecting any settled estates, for any purpose whatsoever, whether involving waste or not, provided the following conditions be observed:

Stat. 19 & 20 Vict. c. 120, s. 2. Court of Chancery may authorize leases of settled estates.

> First. Every such lease shall be made to take effect in possession at or within one year next after the making thereof, and shall be for a term of years not exceeding for an agricultural or occupation lease twenty-one years; for a mining lease, or a lease of water, water-mills, way-leaves, water-leaves or other rights or easements, forty years; and for a building (or repairing (*s*)) lease ninety-nine years; or where the Court shall be satisfied that it is the usual custom of the district and beneficial to the inheritance to grant (any of the above-mentioned leases, except agricultural leases(*t*)), for longer terms, then for such term as the Court shall direct. But nothing in this act shall be construed to empower the Court to authorize any lease beyond the extent to which, in the opinion of the Court, the same might have been authorized in the settlement by the settlor (sect. 27):

Conditions to be observed.

(*r*) As to the interpretation of this term, see sect. 1; also stat. 21 & 22 Vict. c. 77, s. 1, and stat. 27 & 28 Vict. c. 45, s. 3; *In re Laing's Trust*, 35 L. J., Ch. 282; *Re Greene's Settled Estates*, 10 Jur., N. S. 1098. The provisions of the act hereinafter mentioned extend to all settlements, whether made before or after it came in force (s. 44).

(*s*) Stat. 21 & 22 Vict. c. 77, s. 2.

(*t*) Stat. 21 & 22 Vict. c. 77, s. 4.

Secondly. On every such lease shall be reserved the best rent(*u*), or reservation in the nature of rent, either uniform or not, that can be reasonably obtained, to be made payable half-yearly or oftener, without taking any fine or other benefit in the nature of a fine:

Thirdly. Where the lease is of any earth, coal, stone or mineral, a certain portion of the whole rent or payment reserved shall be from time to time set aside and invested as hereinafter mentioned; namely, when the person entitled to the receipt of such rent is entitled to work such earth, &c., for his own benefit, one-fourth part of such rent, and otherwise three-fourth parts thereof, and in every such lease sufficient provision shall be made to ensure such application of the aforesaid portion of the rent, by the appointment of trustees or otherwise, as the Court shall deem expedient:

Fourthly. No such lease shall authorize the felling of any trees, except so far as shall be necessary for the purpose of clearing the ground for any buildings, excavations or other works authorized by the lease:

Fifthly. Every such lease shall be by deed, and the lessee shall execute a counterpart thereof; but the execution of any lease by the lessor or lessee shall be deemed sufficient evidence that a counterpart of such lease has been duly executed by the lessee as required by this act (sect. 34). Every such lease shall contain a condition for re-entry on nonpayment of the rent for a period not less than twenty-eight days after it becomes due, and such covenants,

---

(*u*) See *In re Rawlin's Estate*, L. R., 1 Eq. 286.

conditions and stipulations as the Court shall deem expedient with reference to the special circumstances of the demise (sect. 3).

Any person entitled to the possession or to the receipt of the rents and profits of any settled estates for a term of years determinable on his death, or for an estate for life, or any greater estate, may apply to the Court, by petition in a summary way, to exercise the powers conferred by this act. Sect. 16. Application to be made by petition.

The Court shall require the applicant to produce such evidence as it shall deem sufficient to enable it to ascertain the nature, value and circumstances of the estate, and the terms and conditions on which leases thereof ought to be authorized. Sect. 8. Evidence required.

Subject to the exception contained in the next section, every application to the Court must be made with the concurrence or consent of the following parties; namely, where there is a tenant in tail under the settlement in existence, and of full age, such tenant in tail, or, if there is more than one such tenant in tail, the first of such tenants in tail, and all persons in existence having any beneficial estate or interest under the settlement prior to the estate of such tenant in tail, and all trustees having any estate or interest on behalf of any unborn child prior to the estate of such tenant in tail: Sect. 17. Application to be made with certain consents.

And in every other case the parties to concur or consent shall be all the persons in existence having any beneficial estate or interest under the settlement, and also all trustees having any estate or interest on behalf of any unborn child.

But unless there shall be a person entitled to an estate of inheritance whose consent or concurrence shall have been refused or cannot be obtained, it shall be Sect. 18. Petition may be granted without con-

sent, subject to the rights of non-consenting parties.	lawful for the Court, if it shall think fit, to give effect to any petition, subject to and so as not to affect the rights, estate or interest of any person whose consent or concurrence has been refused or cannot be obtained, or whose rights, estate or interest ought, in the opinion of the Court, to be excepted.
Sect. 40. No person compellable to make or consent to application.	Nothing in this act shall be construed to create any obligation, at law or in equity, on any person to make or consent to any application to the Court, or to exercise any power.
Sects. 19, 20. Notice of application to be given and served.	Notice of any application to the Court under this act shall be inserted in such newspapers as the Court shall direct, and shall be served on all trustees who are seised or possessed of any estate in trust for any person whose consent or concurrence to or in the application is hereby required, and on any other parties who, in the opinion of the Court, ought to be so served, unless the Court shall think fit to dispense with such notice.
Sect. 20. Any person may apply to Court to be heard in opposition to or in support of application under this act.	Any person or body corporate, whether interested in the estate or not, may apply to the Court of Chancery by motion for leave to be heard in opposition to, or in support of, any application which may be made to the Court under this act; and the Court is hereby authorized to permit such person or corporation to appear and be heard in opposition to, or in support of, any such application, on such terms as to costs or otherwise, and in such manner, as it shall think fit.
Sect. 26. Court may exercise powers conferred by act repeatedly. But may not exercise them if negatived in settlement.	The Court shall be at liberty to exercise any of the powers conferred on it by this act, whether the Court shall have already exercised any of the powers conferred by this act in respect of the same property or not; but no such powers shall be exercised if an express declaration or manifest intention that they shall not be exer-

cised is contained in the settlement, or may reasonably be inferred therefrom, or from extrinsic circumstances or evidence; provided always, that the circumstance of the settlement containing powers to effect similar purposes shall not preclude the Court from exercising any of the powers conferred by this act, if it shall think that the powers contained in the settlement ought to be extended. *May exercise them though settlement contains powers for similar purposes.*

The power to authorize leases conferred by this act may be exercised by the Court, either by approving of particular leases, or by ordering that powers of leasing, in conformity with the provisions of this act, shall be vested either in the existing trustees of the settlement or in any other persons; and such powers, when exercised by such trustees, shall take effect in all respects as if the power so vested in them had been originally contained in the settlement, and so as to operate (if necessary) by way of revocation and appointment of the use, or otherwise as the Court shall direct; and the Court, if it shall think fit, may impose any conditions as to consents or otherwise on the exercise of such power (but, except by consent or under special circumstances, not a condition that the leases thereby authorized shall be settled by the Court(*x*)), and may also authorize the insertion of provisions for the appointment of new trustees from time to time for the purpose of exercising such powers of leasing. *Sect. 7. Mode in which leases may be authorized. Sect. 10.*

When a lease or contract for a lease has been approved by the Court, the Court shall direct what person shall execute the same as lessor; and the lease or contract executed by such person shall take effect in all respects as if he was at the time of the execution thereof abso- *Sect. 9. Court to direct who is to be lessor.*

(*x*) Stat. 27 & 28 Vict. c. 45, s. 1.

lutely entitled to the whole estate which is bound by the settlement, and had immediately afterwards settled the same according to the settlement, and so as to operate (if necessary) by way of revocation and appointment of the use, or otherwise, as the Court shall direct.

Sect. 28.
Lease purporting to be made by Court in pursuance of this act not to be invalidated.

After the completion of any lease under the authority of the Court, and purporting to be in pursuance of this act, the same shall not be invalidated on the ground that the Court was not hereby empowered to authorize the same; except that no such lease shall have any effect against any person whose concurrence in or consent to the application ought to have been obtained, and was not obtained.

Sect. 29.
Costs of applications.

It shall be lawful for the Court, if it shall think fit, to order that all or any costs or expenses incident to any application under this act shall be a charge on the hereditaments which are the subject of the application, or on any other hereditaments included in the same settlement and subject to the same limitations; and the Court may also direct that such costs and expenses shall be raised by sale or mortgage of a sufficient part of such hereditaments, or out of the rents or profits thereof, such costs and expenses to be taxed as the Court shall direct.

Sect. 5.
Leases may be surrendered and renewed.

Any leases granted under this act (or otherwise (*y*)) may be surrendered, either for the purpose of obtaining a renewal of the same or not; and the power to authorize leases conferred by this act shall extend to authorize new leases of the whole or any part of the hereditaments comprised in any surrendered lease.

Sect. 43.
Rights of lords of manors not to be affected.

Nothing in this act shall authorize the granting of a lease of any copyhold or customary hereditaments not warranted by the custom of the manor without the con-

(*y*) Stat. 21 & 22 Vict. c. 77, s. 5.

A lease made *after the mortgage* by a mortgagor in possession, though it may be good by way of estoppel between the parties to it (*z*), is, generally speaking, void as against the mortgagee, who may eject the lessee without any previous notice (*a*). In order to create a tenancy between the mortgagee and the tenant let into possession by the mortgagor, there must be some evidence whence it may be inferred that such relation has been raised by mutual agreement (*b*). The mortgagee cannot, by merely giving the lessee notice of the mortgage, make the lessee his tenant (*b*). Mortgagor. Leases by, after the mortgage.

Leases made *before the mortgage* by the mortgagor are binding on the mortgagee (*c*). Leases before the mortgage.

A lease granted by a mortgagee in possession, without the concurrence of the mortgagor, cannot after redemption stand good as against the mortgagor (*d*). If the mortgagee grants a lease and puts the lessee in possession, the mortgagor may file a bill to redeem, and ask for an account against the mortgagee, as in a case of wilful default, and thereby raise the question whether the rent reserved was the best that could have been obtained (*d*). Both mortgagor and mortgagee should therefore concur in leasing the mortgaged property, and in that case the instrument will operate as the Leases by mortgagee in possession.

(*z*) See *post*, p. 42; *Doe* v. *Thompson*, 9 Q. B. 1037.

(*a*) *Thunder* v. *Belcher*, 3 East, 449; *Keech* v. *Hall*, 1 Dougl. 21. See 9 B. & C. 253.

(*b*) 1 Sm. L. C. 570 (6th ed.); *Evans* v. *Elliot*, 9 A. & E. 342; *Brown* v. *Storey*, 1 M. & Gr. 117.

(*c*) *Moss* v. *Gallimore*, 1 Sm. L. C. 561; see *Rogers* v. *Humphreys*, 4 A. & E. 299.

(*d*) See per Lord Romilly, M.R., in *Franklinski* v. *Ball*, 34 L. J., Ch., at p. 154; *S. C.*, 33 Beav. 560.

demise of the mortgagee and the confirmation of the mortgagor (*e*).

Leases by estoppel.

If one makes a lease for years, by indenture, of lands wherein he has no estate at the time when such lease is made, and afterwards purchases those lands, or otherwise acquires a legal interest in them, this will make good and unavoidable his lease, as well as if he had been in the actual possession and seisin thereof at the time when such lease was made; because he having, by indenture, expressly demised those lands, is by his own act estopped from saying he did not demise them (*f*). The tenant and those claiming under him (*g*), so long as they continue in possession under the lease (*h*), are in like manner estopped from disputing the title of the landlord from whom he received possession (*i*), but they may show that such title has expired (*k*). A tenant who has attorned to a person from whom he

---

(*e*) *Doe* v. *Adams*, 2 Cr. & J. 232; 2 Tyr. 289.

(*f*) Bac. Abr. (O.) 189. See *Smith* v. *Low*, 1 Atk. 489; *Webb* v. *Austin*, 8 Sc. N. R. 419; 7 M. & Gr. 701; *Doe* v. *Fuller*, 1 Tyr. & G. 17; *Sturgeon* v. *Wingfield*, 15 M. & W. 224; 15 L. J., Ex. 212; *Doe* v. *Ongley*, 10 C. B. 25; 20 L. J., C. P. 26.

(*g*) *Barwick* v. *Thompson*, 7 T. R. 488; *Taylor* v. *Needham*, 2 Taunt. 278; *Doe* v. *Mills*, 2 A. & E. 17; *Doe* v. *Austin*, 2 Moo. & Sc. 107; *London and North Western Ry. Co.* v. *West*, 36 L. J., C. P. 245; L. R., 2 C. P. 553.

(*h*) *Cuthbertson* v. *Irving*, 4 H. & N. 742; 28 L. J., Ex. 306;

affirmed 6 H. & N. 135; 29 L. J., Ex. 485.

(*i*) See per Bayley, J., 8 B. & C. 475; *White* v. *Foljambe*, 11 Ves., at p. 344; *Parry* v. *House*, Holt, N. P. 489; *Cooper* v. *Blandy*, 1 Bing. N. C. 45; 4 Moo. & Sc. 562; *Doe* v. *Baytup*, 3 A. & E. 188; *Delaney* v. *Fox*, 2 C. B., N. S. 768; 26 L. J., C. P. 248.

(*k*) *England* v. *Slade*, 4 T. R. 682. See per Best, C. J., in 2 Bing. 11; *Neave* v. *Moss*, 1 Bing. 360; *Doe* v. *Edwards*, 5 B. & Ad. 1065; *Doe* v. *Ramsbotham*, 3 M. & S. 516; *Doe* v. *Watson*, 2 Stark. 230; *Mountney* v. *Collier*, 1 E. & B. 630; 22 L. J., Q. B. 124.

did not receive the possession is not estopped from showing want of title in such person (*m*). The estoppel must be mutual, or neither party will be bound by it; hence leases by married women or infants will not operate by way of estoppel (*n*). Moreover if any estate or interest passes by the lease it will not have this effect, though the interest purported to be granted may be greater than the lessor at the time has power to grant (*o*). The doctrine that no estoppel arises where it appears on the face of the deed that the lessor has no legal estate or interest in the premises must be taken to have been overruled (*p*). The estoppels continue no longer on either part than during the lease, for as they began at first by the making of the lease, so by the determination of the lease they are at an end likewise; for then both parts of the indenture belong to the lessor (*o*).

(3) *Restrictions arising from Confidential Relations.*

There are certain classes of persons, standing in confidential relations to the owners of property, who possess peculiar opportunities of obtaining a knowledge of the value of the property with which they are concerned, and peculiar means of influencing the minds of the persons for whom they act. Courts of Equity look with a jealous eye on the transactions of indivi-

(*m*) *Cornish* v. *Scarell*, 8 B. & C. 471.
(*n*) Bac. Abr. (O.) 190; *Smith* v. *Low*, 1 Atk. 489.
(*o*) Bac. Abr. (O.) 191. See *Cuthbertson* v. *Irving*, 4 H. & N. 742; 28 L. J., Ex. 306; affirmed 6 H. & N. 135; 29 L. J., Ex. 485.
(*p*) See *Morton* v. *Woods*, 38 L. J., Q. B. 81, 85; L. R., 4 Q. B. 293; L. R., 3 Q. B. 658. See also S. C., 37 L. J., Q. B. 242, 249; *Jolly* v. *Arbuthnot*, 4 De G. & J. 224; 28 L. J., Ch. 547.

duals occupying this position, and leases granted by principals to agents, by clients to attorneys, by wards to guardians, by cestui que trusts to trustees, or by mortgagors to mortgagees (*q*), will be set aside if the considerations given for the leases are grossly inadequate (*r*), or if any advantage appears to have been taken of the confidential relation in which the parties stand (*s*).

Renewal for his own benefit by person jointly interested with infant in lease.

If a person, jointly interested with an infant in a lease, obtains a renewal to himself only, and the lease proves beneficial, he will be held to have acted as trustee, and the infant may claim his share of the benefit; but if the lease does not prove beneficial, the lessee must take it upon himself (*t*).

Leases by intoxicated persons.

Leases at an inadequate rent made by persons in a state of contrived intoxication will be set aside (*u*).

SECT. III.—*An actual Letting.*

When instruments are construed as mere agreements.

A mere unaccepted proposal (*x*), or a mere agreement, without any words of present demise, will not constitute the relation of landlord and tenant between the parties (*y*). And although words of present demise are

(*q*) *Webb* v. *Rorke*, 2 Sch. & Lef. 661.

(*r*) *Ward* v. *Hartpole*, 3 Bligh, 470; *Dawson* v. *Massey*, 1 B. & Beat. 219.

(*s*) *Aylward* v. *Kearney*, 2 B. & Beat. 463. See the notes to *Huguenin* v. *Baseley*, 2 Wh. & Tud. L. C., Eq. 504.

(*t*) *Ex parte Grace*, 1 B. & P. 376.

(*u*) *Say* v. *Barwick*, 1 V. & B. 195; *Cooke* v. *Claynorth*, 18 Ves. 12. See *Pitt* v. *Smith*, 3 Camp. 33; *Butler* v. *Mulvihill*, 1 Bligh, 137.

(*x*) *Doe* v. *Cartwright*, 3 B. & A. 326. See *Clarke* v. *Fuller*, 16 C. B., N. S. 24.

(*y*) *Clayton* v. *Burtenshaw*, 5 B. & C. 41; *Phillips* v. *Hartley*, 3 C. & P. 121. See *Taylor* v. *Jackson*, 2 C. & K. 22.

made use of, yet if upon the whole instrument (*z*), and having regard to the nature of the subject-matter (*a*), it does not appear to have been intended by the parties to operate as a lease, but only as preparatory and relative to a future lease to be made, the law will rather do violence to the words than break through the intent of the parties (*b*).

Thus, if there are matters to be ascertained, without which the terms of holding will not be perfectly complete (*c*); or if the instrument contains a stipulation that "a clause is to be added in the lease" for a particular purpose (*d*), or a proviso that the instrument shall not be construed or taken to operate as a lease or actual demise (*e*); or if the lease is to take effect only on the performance or happening of a condition (*f*); or if there is a want of certainty as to the time of commencement of the term and of the rent becoming due (*g*), or as to the amount of rent (*g*); or if strong circumstances of inconvenience are apparent on the instrument, if it should be construed as a

(*z*) See per Alderson, B., in *Gore* v. *Lloyd*, 13 L. J., Ex., at p. 372.

(*a*) *Doe* v. *Clare*, 2 T. R. 739, 744; *Perring* v. *Brook*, 7 C. & P. 360; *Fenny* v. *Child*, 2 M. & S. 255, 257; *Doe* v. *Powell*, 8 Sc. N. R. 687; 7 M. & Gr. 980; 14 L. J., C. P. 5.

(*b*) Bac. Abr. (K.) 161; *Doe* v. *Ashburner*, 5 T. R. 163. See *Morgan* v. *Bissell*, 3 Taunt. 65; *Browne* v. *Warner*, 14 Ves. 156; *Doe* v. *Smith*, 6 East, 530; *Tempest* v. *Rawling*, 13 East, 18; *Doe* v. *Powell*, 8 Sc. N. R. 687; 7 M. & Gr. 980; 14 L. J., C. P. 5; *Rawson* v. *Eicke*, 7 A. & E. 451; *Brashier* v. *Jackson*, 6 M. & W. 549; *Chapman* v. *Towner*, 6 M. & W. 100; *Bicknell* v. *Hood*, 5 M. & W. 104.

(*c*) *John* v. *Jenkins*, 1 Cr. & M. 227; *Jones* v. *Reynolds*, 1 Q. B. 506; 10 L. J., Q. B. 193.

(*d*) *Doe* v. *Smith*, 6 East, 530.

(*e*) *Perring* v. *Brook*, 7 C. & P. 360.

(*f*) *Doe* v. *Clarke*, 7 Q. B. 211; 14 L. J., Q. B. 233.

(*g*) *Dunk* v. *Hunter*, 5 B. & A. 322, 325. See *Clayton* v. *Burtenshaw*, 5 B. & C. 41.

lease (*h*); the instrument will be construed as a mere agreement for a lease, although it may contain words of present demise.

When instruments are construed as leases. Instruments not under seal can now operate as leases only when the terms of years to which they relate will end within three years from the making of the instrument, and when the rent reserved during such term amounts to two-third parts at the least of the full improved value of the premises (*i*). An instrument coming within this description, although it may be designated an agreement, and may contain a stipulation for the execution of a future lease (*k*), will nevertheless be held to operate as a lease if it contains words of present demise, such as "I demise," "doth set and let," "doth agree to let"(*l*), "shall enjoy"(*m*), &c., uncontrolled by expressions of a contrary import, a specific rent being reserved, and the time at which the tenancy is to commence being clearly ascertained (*k*). And it would seem, that an agreement for a future lease, under which a person has entered into possession, not containing any words of present demise, but providing that in the meantime, until the lease shall

---

(*h*) *Morgan* v. *Bissell*, 3 Taunt. 65; *Doe* v. *Powell*, 8 Sc. N. R. 687, 700; 7 M. & Gr. 980; 14 L. J., C. P. 5. See *Hayward* v. *Haswell*, 6 A. & E. 265.

(*i*) See *post*, Chap. III., Sect. 2.

(*k*) *Baxter* v. *Browne*, 2 W. Bl. 973; *Poole* v. *Bentley*, 12 East, 168; 2 Camp. 286; *Warman* v. *Faithfull*, 5 B. & Ad. 1042; *Doe* v. *Benjamin*, 9 A. & E. 644, 651; 1 P. & D. 440; *Hancock* v. *Caffyn*, 8 Bing. 358;

368; *Doe* v. *Ries*, 8 Bing. 178; *Pearce* v. *Cheslyn*, 4 A. & E. 225; *Alderman* v. *Neate*, 4 M. & W. 704; 3 Jur. 171; *Wilson* v. *Chisholm*, 4 C. & P. 474; *Chapman* v. *Bluck*, 4 Bing. N. C. 187.

(*l*) *Staniforth* v. *Fox*, 7 Bing. 590; 5 M. & P. 589; *Tarte* v. *Derby*, 15 M. & W. 601; 15 L. J., Ex. 326.

(*m*) *Doe* v. *Ashburner*, 5 T. R. 163.

be executed, the intended lessee shall pay the rent and perform the covenants, with a power of distress for non-payment of rent, will amount to a present demise (*n*).

Sect. IV.—*Exclusive Possession.*

If possession of the premises is to be given up for certain purposes only, the transaction will be construed as a licence, and not a lease (*o*). A mere licence does not confer any estate in the property to which it relates, and is determined by an assignment of the subject-matter in respect of which the privilege is enjoyed (*p*). But a licence to put goods on land involves a permission to the person so licensed to take away the goods and to take a reasonable time to do it (*q*).

An occupation of premises as servant or agent for the more convenient performance of service, or as a mere remuneration for services, is in law the occupa-

Licences.

Occupation as servant or agent.

(*n*) *Hancock* v. *Caffyn*, 8 Bing. 358, 365; 1 Moo. & Sc. 521. See *Pinero* v. *Judson*, 6 Bing. 206; 3 M. & P. 497; *Anderson* v. *Midland Ry. Co.*, 3 E. & E. 614; 30 L. J., Q. B. 94; 7 Jur., N. S. 411; 3 L. T., N. S. 609. But see *Doe* v. *Foster*, 3 C. B. 215; 15 L. J., C. P. 263; *Camden* v. *Batterbury*, 5 C. B., N. S. 808; 28 L. J., C. P. 187; 7 C. B., N. S. 864; 28 L. J., C. P. 335.

(*o*) *Taylor* v. *Caldwell*, 3 B. & S. 826, 832; 32 L. J., Q. B. 164; 11 W. R. 726; 8 L. T., N. S. 356; *Hancock* v. *Austin*, 14 C. B., N. S. 634; 32 L. J., C. P. 252; 11 W. R. 833; 8 L. T., N. S. 429; *Ward* v. *Day*, 4 B. & S. 337; 5 B. & S. 359; 33 L. J., Q. B. 3, 254; *Watkins* v. *Gravesend and Milton Union*, 37 L. J., M. C. 73, 77. See *Jones* v. *Reynolds*, 4 A. & E. 805; *Wood* v. *Manley*, 11 A. & E. 34; 9 L. J., Q. B. 27.

(*p*) *Coleman* v. *Foster*, 1 H. & N. 37.

(*q*) Per Willes, J., in *Cornish* v. *Stubbs*, 39 L. J., C. P., at p. 206. See *Wood* v. *Leadbitter*, 13 M. & W. 838; 14 L. J., Ex. 161.

tion of the master and not of the servant (r), and does not create the relation of landlord and tenant between the parties (s). It has been held, that, in such cases, no notice to quit is necessary, if the service is put an end to (t).

(r) *Bertie* v. *Beaumont*, 16 East, 33, 36; *Rex* v. *Inhabitants of Kelstern*, 5 M. & S. 136; *Rex* v. *Inhabitants of Cheshunt*, 1 B. & A. 473.

(s) See *Doe* v. *Derry*, 9 C. & P. 494; *Mayhew* v. *Suttle*, 4 E. & B. 347; 1 Jur., N. S. 303; 24 L. J., Q. B. 54.

(t) *Doe* v. *Derry*, 9 C. & P. 494. See *Doe* v. *Miles*, 1 Stark. 181.

CHAP. II.

THE DIFFERENT KINDS OF TENANCY.

	PAGE
SECT. I. TENANCY BY SUFFERANCE	49
II. TENANCY AT WILL	50
Where implied	50
Effect of payment of rent	52
III. TENANCY FROM YEAR TO YEAR	53
Where implied	53
How implication may be rebutted	54
Terms consistent with	56
IV. TENANCY FOR YEARS	57
For years, subject to contingency	58
Option to take further term	58
V. TENANCY FOR LIFE	59

SECT. I.—*Tenancy by Sufferance.*

A TENANT by sufferance is one who at first came in by a lawful demise, but after his estate is ended wrongfully holds over (*a*); as, for instance, a tenant for the life of another who continues in possession after the decease of the person for whose life he holds (*b*); or, a tenant for years who holds over after the expiration of his term (*c*); or, an under tenant who continues in possession after the determination of the original lease (*d*); or, a lessee at will who keeps possession after the will has been determined by the death of the lessor (*e*). *[margin: Instances.]*

This so-called tenancy was probably originally a mere device to prevent adverse possession from taking

(*a*) Co. Lit. 57 b.
(*b*) Ibid.
(*c*) Co. Lit. 57 b, 270 b. See *Bayley* v. *Bradley*, 5 C. B. 396; 16 L. J., C. P. 206.
(*d*) *Simpkin* v. *Ashhurst*, 1 Cr., M. & R. 261; 4 Tyr. 781.
(*e*) Co. Lit. 57 b. See *post*, Chap. V., Sect. I.(2). For other instances of tenancy by sufferance, see *Doe* v. *Lawder*, 1 Stark. 308; *Doe* v. *Quigley*, 2 Camp. 505.

F.

place (*f*). It necessarily implies the absence of any agreement between the parties, and by the assent of the owner to the continuance of possession by the tenant will be converted into a tenancy at will (*f*).

Effect of assent of owner.

Against the Crown there can be no tenancy by sufferance (*g*).

Sect. II.—*Tenancy at Will.*

How created.

Expressly.

"Tenant at will is where lands or tenements are let by one man to another, to have and to hold to him at the will of the lessor, by force of which lease the lessee is in possession. In this case the lessee is called tenant at will, because he hath no certain nor sure estate, for the lessor may put him out at what time it pleaseth him"(*h*). But every lease at will must in law be at the will of both parties, and therefore when a lease is made to have and to hold at the will of the lessor, the law implies it to be at the will of the lessee also; and when a lease is made to have and to hold at the will of the lessee, this must be also at the will of the lessor (*i*).

By implication.

Tenancy at will may be created by express agreement (*k*), but it also arises by implication where premises are in the occupation of a person holding them with the consent of the owner, but possessing neither a freehold estate in them, nor a lease for a definite term (*l*). Hence a tenancy at will is implied in the following cases:—

1. Occupation

Where a person lives in a house rent free by the per-

(*f*) Smith L. & T. 31.
(*g*) Co. Lit. 57 b.
(*h*) Lit. sect. 68.
(*i*) Co. Lit. 55 a.
(*k*) *Richardson* v. *Langridge*, 4 Taunt. 128; *Doe* v. *Cox*, 11 Q. B. 122; 17 L. J., Q. B. 3.
(*l*) Smith L. & T. 20. See *Doe* v. *Jones*, 10 B. & C. 718; *Doe* v. *M'Kaeg*, 10 B. & C. 721.

mission of the owner (*m*); provided the occupation is not in the capacity of servant or agent, or as a mere remuneration for services (*n*). *rent free by permission of owner.*

Where possession is taken with the consent of the intended lessor (*o*), under an agreement for a lease (*p*), or under an invalid lease (*q*). *2. Occupation under agreement for lease, or void lease.*

Where possession is taken in pursuance of an agreement for the sale of premises (*r*). In the absence of an agreement to pay for the occupation, no action for use and occupation can be brought against the vendee whilst he is in possession under the contract of sale, because, although a tenant at will, he is not bound to pay rent. After the purchase has gone off, the person remaining in possession still continues tenant at will, but as the payment of the purchase-money, which was to be the compensation for his occupation, is then at an end, he becomes from that time liable to an action for use and occupation (*s*). *3. Occupation under purchase agreement.*

Where a tenant, after his lease has expired, is per- *4. Holding*

(*m*) *Rex* v. *Collett*, R. & R. C. C. 498; *Rex* v. *Jobling*, R. & R. C. C. 525; *Doe* v. *Groves*, 10 Q. B. 486; 16 L. J., Q. B. 297.

(*n*) *Ante*, p. 47.

(*o*) See *Doe* v. *Quigley*, 2 Camp. 505.

(*p*) Judgment of Littledale, J., in *Hamerton* v. *Stead*, 3 B. & C., at p. 483. Judgment of Parke, B., in *Braythwayte* v. *Hitchcock*, 10 M. & W., at p. 497; 12 L. J., Ex., at p. 39. See *Regnart* v. *Porter*, 7 Bing. 451.

(*q*) *Goodtitle* v. *Herbert*, 4 T. R. 680; *Denn* v. *Fearnside*, 1 Wils. 176.

(*r*) *Right* v. *Beard*, 13 East,
210; *Doe* v. *Jackson*, 1 B. & C. 448; *Doe* v. *Miller*, 5 C. & P. 595; *Doe* v. *Rock*, Car. & M. 549; 4 M. & Gr. 30; 11 L. J., C. P. 194; *Ball* v. *Cullimore*, 2 Cr., M. & R. 120; *Doe* v. *Chamberlain*, 5 M. & W. 14; *Howard* v. *Shaw*, 8 M. & W. 118; 10 L. J., Ex. 334.

(*s*) Judgments of Parke, B., and Alderson, B., in *Howard* v. *Shaw*, 10 L. J., Ex., at p. 336; *Hearn* v. *Tomlin*, Peake, N. P. C. 192; *Kirtland* v. *Pounsett*, 2 Taunt. 145; *Winterbottom* v. *Ingham*, 7 Q. B. 611; 14 L. J., Q. B. 298. See *Tew* v. *Jones*, 13 M. & W. 12; 14 L. J., Ex. 94.

mitted to continue in possession pending a treaty for a new lease (*t*).

5. Indefinite letting.

A mere general letting (*u*) or a simple permission to occupy creates a tenancy at will, unless there are circumstances to show an intention to create a tenancy from year to year; as, for instance, an agreement to pay rent by the quarter, or some other aliquot part of the year (*x*).

6. Occupation by cestui que trust.

A *cestui que trust*, who is in possession of an estate by the consent or acquiescence of the trustee, is regarded at law as his tenant at will. But this doctrine only applies where the *cestui que trust* is the actual occupant; where he is merely allowed to receive the rents, or otherwise deal with the estate in the hands of occupying tenants, he is only the agent of the trustee (*y*).

Effect of payment of rent.

In all these cases, however, payment of rent by the tenant with reference to a yearly holding, or an admission by him of a charge of half-a-year's rent in an account between him and his landlord (*z*), will raise a presumption of a change from a tenancy at will into a tenancy from year to year (*a*). But rent may be expressly reserved upon a lease at will, and payment in pursuance of such reservation will not change the character of the tenancy (*b*).

(*t*) *Doe* v. *Stennett*, 2 Esp. 717, 719.

(*u*) Judgment of Chambre, J., in *Richardson* v. *Langridge*, 4 Taunt., at p. 132; *Roe* v. *Lees*, 2 W. Bl., at p. 1173. But see *Doe* v. *Watts*, 7 T. R., at p. 85.

(*x*) Per Parke, B., in *Doe* v. *Wood*, 14 M. & W., at p. 687; *Doe* v. *Gardiner*, 12 C. B. 319; 21 L. J., C. P. 222. See *In re Stroud*, 8 C. B. 502; 16 L. J., C. P. 117; *Fitzmaurice* v. *Bayley*, 8 E. & B., at p. 679.

(*y*) *Melling* v. *Leak*, 16 C. B. 652; 24 L. J., C. P. 187.

(*z*) *Cox* v. *Bent*, 5 Bing. 185.

(*a*) See *post*, p. 53.

(*b*) *Doe* v. *Cox*, 11 Q. B. 122; 17 L. J., Q. B. 3; *Doe* v. *Davies*, 7 Ex. 89; *Anderson* v. *Midland Ry. Co.*, 3 E. & E. 614; 30 L. J., Q. B. 94.

Sect. III.—*Tenancy from Year to Year.*

Tenancy from year to year differs from tenancy at will in the notice required to be given by landlord or tenant in order to determine the tenancy (*c*). A tenant from year to year has a lease for one year certain, with a growing interest during every year thereafter, springing out of the original contract, and parcel of it (*d*). {Distinguished from tenancy at will.}

This tenancy may be either expressly created, by letting premises to hold "from year to year" (*e*); or may arise by implication where rent is paid in respect of the occupation of premises, and with reference to a yearly holding (*f*). {Where implied.}

Where a person has entered into possession of premises and paid rent (*g*) under a void lease (*h*), or under an agreement for a lease (*i*); although such agreement is unwritten, and therefore void (*k*), and no lease has ever been tendered by the lessor or demanded by the {1. Entry and payment of rent under void lease or agreement.}

(*c*) *Post*, Chap. V., Sect. I. (3).

(*d*) *Cattley* v. *Arnold*, 1 J. & H. 651; 28 L. J., Ch. 352.

(*e*) *Post*, Chap. III., Sect. 2, p. 81.

(*f*) Per Parke, B., in *Braythwayte* v. *Hitchcock*, 10 M. & W., at p. 497. See *Doe* v. *Wood*, 14 M. & W. 682; 15 L. J., Ex. 41.

(*g*) See *Cox* v. *Bent*, 5 Bing. 185; *ante*, p. 52.

(*h*) *Doe* v. *Bell*, 5 T. R. 471; *Doe* v. *Watts*, 7 T. R. 83; *Clayton* v. *Blakey*, 8 T. R. 3; *Richardson* v. *Gifford*, 1 A. & E. 52; *Doe* v. *Collinge*, 7 C. B. 939, 960; 18 L. J., C. P. 305; *Lee* v. *Smith*, 9 Ex. 662; 23 L. J., Ex. 198; *Doe* v. *Tanicre*, 12 Q. B. 998, 1013; 18 L. J., Q. B. 49; *Doe* v. *Moffatt*, 15 Q. B. 257; 19 L. J., Q. B. 438; *Tress* v. *Savage*, 4 E. & B. 36; 23 L. J., Q. B. 339.

(*i*) *Doe* v. *Smith*, 1 Man. & Ry. 137; *Mann* v. *Lovejoy*, Ry. & M. 355; *Knight* v. *Bennett*, 3 Bing. 361; *Cox* v. *Bent*, 5 Bing. 185; *Doe* v. *Amey*, 12 A. & E. 476; *Doe* v. *Foster*, 3 C. B. 215; 15 L. J., C. P. 263; *Chapman* v. *Towner*, 6 M. & W. 100; *Braythwayte* v. *Hitchcock*, 10 M. & W. 494; 12 L. J., Ex. 38; *Bennett* v. *Ireland*, E. B. & E. 326; 28 L. J., Q. B. 48. See *Bolton* v. *Tomlin*, 1 N. & P. 247; 5 A. & E. 856.

(*k*) *Knight* v. *Bennett*, 3 Bing. 361, *post*, p. 61.

lessee (*m*), he is presumed to be tenant from year to year upon such of the terms of the instrument as are consistent with that tenancy (*n*). Reference may be made to the instrument to ascertain the terms of the tenancy (*o*).

The tenancy thus implied will cease, without any notice to quit, at the end of the term mentioned in the instrument (*p*).

2. Holding over and payment of rent after expiration of lease.

A tenant who continues in occupation after his lease has expired, and pays rent, is presumed to hold as tenant from year to year on such of the covenants and conditions of the former lease as are applicable to a tenancy from year to year (*q*).

3. Holding over and payment of rent under lease made by tenant for life.

Where the lessee under a lease which becomes void on the death of the lessor continues in possession of the demised premises after that event, and pays rent to the succeeding owner, the latter, by accepting such rent, admits that the person in possession is his tenant from year to year, upon such of the former terms as are consistent with that tenancy (*r*).

Presumption of tenancy from year to

In order to give rise to the presumption of a tenancy from year to year in the above cases it is necessary that

(*m*) *Weakly* v. *Bucknell*, Cowp. 473.

(*n*) *Doe* v. *Bell*, 5 T. R. 471; *Richardson* v. *Gifford*, 1 A. & E. 52; *Doe* v. *Amey*, 12 A. & E. 476; *Mann* v. *Lovejoy*, Ry. & M. 355; *Beale* v. *Sanders*, 3 Bing. N. C. 850; *Tress* v. *Savage*, 4 E. & B. 36; 23 L. J., Q. B. 339.

(*o*) Per Martin, B., in *Lee* v. *Smith*, 9 Ex., at p. 665; *Bolton* v. *Tomlin*, 1 N. & P. 247; 5 A. & E. 856; *De Medina* v. *Polson*, Holt, N. P. 47. See *Cumberland* v. *Glamis*, 15 C. B. 348; 24 L. J., C. P. 46.

(*p*) *Doe* v. *Stratton*, 4 Bing. 446; 3 C. & P. 164; *Doe* v. *Moffat*, 15 Q. B. 257; 19 L. J., Q. B. 438; *Tress* v. *Savage*, 4 E. & B. 36; 23 L. J., Q. B. 339.

(*q*) *Digby* v. *Atkinson*, 4 Camp. 275; *Bishop* v. *Howard*, 2 B. & C. 100; *Hyatt* v. *Griffiths*, 17 Q. B. 505; *Finch* v. *Miller*, 5 C. B. 428. See *Peirse* v. *Shaw*, 2 Man. & Ry. 418.

(*r*) *Doe* v. *Watts*, 7 T. R. 83; *Doe* v. *Morse*, 1 B. & Ad. 365, 369. See *Cornish* v. *Stubbs*, 39 L. J., C. P. 202, 205.

TENANCY FROM YEAR TO YEAR.   55

possession should be taken or kept with intent to hold as tenant (*s*). Whether this intent does or does not exist is a question for a jury to decide on the circumstances of each case (*s*). The rent must also have been paid with reference to a yearly holding (*t*). It is competent to either the payer or receiver of rent to prove the circumstances under which the payment was made, and by such circumstances to repel the legal implication which would arise from the receipt of rent unexplained (*u*). Thus, a landlord who has received rent from a tenant holding over, may show that such rent was accepted by him in ignorance of the death of a person for whose life the premises were held (*v*).

year may be rebutted.
1. By proof that possession was not taken with intent to hold as tenant.
2. By proof of circumstances under which rent was paid or received.

The presumption that the tenancy from year to year implied from holding over after the expiration of a lease is at the former rent, or on the former terms, may be rebutted by evidence of an intention to alter the terms of the tenancy (*x*). A mere alteration in the rent will not, however, rebut the presumption that the tenant holds on the other terms of the former contract (*y*). A reversioner who has received rent under a lease granted by a tenant for life, which determined on his death, may show that she was ignorant of a special covenant on the part of the lessor contained in such lease; and in that case, if there is no other evidence that she agreed to the

Presumption that tenancy is at former terms may also be rebutted.

(*s*) Judgment in *Finlay* v. *Bristol and Exeter Ry. Co.* 7 Ex., at pp. 417, 420.
(*t*) *Braythwayte* v. *Hitchcock*, 10 M. & W. 494, 497. See *Richardson* v. *Langridge*, 4 Taunt. 128, 132; *Doe* v. *Wood*, 14 M. & W. 682; 15 L. J., Ex. 41.
(*u*) Per Wilde, C. J., in *Doe* v. *Crago*, 6 C. B., at p. 98; *Right* v. *Bawden*, 3 East, 260; *Mildmay*

v. *Shirley*, cited in 10 East, 164; *Doe* v. *Francis*, 2 Moo. & R. 57.
(*v*) *Doe* v. *Crago*, 6 C. B. 90; 17 L. J., C. P. 263; Smith, L. & T. 28.
(*x*) *Thetford* v. *Tyler*, 8 Q. B. 95; 15 L. J., Q. B. 33.
(*y*) *Digby* v. *Atkinson*, 4 Camp. 275; *Doe* v. *Raffan*, 6 Esp. 4; *Doe* v. *Geekie*, 5 Q. B. 841; 13 L. J., Q. B. 239.

tenancy continuing on the former terms than such payment and receipt of rent, she will not be bound by the covenant (*z*). Whether the tenant does or does not hold on the former terms is a question of fact for a jury (*z*).

Commencement of implied tenancy.

An implied tenancy from year to year is presumed to commence on the same day of the year as the original tenancy; but this also has been held to be a question for the decision of a jury, upon a consideration of all the facts of each case (*a*).

When it is said that a person becoming tenant from year to year may be deemed to hold over on the terms of a prior lease, that rule cannot be confined to such terms as are necessarily incident to a yearly tenancy, for it would then have no meaning. It must include such

Terms consistent with tenancy from year to year.

terms as may be incident to such a tenancy (*b*). The following terms have been held to be consistent with a tenancy from year to year:— Covenants to keep premises in repair (*c*); to pay rent (damage by fire excepted) (*d*); to keep open a shop, and to use best endeavours to promote the trade of it during the tenancy (*e*); that the tenant may retain and sow forty acres of wheat on the arable land demised at the seed time next after the end of the term, and leave the standing thereof until the harvest then next following, rent free, with the use of premises for threshing, &c.

(*z*) *Oakley* v. *Monck*, 3 H. & C. 706; 34 L. J., Ex. 137; 35 L. J., Ex. 87; L. R., 1 Ex. 159.

(*a*) *Walker* v. *Godè*, 6 H. & N. 594. But see judgment of Martin, B., at p. 600, and observations of Pollock, C. B., in *Oakley* v. *Monck*, 3 H. & C., at p. 714.

(*b*) Per Patteson, J., 17 Q. B. 509.

(*c*) *Richardson* v. *Gifford*, 1 A. & E. 52; *Arden* v. *Sullivan*, 14 Q. B. 832. And see judgment in *Doe* v. *Amey*, 12 A. & E., at p. 479; and per Erle, J., in *Bowes* v. *Croll*, 6 E. & B, at p. 264.

(*d*) *Bennett* v. *Ireland*, E., B. & E. 326; 28 L. J., Q. B. 48.

(*e*) *Sanders* v. *Karnell*, 1 F. & F. 356.

till a certain day (*f*); that the tenant shall be paid for tillages on the expiration of his tenancy (*g*); that the tenant shall leave all the manure upon the farm at the end of his tenancy (*h*); covenants against taking successive crops of corn (*i*); and stipulations for the cultivation of lands on any system (*k*); reservation of the rent payable in advance (*l*); provisoes for re-entry on non-payment of rent, or non-performance of covenants (*m*); or (in the case of a mining lease), that the tenancy may be determined by a six months' notice, expiring at any time (*n*); also a stipulation that the tenancy shall be determinable at a particular time (*o*).

The following terms are inconsistent with a tenancy from year to year:—Covenants by tenant to build, or to do such substantial repairs as are not usually done by tenants from year to year (*p*); to paint once in three years (*q*); to put premises in repair before he commences his occupation (*q*); a stipulation for two years' notice to quit (*r*). *Terms inconsistent with tenancy from year to year.*

Sect. IV.—*Tenancy for a Term of Years.*

Tenancy for a term of years is always the result of an express contract. No limit is imposed by law to *Created only by express contract.*

(*f*) *Hyatt* v. *Griffiths*, 17 Q. B. 505.
(*g*) *Brocklington* v. *Saunders*, 13 W. R. 46.
(*h*) See *Roberts* v. *Barker*, 1 Cr. & M. 808.
(*i*) *Doe* v. *Amey*, 12 A. & E. 476.
(*k*) Per Martin, B., in 1 H. & N. 734.
(*l*) *Lee* v. *Smith*, 9 Ex. 662; 23 L. J., Ex. 198.
(*m*) *Thomas* v. *Packer*, 1 H. & N. 669; 26 L. J., Ex. 207; *Doe* v. *Amey*, 12 A. & E. 476.
(*n*) *Bridges* v. *Potts*, 17 C. B., N. S. 314; 33 L. J., C. P. 338, 343.
(*o*) See per Maule, J., in *Berrey* v. *Lindley*, 3 M. & Gr., at p. 514; 11 L. J., C. P., at p. 32.
(*p*) See per Erle, J., in *Bowes* v. *Croll*, 6 E. & B., at p. 264.
(*q*) See judgments of Tindal, C. J., and Parke, J., in *Pinero* v. *Judson*, 6 Bing., at pp. 210, 211.
(*r*) *Tooker* v. *Smith*, 1 H. & N. 732.

the number of years for which leases may be made by persons possessed of absolute interests, and under no incapacity.

<small>Certainty requisite.</small>

Every contract sufficient to make a lease for years ought to have certainty in three limitations, viz., in the commencement of the term, in the continuance of it, and in the end of it; and these three are in effect but one matter, showing the certainty of the time for which the lessee shall have the land, and if any of these fail, it is not a good lease, for then there wants certainty (*s*).

<small>Lease for years subject to contingency.</small>

The duration of a lease for years may, however, be made to depend upon a contingency, provided a fixed number of years is first specified, for which the lease is to last, if not previously determined by the happening of the condition. Thus, a lease may be granted for twenty-one years if the tenant shall so long continue to occupy the premises(*t*), or for twenty years if the coverture between certain persons named shall so long continue (*u*); or for years dependent upon the duration of a life or lives.

<small>Leases for years determinable at option of lessee or lessor.</small>

Leases for years may be made determinable at specified periods, at the option of the lessor or lessee (*x*). A lease for three, six, or nine years, is a lease for nine years, determinable at the end of three or six years (*y*).

<small>Lease for years, with option to take further term.</small>

Leases may also be granted for fixed terms of years and afterwards from year to year (*z*), or for a term of

(*s*) Plowden's Commentary, 272. See *post*, Chap. III., Sect. 2, p. 79, for construction of provisions as to commencement of leases.
(*t*) *Doe* v. *Clarke*, 8 East, 185. As to the construction of this condition, see *Doe* v. *Steward*, 1 A. & E. 300.
(*u*) Bac. Abr. (L. 3) 177.
(*x*) See *Colton* v. *Lingham*, 1 Stark. 39; *Gray* v. *Friar*, 5 Ex. 584; 4 H. L. Cas. 565.
(*y*) *Goodright* v. *Richardson*, 3 T. R. 462. See *Ferguson* v. *Cornish*, 2 Burr. 1032; 3 T. R. 463, note (*a*). As to the exercise of the option, see *post*, Chap. V., Sect. I, (4).
(*z*) *Brown* v. *Trumper*, 26 Beav. 11; *Jones* v. *Nixon*, 1 H. & C. 48; 31 L. J., Ex. 505.

years with an option to the lessee to take a lease for a further term (a). This option may be exercised by the tenant at any time during the continuance of the tenancy, though after the expiration of the term of years first specified (b), and it will pass to his assignee in bankruptcy (b).

Sect. V.—*Tenancy for Life.*

Leases for life may be made either for the life of the lessee or for the life or lives of some other person or persons, and in the latter case either for their joint lives or for the life of the survivor (c).

If a man grant an estate to a woman while she remains unmarried, or during widowhood, or *quamdiu se bene gesserit*, or to a man and woman during the coverture; in all these cases the lessee has, in judgment of law, an estate for life determinable (d). Estate for life determinable.

If one grant by deed lands or tenements, and express or limit no estate, the grantee has an estate for life (d); unless the whole deed, taken together, suggests a different construction (e). Indefinite grant.

(a) See *Hersey* v. *Giblett*, 18 Beav. 174; 23 L. J., Ch. 818.
(b) *Moss* v. *Barton*, L. R., 1 Eq. 474; *Buckland* v. *Papillon*, 36 L. J., Ch. 81; L. R., 2 Ch. 67.
(c) As to the construction of leases for lives, see *post*, Chap. III., Sect. 2, p. 82.
(d) Co. Lit. 42 a.
(e) See judgment in *Doe* v. *Dodd*, 5 B. & Ad., at pp. 692—694.

CHAP. III.

THE CONTRACT OF TENANCY.

	PAGE
SECT. I. AGREEMENTS FOR LEASES	61
(1) Statutory requisites	61
Essentials of memorandum	61
(2) In what cases parol agreements are enforceable	62
Part performance	62
Fraud	64
Agreement admitted and statute not insisted on.	64
(3) Rights of intended lessee	64
(4) Remedies for breach of agreement	65
Action for damages	65
Specific performance	65
(5) Stamps	66
II. LEASES	67
(1) Statutory requisites	67
In what cases leases may be made by parol	68
(2) In what cases extrinsic evidence is admissible	69
(3) Form and construction of lease	71
Date	73
Recitals	73
Consideration	73
Operative words	74
Parcels	74
Exceptions and reservations	77
Habendum	79
For years	79
From year to year	81
For life	81
Reddendum	82
Covenants	84
Dependent or independent	87
Joint or several	87
Proviso for re-entry	88
Power to resume possession	92
(4) Stamps	93
Effect of want of	93
misstatement of consideration	95
Description and amount of stamp required	97
(5) Counterparts and duplicates	101
Stamps	102
(6) Matters relating to completion of lease	102
Execution	102
Effect of non-execution by lessor	103
„ alterations after execution	104
Registration	105
Custody of lease	105
Costs	106
Entry of lessee	106

Sect. I.—*Agreements for Leases.*

(1) *Statutory Requisites.*

No action shall be brought whereby to charge any person upon any contract or sale of lands, tenements or hereditaments, *or any interest in or concerning them* (*a*), unless the agreement upon which such action shall be brought, or some memorandum or note thereof, shall be in writing, and signed (*b*) by the party to be charged therewith (*c*), or some other person thereunto by him lawfully authorized.

Stat. 29 Car. 2, c. 3, s. 4. Agreements for leases of lands, &c., or some memorandum thereof, must be in writing, and signed by the party to be charged therewith.

It is not necessary that the memorandum or note should be contemporaneous with the agreement (*d*); or that it should have the character of a written contract between the parties, or be delivered to the person who is to have the remedy upon it (*e*). A note or letter written by the lessor to any third person, containing directions to carry the agreement into execution, is sufficient (*f*). The memorandum, however, must not be a mere proposal for a tenancy (*g*); and it must state all the essential terms of the contract (*h*), that is to say,

Essentials of memorandum.

(*a*) See judgment of Littledale, J., in *Evans* v. *Roberts*, 5 B. & C., at p. 839; *Inman* v. *Stamp*, 1 Stark. 12; *Edge* v. *Strafford*, 1 Cr. & J. 391; 1 Tyr. 293. But see *Wright* v. *Stavert*, 2 E. & E. 721; 29 L. J., Q. B. 161; 8 W. R. 413.

(*b*) See *Stokes* v. *Moore*, 1 Cox, 219; *Propert* v. *Parker*, 1 Russ. & M. 625; *Bleakley* v. *Smith*, 11 Sim. 150; *Selby* v. *Selby*, 3 Mer. 2.

(*c*) *Seton* v. *Slade*, 7 Ves. 265; *Fowle* v. *Freeman*, 9 Ves. 351; *Laythoarp* v. *Bryant*, 2 Bing. N. C. 735.

(*d*) Per Lord Ellenborough, C. J., in *Shippey* v. *Derrison*, 5 Esp., at p. 193.

(*e*) See judgment of Willes, J., in *Gibson* v. *Holland*, 35 L. J., C. P., at p. 6.

(*f*) Sug. V. & P. 122 (11th ed.); *Gibson* v. *Holland*, 35 L. J., C. P. 5; L. R., 1 C. P. 1 (a decision on sect. 17).

(*g*) *Clarke* v. *Fuller*, 16 C. B., N. S. 24; 12 W. R. 671; *Forster* v. *Rowland*, 7 H. & N. 103; 30 L. J., Ex. 396.

(*h*) *Williams* v. *Lake*, 2 E. & E. 349, 351; 29 L. J., Q. B. 1.

the subject-matter—describing with certainty the premises to be demised (*i*); the duration of the term (*k*); the amount of the fine (if any) or other consideration (*l*), and of the rent (*m*); and the names of both the parties to the agreement (*n*).

(2) In what cases parol Agreements are enforceable.

Part performance.

Courts of Equity (including the County Courts in cases where the total amount of rent payable during the term does not exceed 500*l*. (*o*)) will enforce performance of unwritten and unsigned agreements for leases, made by persons having power to grant such leases (*p*), provided such agreements are certain and complete (*q*); are either admitted or clearly proved (*r*), and have been partly performed (*s*). Before decreeing specific performance the Court has, first of all, to ascertain that there has been a parol agreement, and to know the terms of that agreement; and if satisfied on these points has then to inquire whether it has been in part performed (*t*).

See *Jackson* v. *Oglander*, 2 Hem. & M. 465; 13 W. R. 936; *Baumann* v. *James*, L. R., 3 Ch. 508; 16 W. R. 877.

(*i*) *Daniels* v. *Davison*, 16 Ves. 249, 255; *Lancaster* v. *De Trafford*, 31 L. J., Ch. 554. See *Ogilvie* v. *Foljambe*, 3 Mer. 53.

(*k*) *Clinan* v. *Cooke*, 1 Sch. & L. 22; *Fitzmaurice* v. *Bayley*, 8 E. & B. 664; 27 L. J., Q. B. 143; 9 H. L. C. 78; 8 W. R. 750.

(*l*) See *Baumann* v. *James*, L. R., 3 Ch. 508; 16 W. R. 877.

(*m*) See *Wain* v. *Warlters*, 5 East, 10; *Saunders* v. *Wakefield*, 4 B. & A. 595.

(*n*) *Williams* v. *Lake*, 2 E. & E. 349; 29 L. J., Q B. 1; judgment in *Warner* v. *Willington*, 3 Drew., at p. 530.

(*o*) Stat. 28 & 29 Vict. c. 99, s. 1 (art. 4); *Willcox* v. *Marshall*, 36 L. J., Ch. 358. But see *Cox* v. *Slater*, 14 W. R. 665.

(*p*) See *Phillips* v. *Edwards*, 33 Beav. 440.

(*q*) See *Thynne* v. *Glengall*, 2 H. L. Cas. 131, 158.

(*r*) *Mortal* v. *Lyons*, 8 Ir. Ch. Rep. 112; see *Reynolds* v. *Waring*, 1 Yo. 346; *Morphett* v. *Jones*, 1 Swanst. 172.

(*s*) *Lester* v. *Foxcroft*, 1 Coll. P. C. 108. See notes in 1 Wh. & Tud. L. C. 693 (3rd ed.).

(*t*) See judgment in *Nunn* v. *Fabian*, 35 L. J., Ch., at p. 141.

To operate as a part performance an act must have been done unequivocally referring to, and resulting from, the agreement (*u*); of such a nature, indeed, that if stated, it would of itself infer the existence of some agreement; and then parol evidence is admitted to show what the agreement is (*x*). The following circumstances have been held to amount to part performance:— *Acts which constitute.*

Where under a parol agreement for a lease, and with distinct reference to such agreement, a person has entered into possession of premises (*y*); and especially where, in pursuance of the agreement, he has expended money in improvements (*z*), with the acquiescence of the landlord (*a*). *1. Entry into possession and expenditure.*

Where under a parol agreement by a landlord to grant to a tenant in possession a lease for a term of years at an increased rent, the tenant has paid rent at the increased rate (*b*). *2. Payment of rent at increased rate.*

Where a person who is already in possession of premises as tenant expends money in alterations in pursuance of a parol agreement for a new lease (*c*), the *3. Expenditure in pursuance of parol agreement.*

(*u*) *Ex parte Hooper*, 19 Ves. 479; judgment in *Morphett* v. *Jones*, 1 Swanst., at p. 181.

(*x*) Per Sir W. Grant, M. R., in *Frame* v. *Dawson*, 14 Ves., at pp. 387, 388.

(*y*) *Bowers* v. *Cator*, 4 Ves. 91; *Pain* v. *Coombs*, 1 De G. & J. 34; see *Wills* v. *Stradling*, 3 Ves., at p. 381; *Boardman* v. *Mostyn*, 6 Ves., at p. 470; *Morphett* v. *Jones*, 1 Swans. 172; *Kine* v. *Balfe*, 2 Ball & B. 343, 348.

(*z*) *Gregory* v. *Mighell*, 18 Ves. 328; *Mundy* v. *Jolliffe*, 5 My. & C. 167; 9 L. J., Ch. 95;

Farrell v. *Davenport*, 3 Giff. 363; 8 Jur., N. S. 862, 1043; see *Surcome* v. *Pinniger*, 3 De G., M. & G. 571.

(*a*) See *Dann* v. *Spurrier*, 7 Ves. 231; *Shillibeer* v. *Jarvis*, 8 De G., M. & G. 79.

(*b*) *Nunn* v. *Fabian*, 35 L. J., Ch. 140; L. R., 1 Ch. 35; see *Wills* v. *Stradling*, 3 Ves. 378, 382.

(*c*) *Sutherland* v. *Briggs*, 1 Hare, 26; 11 L. J., Ch. 36; *Mundy* v. *Jolliffe*, 5 My. & C. 167; 9 L. J., Ch. 95; see *Wills* v. *Stradling*, 3 Ves., at p. 382.

alterations being such as he would not have been liable to make if there had been no agreement (*d*).

4. Under special circumstances, mere retention of possession.

Under special circumstances it would even seem that the mere retention of possession by a tenant after the determination of the original tenancy may amount to part performance (*e*).

Fraud.

If in consequence of fraud an agreement for a lease is not made in compliance with the provisions of the statute, it will be considered in Equity as exempted from the operation of the statute (*f*).

Where agreement is admitted and statute not insisted on.

If a parol agreement is admitted by the defendant, and he does not insist on the statute, Courts of Equity will decree specific performance of such agreement (*g*).

(3) *Rights of intended Lessee.*

As to title.

By agreeing to grant a lease the intended lessor impliedly undertakes that he has title to grant such lease; and if he has not, he is liable to an action at the suit of the intended lessee (*h*). A lessee is a purchaser *pro tanto*, and, it seems, is entitled to call upon the lessor for an inspection of his title (*i*).

As to covenants.

If an agreement for a lease contains no stipulation as

(*d*) See *Frame* v. *Dawson*, 14 Ves. 386.

(*e*) Dart, V. & P. 656; *Dowell* v. *Dew*, 1 Y. & C. C. C. 345; 12 L. J., Ch. 158. *It is to be observed, however, that in this case there was evidence that the tenant had laid out money solely with reference to the agreement.* See 1 Y. & C. C. C. 351; 12 L. J., Ch. 160.

(*f*) See *Pym* v. *Blackburn*, 3 Ves., at p. 38, note; *Whitchurch* v. *Bevis*, 2 Bro. C. C., at p. 565.

(*g*) *Gunter* v. *Halsey*, Amb. 586.

(*h*) *Stranks* v. *St. John*, 36 L. J., C. P. 118; L. R., 2 C. P. 376; *Roper* v. *Coombes*, 6 B. & C. 534; *Gwillim* v. *Stone*, 3 Taunt. 432; explained in 36 L. J., C. P. 120; (the marginal note to this case is incorrect). See *Temple* v. *Brown*, 6 Taunt. 60.

(*i*) 2 Sug. V. & P. 141 (10th ed.); *Keech* v. *Hall*, 1 Dougl. 21; *Purvis* v. *Rayer*, 9 Price, 488.

AGREEMENTS FOR LEASES. 65

to covenants, the person agreeing to take the lease has a right to a lease containing only usual covenants (*k*).

(4) *Remedies for Breach of Agreement.*

Upon the breach of a complete (*l*) and valid (*m*) agreement to grant or take a lease, the person aggrieved thereby may, in an action at law, obtain damages, and also recover back any sum which he may have paid as premium (*n*). 1. Action for damages.

Where a person who has agreed to grant a lease at a future day has disabled himself from doing so by previously making an inconsistent lease, he is considered as having committed a breach of his agreement, and is liable to be sued before such day arrives (*o*).

Instead of bringing an action at law for damages (*p*), the person aggrieved by the breach of an agreement for a lease for years or life may obtain specific performance of such agreement by a suit in equity, provided the contract is complete (*q*), and certain (*r*), and fair and just in all its parts (*s*), and either proved by a memorandum in writing signed by the party to be charged therewith (*m*), or partly performed (*t*). But the exercise of this jurisdiction is entirely in the discretion of the 2. Specific performance.

(*k*) *Propert* v. *Parker*, 3 My. & K. 280. As to what covenants are "usual," see *post*, p. 85.

(*l*) See *Forster* v. *Rowland*, 7 H. & N. 103; 30 L. J., Ex. 396; *Ridgway* v. *Wharton*, 6 H. L. C. 238; 27 L. J., Ch. 46.

(*m*) *Ante*, p. 61.

(*n*) See *Wright* v. *Colls*, 8 C. B. 150; 19 L. J., C. P. 60.

(*o*) *Ford* v. *Tiley*, 6 B. & C. 325, 327.

(*p*) But not in addition to that remedy; see *Sainter* v. *Ferguson*, 1 Mac. & G. 286; 19 L. J., Ch. 170; *Orme* v. *Broughton*, 10 Bing., at p. 538; *Dart*, V. & P. 703.

(*q*) See *Thynne* v. *Glengall*, 2 H. L. C. 131, 158.

(*r*) *Taylor* v. *Portington*, 7 De G., M. & G. 328. See *Parker* v. *Taswell*, 2 De G. & J. 559; 27 L. J., Ch. 812; *Heywood* v. *Cope*, 25 Beav. 140; 27 L. J., Ch. 468.

(*s*) Per Lord Hardwicke, C., in *Buxton* v. *Lister*, 3 Atk., at p. 386.

(*t*) *Ante*, p. 62.

F.

Court (*t*), and it will not in general decree specific performance of a contract for a yearly tenancy (*u*), or of an agreement for a longer term where such term has expired by effluxion of time (*x*), or where there is evidence of general insolvency, showing that the plaintiff is not in a situation to perform the covenants contained in the lease (*y*).

Stat. 21 & 22 Vict. c. 27, s. 2.
Court of Chancery may award damages.

In all cases in which the Court of Chancery has jurisdiction to entertain an application for the specific performance of any covenant, contract, or agreement, it shall be lawful for the same Court, if it shall think fit, to award damages to the party injured, either in addition to, or in substitution for such specific performance, and such damages may be assessed in such manner as the Court shall direct.

(5) *Stamps.*

Where necessary.

A written offer to let, assented to by parol, is admissible in evidence without being stamped (*z*). But where an oral proposal is accepted in writing, such written acceptance must be stamped (*a*).

An agreement for a lease, assented to by the parties to it, but not signed by them, is not admissible in evidence without a stamp (*b*).

Amount of duty.
Stat. 33 & 34 Vict. c. 97, s. 96.

An agreement for a lease (*c*), or with respect to the letting of any lands, tenements, or heritable subjects for

---

(*t*) Per Lord Hardwicke, C., in *Buxton* v. *Lister*, 3 Atk., at p. 386.

(*u*) *Clayton* v. *Illingworth*, 10 Hare, 451.

(*x*) See *Walters* v. *Northern Coal Mining Co.*, 5 De G., M. & G. 629; 25 L. J., Ch. 633.

(*y*) *Neale* v. *Mackenzie*, 1 Keen, 474, 485.

(*z*) *Drant* v. *Brown*, 3 B. & C. 665; see *Turner* v. *Power*, 7 B. & C. 625; M. & M. 131.

(*a*) *Hegarty* v. *Milne*, 14 C. B. 627; 23 L. J., C. P. 151.

(*b*) *Chadwick* v. *Clarke*, 1 C. B. 700; 14 L. J., C. P. 233.

(*c*) Made on or after 1st January, 1871.

any term not exceeding thirty-five years, is to be charged with the same duty as if it were an actual lease made for the term and consideration mentioned in the agreement.

Agreements for leases of lands, &c., not exceeding thirty-five years, to be charged as leases.

A lease made subsequently to, and in conformity with such an agreement duly stamped, is to be charged with the duty of sixpence only.

An agreement, or any memorandum of an agreement, made under hand only, and not otherwise specifically charged with any duty, whether the same be only evidence of a contract, or obligatory upon the parties from its being a written instrument, is chargeable with a duty of sixpence.

Id. Schedule. Duty on agreement under hand, not otherwise charged, sixpence.

An agreement or memorandum the matter whereof is not of the value of 5l. is exempt from duty.

Exemption.

Sect. II.—*Leases.*

(1) *Statutory Requisites.*

Leases of any messuages, manors, lands, tenements or hereditaments made by parol, and not put in writing and signed by the parties making the same, or their agents thereunto lawfully authorized by writing, shall have the force and effect of leases at will only; except nevertheless all leases not exceeding the term of three years from the making thereof, whereupon the rent reserved to the landlord, during such term, shall amount unto two-third parts at the least of the full improved value of the thing demised.

Stat. 29 Car. 2, c. 3, s. 1. Parol leases to be leases at will only.

Sect. 2. Except leases not exceeding three years, and reserving rent amounting to two-thirds of improved value.

A lease, required by law to be in writing, of any tenements or hereditaments, made after the first day of October, 1845, shall be void at law, unless made by deed.

Stat. 8 & 9 Vict. c. 106, s. 3. Leases to be by deed.

The practical effect of these statutory provisions, and of the decisions upon them, may be stated as follows:—

1. Leases of land, &c. to end within three years, and reserving rent equal to two-thirds of full value.

Leases of land, and other corporeal hereditaments, which will end within three years from the time of making (*d*), and whereby there is reserved to the landlord a rent equal to two-third parts at least of the full improved value of the demised premises, may be made verbally (*e*), or by writing not under seal.

2. Leases of land, &c. for more than three years, or reserving less rent than two-thirds of full value.

Leases of land, and other corporeal hereditaments for a longer term than three years, or reserving less rent than two-third parts of the full improved value of the demised premises, must be made by deed. But an instrument not under seal purporting to demise premises for a longer term than three years, or reserving a rent not amounting to two-thirds of the full improved value, though void at law *as a lease*, will be construed by a Court of Equity as an agreement for a lease, of which specific performance may be enforced (*f*). In a Court of Law, also, such an instrument may be available as an agreement (*g*). If the lessee has entered and paid rent under an instrument of this nature, a tenancy from year to year may be created (*h*); and the instrument may indicate ·the terms of such tenancy (*h*).

(*d*) See *Ryley* v. *Hicks,* 1 Stra. 651; *Rawlins* v. *Turner,* 1 Ld. Raym. 736.

(*e*) But verbal leases do not confer the right to sue the lessee for damages for not taking possession. See *Edge* v. *Strafford,* 1 Cr. & J. 391.

(*f*) *Parker* v. *Taswell,* 2 De G. & J. 559; 27 L. J., Ch. 812.

(*g*) *Tidey* v. *Mollett,* 16 C. B., N. S. 298; 33 L. J., C. P. 235; 10 L. T., N. S. 380; *Hayne* v. *Cummings,* 16 C. B., N. S. 421; 10 L. T., N. S. 341; *Bond* v. *Rosling,* 1 B. & S. 371; 30 L. J., Q. B. 227; 9 W. R. 746; *Rollason* v. *Leon,* 7 H. & N. 73; 31 L. J., Ex. 96.

(*h*) *Clayton* v. *Blakey,* 8 T. R. 3; *Doe* v. *Bell,* 5 T. R. 471; *Richardson* v. *Gifford,* 1 A. & E. 52. See *ante,* p. 53.

Leases of rights of common, rights of way, tithes, or other incorporeal hereditaments can only be made by deed (*i*), unless such hereditaments are appurtenant to some corporeal hereditament, in which case they will pass under a demise, even by parol, of such corporeal hereditament (*k*), though nothing is said about them at the time of the demise (*l*). An instrument not under seal demising land, and also purporting to demise incorporeal hereditaments, is not thereby rendered void (*m*).

3. Leases of incorporeal hereditaments.

(2) *In what cases Extrinsic Evidence is admissible.*

Where the contract of lease is reduced into writing, it is presumed that the writing contains all the terms of it (*n*), and, in the absence of fraud, mistake (*o*), or surprise (*p*), verbal or other extrinsic evidence is not in general admissible to contradict or add to the written instrument (*q*). If, for instance, a certain sum is specified therein as the annual rent, parol evidence will not

Exclusion of extrinsic evidence.

(*i*) *Somerset* v. *Fognell*, 5 B. & C. 875; see authorities cited in judgment, at pp. 882, 883; *Gardiner* v. *Williamson*, 2 B. & Ad. 336, 338; *Bird* v. *Higginson*, 2 A. & E. 696; 6 A. & E. 824; *Mayfield* v. *Robinson*, 7 Q. B. 486; *Wood* v. *Leadbitter*, 13 M. & W. 838; 14 L. J., Ex. 161. But agreements for letting the tolls of any turnpike roads, signed by the trustees letting such tolls, or any two of them, or by their clerk or treasurer, and the lessee and his sureties, are valid, notwithstanding the same may not be by deed or under seal. Stat. 3 Geo. 4, c. 126, s. 57.

(*k*) *Skull* v. *Glenister*, 16 C. B., N. S. 81, 102; 33 L. J., C. P. 185;
Dobbyn v. *Somers*, 13 Ir. C. L. R., Q. B. 293.

(*l*) See *Beaudeley* v. *Brook*, Cro. Jac., at p. 190.

(*m*) *Reg.* v. *Hockworthy*, 7 A. & E. 492.

(*n*) See Roscoe's Evidence, 14 (11th ed.).

(*o*) See *Garrard* v. *Frankel*, 30 Beav. 445; 31 L. J., Ch. 604.

(*p*) See Dart's V. & P. (3rd ed.), Ch. 18, sect. 8, p. 664, for the cases in which parol evidence is admitted on these grounds as a defence to a suit for specific performance.

(*q*) See *Woollam* v. *Hearn*, 7 Ves., at p. 218; *Omerod* v. *Hardman*, 5 Ves., at p. 730.

be received to show that the tenant also agreed to pay an additional yearly sum for ground rent (*s*). So also parol evidence is not admissible to show an understanding between the parties that the rent should commence from a later date than that named in the agreement (*t*); and where the lease does not stipulate that the rent is to be a net rent without any deduction, verbal evidence is inadmissible to show the agreement of the parties that it should be such (*u*).

Exceptions.
In the following cases, however, verbal evidence is admitted to add to or explain instruments of lease:—

1. Custom.
Evidence of usage is admitted, where not expressly or impliedly excluded by the terms of the lease (*x*).

2. Latent ambiguity.
Where a deed or instrument seems certain and without ambiguity, for anything that appears upon it, but there is some collateral matter out of the deed or instrument which produces an ambiguity, verbal or other extrinsic evidence is admissible to explain such ambiguity (*y*). Thus, if a person grant his manor of S. to A. B. and the grantor has two manors, of North S. and South S., it being clear that he means to grant one only, whereas both are equally denoted by the words he has used, evidence of previous intention may be received to solve this latent ambiguity (*z*).

3. Technical terms.
Where terms are used which are known and understood by a particular class of persons, in a certain

(*s*) *Preston* v. *Merceau*, 2 W. Bl. 1249.
(*t*) *Henson* v. *Cooper*, 3 Sc. N. R. 48.
(*u*) *Rich* v. *Jackson*, 4 Bro. C. C. 514; see 6 Ves. 334, note (*c*).
(*x*) *Post*, Chap. IV., Sect. 5; Chap. VI., Sect. 3 (1). See *In re Stroud*, 8 C. B. 502; 16 L. J., C.

P. 117.
(*y*) Bac. Maxims, Reg. 23; *Doe* v. *Burt*, 1 T. R. 701; *Osborn* v. *Wise*, 7 C. & P. 761. See *Coker* v. *Guy*, 2 B. & P. 565.
(*z*) Bac. Maxims, Reg. 23. See judgment in *Doe* v. *Hiscocks*, 5 M. & W. 363, 369.

special and peculiar sense, evidence to that effect is admissible (*a*). Thus verbal evidence has been admitted to show that the word " thousand," in a lease of a rabbit warren, by local usage meant 1,200 (*b*); also that the word "level," in a mining lease, was not used in the ordinary sense of a horizontal plane, but in a sense peculiar to mines (*c*). It cannot, however, be inferred as matter of law that words occurring in a lease are used by the parties in a special or technical sense; it is a question for a jury to decide in what sense the words are used in each case (*c*). Where a word is defined by Act of Parliament to mean a precise quantity, or a precise time, the parties using that word, in a lease by deed (*d*), must be presumed to employ it in the sense given to it by the legislature, unless it appears from other parts of the deed that they used it differently (*e*).

In some cases a lease may be explained by parol evidence of the state of the premises at the time when it was granted, and of the mode in which they had been previously enjoyed (*f*).

4. Previous mode of enjoyment of premises.

(3) *Form and Construction of Lease.*

No special form of words is necessary to constitute a lease. Whatever words are sufficient to explain the intent of the parties that the one shall divest himself of the possession (*g*) and the other come into it for a determinate time, such words, whether they run in the

(*a*) 3 Starkie on Evidence, 1033.
(*b*) *Smith* v. *Wilson*, 3 B. & Ad. 728.
(*c*) *Clayton* v. *Gregson*, 6 N. & M. 694; 5 A. & E. 302.
(*d*) See *Doe* v. *Benson*, 4 B. & A. 588.
(*e*) See per Parke, J., in *Smith* v. *Wilson*, 3 B. & Ad., at p. 733; *Doe* v. *Lea*, 11 East, 312.
(*f*) *Hall* v. *Lund*, 1 H. & C. 676; 32 L. J., Ex. 113; 11 W. R. 271. See *Osborn* v. *Wise*, 7 C. & P. 761.
(*g*) See *ante*, p. 47.

form of a licence (*i*), covenant (*k*), or agreement (*l*), are of themselves sufficient, and will in construction of law amount to a lease for years as effectually as if the most proper and pertinent words had been made use of for that purpose; for a lease for years being a contract for the possession and profits of lands on the one side, and a recompense of rent, or other income, on the other, if the words made use of are sufficient to prove such a contract, in what form soever they are introduced, or however variously applicable, the law calls in the intent of the parties, and models and governs the words accordingly (*m*).

By correspondence.

A lease may be made by a correspondence, in which one party offers to take on certain terms fully and definitely stated, and the other unconditionally accepts such offer (*n*).

Lease for life.

Leases for lives of corporeal hereditaments, if not made by a conveyance operating under the Statute of Uses, or in pursuance of a power to lease, must formerly have been perfected by livery of seisin. This ceremony is not now requisite, for all corporeal tenements and hereditaments shall, as regards the conveyance of the immediate freehold thereof, be deemed to lie in grant as well as in livery.

Stat. 8 & 9 Vict. c. 106, s. 2.

Ordinary form of lease.

The ordinary form of lease by deed is technically said to consist of the premises, *habendum, reddendum,* and covenants.

(*i*) *Hall* v. *Sebright*, 1 Mod. 14. See *Doe* v. *Wood*, 2 B. & A. 724.
(*k*) See judgment of Parke, J., in *Doe* v. *Dodd*, 5 B. & Ad., at p. 693; *Whitlock* v. *Horton*, Cro. Jac. 91; *Fenny* v. *Child*, 2 M. & S. 255, 257.
(*l*) See *Lovelock* v. *Franklyn*,
8 Q. B. 371; 16 L. J., Q. B. 182.
(*m*) Bac. Abr. (K.), p. 160. See *Drake* v. *Munday*, Cro. Car. 207; *Walker* v. *Giles*, 6 C. B. 662; 18 L. J., C. P. 323.
(*n*) *Chapman* v. *Bluck*, 4 Bing. N. C. 187; 7 L. J., C. P. 100. See *Jones* v. *Reynolds*, 1 Q. B. 506; 10 L. J., Q. B. 193.

THE PREMISES contain the date, names and descrip- *Premises.*
tions of the parties, recitals, consideration, operative
words, parcels, and the exceptions and reservations.

THE DATE of a deed is not of the substance of the *Date.*
deed; for if it has no date, or a false or impossible date,
yet the deed is good (*o*).

A lease by deed is presumed to be delivered on the
day on which it bears date (*p*); but a party may show
that the deed was delivered on a different day, and in
that case it takes effect from the day of delivery, and
not from the day of the date (*q*).

RECITALS, stating the title of the lessor, are seldom *Recitals.*
necessary, except in the case of an underlease, or where
the lease is made by a tenant for life, or in pursuance
of a power to lease.

THE CONSIDERATION expresses the recompense to be *Consideration.*
rendered by the lessee for the use of the demised premises. This may either consist of the payment of rent
and performance of covenants, or of the payment of a
sum of money as a fine, the execution of improvements
on the demised premises, or in fact any benefit conferred
on the lessor either by the lessee, or by any one else on
his behalf. In leases at a fine made before 1871, the
full amount of the consideration-money must be truly set
forth in words at length, and the lessee may recover
back from the lessor so much of the consideration-money
as is not set forth as aforesaid, or the whole, if no part is
so set forth (*r*). Where in pursuance of an agreement

(*o*) *Goddard's case*, 2 Co. R., at p. 5.
(*p*) *Hall* v. *Denbigh*, Cro. Eliz. 773; see also *House* v. *Laxton*, *ib.* 890.
(*q*) *Steele* v. *Mart*, 4 B. & C. 272, 279, 280.
(*r*) Stats. 48 Geo. 3, c. 149, ss. 22—25; 55 Geo. 3, c. 184, s. 8; *Gingell* v. *Purkins*, 4 Ex. 720; 19 L. J., Ex. 129. Repealed by Stat. 33 & 34 Vict. c. 99.

for a lease, a lease is tendered to the lessor for execution in which the consideration is not truly stated, the lessor is not bound to execute the lease (*s*).

Operative words.

THE OPERATIVE WORDS are those by which the lessor actually lets the premises to the lessee. The terms generally used are "demise and lease," but any words clearly indicating an intention of making a present demise will suffice (*t*). Under the word "demise" there is implied a covenant for quiet enjoyment (*u*).

Parcels.

THE PARCELS contain a description of the property intended to be let. In agricultural leases it is often sufficient to specify the name of the farm, the number of acres it contains, and the parish and county in which it is situated. Where the identity of the demised premises can be perfectly established by this description, other particulars should be omitted, since questions frequently arise as to how far words of particular explanation qualify words of general description (*x*).

"False demonstration."

The rule is clearly settled, that when there is a sufficient description set forth of premises by giving the particular name of a close, or otherwise, a false demonstration,—*i. e.*, an incorrect addition to the description inserted only for the purpose of identifying the property (*y*), may be rejected; but if premises are described in general terms, and a particular description is added, the latter controls the former (*z*).

(*s*) *Vonhollen* v. *Knowles*, 12 M. & W. 602; 13 L. J., Ex. 140.
(*t*) Bac. Abr. (K.) 161; *ante*, pp. 71, 72.
(*u*) *Post*, Chap. IV., Sect. 10 (1).
(*x*) 2 Platt on Leases, 27. See *Doe* v. *Galloway*, 5 B. & Ad. 43; *Dyne* v. *Nutley*, 14 C. B. 122.

(*y*) *Martyr* v. *Lawrence*, 2 De G., J. & S. 261; 12 W. R. 1043; *Manning* v. *Fitzgerald*, 29 L. J., Ex. 24.
(*z*) See per Parke, J., in *Doe* v. *Galloway*, 5 B. & Ad., at p. 51. See *Doe* v. *Greathed*, 8 East, at pp. 103, 104; *Doe* v. *Jersey*, 1 B. & A., at p. 558.

In framing parcels the following particulars should be borne in mind: *Legal meaning of terms of description.*

Land means strictly arable land (*a*); but comprehends in law any ground, soil or earth whatsoever, as meadows (*b*), pastures, moors, marshes, and heath (*c*); and will *primâ facie* include all buildings, woods or water thereupon (*c*). *1. "Land."*

Under the word *water*, it seems that a right of fishing will pass, but the soil will not pass (*d*). To include the soil under the water the description should be *land covered with water* (*d*). But under the word *pond* or *pool*, it seems that the soil will pass (*e*). *2. "Water."*

Farm includes the farm-house, farm buildings, and the lands thereunto belonging, or therewith used (*f*); and may also comprehend woodlands (*g*). *3. "Farm."*

The words *farming buildings*, it seems, include the farm-house (*h*).

Messuage or *house* (the terms are synonymous (*i*)), may comprehend, besides the house and buildings adjoining, a courtyard, garden (*k*), and orchard belonging to the same (*l*), and the stables and other outhouses necessary for the convenient occupation of the house (*m*). *4. "Messuage."*

(*a*) Shep. Touch. 91.
(*b*) *Cooke* v. *Yates*, 4 Bing. 90.
(*c*) Co. Lit. 4 a.
(*d*) Co. Lit. 4 b.
(*e*) Co. Lit. 5 b.
(*f*) Shep. Touch. 93.
(*g*) *Portman* v. *Mill*, 3 Jur. 356.
(*h*) *Cooke* v. *Cholmondeley*, 4 Drew. 326.
(*i*) See 2 T. R. 502.
(*k*) *Carden* v. *Tuck*, Cro. Eliz. 89; *Henson* v. *South Western Ry. Co.*, 8 W. R. 467; *Grosvenor* v. *Hampstead Junction Ry. Co.*, 1 De G. & J. 446; 26 L. J., Ch. 731; *Cole* v. *West London, &c. Ry. Co.*, 27 Beav. 242; 28 L. J., Ch. 767; *Steele* v. *Midland Ry. Co.*, L. R., 1 Ch. 275, 284, 290; 14 W. R. 367; *Marson* v. *London, Chatham and Dover Ry. Co.*, 37 L. J., Ch. 483; L. R., 6 Eq. 101.
(*l*) Shep. Touch. 94; Co. Lit. 5 b.
(*m*) *Doe* v. *Collins*, 2 T. R. 498. See L. R., 1 Ch. 291.

5. "Appurtenances."

To a house.

To land.

The word *appurtenances* will pass only things which have been used together with the house or land demised, or which are reputed or accepted as parcel thereof (*n*). Whether anything is or is not parcel of the premises demised is always matter of evidence (*o*). As appurtenant to a house, a curtilage and a garden (*p*) may pass also a right of turbary (*q*); but, as a general rule, not land (*r*). As appurtenant to land there may pass a sheepwalk (*s*), also a right of turbary (*q*), or of way (*t*); but not an easement which has become extinct, or which does not exist in point of law by reason of unity of ownership (*u*).

Under the words *with all ways to the same belonging or appertaining*, no way will pass unless legally appurtenant; or unless it appears from the grant itself that the parties meant to use the words in a more extended sense than the legal one (*x*). But under the words *with all ways to the demised premises belonging, or with any part thereof used or enjoyed*, it seems that a right of way

---

(*n*) *Bryan* v. *Weatherhead*, Cro. Car. 17; *Kerslake* v. *White*, 2 Stark. 508; see *Maitland* v. *Mackinnon*, 1 H. & C. 607; 32 L. J., Ex. 49; *Smith* v. *Ridgway*, 4 H. & C. 37; 35 L. J., Ex. 11, 198; L. R., 1 Ex. 331.

(*o*) Per Buller, J., in *Doe* v. *Burt*, 1 T. R., at p. 704.

(*p*) *Bettisworth's case*, 2 Co. R., at p. 32.

(*q*) *Solme* v. *Bullock*, 3 Lev. 165; *Dobbyn* v. *Somers*, 13 Ir. C. L. R., Q. B., at p. 300.

(*r*) *Hearn* v. *Allen*, Cro. Car. 57; *Buck* v. *Nurton*, 1 B. & P. 53; but see *Doe* v. *Martin*, 2 W. Bl. 1148.

(*s*) *Hurleston* v. *Woodroffe*, Cro. Jac. 519.

(*t*) Per Lord Mansfield, C. J., in *Morris* v. *Edgington*, 3 Taunt., at p. 30; *Hincheliffe* v. *Kinnoul*, 5 Bing., N. C. 1; *Skull* v. *Glenister*, 16 C. B., N. S. 81; 33 L. J., C. P. 185. But see *Worthington* v. *Gimson*, 2 E. & E. 618; 29 L. J., Q. B. 116; *Harding* v. *Wilson*, 2 B. & C. 96.

(*u*) Per Denman, C. J., in *Plant* v. *James*, 5 B. & Ad., at p. 794; 4 A. & E. 749; *Grymes* v. *Peacock*, 1 Bulstr. 17; *Saunders* v. *Oliffe*, Moo. 467; *Whalley* v. *Tompson*, 1 B. & P. 371; *Clements* v. *Lambert*, 1 Taunt. 205; *Barlow* v. *Rhodes*, 1 Cr. & M. 439.

(*x*) *Barlow* v. *Rhodes*, 1 Cr. & M. 439; 2 Platt on Leases, 34.

which at the time of the granting of the lease is used with any part of the demised premises will pass, although not specifically mentioned (*y*).

The words *more or less*, appended to the measurements in the parcels, being indeterminate, if the land occupied by the tenant exceeds such measurements but corresponds with the abuttals, the tenant has a fair title to insist that it was meant that so much should pass by the demise (*z*). And where the lessor sees the daily progress of a building which covers the land occupied by the tenant, he will not be allowed to claim the overplus beyond the measured distance as an encroachment (*a*). — "More or less."

An EXCEPTION is always of part of the thing granted, but a RESERVATION is always of a thing not *in esse*, but newly created or reserved out of the land or tenement demised (*b*). — Exceptions and reservations.

The words of an exception are usually construed against the lessor and in favour of the lessee (*c*). It seems, however, when a certain number of acres are excepted from a lease, without any specification of the particular acres intended to be excepted, the lessor has, before the lease is actually granted, the right to select the acres to be excepted from the lease (*d*). But if the — Construction of.

(*y*) *Kooystra* v. *Lucas*, 5 B. & A. 830, 834. See *Harding* v. *Wilson*, 2 B. & C., at p. 100.

(*z*) *Neale* v. *Parkin*, 1 Esp. 229, 230; *Cross* v. *Eglin*, 2 B. & Ad., at p. 110.

(*a*) *Neale* v. *Parkin*, 1 Esp. 229. As to the construction of the words "*or thereabouts*," see *Davis* v. *Shepherd*, 35 L. J., Ch. 581, 590; L. R., 1 Ch. 410.

(*b*) Co. Lit. 47 a.

(*c*) Shep. Touch. 100; *Bullen* v. *Denning*, 5 B. & C. 842, 847, 850; *Cardigan* v. *Armitage*, 2 B. & C. 197, 207. See *Chadwick* v. *Marsden*, 36 L. J., Ex. 177; L. R., 2 Ex. 285; 15 W. R. 964. But see *Mitcalfe* v. *Westaway*, 17 C. B., N. S. 658; 34 L. J., C. P. 113.

(*d*) *Jenkins* v. *Green*, 27 Beav. 437; 28 L. J., Ch. 817.

lease has been actually granted in the terms of the agreement, without specifying the lands excepted, the right of selecting the excepted lands will rest with the tenant (*e*). The landlord's right of selection must not be exercised oppressively, so as to interfere with the beneficial enjoyment of the rest of the farm (*e*).

Timber.
An exception of *all the wood and underwood* includes trees both great and small, but not fruit trees (*f*). It extends to the soil on which the trees grow (*g*), if there are no expressions showing that it was intended to confine the exception to the trees themselves (*h*). On the other hand an exception of *all timber-trees*, will comprise only so much of the soil as is sufficient for the vegetation and growth of the trees excepted (*i*). Under an exception of *all and all manner of timber, &c., wood, underwood, bushes and thorns, other than such bushes and thorns as shall be necessary for the repairs of the fences,* all bushes whether forming part of the fences or not, or necessary for repairs or not, are excepted out of the demise (*k*). The meaning of the clause is, that there is reserved to the tenant the right of taking all or parts of the thorns or bushes for repairs when required (*k*).

Where timber is excepted, the lessor is entitled to enter on the demised premises to show it to intending purchasers, and he or his vendee may cut the trees down, and take them away (*l*).

(*e*) *Jenkins* v. *Green*, 27 Beav. 437; 28 L. J., Ch. 817.

(*f*) *London* v. *Southwell*, Hob. 303. See also *Wyndham* v. *Way*, 4 Taunt. 316; note (*a*), p. 318; *Bullen* v. *Denning*, 5 B. & C. 842; Woodfall, L. & T. 129.

(*g*) *Ive* v. *Sams*, Cro. Eliz. 521; 5 Co. R. 11; *Whistler* v. *Pasloe*, Cro. Jac. 487; *Rolls* v. *Rock*, 2 Selw., N. P. 1244 (13th ed.).

(*h*) *Legh* v. *Heald*, 1 B. & Ad. 622; *Pincomb* v. *Thomas*, Cro. Jac. 524.

(*i*) *Whistler* v. *Pasloe*, Cro. Jac. 487. See *Legh* v. *Heald*, 1 B. & Ad. 622; 2 Platt on Leases, 42.

(*k*) *Jenney* v. *Brook*, 13 L. J., Q. B. 376, 385; 6 Q. B. 323.

(*l*) Shep. Touch. 100; *Liford's Case*, 11 Co. R., at p. 52; *Hewitt*

The word *minerals*, in its proper sense, comprehends Minerals.
all fossil bodies dug out of mines or quarries (*m*); hence
it includes stones dug from quarries (*n*). Under an exception of mines, everything is excepted that is necessary for working them, including way-leave for carrying
away the minerals (*o*); but a reservation of mines and
quarries, with full power to win and work the same,
does not include the right of so working them as to let
the surface down (*p*).

A reservation of the exclusive *right of hunting*, Sporting. *shooting, fishing and sporting* over the demised premises
includes whatever is ordinarily known as hunting,
shooting, fishing and sporting; and a tenant under a
lease containing such a reservation is not entitled to
shoot rabbits (*q*).

The proper office of the HABENDUM is to restrain Habendum.
the generality of the premises (*r*). It limits and ascertains the estate of the lessee by specifying the time of
commencement, and the duration of the interest granted
to him.

Leases for years may be made to commence either 1. For years.
immediately, or from a past (*s*) or future day. Where Commencement of lease.
leases are made to commence from the day of the date
of the instrument of lease, the word *from* is construed

v. *Isham*, 7 Ex. 77; 21 L. J., Ex. 35.

(*m*) *Rosse* v. *Wainman*, 14 M. & W. 859; 15 L. J., Ex. 67; aff. 2 Ex. 800.

(*n*) *Micklethwait* v. *Winter*, 6 Ex. 644; 20 L. J., Ex. 313.

(*o*) Judgment in *Proud* v. *Bates*, 34 L. J., Ch., at p. 411; *Cardigan* v. *Armitage*, 2 B. & C. 197, 207.

(*p*) Judgment in *Proud* v. *Bates*, 34 L. J., Ch., at p. 412.

(*q*) *Jeffryes* v. *Evans*, 19 C. B., N. S. 246; 34 L. J., C. P. 261. See *post*, Chap. IV., Sect. 14.

(*r*) Per Tindal, C. J., in *Burton* v. *Barclay*, 7 Bing., at p. 757. See Hob. 170, 171.

(*s*) See *Enys* v. *Donnithorne*, 2 Burr. 1190.

to mean either inclusive or exclusive, according to the context and subject-matter, and so as to effectuate the deeds of parties and not to destroy them (*t*).

Leases by deed made to commence from an event which has never happened, or from the date of the deed, where the deed has either no date or an impossible date (*u*), take effect from the time of the delivery of the deed (*x*). Leases to commence *from henceforth* begin from the delivery of the deed, and not from its date (*y*). A lease made to begin after the end or determination of a previous lease, where there is no previous lease, or such previous lease has determined or become void, will begin immediately (*z*).

The habendum of a lease must be construed as taking effect from the time of its execution, though the duration of the term is to be computed from a prior day (*a*). Hence the interest of the lessee, and his liability for breaches of covenant, commence only from the day of the execution of the deed (*b*).

It will be sufficient if the date at which the lease is to commence is capable of being ascertained with certainty at the time when the lease is to take effect in possession, though up to that time the period of commencement may be uncertain (*c*). Thus, if a lease be granted for twenty-one years after three lives in being; though it is uncertain at first when the term will com-

(*t*) *Pugh* v. *Leeds*, 2 Cowp. 714. See also *Doe* v. *Day*, 10 East, 427.

(*u*) See *Chapman* v. *Beecham*, 3 Q. B. 723; 12 L. J., Q. B. 42.

(*x*) Bac. Abr. (L.) 168; *Styles* v. *Wardle*, 4 B. & C. 908, 911.

(*y*) *Clayton's Case*, 5 Co. Rep. 1. See *Steele* v. *Mart*, 4 B. & C. 272, 278.

(*z*) Bac. Abr. (L.) 170; *Miller* v. *Maynwaring*, Cro. Car. 397, 399.

(*a*) Per Parke, B., in *Jervis* v. *Tomkinson*, 1 H. & N., at p. 206.

(*b*) *Jervis* v. *Tomkinson*, 1 H. & N. 195; 26 L. J., Ex. 41; *Shaw* v. *Kay*, 1 Ex. 412; 17 L. J., Ex. 17. See *Wyburd* v. *Tuck*, 1 B. & P. 464.

(*c*) Shep. Touch. 272.

mence, because the lives are in being, yet when they die it is reduced to a certainty ; and *id certum est quod certum reddi potest* (*d*).

The duration of the lease must also be ascertained either by the express limitation of the parties at the time of making the lease, or by reference to some collateral or subsequent act or event which may with equal certainty measure the continuance thereof (*e*). A lease for an indefinite term is *primâ facie* a lease at will (*f*), but a general letting at a yearly rent usually gives rise to an implied tenancy from year to year (*f*).

Duration of leases.

Where it is intended to create an express tenancy from year to year the words of the habendum should be *from year to year*. A lease *for one year certain, and so on from year to year*, has been held to contemplate a tenancy for two years at the least (*g*). A letting *not for one year only, but from year to year*, enures as a demise for two years at least (*h*). A lease *for a year*, or *for one year and no longer*, creates a tenancy expiring at the end of the year without notice to quit (*i*).

2. From year to year.

A lease for life of corporeal hereditaments could not by the common law be made to commence *in futuro*, because livery of seisin was formerly essential to the creation of an estate of freehold, and present livery could not be

3. For life.

(*d*) Per Ld. Kenyon, C. J., in *Goodright* v. *Richardson*, 3 T. R., at p. 463.

(*e*) Bac. Abr. (L. 3) 176; *Bishop of Bath's Case*, 6 Co. R., at pp. 35, 35 a. *Ante*, p. 58.

(*f*) *Ante*, p. 52. But see *Say* v. *Smith*, Plowden, 271; *Gwynne* v. *Maynstone*, 3 C. & P. 302.

(*g*) *Doe* v. *Green*, 9 A. & E. 658. See *Reg.* v. *Chawton*, 1 Q. B. 247.

(*h*) *Denn* v. *Cartwright*, 4 East, 29, 33.

(*i*) *Cobb* v. *Stokes*, 8 East, 358. See judgment in *Messenger* v. *Armstrong*, 1 T. R., at p. 54; also judgment in *Right* v. *Darby*, *Ib.*, at p. 162.

F.

G

made to a future estate (*l*). It would appear, however, that livery of seisin is not now necessary to the creation of a freehold interest (*m*). As a use may be limited *in futuro*, a lease for life may be made to commence at a future day by limitations operating under the Statute of Uses, as, for instance, where the lease is made in pursuance of a power to lease (*n*).

A lease for term of life, without mentioning for whose life, shall be deemed to be for the life of the lessee (*o*). When A. demises to B. for the term of *his* life, the word *his*, in ordinary construction, would apply to B. as the last antecedent. But instances perpetually occur where that word is used, and does not refer to the last party named. The words of the demise are ambiguous, and may derive explanation from the other parts of the instrument. A covenant for quiet enjoyment during the life of the lessor tends very strongly to expound the intention of the parties (*p*). A lease made to A. during the life of B. and C. will continue during the life of the survivor (*q*); but a lease for a term of years if A. and B. shall so long live will determine on the death of one of them (*q*).

Reddendum.

THE REDDENDUM fixes the amount and kind of recompense to be paid by the lessee to the lessor for the possession of the demised premises, and usually speci-

---

(*l*) *Barwick's Case*, 5 Co. R., at p. 94 a; 2 Black. Com. 165. See *Greenwood* v. *Tyber*, Cro. Jac. 563; *Freeman* v. *West*, 2 Wils. 165.

(*m*) Stat. 8 & 9 Vict. c. 106, s. 2. *Ante*, p. 72.

(*n*) 1 Sanders on Uses, 142 (5th ed.); 1 Platt on Leases, 692.

(*o*) Co. Lit. 42 a.

(*p*) Per Taunton, J., in *Doe* v. *Dodd*, 5 B. & Ad., at p. 693.

(*q*) *Brudnel's Case*, 5 Co. R. 9.

fies the periods at which such recompense is to be paid or rendered.

No special form of words is essential. A proviso (*r*), or a covenant (*s*), may constitute a good reservation of rent, and a letting *at and under the rent of* 80*l.* is an agreement by the tenant to pay that rent (*t*). Under the words *yielding and paying* a covenant for payment of the rent is implied (*u*).

Rent may be made payable in advance, but in that case the reddendum should state expressly that the rent is so payable *from time to time,* or *always,* in advance, or the stipulation for payment in advance may be held to relate to the first quarter's rent only (*x*). *Rent payable in advance.*

The amount of the rent must be either expressly stated, or otherwise rendered capable of being ascertained with certainty (*y*). In some cases there may be a certainty in uncertainty; as a man may hold of his lord to shear all the sheep depasturing within his lord's manor; and this is certain enough, although the lord has sometimes a great, and sometimes a small number there (*z*). A royalty of so much quarterly per solid yard for marl got, and so much per thousand for all bricks made by the tenant, is a rent capable of being ascertained with certainty (*a*). *Certainty as to amount of rent.*

The rent must be reserved to the lessor and his heirs, and not to a stranger (*b*). But the law uses all industry

(*r*) *Harrington* v. *Wise,* Cro. Eliz. 486.
(*s*) *Drake* v. *Munday,* Cro. Car. 207.
(*t*) *Doe* v. *Kneller,* 4 C. & P. 3.
(*u*) Judgment in *Iggulden* v. *May,* 9 Ves., at p. 330; *Hellier* v. *Casbard,* 1 Sid. 266; *Porter* v. *Swetnam,* Styles, 406.
(*x*) See *Holland* v. *Palser,* 2 Stark. 161.
(*y*) Co. Lit. 142 a.
(*z*) Co. Lit. 96 a.
(*a*) *Daniel* v. *Gracie,* 6 Q. B. 145; 13 L. J., Q. B. 309. See judgment in *Watson* v. *Waud,* 8 Ex., at p. 339.
(*b*) Lit. s. 346; 2 Wms. Saund. 370. *Post,* Chap. IV., Sect. 1 (2), p. 112.

imaginable to conform the reservation to the estate (*c*). Hence a reservation to the lessor, entitled in fee, his heirs, *executors*, and assigns will not prevent the rent from following the reversion and going to the heir (*d*).

Mode of reservation.

The most clear and sure mode of reservation is to reserve rent yearly during the term, and leave the law to make the distribution, without an express reservation to any person (*e*). A reservation of rent to the lessor only, not mentioning his heirs, &c., will enure only during the life of the lessor (*f*), unless the reservation be expressly to the lessor *during the term*, in which case rent will continue payable to the end of the term (*g*).

"Net rent."

A stipulation for a *net rent* means a rent clear of all deductions (*h*); hence the tenant under a lease containing this reservation will be liable to pay land tax and sewer's rates (*h*).

Covenants. How constituted.

A COVENANT is nothing more than an agreement of the parties under seal (*i*). Hence, in order to constitute a covenant, no technical language is necessary (*k*); any words in a deed which show an agreement to do a thing amount to a covenant (*l*). A recital (*m*), or an

(*c*) Judgment in *Sacheverell* v. *Froggatt*, 1 Vent., at p. 161.
(*d*) *Drake* v. *Munday*, Cro. Car. 207. See *Sacheverell* v. *Froggatt*, 2 Wms. Saund. 367 a.
(*e*) *Whitlock's Case*, 8 Co. R., at p. 71.
(*f*) Co. Lit. 47 a.
(*g*) *Sacheverell* v. *Froggatt*, 2 Wms. Saund. 367 a.
(*h*) See judgment of Ld. Tenterden, C. J., in *Bennett* v. *Womack*, 7 B. & C., at p. 629; 3 C. & P. 96; *Bradbury* v. *Wright*, 2 Dougl. 624.

(*i*) Per Ld. Ellenborough, C. J., in *Randall* v. *Lynch*, 12 East, at p. 182.
(*k*) *Lant* v. *Norris*, 1 Burr. 287, 290. See also *Saltoun* v. *Houstoun*, 1 Bing., at p. 440.
(*l*) *Easterby* v. *Sampson*, 6 Bing. 644, 650; 9 B. & C. 505; *Stevenson's Case*, 1 Leon. 324; 12 East, 182, note (*a*); *Hollis* v. *Carr*, 2 Mod. 87; *St. Albans* v. *Ellis*, 16 East, 352; *Cannock* v. *Jones*, 3 Ex. 233.
(*m*) *Sampson* v. *Easterby*, 9 B. & C. 505; 6 Bing. 644; *Furrall*

exception, may constitute a covenant, where it appears from the rest of the deed to be the intention of the parties that it should do so (*n*).

An express covenant for payment of rent should be inserted in every lease, because this covenant makes the tenant chargeable with rent during the whole of the term, and if he assigns the lease gives the landlord a remedy against him as well as against the assignee (*o*). If it is agreed that the rent shall cease to be payable in case the demised premises shall be burnt down, or shall become uninhabitable, an express exception to that effect should be inserted in the covenant for payment of rent. An exception of damage by fire contained in the covenant to repair does not limit the operation of the covenant for payment of rent (*p*). Covenant for payment of rent.

Where it is intended that the liability to perform, and the right to take advantage of covenants, shall pass with the land to the assignee, the *assigns* should always be expressly named; for though some covenants will bind assigns though not named, and others will not bind them though named, yet as there is a middle class, in which assigns are bound if named, and not otherwise, it is prudent to provide for the possibility of a covenant being held to belong to this class (*q*). Where assigns should be named.

Where an agreement for a lease contains no stipulation as to the covenants to be inserted in the lease, or stipulates for the *usual covenants*, it seems that the lessor is entitled to have introduced into the lease a "Usual covenants."

v. *Hilditch*, 5 C. B., N. S. 840; *Lay* v. *Mottram*, 19 C. B., N. S. 479.

(*n*) *St. Albans* v. *Ellis*, 16 East, 352; Woodfall L. & T. 127.

(*o*) 2 Platt on Leases, 163. See *post*, Chap. IV., Sect. 12.

(*p*) *Hare* v. *Groves*, 3 Anst. 687; 2 Platt on Leases, 166. See *post*, Chap. IV., Sect. 2.

(*q*) 4 Jarm. Conv., by Sweet, 428. See *post*, Chap. IV., Sect. 12.

covenant by the tenant to repair, without exception in case of damage by fire or tempest (*r*); but the lessor cannot require the insertion of a covenant by the lessee not to assign or underlet without licence (*s*); or a covenant not to exercise particular trades on the demised premises (*t*). The question of what covenants are usual appears, however, to be one of fact, and not of law (*u*). A covenant by the tenant to pay land tax and sewer's rate is a usual covenant in a lease, reserving a net rent (*u*); and a proviso for re-entry is usual in leases of public-houses (*x*). A covenant that in case the demised premises shall be blown down or burned, the lessor shall rebuild, or otherwise the tenant shall be at liberty to quit, is not a usual covenant (*y*).

Construction of covenants.

Every covenant is to be expounded with a regard to its context, and such exposition must be upon the whole instrument, *ex antecedentibus et consequentibus*, and according to the reasonable sense and construction of the words (*z*). Hence, if a man acts contrary to the intention of his covenant a breach will be committed, although he literally performs it; as, if a man covenants to leave all the trees upon the land, and he cuts them down and leaves them there (*a*). If the meaning of the words of a covenant be doubtful, it would seem that

(*r*) *Kendall* v. *Hill*, 6 Jur., N. S. 968; *Sharp* v. *Milligan*, 23 Beav. 419.

(*s*) *Henderson* v. *Hay*, 3 Bro. C. C. 632; *Vere* v. *Loreden*, 12 Ves. 179; *Church* v. *Brown*, 15 Ves. 258; *Browne* v. *Raban, Ib.* 528; judgment in *Buckland* v. *Papillon*, 30 L. J., Ch., at p. 83.

(*t*) *Propert* v. *Parker*, 3 My. & K. 280; *Van* v. *Corpe, Ib.* 269.

(*u*) *Bennett* v. *Womack*, 3 C. & P. 96; 7 B. & C. 627. See *Doe* v. *Williams*, 11 Q. B. 688; 17 L. J., Q. B. 154.

(*x*) *Bennett* v. *Womack*, 7 B. & C. 627; *Haines* v. *Burnett*, 27 Beav. 500; 29 L. J., Ch. 289.

(*y*) *Doe* v. *Sandham*, 1 T. R. 705; *Medwin* v. *Sandham*, 3 Swanst. 685.

(*z*) Per Ld. Ellenborough, C. J., in *Iggulden* v. *May*, 7 East, at p. 241.

(*a*) Com. Dig. *Covenant* (E. 2); Smith L. & T. 122.

such construction will be made as is most strong against the covenantor (*b*).

Covenants are construed as dependent or independent according to the fair intention of the parties, to be collected from the instrument, and technical words (if there be any to encounter such intention) should give way to that intention (*c*). As furnishing a guide to the discovery of the intention of the parties (*d*), it has been laid down as a rule that where a covenant goes only to part of the consideration on both sides, and a breach of such covenant may be paid for in damages, it is an independent covenant (*e*). Whether dependent or independent.

Covenants entered into with several persons, although they may appear *primâ facie* to be joint, yet may be construed as separate, if the interest of the parties in the deed appears to be separate. If the words are ambiguous, they may be construed according as the interest of the parties appears to be joint or several, but if they are expressly and clearly joint or several, they cannot be so controlled (*f*). It has been held, that where a demise is joint, and the covenants upon which an action is brought are entire, and are made Whether joint or several.

(*b*) Bac. Abr. *Covenant* (F.); judgment in *Doe* v. *Stevens*, 3 B. & Ad., at p. 303. But see *Rhodes* v. *Bullard*, 7 East, 116.

(*c*) See judgment of Ld. Kenyon, C. J., in *Porter* v. *Shephard*, 6 T. R., at p. 668; judgment of Ld. Chelmsford in *Roberts* v. *Brett*, 34 L. J., C. P., at p. 247.

(*d*) Per Ld. Chelmsford, 34 L. J., C. P., at p. 247.

(*e*) *Boone* v. *Eyre*, 1 H. Bl. 273, note (*a*); *St. Albans* v. *Shore*, *Ib.* 270; *Pordage* v. *Cole*, 1 Wms. Saund. 320 b; *Carpenter* v. *Cresswell*, 4 Bing. 409, 411. See *Baggallay* v. *Pettit*, 5 C. B., N. S. 637; 28 L. J., C. P. 169. See also *post*, Chap. IV., Sect. 2 (2).

(*f*) Per Parke, B., in *Sorsbie* v. *Park*, 13 L. J., Ex., at p. 11; 12 M. & W., at p. 158; *Bradburne* v. *Botfield*, 14 M. & W. 559, 572; 14 L. J., Ex. 330; *Keightley* v. *Watson*, 3 Ex. 716, 722. See *Slingsby's Case*, 5 Co. R. 18 a; *Eccleston* v. *Clipsham*, 1 Wms. Saund. 153; *Anderson* v. *Martindale*, 1 East. 497; *James* v. *Emery*, 8 Taunt. 245; *Withers* v. *Bircham*, 3 B. & C. 254.

with both the lessors, the cause of action is joint, and both of the covenantees ought to sue, though as between themselves their interests may be separate (*g*). Hence, the benefit of a covenant to repair in a joint lease made by tenants in common, will run with the entire reversion, and the representatives of all the tenants in common must join in suing for a breach of such covenant (*h*).

Provisoes for re-entry.

A PROVISO FOR RE-ENTRY on the whole of the demised premises, on breach of any covenant in the lease, is not unreasonable (*i*). A proviso for re-entry on the bankruptcy of the lessee (*k*), or on his contracting a debt upon which judgment should be signed and execution issue (*l*), is lawful.

It is not essential that leases containing provisoes or conditions for re-entry should be made by deed (*m*).

How framed.

A person who demises land by an instrument not under seal may introduce a condition into it, provided he use apt and proper words for the purpose. In a lease for years, no precise form of words is necessary to make a condition. It is sufficient, if it appear that the words used were intended to have the effect of creating a condition (*n*). The right of entry should be reserved to the owner of the legal estate in the premises (*o*).

(*g*) Per Ld. Denman, C. J., in *Foley* v. *Addenbrooke*, 12 L. J., Q. B., at p. 165; 4 Q. B., at p. 207.

(*h*) *Thompson* v. *Hakewill*, 19 C. B., N. S. 713; 35 L. J., C. P. 18.

(*i*) See *Haberdashers' Company* v. *Isaac*, 3 Jnr., N. S. 611.

(*k*) *Roe* v. *Galliers*, 2 T. R. 133. See *Church* v. *Browne*, 15 Ves., at p. 268.

(*l*) See *Davis* v. *Eyton*, 7 Bing. 154. As to the construction of these provisoes, see *Doe* v. *Pritchard*, 5 B. & Ad. 765; *Doe* v. *Davies*, 6 C. & P. 614; 1 Cr. M. & R. 405; *Doe* v. *Rees*, 4 Bing. N. C. 384.

(*m*) See *Hayne* v. *Cummings*, 16 C. B., N. S. 421; 10 L. T., N. S. 341.

(*n*) Per Bayley, J., in *Doe* v. *Watt*, 8 B. & C., at p. 315.

(*o*) Lit. s. 347; *Doe* v. *Law-*

Provisoes for re-entry are construed according to the letter, unless a decisive reason is shown for departing from it (*p*), such as a clear intention of the parties. The rule that the words of a covenant must be taken against the covenantor, applies more strongly to a proviso for re-entry, which contains a condition that destroys or defeats the estate (*q*). Where a proviso is insensible, it seems that the Courts will not find out a meaning for it (*r*).

Construction of provisoes for re-entry.

PROVISO *for re-entry for breach of covenants " hereinafter contained."* The lessor cannot re-enter for breach of a covenant placed *before* the proviso in the lease, although there are no covenants by the lessee after the proviso (*s*).

PROVISO *for re-entry " if the lessee shall do or cause to be done any act, matter or thing whatsoever contrary to, or in breach of any of the covenants."* Does not apply to a breach of a covenant to repair, the omission to repair not being *an act done* within the meaning of the proviso (*t*).

PROVISO *for re-entry " if the lessee shall, by the space of thirty days next after notice, make default in performance of any of the clauses or agreements herein contained."* Does not apply to the breach of a covenant not to allow alterations in the premises, or permit new buildings to be made upon them without permission (*u*).

---

rence, 4 Taunt. 23; *Saunders* v. *Merryweather*, 3 H. & C. 902; 35 L. J., Ex. 115; 13 W. R. 814.

(*p*) Per Ld. Ellenborough, C. J., in *Doe* v. *Godwin*, 4 M. & S., at p. 269; *Doe* v. *Marchetti*, 1 B. & Ad. 715, 720. But see *Doe* v. *Elsam*, Moo. & M. 189; *Croft* v. *Lumley, post*, p. 90, note (*x*).

(*q*) Per Ld. Tenterden, C. J., in *Doe* v. *Stevens*, 3 B. & Ad., at p. 303.

(*r*) *Doe* v. *Carew*, 2 Q. B. 317; 11 L. J., Q. B. 5.

(*s*) *Doe* v. *Godwin*, 4 M. & S. 265.

(*t*) *Doe* v. *Stevens*, 3 B. & Ad. 299.

(*u*) *Doe* v. *Marchetti*, 1 B. & Ad. 715.

PROVISO *for re-entry "if the lessee shall make default in the performance of any other covenants which on his part are or ought to be observed, performed or kept."* Applies to and forbids the breach of a negative as well as a positive covenant (*x*).

PROVISO *for re-entry "if the lessee shall be duly found and declared a bankrupt."* Does not apply where the tenant is found and declared a bankrupt without a proper petitioning creditor's debt (*y*).

PROVISO *for re-entry "if the lessee shall happen to become insolvent and unable in circumstances to go on with the management of the farm."* It is doubtful whether the attainder of the tenant is a forfeiture of the lease (*z*).

PROVISO *for re-entry "if the lessee, his executors, administrators or assigns, should become bankrupt or insolvent, &c."* The right of re-entry accrues on the bankruptcy of the survivor of certain executors to whom the tenant, dying during the term, has bequeathed the premises on trust (*a*).

PROVISO *for re-entry "in case the term of years hereby granted shall be extended or taken in execution."* Seizure by the sheriff under a writ of extent against the lessee at the suit of the Crown is a taking in execution within this proviso (*b*).

(*x*) *Croft* v. *Lumley*, 4 Jur., N. S. 903; 6 H. L. C. 672; 27 L. J., Q. B. 321.

(*y*) *Doe* v. *Ingleby*, 15 M. & W. 465.

(*z*) *Doe* v. *Pritchard*, 5 B. & Ad. 765.

(*a*) *Doe* v. *David*, 1 Cr. M. & R. 405; 6 C. & P. 614.

(*b*) *Rex* v. *Topping*, M'Clel. & Y. 544.

PROVISO *for re-entry " in case of breach of any of the agreements herein contained," (in a written agreement whereby premises are let for a term, " at and under the rent of* 80*l.*") The lessor may re-enter for nonpayment of rent, although there is no express agreement to pay rent (*c*).

PROVISO *for re-entry upon breach of any of the covenants, enumerating all the covenants except a covenant not to carry off hay, &c., under a penalty of* 5*l. per ton.* The meaning is, that if the hay be removed without payment of that sum, the right of re-entry shall accrue (*d*).

PROVISO *for re-entry if the tenant does not execute certain repairs to the satisfaction of the surveyor of the lessor.* It is sufficient if the jury think that the surveyor ought to have been satisfied with the repairs which are done, and although he is not in fact satisfied, no forfeiture will be incurred (*e*).

PROVISO *for re-entry " in case no sufficient distress can be found upon the premises."* Search must be made in every part of the premises (*f*).

PROVISO *for re-entry " if the lessee shall commit waste to the value of* 10*s."* The waste contemplated in the proviso is waste producing an injury to the reversion (*g*).

PROVISO *for re-entry " in default of making it appear, by a good and sufficient certificate, that a certain person in a foreign country is living."* The fact

(*c*) Doe v. Kneller, 4 C. & P. 3.
(*d*) Doe v. Jepson, 3 B. & Ad. 402, 403.
(*e*) Doe v. Jones, 2 C. & K. 743.
(*f*) Rees v. King, Forrest, 19. See 2 B. & B. 514.
(*g*) Doe v. Bond, 5 B. & C. 855.

cannot be properly certified by hearsay, or presumptive evidence (*h*).

Power to resume possession of part of demised premises.

Sometimes there is inserted in a lease a proviso enabling the lessor to resume possession of any portion, or certain specified portions, of the demised land on giving notice to the lessee.

Construction of provisoes.

PROVISO *empowering the lessor to resume any portion of the demised land which may be required for the purpose of " building, planting, accommodation or otherwise."* The words *or otherwise* must be held to refer to some purposes of the same character as those before specified, and the proviso will not enable the lessor to resume a portion of the land for the purpose of conveying it to a railway company (*i*).

PROVISO *giving the lessor's son power to take the demised house for himself when he comes of age.* The son must make his election in a reasonable time after he comes of age. The delay of a year is unreasonable (*k*).

COVENANT *that if lessor shall be desirous, during the term, to take all or any part of the land for building thereon it shall be lawful for her to enter upon all or any part to make such buildings as she shall think proper, and to do all necessary acts without interruption by the lessee, provided the lessor give six months' notice of such intention.* This is not merely a covenant that the lessor may come upon the land in order to build

---

(*h*) *Randle* v. *Lory*, 6 A. & E. 218.

(*i*) *Johnson* v. *Edgware, Highgate and London Ry. Co.*, 35 L. J., Ch. 322.

(*k*) *Doe* v. *Smith*, 2 T. R. 436.

upon it, but she may take the whole of the land back for the purpose of building (*l*).

STIPULATION *in an agreement to let (in which there was no clause of re-entry) that in case the landlord should want any part of the demised land to build, or otherwise, the lessee will give up that part on a proportionate abatement being made in the rent, the fences being paid for and six months' notice being given.* This is a covenant and not a condition operating in defeasance of the estate (*m*).

STIPULATION *in a lease, by the Commissioners of Woods and Forests, that if the Commissioners, for the time being, shall, at any time during the term, be desirous to determine the demise, and of such desire shall cause "one calendar month's notice in writing, under their hands," to be given to the lessee, the lease, at the expiration of such notice, shall cease, determine and be absolutely void.* The lease may be determined by a notice signed by two only of three commissioners by virtue of stat. 10 Geo. 4, c. 50, s. 92 (*n*).

(4) *Stamps on Leases.*

Though a parol lease of land, not exceeding three years, and reserving as rent two third parts of the full annual value, is good; yet if a man, through caution, reduce it into writing he must pay for the stamp, or the Courts will not receive the instrument in evidence (*o*). Where necessary.

The want of a proper stamp does not invalidate a Effect of want of stamp.

(*l*) Doe v. *Abel*, 2 M. & S. 541, 549. See *Doe* v. *Kennard*, 12 Q. B. 244.
(*m*) Doe v. *Phillips*, 2 Bing. 13.
(*n*) *Coombes* v. *Dutton*, 5 M. & W. 469.
(*o*) *Prosser* v. *Phillips*, Bull. N. P. 269.

lease, but renders it inadmissible as evidence (*p*) except on payment of penalties.

Stat. 33 & 34 Vict. c. 97, s. 15.
Instruments may be stamped after execution, on payment of unpaid duty and penalties.

(1.) Except where express provision to the contrary is made by this or any other act, any unstamped or insufficiently stamped instrument may be stamped after the execution thereof, on payment of the unpaid duty and a penalty of ten pounds, and also by way of further penalty, where the unpaid duty exceeds ten pounds, of interest on such duty, at the rate of five pounds per centum per annum, from the day upon which the instrument was first executed up to the time when such interest is equal in amount to the unpaid duty.

And the payment of any penalty or penalties is to be denoted on the instrument by a particular stamp.

(2.) Provided as follows:

As to instruments executed abroad.

(*a.*) Any unstamped or insufficiently stamped instrument, which has been first executed at any place out of the United Kingdom, may be stamped, at any time within two months after it has been first received in the United Kingdom, on payment of the unpaid duty only:

Penalties may be remitted.

(*b.*) The commissioners may, if they think fit, at any time within twelve months after the first execution of any instrument, remit the penalty or penalties, or any part thereof.

Sect. 16.
Unstamped or insufficiently stamped instruments may be received in evidence in any court, on

(1.) Upon the production of an instrument chargeable with any duty as evidence in any court of civil judicature in any part of the United Kingdom, the officer whose duty it is to read the instrument shall call the attention of the judge to any omission or insuffi-

(*p*) See *Turner* v. *Power*, 7 B. & C. 625; M. & M. 131.

ciency of the stamp thereon; and if the instrument is one which may legally be stamped after the execution thereof, it may, on payment to the officer of the amount of the unpaid duty, and the penalty payable by law on stamping the same as aforesaid, and of a further sum of one pound, be received in evidence, saving all just exceptions on other grounds. *[payment of duty and penalties.]*

(2.) The officer receiving the said duty and penalty shall give a receipt for the same, and make an entry in a book kept for that purpose of the payment and of the amount thereof, and shall communicate to the commissioners the name or title of the cause or proceeding in which, and of the party from whom, he received the said duty and penalty, and the date and description of the instrument, and shall pay over to the receiver general of inland revenue, or to such other person as the commissioners may appoint, the money received by him for the said duty and penalty. *[The officer of the court to account for duties and penalties.]*

(3.) Upon production to the commissioners of any instrument in respect of which any duty or penalty has been paid as aforesaid, together with the receipt of the said officer, the payment of such duty and penalty shall be denoted on such instrument accordingly.

Save and except as aforesaid, no instrument executed in any part of the United Kingdom, or relating, wheresoever executed, to any property situate, or to any matter or thing done or to be done, in any part of the United Kingdom, shall, except in criminal proceedings, be pleaded or given in evidence, or admitted to be good, useful, or available in law or equity, unless it is duly stamped in accordance with the law in force at the time when it was first executed. *[Sect. 17. Instrument not duly stamped inadmissible.]*

The amount of the *ad valorem* stamp duty on a lease *[Effect of mis-]*

THE CONTRACT OF TENANCY.

statement of consideration.

made before 1871, was regulated by the consideration (whether fine or rent) expressed to be paid, and not by that which was actually paid (*q*). The recent Stamp Act would appear to have effected a change in this respect (*r*).

Stat. 33 & 34 Vict. c. 97, s. 10.

All facts affecting ad valorem duty to be set forth.

All the facts and circumstances affecting the liability of any instrument to *ad valorem* duty, or the amount of the *ad valorem* duty with which any instrument is chargeable, are to be fully and truly set forth in the instrument; and every person who, with intent to defraud her Majesty, or her heirs or successors,

(1.) Executes any instrument in which all the said facts and circumstances are not fully and truly set forth:

(2.) Being employed or concerned in or about the preparation of any instrument, neglects or omits fully and truly to set forth therein all the said facts and circumstances;

shall forfeit the sum of ten pounds.

Effect of mis-statement of consideration.

The mis-statement of the consideration, though it subjects the parties to the lease, and the attorney preparing it, to penalties, does not avoid the instrument (*s*). The statute 55 Geo. 3, c. 184, s. 8, requiring the consideration to be set out, and imposing an *ad valorem* duty on the consideration, applied only to the case of a consideration passing between the lessor and the lessee (*t*).

(*q*) *Doe* v. *Lewis*, 10 B. & C. 673; *Duck* v. *Braddyll*, 13 Price, 455. See *Steer* v. *Crowley*, 14 C. B., N. S. 337, 357; 32 L. J., C. P. 191.

(*r*) See stat. 33 & 34 Vict. c. 97, *Schedule*, tit. Conveyance; compare judgment in *Doe* v. *Lewis*, 10 B. & C., at p. 675.

(*s*) *Doe* v. *Hobson*, 3 D. & R. 186; *Robinson* v. *Macdonnell*, 5 M. & S., at p. 234.

(*t*) *Boone* v. *Mitchell*, 1 B. & C. 18, 20.

If a lease made before 1871 contains a demise of two different subject-matters and reserves two separate rents, but the letting is one transaction, one *ad valorem* stamp on the aggregate amount of both rents is sufficient (*y*). But if a certain rent is reserved for a house and land, and by a separate reservation in the same lease another rent is made payable for furniture and fixtures, an *ad valorem* stamp on the rent of the house and land only is not sufficient (*z*). A lease containing an agreement, giving the lessee the option of purchasing the premises demised for a specified sum, requires only a lease stamp (*a*); unless the agreement to purchase relates to other premises besides those which are the subject of the lease, in which case an agreement stamp also will be necessary (*b*). A lease, containing a contract for the purchase of fixtures, cannot be given in evidence to prove the value of the fixtures unless it has a lease stamp, although it has an agreement stamp (*c*). A mere acknowledgment of an antecedent tenancy does not require a lease stamp (*d*).

1. *As to leases before* 1871. Where two stamps are requisite.

An instrument containing or relating to several distinct matters is to be separately charged with duty in respect of each of such matters.

An instrument made for any consideration, in respect whereof it is chargeable with *ad valorem* duty, and also for any other valuable consideration, is to be charged with duty in respect of such last-mentioned consideration.

2. *As to leases made on or after 1st January,* 1871. Stat. 33 & 34 Vict. c. 97, s. 8. Duty chargeable on every distinct matter or consideration.

(*y*) *Boase* v. *Jackson*, 3 B. & B. 185; *Blount* v. *Pearman*, 1 Bing. N. C. 408; *Parry* v. *Deere*, 5 A. & E. 551; *Reg.* v. *Hockworthy*, 7 A. & E. 492.
(*z*) *Coster* v. *Cowling*, 7 Bing. 456.
(*a*) *Worthington* v. *Warrington*, 5 C. B. 635; 17 L. J., C. P. 117. See *post*, p. 100.

(*b*) See *Lovelock* v. *Franklyn*, 8 Q. B. 371; 16 L. J., Q. B. 182.
(*c*) *Corder* v. *Drakeford*, 3 Taunt. 382.
(*d*) *Eagleton* v. *Gutteridge*, 11 M. & W. 465; 12 L. J., Ex. 359. See *Hill* v. *Ramm*, 5 M. & Gr. 789; *Barry* v. *Goodman*, 2 M. & W. 768.

THE CONTRACT OF TENANCY.

Stat. 33 & 34 c. 97.
Amount of duty.

LEASE OR TACK—   £ s. d.
  (1.) For any definite term less than a year:
    (*a.*) Of any dwelling-house or tenement, or part of a
      dwelling-house or tenement, at a rent not ex-
      ceeding the rate of 10*l.* per annum 0 0 1
    (*b.*) Of any furnished dwelling-house or apartments
      where the rent for such term exceeds 25*l.* .. 0 2 6
    (*c.*) Of any lands, tenements, or heritable subjects { The same duty as a lease for a year at the rent reserved for the definite term.
      except or otherwise than as aforesaid

  (2.) For any other definite term or for any indefinite term:
  Of any lands, tenements or heritable subjects—
    Where the consideration, or any part of the consi-
    deration, moving either to the lessor or to any
    other person, consists of any money, stock or
    security:

    In respect of such consideration..   .. { The same duty as a conveyance on a sale for the same consideration (*f*).

    Where the consideration or any part of the con-
    sideration is any rent:

(*f*) *I. e.*—Where the amount or value of the consideration   £ s. d.
    for the sale does not exceed 5*l.* 0 0 6
  Exceeds 5*l.* and does not exceed 10*l.* .. 0 1 0
    „ 10*l.*   „   „   15*l.* .. 0 1 6
    „ 15*l.*   „   „   20*l.* .. 0 2 0
    „ 20*l.*   „   „   25*l.* .. 0 2 6
    „ 25*l.*   „   „   50*l.* .. 0 5 0
    „ 50*l.*   „   „   75*l.* .. 0 7 6
    „ 75*l.*   „   „   100*l.* .. 0 10 0
    „ 100*l.* „   „   125*l.* .. 0 12 6
    „ 125*l.* „   „   150*l.* .. 0 15 0
    „ 150*l.* „   „   175*l.* .. 0 17 6
    „ 175*l.* „   „   200*l.* .. 1 0 0
    „ 200*l.* „   „   225*l.* .. 1 2 6
    „ 225*l.* „   „   250*l.* .. 1 5 0
    „ 250*l.* „   „   275*l.* .. 1 7 6
    „ 275*l.* „   „   300*l.* .. 1 10 0
    „ 300*l.*
  For every 50*l.*, and also for any fractional
    part of 50*l.*, of such amount or value .. 0 5 0

LEASES.

(2.) For any other definite term, &c.—*continued.*
    In respect of such consideration:
        If the rent, whether reserved as a yearly rent
        or otherwise, is at a rate or average rate:

	If the term is definite and does not exceed 35 years, or is indefinite.			If the term being definite exceeds 35 years but does not exceed 100 years.			If the term being definite exceeds 100 years.		
	£	s.	d.	£	s.	d.	£	s.	d.
Not exceeding 5*l*. per annum	0	0	6	0	3	0	0	6	0
Exceeding—									
5*l*. and not exceeding 10*l*.	0	1	0	0	6	0	0	12	0
10*l*. ,, ,, 15*l*.	0	1	6	0	9	0	0	18	0
15*l*. ,, ,, 20*l*.	0	2	0	0	12	0	1	4	0
20*l*. ,, ,, 25*l*.	0	2	6	0	15	0	1	10	0
25*l*. ,, ,, 50*l*.	0	5	0	1	10	0	3	0	0
50*l*. ,, ,, 75*l*.	0	7	6	2	5	0	4	10	0
75*l*. ,, ,, 100*l*.	0	10	0	3	0	0	6	0	0
100*l*. For every full sum of 50*l*., and also for any fractional part of 50*l*. thereof ..	0	5	0	1	10	0	3	0	0
(3.) Of any other kind whatsoever not hereinbefore described							0	10	0

(1.) Where the consideration, or any part of the consideration, for which any lease or tack is granted or agreed to be granted, does not consist of money, but consists of any produce or other goods, the value of such produce or goods is to be deemed a consideration in respect of which the lease or tack or agreement is chargeable with *ad valorem* duty, and where it is stipulated that the value of such produce or goods is to amount at least to, or is not to exceed, a given sum, or where the lessee is specially charged with, or has the option of paying after, any permanent rate of conversion, the value of such produce or goods is, for the purpose of assessing the *ad valorem* duty, to be estimated at such given sum, or according to such permanent rate.

Sect. 97.
Where produce or goods are reserved as rent, duty to be chargeable on value thereof.

Where value is ascertained by stipulation in lease, duty to be assessed thereon.

Leases stamped in accordance with statement of value to be deemed duly stamped till contrary is shown.	(2.) A lease or tack or agreement made either entirely or partially for any such consideration, if it contains a statement of the value of such consideration, and is stamped in accordance with such statement, is, so far as regards the subject-matter of such statement, to be deemed duly stamped, unless or until it is otherwise shown that such statement is incorrect, and that it is in fact not duly stamped.
Sect. 98. No duty chargeable in respect of penal rent;	(1.) A lease or tack, or agreement for a lease or tack, or with respect to any letting, is not to be charged with any duty in respect of any penal rent, or increased rent in the nature of a penal rent, thereby reserved or agreed to be reserved or made payable, or by reason of
or of surrender of prior lease;	being made in consideration of the surrender or abandonment of any existing lease, tack, or agreement of or relating to the same subject-matter.
or of covenant relating to matter of lease.	(2.) No lease made for any consideration or considerations in respect whereof it is chargeable with *ad valorem* duty, and in further consideration either of a covenant by the lessee to make, or of his having previously made, any substantial improvement of or addition to the property demised to him, or of any covenant relating to the matter of the lease, is to be charged with any duty in respect of such further consideration.
Duty on leases by ecclesiastical corporations.	(3.) No lease for a life or lives not exceeding three, or for a term of years determinable with a life or lives not exceeding three, and no lease for a term absolute not exceeding twenty-one years, granted by an ecclesiastical corporation aggregate or sole, is to be charged with any higher duty than thirty-five shillings.
On leases by Trinity College, Dublin.	(4.) No lease for a definite term exceeding thirty-five years granted under ' The Trinity College (Dublin)

Leasing and Perpetuity Act, 1851,' is to be charged with any higher duty than would have been chargeable thereon if it had been a lease for a definite term not exceeding thirty-five years.

(5.) No lease or tack, or agreement for a lease or tack, in Scotland, of any dwelling-house or tenement, or part of a dwelling-house or tenement, for any definite term not exceeding a year, at a rent not exceeding the rate of ten pounds per annum, is to be charged with any higher duty than one penny. *On leases of dwelling-houses for term not exceeding a year at rent not exceeding 10l. per annum.*

The duty upon an instrument chargeable with duty as a lease or tack for any definite term less than a year of— *Sect. 99. Duty in certain cases may be denoted by adhesive stamp.*

(1.) Any dwelling-house or tenement, or part of a dwelling-house or tenement, at a rent not exceeding the rate of ten pounds per annum;

(2.) Any furnished dwelling-house or apartments;

Or upon the duplicate or counterpart of any such instrument, may be denoted by an adhesive stamp, which is to be cancelled by the person by whom the instrument is first executed.

(1.) Every person who executes, or prepares, or is employed in preparing any instrument upon which the duty may, under the provisions of the last preceding section, be denoted by an adhesive stamp, and which is not, at or before the execution thereof, duly stamped, shall forfeit the sum of five pounds. *Sect. 100. Penalty on not affixing adhesive stamp before execution.*

(2.) Provided that nothing in this section contained shall render any person liable to the said penalty of five pounds in respect of any letters or correspondence.

(5) *Counterparts and Duplicates.*

Counterpart. Leases are often prepared in two parts, known respectively as the lease and counterpart. The lease is executed by the lessor alone, and is kept by the lessee (g). The counterpart is executed by the lessee alone, and is kept by the lessor. The production of a counterpart, properly stamped and executed by the lessee, is presumptive evidence of the execution of a lease (h).

Duplicate. Where copies of a lease are each executed by both lessor and lessee they are termed duplicates.

Stat. 33 & 34 Vict. c. 97, s. 93.

Denoting stamp necessary.

The duplicate or counterpart of an instrument chargeable with duty (except the counterpart of an instrument chargeable as a lease, such counterpart not being executed by or on behalf of any lessor or grantor,) is not to be deemed duly stamped unless it is stamped as an original instrument, or unless it appears by some stamp impressed thereon that the full and proper duty has been paid upon the original instrument of which it is the duplicate or counterpart.

Id. *Schedule.* Amount of duty.

DUPLICATE or COUNTERPART of any instrument chargeable with any duty.

Where such duty does not amount to 5s. .. { The same duty as the original instrument.

£ s. d.
In any other case 0 5 0

(6) *Matters relating to the completion of Leases.*

Execution of leases by deed. Leases by deed should be signed, sealed and delivered by the parties, or their agents, duly authorized by power of attorney under seal (i). It is not clear, however,

(g) *Post*, p. 105.
(h) *Hughes* v. *Clark*, 10 C. B. 905; *Houghton* v. *Kœnig*, 18 C. B. 235; 25 L. J., C. P. 218. See *Doe* v. *Austin*, 2 Moo. & Sc. 107.
(i) *Ante*, p. 31.

that signature, though usual and desirable, is essential to leases by deed (*k*). No formal mode of delivery is necessary. A deed may be delivered by handing it over to the party to whom it is made, without words; or by words without any act of delivery (*l*).

The delivery may be qualified by express words, so as to prevent it from operating until the performance of some condition, as, for instance, the payment of a sum of money. Or an agreement to that effect may be inferred from circumstances; and in that case, though there is no express delivery as an escrow, the instrument will not operate as a deed until the condition has been performed (*m*).

Leases made by agents should be executed by them in the names of their principals, thus,—*A. B., by C. D., his agent.* An agent who executes a lease or agreement in his own name only may be held personally liable, even where the instrument is expressed to be made by him for and on behalf of the principal (*n*).

Execution of leases by agents.

It is desirable that leases by deed should be attested by two witnesses, but, unless the deed is made in pursuance of a power requiring witnesses, the want of attestation will not render it void (*o*).

Attestation.

Until the lessor has executed the lease, the lessee is not bound by the covenants to repair or to pay rent, because until then he has not the consideration for which he has stipulated (*p*). But when, in a mortgage deed

Effect of non-execution by lessor.

(*k*) *Aveline* v. *Whisson*, 4 M. & Gr. 801; 12 L. J., C. P. 58. See *Couch* v. *Goodman*, 2 Q. B., at p. 596; 11 L. J., Q. B. 225, 227; 2 Platt on Leases, 9.

(*l*) Co. Lit. 36 a.

(*m*) *Gudgen* v. *Besset*, 6 E. & B. 986; 26 L. J., Q. B. 36.

(*n*) *Norton* v. *Herron*, 1 C. & P. 648; Ry. & M. 229; *Tanner* v. *Christian*, 4 E. & B. 591; 24 L. J., Q. B. 91.

(*o*) 2 Black. Com. 307.

(*p*) *Swatman* v. *Ambler*, 8 Ex. 72; 22 L. J., Ex. 81; *Pitman* v. *Woodbury*, 3 Ex. 4.

not executed by the mortgagee, the mortgagor has attorned and has occupied as tenant to the mortgagee at a fixed rent payable half-yearly, and has made several half-yearly payments, the relation of landlord and tenant is created, and a distress for rent may be made by the mortgagee (*q*). Rent is recoverable from sureties under a lease of the wife's lands executed by husband and wife, but not acknowledged by the wife, nor made according to the provisions of stat. 19 & 20 Vict. c. 120, s. 32 (*r*); provided there is nothing to show that the parties bargained for a lease which it should be impossible for the wife to dispute(*s*). A lease purporting to be made by a tenant for years determinable with his life and the reversioner, not executed by the reversioner, but containing a clause expressly stating that the parties demise, so far only as they lawfully can, according only to their respective estates and interests, is binding on the lessee, who has entered into possession (*t*).

Effect of alterations in a lease after execution.

If any alteration is made in a lease after it has been executed by the lessor and lessee, it will require a fresh stamp; unless, perhaps, in cases where such alteration is made with the consent of both parties, and is merely an expression of what was before implied, as, for instance, the addition of the words "house and buildings" to a proviso for giving up a farm (*u*). If a deed is altered, after execution, in a point material by one party without the privity of the other, it thereby

---

(*q*) *West* v. *Fritch*, 3 Ex. 216; 18 L. J., Ex. 50. See judgment of Cockburn, C. J., in *Morton* v. *Woods*, 37 L. J., Q. B., at p. 247; L. R., 3 Q. B., at p. 667. See S. C., 38 L. J., Q. B. 81; L. R., 4 Q. B. 293.

(*r*) *Ante*, p. 9.

(*s*) *Toler* v. *Slater*, 37 L. J., Q. B. 33; L. R., 3 Q. B. 42.

(*t*) *How* v. *Greek*, 3 H. & C. 391; 34 L. J., Ex. 4, 6.

(*u*) *Doe* v. *Houghton*, 1 Man. & Ry. 208; Woodfall, L. & T. 134.

becomes void (*x*). But an alteration made before execution by the lessor and lessee does not affect the validity of the deed, although it has been previously executed by other persons parties thereto (*y*).

A memorial of a lease by deed of lands situate in the counties of Middlesex, or York, or in the town of Kingston-upon-Hull, should be entered on the respective registers provided for the purpose; unless the lease is at a rack-rent, or does not exceed twenty-one years where the possession and occupation go along with the lease, *i.e.* where the lessee is also the occupier of the premises (*z*). Registration.
Stats. 7 Anne, c. 20 (Middlesex); 2 & 3 Anne, c. 4; 5 Anne, c. 18 (West Riding); 6 Anne, c. 35 (East Riding and Hull); 8 Geo. 2, c. 6 (North Riding).

Copyholds are excepted from the Registry Acts, but it has been thought to be advisable to register such leases of copyhold estates as would require registration if the estate were freehold (*a*).

No lease of lands within the Bedford Level, except leases for seven years or under in possession, shall be of force but from the time it shall be entered with the registrar. Stat. 15 Car. 2, c. 17, s. 8.

During the continuance of the demise, the indenture of lease belongs to the lessee, and the counterpart to the lessor (*b*). The lessee is entitled to possession of the instrument of lease after his interest in the demised premises has expired or been determined by forfeiture (*c*). Where a lease is in the hands of the tenant, Custody of lease.

(*x*) *Pigot's Case*, 11 Co. R. 26 a, 27.
(*y*) *Hall* v. *Chandless*, 4 Bing. 123.
(*z*) Dart's V. & P. 457 (4th ed.).
(*a*) Sug. V. & P. 732 (14th ed.); Rigge on Registration of Deeds, 87, note (*m*).
(*b*) See judgment in *Hall* v. *Ball*, 10 L. J., C. P. at p. 287.
(*c*) *Hall* v. *Ball*, 3 M. & Gr. 242; 10 L. J., C. P. 285; *Elworthy* v. *Sandford*, 3 H. & C. 330; 34 L. J., Ex. 42.

and no counterpart can be found, it seems that the landlord is entitled to inspect and take a copy of the lease (*d*). It is a common application at chambers, on the part of lessors, for a copy of the lease in the possession of the lessee, and the order is frequently made, on the ground that the lessee is a trustee for the lessor (*e*). If a lessee against whom an action of ejectment for a forfeiture is brought has no duplicate or copy of the lease, he may, independently of stat. 14 & 15 Vict. c. 99, s. 6, obtain from a judge an order to inspect and take a copy of the lease (*f*).

Costs of preparing lease.

The usual course is for the lessor's attorney to prepare the lease, and for the lessee to pay the costs (*g*). If the lease is prepared by the attorney of the lessor, who is not employed by the lessee for that purpose, the lessor is the person liable, in the first instance, to pay the attorney, but the lessor can recover the amount from the lessee whether the lessee takes up the lease or refuses to do so (*h*). The lessor must bear the expense of the counterpart unless the lessee has expressly agreed to pay for it (*i*). Generally, however, the lessee agrees to pay all the costs of both lease and counterpart (*k*).

Entry of lessee.

At common law no lease for years, whether with or without any reservation of rent, is looked upon as com-

---

(*d*) *Doe* v. *Slight*, 1 Dowl. 163. See *Woodcock* v. *Worthington*, 2 Y. & J. 4; *Portmore* v. *Goring*, 4 Bing. 152.

(*e*) Per Martin, B., 34 L. J., Ex. 44.

(*f*) *Doe* v. *Roe*, 1 E. & B. 279; 22 L. J., Q. B. 102.

(*g*) *Grissell* v. *Robinson*, 3 Scott, 329; 3 Bing. N. C. 10.

(*h*) *Baker* v. *Meryweather*, 2 C. & K. 737; *Grissell* v. *Robinson*, 3 Bing. N. C. 10.

(*i*) *Jennings* v. *Major*, 8 C. & P. 61.

(*k*) Woodfall, L. & T. p. 144.

plete till actual entry has been made by the lessee (*l*). A lease in the usual form, not operating under the Statute of Uses, does not of itself vest any estate in the lessee, but only gives him a right of entry on the tenement, called his interest in the term, or *interesse termini* (*m*).

The right upon a lease to commence immediately is (except under the Statute of Uses) until entry an *interesse termini* only, and so is the right upon a lease to commence at a future time; and the same rules are applicable to both. Each is a *right* only, not an *estate*. The whole estate, notwithstanding such right, is in the lessor. In neither case will a conveyance by the lessee to the lessor operate as a surrender, nor will a release from the lessor to the lessee operate by way of enlarging the estate. The right may be granted away as a right or extinguished by a release; but it cannot be conveyed as an estate; it has all the properties and consequences of a right only, and not of an estate (*n*).

Nature of lessee's interest before entry.

At any time during the term, even after the death of the lessor, the lessee or his assignee, or personal representatives, may perfect the lease by entry, or some act equivalent thereto (*o*). Until this has been done, neither the lessee nor his assignee can maintain an action of trespass in respect of the demised premises (*p*); but he

(*l*) Bac. Abr. (M.) p. 183.
(*m*) 2 Black. Com. 144; Co. Lit. 46 b. See judgment in *Copeland* v. *Stephens*, 1 B. & A., at p. 605.
(*n*) Judgment in *Doe* v. *Walker*, 5 B. & C., at p. 118. See *Saffyn's Case*, 5 Co. R., at p. 124.
(*o*) Co. Lit. 46 b; *Copeland* v.

Stephens, 1 B. & A., at p. 607.
(*p*) Bac. Abr. (M.), p. 183; *Turner* v. *Cameron's, &c. Co.*, 5 Ex. 932; 20 L. J., Ex. 71; *Wheeler* v. *Montefiore*, 2 Q. B. 133; 11 L. J., Q. B. 34. See *Harrison* v. *Blackburn*, 17 C. B., N. S. 678; 34 L. J., C. P. 109.

may bring an action of ejectment (*q*). An action for use and occupation cannot be maintained against him until he has entered (*r*).

(*q*) *Doe* v. *Day*, 2 Q. B. 147, 156; 12 L. J., Q. B. 86, 88. See observations of Byles, J., in *Harrison* v. *Blackburn*, 34 L. J., C. P., at p. 113.

(*r*) *Edge* v. *Strafford*, 1 Cr. & J. 391; *Lowe* v. *Ross*, 5 Ex. 553; 19 L. J., Ex. 318; *Towne* v. *D'Heinriche*, 13 C. B. 892; 22 L. J., C. P. 219.

CHAP. IV.

TERMS OF TENANCY.

		PAGE
SECT. I. RENT		109
(1) What may be reserved as rent		109
(2) Payments which are not rent		110
(3) When rent is payable		112
(4) Where payable		115
(5) To whom payable		115
(6) Amount payable		117
(7) Apportionment		126
(8) Payment and remittance		128
(9) Effect of payment		129
(10) Remedies for recovery of rent		130
II. REPAIRS		189
III. WASTE		198
IV. MODE OF USING PREMISES		200
V. CULTIVATION		207
VI. FENCES		214
VII. TREES		217
VIII. INSURANCE		220
IX. TAXES		223
X. QUIET ENJOYMENT		229
XI. UNDERLEASES		235
XII. ASSIGNMENTS		239
XIII. LIVE STOCK		258
XIV. GAME		259

SECT. I.—*Rent.*

(1) *What may be reserved as Rent.*

IT is not essential that rent should consist of the payment of money. The delivery of hens, horses, wheat, &c., may constitute a rent (*a*), and so also may the

Need not be money.

(*a*) Co. Lit. 142 a.

performance of personal services, such as shearing sheep (*b*), carrying coals (*c*), or cleaning a church (*d*).

Must not be part of demised premises.
Parcel of the annual profits of the premises demised, as, for instance, the herbage of land, cannot be reserved as rent (*e*). A royalty payable to the owner of a brickfield upon the bricks made, is, however, a rent, although the land is in course of being wholly consumed (*f*).

(2) *Payments which are not Rent.*

The following payments are not, properly speaking, rent, and, though recoverable by action, cannot be distrained for, unless an express power to distrain is contained in the lease:

1. Sums reserved on leases of incorporeal hereditaments.
Payments reserved by way of rent on a lease of an incorporeal hereditament (*g*). But rent may be reserved out of reversions and remainders (*h*), and the sovereign may reserve a rent out of any incorporeal hereditament (*h*).

2. Sums reserved on leases of chattels.
Payments reserved by way of rent on a lease of personal chattels (*i*). But a mixed payment of rent for land and goods will be held to issue out of the land alone (*k*); hence rent for furnished lodgings (*l*), or for

---

(*b*) Co. Lit. 96 a.
(*c*) *Doe* v. *Morse*, 1 B. & Ad. 365. See *Lanyon* v. *Carne*, 2 Saund. 165, 167.
(*d*) *Doe* v. *Benham*, 7 Q. B. 976; 14 L. J., Q. B. 342.
(*e*) Co. Lit. 142 a; 2 Black. Com. 41.
(*f*) *Reg.* v. *Westbrook*, 10 Q. B. 178; 16 L. J., M. C. 87; *Reg.* v. *Everist*, Ib. See *Daniel* v. *Gracie*, 6 Q. B. 145; 13 L. J., Q. B. 309; *Barrs* v. *Lea*, 33 L. J., Ch. 437; 12 W. R. 525.

(*g*) Co. Lit. 47 a; *Gardiner* v. *Williamson*, 2 B. & Ad. 336, 339.
(*h*) Co. Lit. 47 a; see note 284.
(*i*) *Spencer's Case*, 5 Co. R., at p. 17.
(*k*) *Collins* v. *Harding*, Cro. Eliz., at p. 607; *Farewell* v. *Dickinson*, 6 B. & C. 251. See *Salmon* v. *Matthews*, 8 M. & W. 827.
(*l*) *Newman* v. *Anderton*, 2 B. & P., N. R. 224.

the exclusive occupation of part of a room together with a supply of steam power, may be distrained for (*m*).

Payments reserved by way of rent in a mere licence to use premises for a particular purpose (*n*). A distress cannot be made for rent reserved on a letting of a standing for machinery, with a supply of steam power (*o*), unless the letting is of a defined portion of a room in a factory, partitioned off from the rest, with the intention of giving the exclusive occupation to the person to whom it is let (*p*).

<small>3. Sums reserved in a mere licence.</small>

Payments reserved by way of rent on a mere agreement for a lease, where no tenancy has been created by payment of rent or otherwise (*q*). Where a tenant holds over after notice to quit given by the landlord, rent subsequently accruing due cannot be distrained for until a new tenancy has been expressly or impliedly created (*r*).

<small>4. Sums reserved on a mere agreement for a lease.</small>

Payments by way of increased rent which a tenant under a lease for a term of years agrees by parol with his lessor to make during the remainder of the term, in consideration of the lessor's executing improvements on the demised premises (*s*). Though the word rent is used, the agreement is held to amount only to a personal contract to pay an additional sum yearly (*t*).

<small>5. Additional rent for improvements.</small>

(*m*) *Selby* v. *Greaves*, L. R., 3 C. P. 594; 37 L. J., C. P. 251.

(*n*) See *ante*, p. 47.

(*o*) *Hancock* v. *Austin*, 14 C. B., N. S. 634; 32 L. J., C. P. 252.

(*p*) *Selby* v. *Greaves*, L. R., 3 C. P. 594; 37 L. J., C. P. 251.

(*q*) Woodfall, L. & T. 375; *Hegan* v. *Johnson*, 2 Taunt. 148; *Dunk* v. *Hunter*, 5 B. & A. 322; *Regnart* v. *Porter*, 7 Bing. 451. See *ante*, p. 53; also p. 47, note (*n*).

(*r*) *Alford* v. *Vickery*, Car. & M. 280; *Jenner* v. *Clegg*, 1 Moo. & R. 213; *Sullivan* v. *Bishop*, 2 C. & P. 359; *ante*, p. 54.

(*s*) *Hoby* v. *Roebuck*, 7 Taunt. 157; *Donellan* v. *Read*, 3 B. & Ad. 899; *Lambert* v. *Norris*, 2 M. & W. 333. See *Foquet* v. *Moor*, 7 Ex. 870; 22 L. J., Ex. 35.

(*t*) See judgment in *Donellan* v. *Read*, 3 B. & Ad., at p. 905.

6. Payments "over and above the rent."
7. Payments reserved upon the assignment of a lease.
8. Payments reserved to a stranger.

Payments agreed to be made by the lessee to the lessor annually, "over and above the rent"(*u*).

Payments by way of rent reserved upon the assignment of a lease (*x*).

Payments by way of rent reserved to a stranger to the reversion (*y*). But such a reservation may be good by estoppel (*z*); and it seems that the sovereign may reserve rent to a stranger (*a*).

(3) *When Rent is payable.*

1. Where there is no express stipulation as to days of payment.

A yearly rent is payable only once in a year, and not until the end of the year, unless the reservation be qualified by subsequent words, making the rent payable in advance (*b*), or at shorter intervals than a year; as, for instance, half-yearly or quarterly (*c*). A clause making a lease determinable by notice expiring on any quarter day will not constitute a quarterly reservation of rent (*d*).

Sometimes by the custom of the country rent may be due in advance (*e*).

2. Construc-

RENT PAYABLE *quarterly, or half-quarterly, if re-*

(*u*) *Morrice* v. *Antrobus*, Hardr. 325; *Smith* v. *Mapleback*, 1 T. R. 441, 445. But see *Harre* v. *Lea*, 33 L. J., Ch. 437; 12 W. R. 525.

(*x*) *Witton* v. *Bye*, Cro. Jac. 486; *Poulteney* v. *Holmes*, 1 Stra. 405; *Parmenter* v. *Webber*, 8 Taunt. 593; ⸺ v. *Cooper*, 2 Wils. 375; *Preece* v. *Corrie*, 5 Bing. 24. See *Langford* v. *Selmes*, 3 K. & J. 220.

(*y*) Co. Lit. 143 b; *Oates* v. *Frith*, Hob. 130; 2 Rol. Abr. 447, pl. 3. See *Gilbertson* v. *Richards*, 4 H. & N. 277; 28 L. J., Ex. 158.

(*z*) See *ante*, p. 42.

(*a*) Co. Lit. 143 b.

(*b*) See *Finch* v. *Miller*, 5 C. B. 428; *ante*, p. 83.

(*c*) *Coomber* v. *Howard*, 1 C. B. 440. See *Turner* v. *Allday*, Tyr. & Gr. 819.

(*d*) *Collett* v. *Curling*, 10 Q. B. 785; 16 L. J., Q. B. 390.

(*e*) *Buckley* v. *Taylor*, 2 T. R. 600. But see *Doe* v. *Weller*, 1 Jur., O. S. 622.

quired. Where the landlord has received the rent quarterly for a year, a previous demand is necessary to make it payable half-quarterly (*f*). A distress is not equivalent to a demand, and cannot be made before a demand in fact (*g*). tion of express stipulation.

RENT PAYABLE *at the "two usual feasts of the year."* Is due at Michaelmas and Lady Day (*h*).

RENT PAYABLE *from the following Lady Day, upon a parol demise.* Where there is a custom of the country respecting the meaning of "Lady Day," that term is considered as used *primâ facie* consistently with the custom, and evidence of such custom is admissible (*i*).

RENT PAYABLE *on a specified day, or within a certain number of days afterwards.* Is not due, during the continuance of the lease (*k*), until the expiration of the last of the days of grace (*l*).

RENT PAYABLE *at the "feasts of the Annunciation and St. Michael," in a lease made in August.* The words will be transposed, and the first instalment of the rent payable at Michaelmas (*m*).

RENT PAYABLE *quarterly, " the first payment to be made on the 25th of March following," in agreement dated 8th September.* Only a quarter's rent is due on 25th March, the first quarter's

(*f*) *Mallam* v. *Arden*, 10 Bing. 299. See *Clarke* v. *Holford*, 2 C. & K. 540.
(*g*) Per Alderson, J., 10 Bing. 300.
(*h*) 2 Rol. Abr. 450 (M.), pl. 2.
(*i*) *Doe* v. *Benson*, 4 B. & A. 588, 589.
(*k*) See *Barwick* v. *Foster*,
Cro. Jac. 227, 233; Yelv. 167.
(*l*) *Clun's Case*, 10 Co. R. 127 a, 128 a; *Blunden's Case*, Cro. Eliz. 565; *Pilkington* v. *Dalton*, Cro. Eliz. 575.
(*m*) *Hill* v. *Grange*, Plowden, 164, 171; incorrectly cited in *Mallory's Case*, 5 Co. R. 111 b.

rent being either forgiven altogether, or postponed to the end of the term (*n*).

RENT PAYABLE "*yearly and every year during the term by four equal quarterly payments, on 25th March, 24th June, 29th September and 25th December in every year, commencing from 25th March then instant,*" in a lease for seven years from 25th March, by indenture dated 21st March. There must be seven payments of the annual rent; the rent will either be treated as a forehand rent, the first payment to be made on entering; or as payable on the days named, although one of them is after the expiration of the term (*o*).

Payment before the rent-day.
If a tenant pays his rent before the day on which it is due, the payment is voluntary, and at law does not operate as a discharge (*p*). But advances made by a tenant on account of rent not due at the time are an equitable defence to an action for such rent (*q*).

Payment on the rent-day.
Payment of rent on the morning of the rent-day will be valid as against the heir of the landlord in case the latter should die on the same day (*r*). But the tenant has the whole of the day to pay his rent in, and it is not in arrear until after midnight (*s*).

(*n*) *Hutchins* v. *Scott*, 2 M. & W. 809, 810.

(*o*) *Hopkins* v. *Helmore*, 8 A. & E. 463.

(*p*) *Clun's Case*, 10 Co. R. 127 a; *Cromwell* v. *Andrews*, Cro. Eliz. 15.

(*q*) *Nash* v. *Gray*, 2 F. & F. 391. See *Rockingham* v. *Penrice*, 1 Swanst. 345, note; 1 P. W. 177.

(*r*) *Clun's Case*, 10 Co. Rep. 127.

(*s*) *Dibble* v. *Bowater*, 2 E. & B. 564; 22 L. J., Q. B. 396. See *Duppa* v. *Mayo*, 1 Wms. Saund., at p. 287; judgment of Blackstone, J., in *Cutting* v. *Derby*, 2 W. Bl., at p. 1077.

(4) *Where Rent is payable.*

If no other place is appointed by agreement, rent must be paid upon the land demised (*t*); but if the tenant has expressly covenanted to pay rent, it is his duty to seek out the person to whom the rent is to be paid, and to pay it, or tender it to him, on the appointed day (*u*). If the sovereign makes a lease for years rendering rent, without appointing any place for payment, the lessee may pay the rent either at the exchequer or to the bailiffs or receivers authorized by the sovereign to receive it (*t*).

Where there is no express agreement.

On lease by sovereign.

(5) *To whom Rent is payable.*

A tender to an agent authorized to receive payment is as good as a tender to the landlord in person (*x*). The landlord's wife, who has acted as his agent on similar occasions before, when her authority was acknowledged, retains such authority till it is countermanded (*y*). A clause in a lease by deed, whereby the landlord agrees that K. is to receive all rent from the tenant at all times when it becomes due during the term, and his receipt is to be a full and sufficient discharge from all liability, has been interpreted as a bare authority to receive the rent, and therefore revocable by the landlord (*z*).

1. Agents.

A tenant under a lease made by a mortgagor *before* the mortgage may without prejudice pay rent to the mortgagor until he has notice of the mortgage from the

2. Mortgagor.

(*t*) *Boroughes' Case*, 4 Co. R., at p. 73 a.
(*u*) *Haldane* v. *Johnson*, 8 Ex. 689, 695; 22 L. J., Ex. 264.
(*x*) *Goodland* v. *Blewitt*, 1 Camp. 477, 478. See *post*, p. 166;

Roscoe's Evidence, 408 (11th ed.).
(*y*) *Browne* v. *Powell*, 4 Bing. 230, 232. See *Dodd* v. *Acklom*, 6 M. & Gr. 672; 13 L. J., C. P. 11.
(*z*) *Venning* v. *Bray*, 2 B. & S. 502; 31 L. J., Q. B. 181.

mortgagee (a). After the mortgagee has given such notice he is entitled to and may distrain for all rent in arrear and not previously paid to the mortgagor, as well as all rent accruing afterwards (b). A tenant who comes into possession under a demise from a mortgagor, *after* a mortgage executed by him, may consider the mortgagor as his landlord so long as the mortgagee allows the mortgagor to receive the rents (c). But after notice of the mortgage and a demand of payment by the mortgagee, the tenant is justified in paying to the mortgagee all rent due since the mortgage, not already paid to the mortgagor, and all rent subsequently accruing due (d). The mere fact of the mortgagee's having given notice to the tenant to pay rent to him, not accompanied by actual payment, is, however, no defence to an action or distress for rent by the mortgagor (e).

3. Joint tenants.
4. Tenants in common.

Upon a lease by several joint tenants, one of them may recover the whole rent and give a discharge for it (f). Upon a lease by tenants in common, the survivor may sue for the whole rent, although the reservation is to the lessors according to their respective interests (g). But if a lessee holding under two tenants in common pays the whole rent to one after notice

(a) Stat. 4 Anne, c. 16, s. 10; *post*, p. 117; *Trent* v. *Hunt*, 9 Ex. 14, 23; 22 L. J., Ex. 318.

(b) *Moss* v. *Gallimore*, 1 Dougl. 279; *Rogers* v. *Humphreys*, 4 A. & E. 299; *Burrows* v. *Gradin*, 1 D. & L. 213; 12 L. J., Q. B. 333. See *Whitmore* v. *Walker*, 2 C. & K. 615.

(c) Per Bayley, J., in *Pope* v. *Biggs*, 9 B. & C., at p. 251.

(d) *Pope* v. *Biggs*, 9 B. & C. 245; *Johnson* v. *Jones*, 9 A. & E.

809; *Waddilove* v. *Barnett*, 2 Bing., N. C. 538. But see *Alchorne* v. *Gomme*, 2 Bing. 54.

(e) *Wheeler* v. *Branscombe*, 5 Q. B. 373; 13 L. J., Q. B. 83; *Wilton* v. *Dunn*, 17 Q. B. 294; 21 L. J., Q. B. 60. See *Hickman* v. *Machin*, 4 H. & N. 716; 28 L. J., Ex. 310.

(f) *Robinson* v. *Hoffman*, 4 Bing. 562, 565.

(g) *Wallace* v. *M'Laren*, 1 Man. & Ry. 516. See *ante*, p. 88.

from the other not to pay it, the tenant in common who gave the notice may distrain for his share (*h*).

All grants of any manors or rents, or of the reversion or remainder of any messuages or lands, shall be good and effectual to all intents and purposes, without any attornment of the tenants of any such manors or of the land out of which such rent shall be issuing, or of the particular tenants upon whose particular estates any such reversions or remainders shall be expectant or depending, as if their attornment had been made. {5. Assignee of reversion. Stat. 4 Anne, c. 16, s. 9. Conveyances to be good without attornment of tenants.}

But no such tenant shall be prejudiced or damaged by payment of any rent to any such grantor, or by breach of any condition for non-payment of rent, before notice shall be given to him of such grant by the grantee. {Sect. 10. Tenant not to be prejudiced by payment of rent to grantor before notice.}

Payment of rent to a person not entitled to it, with the acquiescence, under a false apprehension, of the person really entitled, will not exonerate the tenant from the duty of paying it to the latter (*i*). Rent paid by mistake, in ignorance of the death of a person for whose life the premises are held, may be recovered back (*k*). {Payment of rent to person not entitled to it.}

(6) *Amount of Rent payable.*

Where there is a written agreement between landlord and tenant, that for certain premises the tenant shall pay 170*l.* a-year, and afterwards an arrangement is made by parol that 30*l.* a-year shall be allowed out of {Parol agreement for reduction of rent.}

(*h*) *Harrison* v. *Barnby*, 5 T. R. 246. See *Powis* v. *Smith*, 5 B. & A. 850.
(*i*) *Williams* v. *Bartholomew*,
1 B. & P. 326.
(*k*) *Barber* v. *Brown*, 1 C. B., N. S. 121; 26 L. J., C. P. 41.

the rent, because the landlord is to occupy a certain part for a time, such arrangement does not vary the agreement so as to reduce the rent payable under it (*l*); and, notwithstanding the tenant has paid rent at the reduced rate, the original rent will continue to be the rent payable for the premises (*m*).

Increased rent. An additional rent is frequently reserved in case the tenant violates the provisions of his lease; as, for instance, a yearly rent for every acre of land above a certain quantity which he ploughs up or converts into tillage. A sum thus reserved is not deemed a penalty, but a liquidated satisfaction fixed and agreed upon by the parties (*n*). Courts of equity will not relieve the lessee from payment of these sums (*o*), or restrain him by injunction from committing the acts upon which such sums become payable; for the parties themselves are considered as having agreed to the damage (*p*). Sums thus reserved, after they have once become payable, are payable as rent annually during the residue of the term (*q*).

General rule as to set-off against rent. A tenant cannot, in general, set off against the rent sums due to him from his landlord, or payments made on behalf of his landlord, unless there is a special agreement to that effect; for although the sum due to the

(*l*) *Hilton* v. *Goodkind*, 2 C. & P. 591.

(*m*) See *Crowley* v. *Vitty*, 7 Ex. 319; 21 L. J., Ex. 135.

(*n*) *Rolfe* v. *Peterson*, 2 Bro. P. C. 436; *Farrant* v. *Olmius*, 3 B. & A. 692. See *Jones* v. *Green*, 3 Y. & J. 298; *Denton* v. *Richmond*, 1 Cr. & M. 734, 742.

(*o*) *Rolfe* v. *Peterson*, 2 Bro. P. C. 436.

(*p*) *Woodward* v. *Gyles*, 2 Vern. 119; judgment in *Aylet* v. *Dodd*, 2 Atk., at p. 239; judgment in *Benson* v. *Gibson*, 3 Atk., at p. 396. See *Legh* v. *Lillie*, 6 H. & N. 165, 169; 30 L. J., Ex. 25.

(*q*) *Farrant* v. *Olmius*, 3 B. & A. 692; *Birch* v. *Stephenson*, 3 Taunt., at p. 478; *Bowers* v. *Nixon*, 13 Jur. 334; 12 Q. B., at p. 558.

RENT.   119

tenant may be of greater amount than the rent, yet if the rent is not paid the landlord may distrain for it (*r*).

A tenant cannot obtain an injunction in equity against his landlord to restrain proceedings upon a replevin bond on the ground of set-off against the rent distrained for (*s*).

If, however, the landlord, instead of distraining, sues for rent, the defendant may plead a set-off (*t*). But in an action of covenant for rent the defendant cannot set off any *uncertain* damages that he may be entitled to recover against the landlord on any of the covenants in the lease (*u*).

The following payments may be deducted by the tenant from his rent:—Sums paid by the tenant for the landlord's share of property tax (*x*) during the half-year immediately preceding the rent-day (*y*). This deduction may be made although the tenant has covenanted or agreed to pay the rent in full without any deduction for property tax (*z*). As soon as the tenant has paid the property tax, it is in effect a payment by him of so much of the next rent due to his landlord (*a*). But the deduction must be made from the next pay-

Deductions which may be made from rent.
1. Property tax.

(*r*) *Absolom* v. *Knight*, Bull. N. P. 181; 2 Barnes, 356; *Laycock* v. *Tuffnell*, 2 Chit. 531; judgment of Park, J., in *Andrew* v. *Hancock*, 1 B. & B., at p. 46; *Willson* v. *Davenport*, 5 C. & P. 531.

(*s*) *Pratt* v. *Keith*, 33 L. J., Ch. 528. See *Townrow* v. *Benson*, 3 Madd. 203.

(*t*) Stats. 2 Geo. 2, c. 22, s. 13; 8 Geo. 2, c. 24, ss. 4, 5. See Roscoe's Evidence, 415 (11th ed.).

(*u*) *Weigall* v. *Waters*, 6 T. R. 488. See *Gower* v. *Hunt*, 1 Barnes, 203.

(*x*) See *Gabell* v. *Sherell*, 5 Taunt. 81.

(*y*) See *Franklin* v. *Carter*, 1 C. B. 750; 14 L. J., C. P. 241.

(*z*) Stat. 5 & 6 Vict. c. 35, s. 103; *Fuller* v. *Abbot*, 4 Taunt. 105; *Tinckler* v. *Prentice*, 4 Taunt. 549. See *post*, Sect. 9 of this Chapter, p. 225.

(*a*) See per Abbott, J., in *Denby* v. *Moore*, 1 B. & A., at p. 129.

ment of rent, or the amount cannot afterwards be recovered at law (*b*). It is only on the production of a certificate of the tax being paid that the landlord is bound to make the allowance (*c*). A succeeding occupier may tender in part payment of his rent a receipt for property tax which has become due since the last payment of rent, and has been paid by the former occupier (*d*).

2. Land tax. Sums paid by the tenant for the landlord's proportion of the land tax (*e*); provided there is no agreement to the contrary. A payment of land tax can only be deducted from the rent which has then accrued, or is then accruing due; for the law considers the payment of the land tax as a payment of so much of the rent then due, or growing due, to the landlord; and if afterwards the tenant pays the rent in full, he cannot at a subsequent time deduct that overpayment from the rent (*f*).

3. Sewers rate.
4. Tithe rent-charge. Sums paid by the tenant for the landlord's proportion of a sewers rate (*g*); also rent-charge in lieu of tithes paid by the tenant (*h*); unless the tenant has expressly agreed to pay the rate or rent-charge. These deduc-

(*b*) *Denby* v. *Moore*, 1 B. & A. 123; *Cumming* v. *Bedborough*, 15 M. & W. 438.

(*c*) *Pocock* v. *Eustace*, 2 Camp. 181; *Baker* v. *Davis*, 3 Camp. 474.

(*d*) *Clennel* v. *Read*, 7 Taunt. 50.

(*e*) See judgment of Bayley, J., in *Stubbs* v. *Parsons*, 3 B. & A. 519; *Whitfield* v. *Brandwood*, 2 Stark. 440; *Hyde* v. *Hill*, 3 T. R. 377; stat. 38 Geo. 3, c. 5, s. 17.

(*f*) Per Bayley, J., in *Stubbs* v. *Parsons*, 3 B. & A., at p. 520; *Andrew* v. *Hancock*, 1 B. & B. 37; *Saunderson* v. *Hanson*, 3 C. & P. 314; see *Bramston* v. *Robins*, 4 Bing. 11; *Waller* v. *Andrews*, 3 M. & W. 312; *post*, p. 122.

(*g*) Stat. 24 & 25 Vict. c. 133, s. 38; *Smith* v. *Humble*, 15 C. B. 321.

(*h*) See stat. 6 & 7 Will. 4, c. 71, s. 70; *Griffinhoofe* v. *Daubuz*, 4 E. & B. 230; 5 E. & B. 746; 25 L. J., Q. B. 237.

tions must be made from the next payment of the rent (*i*).

Compulsory payments made by an under-tenant of arrears of rent due from the original tenant to the original landlord, for which the goods of the under-tenant are liable to be distrained (*k*). A payment of such rent by the occupier, in default of the original tenant, is not the less a compulsory payment, because the original landlord on demanding it allows the occupier time to pay (*l*). To make the payment compulsory, it is not essential that the original landlord should have threatened to distrain upon the occupier; it is enough that he has demanded payment, for a demand by one who has the power to distrain is treated as equivalent to a threat of distress (*m*). A payment under such circumstances is no more voluntary than a donation to a beggar who presents a pistol (*n*).

<small>5. Rent due to original landlord.</small>

Rent growing due may be discharged by such payments as well as rent actually due (*l*).

If premises are liable to a distress, the tenant has a right to pay the charge to which they are liable, and to deduct from his rent the sum so paid (*o*). Payment by a tenant of an annuity or a legacy secured by power of distress (*p*); or of interest due on a mortgage made before the commencement of the tenancy (*q*), is considered as equivalent to payment of so much rent to

<small>6. Other compulsory payments.</small>

(*i*) See *Andrew* v. *Hancock*, 1 B. & B. 37; *Saunderson* v. *Hanson*, 3 C. & P. 314.

(*k*) *Sapsford* v. *Fletcher*, 4 T. R. 511; *Carter* v. *Carter*, 5 Bing. 406; *Sturgess* v. *Farrington*, 4 Taunt. 614.

(*l*) *Carter* v. *Carter*, 5 Bing. 406.

(*m*) Smith, L. & T. 171.

(*n*) Per Best, C. J., in *Carter* v. *Carter*, 5 Bing., at p. 409.

(*o*) Per Burrough, J., in *Taylor* v. *Zamira*, 6 Taunt., at p. 529.

(*p*) *Taylor* v. *Zamira*, 6 Taunt. 524; *Whitmore* v. *Walker*, 2 C. & K. 615.

(*q*) *Johnson* v. *Jones*, 9 A. & E. 809, 814; *Dyer* v. *Bowley*, 2 Bing. 94.

the landlord. But in order to operate as a deduction from rent, the money must have been actually paid(*r*); and it would seem that the payment must have been preceded by a demand, accompanied by a threat, in case of non-payment, to distrain, or to eject, or to "put the law in force"(*s*). The payment, moreover, must be made either to relieve the tenant of an incumbrance on the land, or to discharge a debt due by the landlord(*t*). A deduction permitted, for several years, by mistake by the landlord or his agent, the landlord having the means of knowing all the facts, and there being no fraud or misrepresentation on the part of the tenant, will operate as a payment of so much rent, and the landlord cannot afterwards distrain for sums so deducted, or recover them by action as arrears of rent(*u*).

<small>Construction of express covenants as to amount of rent.</small>

COVENANT *to pay as rent "one-third part of the money that shall arise, be made, received, or produced from the sale of coals," also to " keep true accounts of all coal daily raised, and deliver true copies thereof."* The rent is to be calculated on the amount of coal sold, not on the amount of money actually received(*x*).

COVENANT *to deliver quarterly to the lessor two equal thirteenth parts of all coal raised, or pay him quarterly the value thereof in money; and that in case at the end of the first quarter of any*

(*r*) *Ante*, pp. 116, 120, note (*c*). See *Ryan* v. *Thompson*, 37 L. J., C. P. 134; L. R., 3 C. P. 144.

(*s*) *Whitmore* v. *Walker*, 2 C. & K. 615; *Taylor* v. *Zamira*, 6 Taunt. 524. But see *ante*, p. 121.

(*t*) See judgment of Cresswell, J., in *Boodle* v. *Cambell*, 13 L. J., C. P., at p. 145; 7 M. & Gr. 386; *Graham* v. *Allsopp*, 3 Ex. 186; 18 L. J., Ex. 85.

(*u*) *Bramston* v. *Robins*, 4 Bing. 11; *Waller* v. *Andrews*, 3 M. & W. 312.

(*x*) *Edwards* v. *Rees*, 7 C. & P. 340, 341.

year such quarterly deliveries should not have equalled in value or amount 38*l.* 10*s. the lessees should also pay at the end of any such past quarter such additional rent or sum as would make up* 38*l.* 10*s., with similar provisions for the payment of such further sums as would make up at the end of the second quarter* 75*l.*, *at the end of the third quarter* 111*l.* 10*s.*, *and at the end of the fourth quarter* 150*l.*, " *it being the intent and meaning of the parties that the royalties reserved shall always amount to* 150*l. per annum at the least.*" The rent is to be made up every quarter, and the landlord is not to have less than 150*l.* a year. If the royalty in any quarter falls short of 38*l.* 10*s.* it must be made up to that sum; but, if the royalty in any quarter exceeds that sum, the surplus is not to be given back to the lessees (*y*).

COVENANT *to raise* 13,000 *tons of coal in each year and pay* 8*d. per ton royalty for the same, or to pay that amount of money, viz.* 433*l.* 6*s.* 8*d., each year as a fixed rent, whether the coals are wrought or not.* The covenant does not carry with it, by implication, a condition that there shall be coals to the amount mentioned in it capable of being wrought; and the whole rent claimed is payable, although the mine is so exhausted that the lessee cannot raise 13,000 tons of coal in a year (*z*).

COVENANT *by lessee of a coal mine to pay one-half of*

(*y*) *Bishop* v. *Goodwin*, 14 M. & W. 260, 263, 264; 14 L. J., Ex. 290.

(*z*) *Bute* v. *Thompson*, 13 M. & W. 487; 14 L. J., Ex. 95. See *Jervis* v. *Tomkinson*, 1 H. & N. 195; 26 L. J., Ex. 41; *Ridgway* v. *Sneyd*, 1 Kay, 627.

all such sums of money as the cannel to be got should sell for at the pit's mouth over and above 4*d.* the basket. The lessee is not liable to pay to the lessor any part of the money produced by the sale of coals elsewhere than at the pit's mouth (*a*).

AGREEMENT *that lessee shall spend a specified sum in repairs, to be inspected and approved of by the lessor, and to be done in a substantial manner; the lessee to be allowed to retain the sum out of the first year's rent of the premises.* The lessor's approval is not a condition precedent to the lessee's retaining the rent (*b*).

Premises destroyed by fire, &c.

If the demised premises are destroyed or rendered uninhabitable by fire, the full rent will nevertheless, in the absence of an express stipulation to the contrary, continue to be payable throughout the term granted by the lease (*c*), although the landlord has received insurance money which he refuses to apply in rebuilding (*d*). The Court of Chancery will not, under these circumstances, grant an injunction to restrain the landlord from suing for the rent (*e*). Where an agreement for a lease, under the terms of which a person has become tenant from year to year, provides that the lease shall contain covenants on the part of the tenant to pay

---

(*a*) *Gerrard* v. *Clifton*, 7 T. R. 676; 1 B. & P. 524; *Clifton* v. *Walmesley*, 5 T. R. 564.

(*b*) *Dallman* v. *King*, 4 Bing. N. C. 105.

(*c*) *Baker* v. *Holtzpaffel*, 4 Taunt. 45; *Izon* v. *Gorton*, 5 Bing. N. C. 501; 7 Scott, 537; *Monk* v. *Cooper*, 2 Stra. 763; *Belfour* v. *Weston*, 1 T. R. 310;

Hare v. *Groves*, 3 Anstr. 687. See *Packer* v. *Gibbins*, 1 Q. B. 421.

(*d*) *Leeds* v. *Cheetham*, 1 Sim. 146; *Lofft* v. *Dennis*, 1 E. & E. 474; 28 L. J., Q. B. 168.

(*e*) *Holtzapffel* v. *Baker*, 18 Ves. 115; *Leeds* v. *Cheetham*, 1 Sim. 146.

rent, damage by fire excepted, and that until the lease shall be granted the lessor may distrain for all or any part of the rent agreed to be paid, the effect of the destruction by fire of any part of the premises will be to entitle the tenant to a deduction from the rent according to the proportion which the annual value of the destroyed part bears to the annual value of the whole; taking the whole to be the premises as originally demised, not as improved by subsequent additions made by the tenant(f).

On the same principle the tenant of a building is liable to pay rent after it has been carried away by a flood(g) or occupied by an alien enemy(h); and the tenant of land must also pay rent, though the land is covered with water by an inundation (i).

If a person contracts for the use and occupation of land for a specified time and at a specified rent, he is bound by his bargain, though the land may not answer the purpose for which he took it. If, for instance, the land should turn out to be wet, or the grass, from any reason, should prove to be deleterious to cattle, that would be no excuse for not paying the lessor's rent(j). So also, in the absence of fraud, the tenant is not exonerated from payment of rent though a dwelling-house taken by him for immediate occupation is unfit for habitation (k).

Premises unfit for use or habitation.

It is no defence to an action for rent that the landlord is under an implied contract to repair the demised

Non-repair by landlord.

(f) *Bennet* v. *Ireland*, E. B. & E. 326; 28 L. J., Q. B. 48.

(g) *Carter* v. *Cummins*, cited in *Harrison* v. *North*, 1 Cb. Cas., at p. 84.

(h) *Paradine* v. *Jane*, Alcyn, 26; see *Harrison* v. *North*, 1 Ch. Cas. 83.

(i) 1 Roll. Abr. 236 (C.)

(j) Per Lord Abinger, C. B., in *Sutton* v. *Temple*, 13 L. J., Ex., at p. 22; 12 M. & W., at p. 62.

(k) *Hart* v. *Windsor*, 12 M. & W. 68; 13 L. J., Ex. 129. See *post*, Sect. 4 (1).

premises, and that by his neglect they have become useless to the tenant (*l*).

Eviction by landlord.

An eviction of the tenant by the landlord will constitute a defence to an action for rent (*m*); but the defendant is bound to show that the eviction took place before the rent became due (*n*). An eviction of the tenant by the landlord from part of the demised premises operates as a suspension of the entire rent during the continuance of the eviction (*o*).

(7) *Apportionment of Rent.*

In respect of estate.
1. On grant or devise of part of reversion.
2. On severance of reversion on death of lessor intestate.

Rent is apportionable in the following cases:—Where the lessor has granted (*p*) or devised (*q*) part of the reversion to the lessee or a stranger; where, in the case of a lease including both freehold and leasehold premises, upon the death of the lessor intestate the reversion in the demised premises is divided by operation of law between his real and personal representatives (*r*); where the reversion descends to coparceners, and a partition is made between them (*q*); where the lessee

3. On tenant's losing possession of part of premises.

has surrendered part of the demised premises to the lessor (*s*), or has been lawfully evicted from part of the demised premises by a person having a title paramount to that of the lessor (*t*); or where the lessor has entered

---

(*l*) *Surplice* v. *Farnsworth*, 7 M. & Gr. 576; 13 L. J., C. P. 215.
(*m*) See *post*, p. 230.
(*n*) See *Boodle* v. *Cambell*, 7 M. & Gr. 386; 13 L. J., C. P. 142.
(*o*) *Morrison* v. *Chadwick*, 7 C. B. 266; 18 L. J., C. P. 189.
(*p*) Co. Lit. 148 a; Litt. s. 222; *Collins and Harding's Case*, 13 Co. R. 57.
(*q*) See *Ewer* v. *Moyle*, Cro. Eliz. 771.
(*r*) *Moodie* v. *Garnance*, 3 Bulstr. 153.
(*s*) Co. Lit. 148 a; per Popham, J., in *Smith* v. *Malings*, Cro. Jac. 160.
(*t*) See *Stevenson* v. *Lombard*, 2 East, 575; *Doe* v. *Meylor*, 2 M. & S. 276; *Tomlinson* v. *Day*, 2 B. & B. 680; Co. Lit. 148 b.

upon part of the demised premises upon a forfeiture under a special condition for re-entry into part (*u*). But where a lessee under a parol lease of one hundred acres of land accepted the lease and entered upon the land, but upon his entry found eight acres in the possession of a person entitled under a prior lease from the lessor for a term exceeding the duration of the later lease, and that person kept possession of the eight acres until half-a-year's rent became due, and excluded the lessee from the enjoyment during that period, the lessee continuing in possession of the remainder; it was held, that the latter demise was wholly void as to the eight acres; that the rent was not apportionable, and that the lessor was not entitled to distrain for the whole rent or any part of it (*x*).

All rents (*y*) (whether reserved under an instrument in writing or otherwise) shall, like interest on money lent, be considered as accruing from day to day, and shall be apportionable in respect of time accordingly. *Apportionment in respect of time. Stat. 33 & 34 Vict. c. 35, s. 2.*

The apportioned part of any such rent shall be payable or recoverable in the case of a continuing rent when the entire portion of which such apportioned part shall form part shall become due and payable, and not before; and in the case of a rent determined by re-entry, death or otherwise, when the next entire portion of the same would have been payable if the same had not so determined, and not before. *Sect. 3. Apportioned part to be payable at time when entire portion is payable.*

All persons and their respective heirs, executors, administrators and assigns, and also the executors, ad- *Sect. 4. Same remedies for recovering*

(*u*) *Walker's Case*, 3 Co. R., at p. 22 a; *Collins and Harding's Case*, 13 Co. R., at p. 58.

(*x*) *Neale* v. *Mackenzie*, 1 M. & W. 747. See 2 Cr. M. & R. 84.

(*y*) Including rent service, rent-charge and rent seck, and also tithes and all periodical payments or renderings in lieu of or in the nature of rent or tithe. Sect. 5.

ministrators and assigns respectively of persons whose interests determine with their own deaths, shall have the same remedies at law and in equity for recovering such apportioned parts as aforesaid when payable (allowing proportionate parts of all just allowances) as they respectively would have had for recovering such entire portions as aforesaid if entitled thereto respectively; provided that persons liable to pay rents reserved out of or charged on lands or other hereditaments of any tenure, and the same lands or other hereditaments shall not be resorted to for any such apportioned part forming part of an entire or continuing rent as aforesaid specifically, but the entire or continuing rent, including such apportioned part, shall be recovered and received by the heir or other person who, if the rent had not been apportionable under this act or otherwise, would have been entitled to such entire or continuing rent, and such apportioned part shall be recoverable from such heir or other person by the executors or other parties entitled under this act to the same by action at law or suit in equity.

<small>apportioned parts as for entire portion.</small>

<small>But lessee not to be resorted to for payment of apportioned part specifically.</small>

<small>Sect. 7. Act not to operate where apportionment expressly negatived.</small>

The provisions of this act shall not extend to any case in which it is or shall be expressly stipulated that no apportionment shall take place.

<small>How apportionment may be made.</small>

Apportionment may be made by the lessor, with the consent of the lessee, or by the verdict of a jury in an action of debt brought by a reversioner for the rent (z).

(8) *Payment of Rent.*

<small>Bill or note.</small>

A bill of exchange, or promissory note, given by a tenant to his landlord for rent in arrear, will not,

---

(z) *Bliss* v. *Collins*, 5 B. & A. 876.

until payment is actually made, operate as a satisfaction of the rent, or take away, or even postpone, the right of the landlord to distrain, or to avail himself of his other remedies for recovering the rent, unless there is a distinct agreement to that effect (*a*). An agreement by the landlord to accept interest on rent in arrear does not postpone the right of distress (*b*). Agreement to take interest.

If a landlord has directed his tenant to remit his rent by post, or perhaps if rent is so remitted in the usual way of transacting business of this nature between the parties, the money is remitted at the peril of the landlord (*c*); provided the tenant has used due caution in delivering the letter at a post office (*d*). Remittance.

(9) *Effect of Payment of Rent.*

Payment of rent raises a presumption that the party receiving it has a good title to the rent; but if made to a person from whom the tenant did not originally receive possession of the demised premises, the presumption may be rebutted (*e*). Hence, a tenant who has come into possession under a former owner, and has paid, or agreed to pay, rent to a person who claims to be succeeding owner, in ignorance of a defect in the title of such person, may show that he is not As evidence of attornment.

(*a*) *Davis* v. *Gyde*, 2 A. & E. 623; *Harris* v. *Shipway*, Bull. N. P. 182; *Drake* v. *Mitchell*, 3 East, 251. See *Parrot* v. *Anderson*, 7 Ex. 93, 95; 21 L. J., Ex. 291.

(*b*) *Sherry* v. *Preston*, 2 Chit. 245.

(*c*) *Warwicke* v. *Noakes*, Peake, N. P. C. 67.

(*d*) *Hawkins* v. *Rutt*, Peake, N. P. C. 186.

(*e*) Judgment of Gibbs, C. J., in *Rogers* v. *Pitcher*, 6 Taunt., at p. 208; *Cornish* v. *Searell*, 8 B. & C. 471; *Doe* v. *Clarke*, Peake's Add. Cas. 239; *Cox* v. *Knight*, 18 C. B. 645; 25 L. J., C. P. 314.

F. K

the landlord (*g*). Payment of rent by a lessee to a lessor after the lessor's title has expired, and after the lessee has notice of an adverse claim, does not amount to an acknowledgment of title in the lessor, or to a virtual attornment, unless at the time of payment the lessee knows the precise nature of the adverse claim, or the manner in which the lessor's title has expired (*h*). Before the lessee can be bound by such payment, the lessor must say openly, " My former title is at an end; will you, notwithstanding, go on?"(*i*).

Payment of rent by a tenant to an authorized agent, who does not disclose his principal's name at the time, but pays over the rent to his principal, is evidence as against the tenant of the principal's title, to support an avowry for rent (*k*).

(10) *Remedies for Recovery of Rent.*

	PAGE
(a) *Distress*	131
1. Requisites to..	131
Certain and proper rent	131
Rent in arrear	132
Reversion in person distraining	132
Goods liable to distress	137
2. Where made..	144
3. When made ..	149
4. Amount for which made	151
5. Mode of making	152
Entry	154
Seizure	156
Impounding	158
6. Requisites to sale	164
Notice	164
Appraisement	167
7. Sale	169
8. Costs of distress	173

(*g*) *Gregory* v. *Doidge*, 3 Bing. 474, 475; *Claridge* v. *Mackenzie*, 4 M. & Gr. 143, 155.

(*h*) *Fenner* v. *Duplock*, 2 Bing. 10; 3 Bing. 475. But see *Doe* v. *Wilkinson*, 3 B. & C. 413.

(*i*) Judgment of Best, C. J., in 2 Bing. 11.

(*k*) *Hitchings* v. *Thompson*, 5 Ex. 50; 19 L. J., Ex. 146.

(a) *Distress*—continued.

		PAGE
9. Remedies for illegal distresses		.. 175
Rescue		.. 175
Replevin..		.. 176
Action of trespass, &c.		.. 178
In Metropolitan Police District		.. 179
10. Remedy for irregular distresses		.. 180
(b) *Remedy on Execution against Tenant*..		.. 181
(c) *Remedy on Bankruptcy of Tenant*		.. 185
(d) *Remedy by Action.*		.. 187

1. *Requisites to Distress.*

Unless a power to distrain is expressly conferred upon the landlord (*l*), the following circumstances must exist to enable him to avail himself of that remedy:—

The rent for which the distress is made must be reserved upon an actual and existing demise of a corporeal hereditament (*m*). No distress can be made for rent due under a mere agreement for a lease, or accruing after the expiration of a notice to quit, unless a tenancy has been expressly or impliedly created (*m*). Moreover, before a landlord takes into his hand the speedy remedy of distress, he must see that the amount of rent to be demanded has been settled with precision (*n*). He has no right to distrain, unless a fixed rent has been expressly or impliedly (*o*) agreed upon; if there is no fixed rent, the law gives him a remedy by the action for use and occupation (*p*). A rent which, though of fluctuating amount, is ascertainable with certainty, may be distrained for (*q*); as, for instance, a rent of so much per cubic yard for marl got, and so

Marginal note: 1. A certain and proper rent.

(*l*) *Post*, p. 132.
(*m*) See *ante*, pp. 110—112.
(*n*) Per Tindal, C. J., in *Regnart* v. *Porter*, 7 Bing., at p. 454.
(*o*) See *Knight* v. *Benett*, 3 Bing. 361.
(*p*) See judgment of Abbott, C. J., in *Dunk* v. *Hunter*, 5 B. & A., at p. 325. Double value cannot be recovered by distress, *post*, Chap. VI., Sect. 5 (2).
(*q*) Co. Lit. 96 a; *Daniel* v. *Gracie*, 6 Q. B. 145; 13 L. J., Q. B. 309.

much per thousand for bricks made (*r*). A distress may be made for an increased rent of so much per acre for every acre of land converted into tillage (*s*).

By express agreement, however, a power may be conferred to distrain for payments which are not rent (*t*). Thus, a sum payable by way of punishment for not spending the produce on the land demised, may be made recoverable by distress in the same way as a distress is made for rent in arrear (*t*).

2. Rent in arrear.

There can be no distress till the rent is in arrear, and rent, though due on the day appointed for payment, is not in arrear until that day has elapsed (*u*); hence, no distress can be made until the day after the rent-day (*u*). Where by custom or express reservation rent is payable in advance (*x*), the landlord may distrain for it as soon as the half-year, or other period for which it is paid, has begun (*y*). The landlord, by taking a bill or note for the rent in arrear, or by accepting interest upon it, will not necessarily deprive himself of his right to distrain (*z*).

3. Reversion in person distraining.

In general, the person who distrains, or on whose behalf the distress is made, must possess a reversion (*a*); hence, rent reserved on the assignment of a lease cannot be distrained for (*a*). But the reversion, to support a

---

(*r*) *Daniel* v. *Gracie*, 6 Q. B. 145; 13 L. J., Q. B. 309.

(*s*) See *Roulston* v. *Clarke*, 2 H. Bl. 563; *ante*, p. 118.

(*t*) *Pollitt* v. *Forrest*, 11 Q. B. 949; 16 L. J., Q. B. 424.

(*u*) *Dibble* v. *Bowater*, 2 E. & B. 564, 568; 22 L. J., Q. B. 396. See 2 Wms. Saund. 287.

(*x*) *Ante*, pp. 83, 112.

(*y*) *Buckley* v. *Taylor*, 2 T. R. 600; *Harrison* v. *Barry*, 7 Price, 690, 698; *Lee* v. *Smith*, 9 Ex. 662, 665. As to rent payable in advance *if demanded*, see *Clarke* v. *Holford*, 2 C. & K. 540; *Williams* v. *Holmes*, 8 Ex. 861; 22 L. J., Ex. 283; *Witty* v. *Williams*, 12 W. R. 755; 10 L. T., N. S. 457; *ante*, p. 113, note (*f*).

(*z*) *Ante*, p. 128.

(*a*) See cases cited *ante*, in notes (*x*), (*y*), p. 112.

distress, need not be an actual reversion; it is sufficient if it be a reversion by estoppel (*b*), and if a tenant is actually let into occupation, there is a reversion which he is estopped from denying (*c*). Hence, if a mortgagor, who has executed a second mortgage, has attorned to the second mortgagee, and occupied as tenant to him, a distress may be made by such mortgagee, although he has no legal reversion (*d*). So also, a mortgagor may distrain for rent due under a lease made by him after the mortgage (*e*); but he must bear in mind, that compulsory payments previously made by his tenant to the mortgagee for interest due on the mortgage, are equivalent to payment of so much rent (*f*). The mortgagee cannot distrain for rent due under a lease made by the mortgagor after the mortgage, until a new tenancy has been expressly or impliedly created between the mortgagee and the tenant (*g*). Notice by the mortgagee to the tenant to pay the rent to him does not constitute a tenancy between the parties, so as to enable the mortgagee to distrain for rent accruing due after the notice (*g*).

After a mortgagee has given notice of the mortgage to the lessee in possession under a lease made before the mortgage, he is entitled to, and may distrain for, rent in arrear at the time of the notice, and rent subsequently becoming due (*h*). A mortgagor cannot, strictly speak-

Distress for rent under lease after mortgage.

Distress for rent due on lease prior to mortgage.

(*b*) See *ante*, p. 42.
(*c*) Judgment of Blackburn, J., in *Morton* v. *Woods*, 37 L. J., Q. B., at p. 248.
(*d*) *Morton* v. *Woods*, 37 L. J., Q. B. 242; L. R., 3 Q. B. 658. Aff. 38 L. J., Q. B. 81; L. R., 4 Q. B. 293.
(*e*) *Alchorne* v. *Gomme*, 2 Bing. 54.

(*f*) *Ante*, p. 121.
(*g*) *Evans* v. *Elliott*, 9 A. & E. 342; *Rogers* v. *Humphreys*, 4 A. & E. 299; *ante*, p. 41.
(*h*) *Moss* v. *Gallimore*, 1 Dougl. 279; *Rogers* v. *Humphreys*, 4 A. & E. 299; *Burrows* v. *Gradin*, 1 D. & L. 213; 12 L. J., Q. B. 333; *ante*, p. 116.

ing, distrain for rent due under a lease made *before* the mortgage; but if permitted by the mortgagee to continue in the receipt of such rent, he is during such permission, *præsumptione juris* authorized, if it should become necessary, to realize the rent by distress, and to distrain for it in the mortgagee's name, and as his bailiff. He may justify the distress as bailiff, although he said at the time of taking, that he distrained for rent due to himself (*i*).

Receiver.

A receiver appointed by mortgagor and mortgagee to receive the rents of the mortgaged property, and to use such remedies by way of entry and distress as should be requisite, and to whom the mortgagor has attorned as tenant, may distrain on the goods belonging to the mortgagor on the mortgaged premises (*k*).

An authority to tenants to pay rent to a person, whose receipt is to be their discharge, may perhaps authorize that person to demand, but not to distrain for the rent (*l*).

Receivers appointed by the Court of Chancery have a power, where they see it necessary, to distrain for rent, and need not apply first to the Court for a particular order for that purpose (*m*). But if there should be any doubt as to who has a legal right to the rent, then the receiver, as he must distrain in the name of the person who has that right, may very properly make an application to the Court for an order (*m*).

Distress for

If any man shall have, in the right of his wife, any

(*i*) *Trent* v. *Hunt*, 9 Ex. 14, 24; 22 L. J., Ex. 318.
(*k*) *Jolly* v. *Arbuthnot*, 4 De G. & J. 224; 28 L. J., Ch. 547. See *Dancer* v. *Hastings*, 4 Bing. 2.
(*l*) *Ward* v. *Shew*, 9 Bing. 608.

(*m*) Per Lord Hardwicke in *Pitt* v. *Snowden*, 3 Atk. 750; *Bennett* v. *Robins*, 5 C. & P. 379; *Brandon* v. *Brandon*, 5 Madd. 473.

estate in fee simple, fee tail, or for term of life in any rents, and the same rents shall be due, behind and unpaid in the said wife's life, the husband, after the death of his wife, may distrain for the said arrearages, in like manner as he might have done if his said wife had been then living.

<small>Arrears of rent of wife's freeholds. Stat. 32 Hen. 8, c. 37, s. 3. Husband may distrain for arrears due during wife's life.</small>

Under this statute the husband may distrain for all arrears of rent which have become due either before the marriage or during its continuance (*n*). If he becomes tenant by the curtesy, he may distrain for rent due after the coverture; and it has been said that a man who has made a lease for years rendering rent of lands of which he is seised in right of his wife, although on her death he does not become tenant by the curtesy, but his estate is determined, may nevertheless distrain for the rent until her heir has entered (*o*).

It shall be lawful to every executor or administrator of any (tenant in fee, in fee tail or for life (*p*) of rents issuing out of freehold lands (*q*)), unto whom such rent shall be due and not paid at the time of his death, to distrain for the arrearages of all such rents upon the lands charged with the payment of such rents, so long as the said lands continue in the possession of the tenant who ought to have paid the said rent, or any person claiming from the same tenant.

<small>Executors and administrators. Stat. 32 Hen. 8, c. 37, s. 1. Executors, &c. of lessor who has leased for life may distrain.</small>

It shall be lawful for the executors or administrators <small>Stat. 3 & 4</small>

(*n*) *Ognel's Case*, 4 Co. R., at p. 51; Co. Lit. 162 b, 351 b.

(*o*) Bac. Abr. (C. 1), 17; *Dixon* v. *Harrison*, Vaugh. 46; Woodfall, L. & T. 228. See *Howe* v. *Scarrott*, 4 H. & N. 723; 28 L. J., Ex. 325; but consider *Blake* v. *Foster*, 8 T. R. 487; judgment of Bayley, J., in *Hill* v. *Saunders*, 4 B. & C., at p. 535.

(*p*) Co. Lit. 162 b; *Prescott* v. *Boucher*, 3 B. & Ad. 849; *Jones* v. *Jones*, ib. 967.

(*q*) *Appleton* v. *Doily*, Yelv. 135; 2 Williams on Exors. 836.

Will. 4, c. 42, s. 37.
Executors, &c. of landlord may distrain for rent due in his life.

of any landlord to distrain upon the lands demised for any term, or at will, for the arrearages of rent due to such lessor or landlord in his lifetime, in like manner as such lessor or landlord might have done in his lifetime.

Sect. 38. Arrears may be distrained for within six months after end of lease.

Such arrearages may be distrained for after the end or determination of such term or lease at will, in the same manner as if such term or lease had not been ended or determined; provided that such distress be made within the space of six calendar months after the determination of such term or lease, and during the continuance of the possession of the tenant from whom such arrears became due.

An executor, before probate, may distrain for rent due to the testator (*s*).

Tenant from year to year.

A tenant from year to year, underletting from year to year, has a sufficient reversion to support a distress (*t*).

Tenant at will.

A right to distrain always exists in a tenancy at will where a rent is reserved (*u*).

Joint tenants.

One of several joint tenants or coparceners may distrain for the whole rent without any express authority from the rest (*x*); but he must avow in his own right and as bailiff to the rest (*x*).

After a severance of the reversion by a conveyance of the shares of some of several joint tenants who have demised at a single rent, no distress can be made for arrears of such rent due before the severance (*y*).

(*s*) *Whitehead* v. *Taylor*, 10 A. & E. 210; 1 Williams on Exors. 256.

(*t*) *Curtis* v. *Wheeler*, Moo. & M. 493. See *Oxley* v. *James*, 13 M. & W. 209; 13 L. J., Ex. 358, 360.

(*u*) Per Blackburn, J., 37 L. J., Q. B. 247.

(*x*) *Pullen* v. *Palmer*, 3 Salk. 207; *Leigh* v. *Shepherd*, 2 B. & B. 465; *Robinson* v. *Hofman*, 4 Bing. 562.

(*y*) *Staveley* v. *Allcock*, 16 Q. B. 636; 20 L. J., Q. B. 320.

Tenants in common are entitled to separate distresses for their several shares of the rent (*z*). It has been said that they may all join in one distress (*a*); but in that case they must avow separately (*a*).

Tenants in common.

An instrument whereby a person acknowledges that he is indebted to another as agent of his landlord, in a specified sum for arrears of rent, and pays a sum on account and in part of such rent, and undertakes to pay a specified sum per annum for the premises, is an acknowledgment of an antecedent tenancy, and shows an authority to distrain (*b*). An agreement for the sale of premises, under which the purchaser has entered into possession, and whereby for the purpose of securing the due performance of the several agreements therein contained, the purchaser admits himself to be a tenant from week to week of the vendor of the hereditaments thereby agreed to be sold, at a specified weekly rent payable in advance, entitles the vendor to distrain for the sum payable as weekly rent (*c*).

Acknowledgment of antecedent tenancy.

Generally speaking, the landlord may distrain for rent all moveable chattels which are upon the demised premises at the time when the distress is made. Whether such goods are the property of the tenant or of a stranger is perfectly immaterial, provided they are on the premises, and are not privileged from distress (*d*).

4. *Goods liable to be distrained.*

Goods belonging to third persons.

It shall be lawful for any person having rent arrear, and due upon any demise, to seize and secure any

Stat. 2 Will. & M. sess. 1, c. 5, s. 3.

(*z*) *Whitley* v. *Roberts*, M'Clel. & Y. 107.

(*a*) Bullen on Distress, 48; Woodfall, L. & T. 384.

(*b*) Per Alderson, B., in *Eagleton* v. *Gutteridge*, 12 L. J., Ex., at p. 361. See *Gladman* v. *Plumer*, 15 L. J., Q. B. 79.

(*c*) *Yeoman* v. *Ellison*, 36 L. J., C. P. 326; L. R., 2 C. P. 681.

(*d*) Per Buller, J., in *Gorton* v. *Falkner*, 4 T. R., at p. 568. See *Muspratt* v. *Gregory*, 1 M. & W. 633; 3 M. & W. 677; *Cramer* v. *Mott*, 39 L. J., Q. B. 172; L. R., 5 Q. B. 357.

Sheaves of corn or hay may be distrained.

sheaves or cocks of corn, or corn loose, or in the straw, (whether threshed or not (*e*)), or hay lying or being in any barn or granary, or upon any hovel, stack or rick, or otherwise upon any part of the land or ground charged with such rent (*f*).

Stat. 11 Geo. 2, c. 19, s. 8.

It shall be lawful for every landlord, or his steward, bailiff, receiver or other person empowered by him, to seize as a distress for arrears of rent any cattle or stock of their respective tenant, feeding or depasturing upon any common, appendant or appurtenant, or any ways belonging to all or any part of the premises demised or holden; and also to seize all sorts of corn and grass, hops, roots, fruits, pulse or other product whatsoever (of a similar nature (*g*)) growing on any part of the estates demised, as a distress for arrears of rent.

Growing crops may be distrained.

Property absolutely privileged from distress.
1. Fixtures.

The following kinds of property are not liable to distress:—

"Things annexed to the freehold" (*h*); including tenant's fixtures, such as kitchen ranges, stoves, coppers, grates, &c. (*i*); also trees growing in a nurseryman's grounds (*k*).

The temporary removal of fixtures out of their proper place, for repairs, does not deprive them of this privilege (*l*). But machinery used for manufacture, which is merely fixed to the freehold for the purpose of rendering it steadier and more capable of convenient use,—as,

---

(*e*) *Belasyse* v. *Burbridge*, Lutw. 66.
(*f*) See *post*, p. 159.
(*g*) *Clark* v. *Gaskarth*, 8 Taunt. 431; *Clark* v. *Calvert*, 3 Moo. 96.
(*h*) *Simpson* v. *Hartopp*, Willes, 512; 1 Smith, L. C. 385 (6th ed.); *Gorton* v. *Falkner*, 4 T. R., at p.

569; Co. Lit. 47 b.
(*i*) *Darby* v. *Harris*, 1 Q. B. 895; 10 L. J., Q. B. 294. See *post*, Chap. VI. (1).
(*k*) *Clark* v. *Gaskarth*, 8 Taunt. 431; *Clark* v. *Calvert*, 3 Moo. 96.
(*l*) See judgment in *Gorton* v. *Falkner*, 4 T. R., at p. 567.

for instance, machines fastened by bolts to the floor of a factory—may be distrained for rent (*m*). In determining whether the thing distrained is a personal chattel or a fixture, it is important to consider the mode and degree of annexation to the soil or fabric; that is, whether it can easily be removed *integrè, salvè, et commodè*, without injury to itself or to the fabric of the building; and in the next place, whether it was for the permanent and substantial improvement of the freehold, or merely for a temporary purpose, and the more complete enjoyment and use of it as a chattel (*n*). Railways formed by rails, fixed to wooden sleepers embedded in ballast, cannot be distrained (*o*).

Title deeds (*p*) and keys (*p*).

" Things delivered to a person exercising a public trade to be managed in the way of his trade" (*q*).

Under this head are included corn sent to a miller to be ground (*r*); materials sent to a manufacturer to be worked up (*s*); beasts sent to a butcher to be slaughtered (*t*); goods deposited for the purpose of sale with a factor (*u*), commission agent (*x*) or auctioneer (*y*);

2. Title-deeds, &c.
3. Goods sent to tenant to be manufactured.

(*m*) *Hellawell* v. *Eastwood*, 6 Ex. 295; 20 L. J., Ex. 154. See *Duck* v. *Braddyll*, M'Clel. 217; judgment in *Turner* v. *Cameron*, 39 L. J., Q. B., at p. 131.

(*n*) Per Parke, B., in *Hellawell* v. *Eastwood*, 6 Ex., at p. 312. See 39 L. J., Q. B. 130.

(*o*) *Turner* v. *Cameron*, 39 L. J., Q. B. 125; L. R., 5 Q. B. 306.

(*p*) See *Hellawell* v. *Eastwood*, 6 Ex., at pp. 306, 311.

(*q*) *Simpson* v. *Hartopp*, Willes, 512. See judgment of Erle, C. J., in *Swire* v. *Leach*, 34 L. J., C. P., at p. 151; *Gisbourn* v. *Hurst*, 1 Salk. 249.

(*r*) Co. Lit. 47 a.

(*s*) *Gibson* v. *Ireson*, 3 Q. B. 39. See *Wood* v. *Clarke*, 1 Cr. & J. 484.

(*t*) *Brown* v. *Shevill*, 2 A. & E. 138.

(*u*) *Gilman* v. *Elton*, 3 Br. & B. 75; *Mathias* v. *Mesnard*, 2 C. & P. 353.

(*x*) *Findon* v. *M'Laren*, 6 Q. B. 891; 14 L. J., Q. B. 183.

(*y*) *Adams* v. *Grane*, 1 Cr. & M. 380; *Brown* v. *Arundell*, 10 C. B. 54; 20 L. J., C. P. 30; *Williams* v. *Holmes*, 8 Ex. 861; 22 L. J., Ex. 283.

or placed for safe custody in the warehouse of a wharfinger (*z*); or pledged with a pawnbroker (*a*); also the goods of guests brought into an inn (*b*), and goods delivered to a carrier to be conveyed by him to some place (*c*). But goods placed in the hands of the tenant, merely with the intent that they shall remain on the premises, are not privileged from distress (*d*). Hence, brewers' casks sent to a public-house, and left with the publican till they are empty, may be distrained by the owner of the public-house (*e*); a boat left in the care of the tenant of saltworks, may be distrained by the owner of the salt works (*f*); and carriages and horses standing at livery may be distrained by the landlord for rent due by the livery stable-keeper (*g*). It has recently been held, that wine sent to the warehouse of a wine-warehouseman to be matured, is liable to be distrained for rent due to the landlord of the premises where it is deposited (*h*).

4. Wild animals.

Animals *feræ naturæ* (*i*). But deer in an inclosed ground may be distrained (*k*).

5. Goods in actual use.

Things in actual use: as, for instance, a horse, while it is drawing a cart (*l*) or being ridden (*m*); tools,

(*z*) *Thompson* v. *Mashiter*, 1 Bing. 283.
(*a*) *Swire* v. *Leach*, 18 C. B., N. S. 479; 34 L. J., C. P. 150; 13 W. R. 385.
(*b*) *Crosier* v. *Tomkinson*, 2 Ld. Ken. 439. See *Fowkes* v. *Joyce*, 3 Lev. 260; 2 Vern. 129.
(*c*) *Gisbourn* v. *Hurst*, 1 Salk. 249.
(*d*) See judgment of Wilde, B., in *Parsons* v. *Gingell*, 4 C. B., at p. 558.
(*e*) *Joule* v. *Jackson*, 7 M. & W. 450; 10 L. J., Ex. 142.

(*f*) *Muspratt* v. *Gregory*, 1 M. & W. 633; 3 M. & W. 677.
(*g*) *Francis* v. *Wyatt*, 1 W. Bl. 483; 3 Burr. 1498; *Parsons* v. *Gingell*, 4 C. B. 545; 16 L. J., C. P. 227.
(*h*) *Ex parte Russell*, 18 W. R. 753.
(*i*) Co. Litt. 47 a.
(*k*) See *Davies* v. *Powell*, Willes, 48.
(*l*) *Field* v. *Adames*, 12 A. & E. 649; 10 L. J., Q. B. 2.
(*m*) *Storey* v. *Robinson*, 6 T. R. 138; Co. Litt. 47 a.

while a man is working with them (*n*); and, it seems, wearing apparel, while in actual use.

But a horse, which a man is leading (*o*), and clothes, not actually worn (*p*), may be distrained.

Perishable goods, such as milk or meat, which cannot be restored, upon a replevin, in the same condition as that in which they were taken (*q*).   6. Perishable goods.

Goods which have been distrained *damage feasant*, or are in the possession of the sheriff (*r*) under an execution (*s*).   7. Goods in custody of law.

In case all or any part of the growing crops of the tenant of any farm or lands shall be seized and sold by any sheriff or other officer by virtue of any writ of execution, such crops, so long as the same shall remain on the farm or lands, shall, in default of sufficient distress of the goods and chattels of the tenant, be liable to the rent which may accrue and become due to the landlord after any such seizure and sale, and to the remedies by distress for recovery of such rent; and that notwithstanding any bargain, sale or assignment which may have been made or executed of such growing crops by any such sheriff or other officer.   Stat. 14 & 15 Vict. c. 25, s. 2. Growing crops seized and sold under execution to be liable to distress for rent accruing after seizure and sale.

Where any purchaser of any crops or produce hereinbefore mentioned (*t*) shall have entered into any agreement with such sheriff or other officer, touching the use and expenditure thereof on lands let to farm, it   8. Produce sold by sheriff subject to agreement to consume it on land.

(*n*) *Simpson* v. *Hartopp*, Willes, 512; Co. Lit. 47 a.

(*o*) *Wagstaff* v. *Clack*, cited in Woodfall, L. & T. 394, n. (*x*).

(*p*) *Baynes* v. *Smith*, 1 Esp. 206; *Bisset* v. *Caldwell*, *id.* note; Peake, N. P. C. 36.

(*q*) *Morley* v. *Pincombe*, 2 Ex. 101; 18 L. J., Ex. 272.

(*r*) *Blades* v. *Arundale*, 1 M.

& S. 711. See *Smith* v. *Russell*, 3 Taunt. 400.

(*s*) Co. Lit. 47 a; *Wharton* v. *Naylor*, 12 Q. B. 673; 17 L. J., Q. B. 278. As to the means to be adopted by the landlord, where his tenant's goods are taken in execution, see *post*, p. 181.

(*t*) See *post*, p. 209.

Stat. 56 Geo. 3, c. 50, s. 6. Landlord not to distrain on produce so sold.	shall not be lawful for the owner or landlord of such lands to distrain for any rent on any corn, hay, straw or other produce thereof, which, at the time of such sale and the execution of such agreement, entered into under the provisions of this act, shall have been severed from the soil and sold, subject to such agreement, by such sheriff or other officer; nor on any turnips, whether drawn or growing (*t*), if sold according to the provisions of this act; nor on any horses, sheep or other cattle, nor on any beast whatsoever, nor on any waggons, carts or other implements of husbandry, which any person shall employ, keep or use on such lands, for the purpose of threshing out, carrying or consuming any such corn, hay, straw, turnips or other produce, under the provisions of the act, and the agreement or agreements directed to be entered into between the sheriff or other officer and the purchaser of such crops and produce.
9. Frames, materials, &c. entrusted to workmen. Stat. 6 & 7 Vict. c. 40, s. 18. Not to be distrained except for rent due by owner.	No frame, loom or machine, materials, tools or apparatus entrusted for the purpose of being used or worked in any of the said manufactures (the woollen, worsted, linen, cotton, flax, mohair or silk manufactures (ss. 1, 2)), or any work connected therewith, or any parts or processes thereof, whether such frame, &c. shall or shall not be rented or taken by the hire, shall be distrained for rent, unless the rent be due by the owner of the said frame, &c., or of any part thereof.
Sect. 19. Remedy of owner of frame, &c.	If any landlord shall distrain any frame, &c., belonging to any other person which shall have been entrusted for the purpose of being used in any of the said manufactures, and shall refuse to restore possession of all such frames, &c., to the person entrusting the same, when demanded by him (any two or more justices of the peace may order the property to be forthwith restored).

(*t*) See now stat. 14 & 15 Vict. c. 25, s. 2, last page.

The goods or chattels of an ambassador (*u*).   10. Goods of ambassador.

Where any company is being wound up by the Court, or subject to the supervision of the Court, any distress put in force against the estate or effects of the company after the commencement of the winding-up (*i. e.*, after the presentation of the petition for the winding-up (s. 84)) shall be void.   11. Effects of company being wound up. Stat. 25 & 26 Vict. c. 89, s. 163. Distress after commencement of winding-up to be void.

It seems that this prohibition against enforcing a distress does not apply where premises are demised to persons who afterwards declare themselves trustees for a company (*x*). With the leave of the Court, however, a distress may be proceeded with, subject to such terms as the Court may impose (*y*). But it appears that in all cases in which the Court has allowed execution to proceed it had issued before the winding-up order was made (*z*).

The following kinds of property cannot be distrained if there are sufficient goods of other kinds on the premises to satisfy the distress.   *Property conditionally privileged from distress.*

Implements of trade not in actual use (*a*).   1. Implements of trade.

No man shall be distrained by his beasts that gain his land (cart-colts and young steers, not broken in or used for harness or the plough, are not within these words (*b*)), nor by his sheep (or the sheep of his under-   2. Cattle and sheep. Stat. 51 Hen. 3, stat. 4.

(*u*) See stat. 7 Anne, c. 12, s. 3.

(*x*) *In re Exhall Coal Mining Co. Limited*, 33 L. J., Ch. 595.

(*y*) Sect. 87. See 33 L. J., Ch. 596, note; 35 L. J., Ch. 425.

(*z*) Judgment of Lord Romilly, M. R., in *In re Progress Assurance Co.*, 39 L. J., Ch. 504; L. R., 9 Eq. 372. See *In re Great Ship Co.*, 33 L. J., Ch. 245; *In re*

London Cotton Co., 35 L. J., Ch. 425; L. R., 2 Eq. 53; *In re Bastow & Co.*, 36 L. J., Ch. 899; L. R., 4 Eq. 618.

(*a*) *Gorton* v. *Falkner*, 4 T. R., 565; *Fenton* v. *Logan*, 9 Bing. 676; *Nargett* v. *Nias*, 1 E. & E. 439; 28 L. J., Q. B. 143.

(*b*) *Keen* v. *Priest*, 4 H. & N. 236.

tenant(*b*)), for the king's debt, nor the debt of any other man, nor for any other cause, by the king's, or other bailiffs, but until they can find another distress, or chattels sufficient whereof they may levy the debt, or that are sufficient for the demand (*c*).

<small>Not to be distrained if there is other sufficient distress on premises.</small>

Cattle, &c. may be distrained if there is no other sufficient distress upon the demised premises besides growing crops (*d*). Cattle at agistment are liable to a distress (*e*). Where a stranger's cattle escape into another's land by breaking fences in which there is no defect; or by breaking defective fences, if the tenant of the land where the distress is taken is not bound to repair such fences, the cattle may be immediately distrained for rent (*f*). But if the beasts come on the premises through defect of fences, which the tenant of the land on which they stray is bound to repair, they cannot be distrained by the landlord for rent, unless the owner of the cattle, after notice that they are in the land, neglects or refuses to drive them away (*f*).

2. *Where Distress must be made.*

<small>General rule.</small>

Generally speaking, a thing cannot be distrained for rent-arrear except on the premises demised (*g*).

<small>Stat. 52 Hen. 3, c. 15. Subject not to take distresses out of his fee.</small>

It shall be lawful for no man, from henceforth, for any manner of cause, to take distresses out of his fee, nor in the king's highway, nor in the common street, but

---

(*b*) *Keen* v. *Priest*, 4 H. & N. 236; 28 L. J., Ex. 157.

(*c*) See *Jenner* v. *Yolland*, 6 Price, 3; *post*, p. 170.

(*d*) *Pigott* v. *Birtles*, 1 M. & W. 441.

(*e*) 1 Roll. Abr. 669, pl. 23; Woodfall, L. & T. 399; 3 Black. Com. 8, note.

(*f*) *Poole* v. *Longueville*, 2 Saund. 290, n. (7). See *Goodwyn* v. *Chereley*, 4 H. & N. 631; 28 L. J., Ex. 298.

(*g*) Per Best, C. J., in *Buzzard* v. *Capel*, 4 Bing., at p. 140. See *Capel* v. *Buzzard*, 6 Bing. 150, 161; 8 B. & C. 141; *Gillingham* v. *Gryer*, 16 L. T., N. S. 640.

only to the king or his officers having special authority to do the same (*h*).

In the following cases, however, the landlord may distrain goods not upon the demised premises:— *Exceptions.*

It shall be lawful for every landlord, or his bailiff, to seize, as a distress for rent, any cattle or stock of (his) tenant feeding upon any common appendant or appurtenant or anyways belonging to all or any part of the premises demised. 1. Stock feeding on common.
Stat. 11 Geo. 2, c. 19, s. 8.

If the landlord comes to distrain cattle which he sees then within his fee, but the tenant, or any other person, to prevent the landlord from distraining, drives the cattle out of the fee, the landlord may follow and distrain them (*i*). But the landlord cannot distrain cattle out of his fee if, when coming to distrain, he did not see them within his fee, or if the cattle of themselves, after the landlord has seen them, go out of the fee, or if, after the landlord has seen the cattle, the tenant removes them for any other cause than to prevent the landlord from distraining (*i*). 2. Cattle which landlord, coming to distrain, sees on demised premises.

In case any tenant for life, years, at will, sufferance or otherwise of any messuages, lands, tenements or hereditaments, upon the demise or holding whereof any rent shall be reserved, due, or made payable (*k*), shall fraudulently (either openly, with notice given to the landlord (*l*) or clandestinely convey away or carry off or from such premises (*m*) his goods or chattels, to prevent the landlord from distraining the same for arrears of rent so reserved, due, or made payable, it shall be lawful for every 3. Fraudulent removal.
Stat. 11 Geo. 2, c. 19, s. 1.

Landlord may, within thirty days, seize and sell goods fraudulently carried off.

(*h*) See also stat. 3 Edw. 1, c. 16.
(*i*) Co. Lit. 161 a.
(*k*) See *Anderson* v. *Midland Ry. Co.*, 3 E. & E. 614; 30 L. J., Q. B. 94.
(*l*) *Opperman* v. *Smith*, 4 D. & R. 33.
(*m*) See *Stanley* v. *Wharton*, 9 Price, 301.

F.   L.

landlord, or any person by him for that purpose lawfully empowered, within thirty days next ensuing such conveying away or carrying off, to seize such goods and chattels, wherever the same shall be found, as a distress for the said arrears of rent, and the same to sell or otherwise dispose of in such manner as if the said goods and chattels had actually been distrained by such landlord upon such premises for such arrears of rent (*n*).

Sect. 2.
Exception in case goods are bonâ fide sold before seizure.

No landlord, or other person entitled to such arrears of rent, shall seize any such goods or chattels as a distress for the same which shall be sold *bonâ fide*, and for a valuable consideration, before such seizure made, to any person not privy to such fraud as aforesaid (*o*).

Sect. 7.
Landlords may break open houses, &c. in which goods fraudulently removed are secured.

Where any goods or chattels fraudulently or clandestinely conveyed or carried away by any tenant, or other person aiding or assisting therein, shall be put in any house, barn, stable, outhouse, yard, close or place locked up, fastened or otherwise secured, so as to prevent such goods or chattels from being seized as a distress for arrears of rent, it shall be lawful for the landlord, his steward, bailiff, receiver or other person empowered, to seize, as a distress for rent, such goods and chattels,—first calling to his assistance the constable or other peace officer of the hundred, borough, parish, district or place where the same shall be suspected to be concealed (or a special constable appointed for the occasion (*p*)), who are hereby required to aid and assist therein; and, in case of a dwelling-house, oath being also first made before some justice of the peace of a reasonable ground to suspect that such goods or chattels are therein,—in the daytime (without any previous re-

(*n*) See also stat. 8 Anne, c. 14, s. 2.
(*o*) See *Williams* v. *Roberts*, 7
Ex. 618; 22 L. J., Ex. 61.
(*p*) *Cartwright* v. *Smith*, 1 Moo. & Rob. 284.

quest (*q*)), to break open and enter into such house, barn, stable, outhouse, yard, close and place, and to seize such goods and chattels for the said arrears of rent, as he might have done by virtue of this or any former act if such goods and chattels had been put in any open field or place.

If any tenant shall fraudulently remove and convey away (or, without actual participation, shall be privy to the removal of (*r*)) his goods or chattels as aforesaid, or if any person shall wilfully and knowingly (being privy to the fraudulent intent (*s*)) aid or assist any such tenant in such fraudulent conveying away or carrying off of any part of his goods or chattels, or in concealing the same (although no distress may be in progress or contemplated at the time (*t*)), every person so offending shall forfeit to the landlord double the value of the goods by him carried off or concealed as aforesaid; to be recovered by action of debt, or (as an alternative remedy (*u*)), where the goods and chattels so fraudulently carried off or concealed shall not exceed the value of fifty pounds, the landlord, his bailiff, servant or agent in his behalf (may) exhibit a complaint in writing against such offender before two or more justices of the peace of the same county, riding or division of such county, residing near the place whence such goods and chattels were removed, or near the place where the same were found, not being interested in the lands or tenements whence such goods were removed, (who, after examining the parties concerned upon oath,) may, by order under

Sect. 3.
Penalty on tenant or person assisting in fraudulent removal of goods.

Sect. 4.

(*q*) *Williams* v. *Roberts*, 7 Ex. 618; 22 L. J., Ex. 61.

(*r*) *Lyster* v. *Brown*, 1 C. & P. 121.

(*s*) *Brooke* v. *Noakes*, 8 B. & C. 537, 542.

(*t*) *Stanley* v. *Wharton*, 10 Price, 138.

(*u*) *Bromley* v. *Holden*, M. & M. 175; *Horsefall* v. *Davy*, 1 Stark. 169.

their hands and seals, adjudge the offender to pay double the value of the said goods and chattels to such landlord at such time as the said justices shall appoint.

<small>Requisites to proceedings under this statute.</small>

Before availing himself of the provisions of this statute, the landlord should ascertain the following particulars:—

<small>1. Goods belonging to tenant.</small>

That the goods removed belonged to the tenant. A stranger or lodger has a right to remove his goods off the premises at any time, or under any circumstances (x), before the commencement of a distress (y).

<small>2. Fraudulent intent.</small>

That the goods were carried off with a view to deprive the landlord of his remedy by distress (z), and that no sufficient goods remained on the premises to satisfy the rent then due (a). The mere removal of goods by the tenant from the demised premises, when rent is in arrear, is not of itself fraudulent as against the landlord (b); nor is every conveying away of the goods of a tenant penal, although it may operate to defeat the landlord's right (c). To constitute a fraudulent removal, the fraud must be that of the tenant or person removing the property for his benefit (c). The statute was never meant to extend to a creditor who is seeking payment of his debt *bonâ fide;* and such creditor may, for the purpose of satisfying such debt and with the assent of the debtor, take possession of his goods,

---

(x) Per Martin, B., in *Foulger* v. *Taylor*, 5 H. & N., at p. 210; *Thornton* v. *Adams*, 5 M. & S. 38; *Postman* v. *Harrell*, 6 C. & P. 225; *Fletcher* v. *Marillier*, 9 A. & E. 457.

(y) *Wood* v. *Nunn*, 5 Bing. 10.

(z) *Parry* v. *Duncan*, 7 Bing. 243, 246; *John* v. *Jenkins*, 1 Cr. & M. 227.

(a) *Opperman* v. *Smith*, 4 D. & R. 33; *Parry* v. *Duncan*, 7 Bing. 243. But see *Gilham* v. *Arkwright*, 16 L. T. 88; Woodfall, L. & T. 422.

(b) *Parry* v. *Duncan*, 7 Bing. 243, 246.

(c) *Bach* v. *Meats*, 5 M. & S. 200, 204–206.

and remove them from the premises without incurring any penalty under the statute, even though he knows that the debtor is in distressed circumstances, and is apprehensive that his goods may be distrained (c).

That the goods were carried off *after* rent had become due (d). The landlord is, however, justified in following and distraining goods which have been removed on the morning of the day on which rent became due (e).

3. Rent due.

3. *When Distress must be made.*

It shall be lawful for any person or persons, having any rent in arrear or due upon any lease for life or for years or at will ended or determined, to distrain for such arrears after the determination of the said respective leases, in the same manner as they might have done if such lease had not been ended or determined; provided that such distress be made within the space of six calendar months after the determination of such lease, and during the continuance of such landlord's title, and during the possession of the tenant from whom such arrears became due (f) (or of his administrator, if the tenancy continues after the death of the tenant (g)).

Stat. 8 Anne, c. 14, s. 6. Landlord may distrain for rent after determination of lease.

Sect. 7. Distress to be made within six months after determination of lease and during possession of tenant.

There is nothing in this statute confining its operation to a wrongful holding over, or to a holding of the whole of the demised premises (h). Hence, where a

---

(c) *Bach* v. *Meats,* 5 M. & S. 200, 204, 206.

(d) *Watson* v. *Main,* 3 Esp. 15; *Furneaux* v. *Fotherby and Clarke,* 4 Camp. 136; *Rand* v. *Vaughan,* 1 Bing. N. C. 767.

(e) *Dibble* v. *Bowater,* 2 E. & B. 564; 22 L. J., Q. B. 396. See ante, pp. 114, 132.

(f) See *Coupland* v. *Maynard,* 12 East, 134; *Taylerson* v. *Peters,* 7 A. & E. 110.

(g) *Turner* v. *Barnes,* 2 B. & S. 435; 31 L. J., Q. B. 170.

(h) Judgment in *Nuttall* v. *Staunton,* 4 B. & C., at p. 56.

tenant, by permission of the landlord, remains in possession of part of a farm after the expiration of his tenancy, the landlord may distrain on that part within six months after the expiration of the tenancy (*i*). The statute, however, does not apply where the interest under the lease is undetermined. A custom of the country under which the tenant is entitled to leave his awaygoing crops in the barns, or to use the barns to thrash his corn and fodder his cattle, for a certain time after the expiration of the lease, operates as a prolongation of the term, and during such prolongation the landlord may distrain independently of the statute (*j*).

<small>Stat. 3 & 4 Will. 4, c. 27, s. 2.
Distress for rent-charge to be made within twenty years after right to distrain accrues.</small>

No person shall make a distress to recover any rent (charge (*k*)), but within twenty years next after the time at which the right to make such distress shall have first accrued to some person through whom he claims; or if such right shall not have accrued to any person through whom he claims, then within twenty years next after the time at which the right to make such distress shall have first accrued to the person making the same (*i.e.*, twenty years from the last payment of rent (*l*)).

<small>Time at which distress must be made.</small>

A distress must be made in the daytime (*m*). If made before sunrise, or after sunset, it will be illegal, although at the time there may be ample daylight (*n*). Persons who distrain ought not, however, to go so near these limits as to raise any doubt on the subject (*o*).

<small>Postponement</small>

A landlord may expressly agree not to distrain for

(*i*) *Nuttall* v. *Staunton*, 4 B. & C. 51.

(*j*) *Beavan* v. *Delahay*, 1 H. Bl. 5, see note (*a*), p. 7; *Boraston* v. *Green*, 16 East, at p. 81; *Knight* v. *Benett*, 3 Bing. 364, 366. See *post*, Chap. VI., Sect. 2 (2).

(*k*) See *Grant* v. *Ellis*, 9 M. & W. 113.

(*l*) Sect. 3; *Owen* v. *De Beauvoir*, 16 M. & W. 547; 5 Ex. 166.

(*m*) See *ante*, p. 132, as to the day on which it must be made.

(*n*) *Aldenburgh* v. *Peaple*, 6 C. & P. 212; *Tutton* v. *Darke*, 5 H. & N. 647; 29 L. J., Ex. 271.

(*o*) Per Martin, B., 5 H. & N., at p. 655.

a certain time (*p*). Where there is no express contract, such an agreement may sometimes be implied; thus, on proof that the landlord of a farm permitted a sale by the tenant of the eatage of a pasture for a specified period, on condition that the amount produced by such sale was to be paid to the landlord, a contract may be inferred on his part not to distrain the cattle of the purchaser (*q*).

of right to distrain.

4. *Amount for which Distress may be made.*

No arrears of rent, or any damages in respect of such arrears of rent, shall be recovered by any distress, action or suit, but within six years next after the same respectively shall have become due, or next after an acknowledgment of the same in writing shall have been given to the person entitled thereto, or his agent, signed by the person by whom the same was payable, or his agent.

Stat. 3 & 4 Will. 4, c. 27, s. 42.

Six years' arrears of rent only recoverable by distress.

So long as the relation of landlord and tenant subsists, the right of the landlord to rent is not barred by non-payment, but under the above statute the amount recoverable is limited to six years' arrears (*r*).

The common law does not cast any obligation on the person distraining to inform the tenant what is the amount of arrears for which the distress is made (*s*). The person distraining is entitled to a tender of the amount really due, and upon his refusal to accept that sum, the tenant's course is to replevy the goods (*t*). Hence no action can be maintained for distraining for more rent than is due, even when it is alleged to

Distress for more rent than is due.

(*p*) *Giles* v. *Spencer*, 3 C. B., N. S. 244; 26 L. J., C. P. 237. See *Welsh* v. *Rose*, 6 Bing. 638.
(*q*) *Horsford* v. *Webster*, 1 Cr. M. & R. 696.
(*r*) *Archbold* v. *Scully*, 9 H. L.
C. 360.
(*s*) Judgment in *Tancred* v. *Leyland*, 16 Q. B., at p. 680. See also 11 Ex. 879.
(*t*) *Glynn* v. *Thomas*, 11 Ex. 870; 25 L. J., Ex. 125.

have been done maliciously (*u*), unless it appears that the goods seized and sold were of greater value than was necessary to satisfy the arrears of rent actually due (*x*).

Distress after bankruptcy.

A distress for rent levied after the commencement of the bankruptcy of the tenant is available only for one year's rent accrued due prior to the date of the order of adjudication (*y*).

5. *Mode of making Distress.*

Warrant of distress.

The landlord may, of course, distrain in person; but the more prudent course is to employ an experienced bailiff, who should be authorized by a warrant of distress signed by the landlord (*z*). The indemnity to

Implied indemnity to bailiff.

the bailiff, implied from the warrant of distress, extends only to acts properly done by him in the exercise of his authority (*a*). The duty of using proper care and diligence in ascertaining that the distress may be safely made is cast upon the bailiff in cases of ordinary distresses for rent, unless the landlord by his conduct has dispensed with it (*b*). The land-

---

(*u*) *Stevenson* v. *Newnham*, 13 C. B. 285; 22 L. J., C. P. 110.

(*x*) *Wilkinson* v. *Terry*, 1 Moo. & Rob. 377; *Tancred* v. *Leyland*, 16 Q. B. 669; 20 L. J., Q. B. 316; *Glynn* v. *Thomas*, 11 Ex. 870; 25 L. J., Ex. 125; *French* v. *Phillips*, 1 H. & N. 564; 26 L. J., Ex. 82.

(*y*) Stat. 32 & 33 Vict. c. 71, s. 34. See *post*, p. 186.

(*z*) *Form of Warrant.*
To Mr. A. B., my bailiff.
Distrain such of the goods and chattels as may lawfully be distrained for rent in and upon the house [*or* farm] and premises occupied by C. D., situate at ——, in the parish of ——, in the county of ——, for £——, being the amount of [one half-year's] rent due to me in respect of the same, on the —— day of —— last, and proceed thereon for the recovery of the said rent as the law directs.

E. F.

Dated the —— day of ——, 18—.

An authority to distrain does not require a stamp. *Pyle* v. *Partridge*, 15 M. & W. 20; 15 L. J., Ex. 129.

(*a*) See Bullen & Leake's Pleadings, 152, n. (*a*) (2nd ed.).

(*b*) Judgment in *Toplis* v. *Grane*, 5 Bing. N. C., at p. 651.

lord may recover from the bailiff damage occasioned by his negligence or misconduct (*c*). An express indemnity is frequently appended to the distress-warrant. After an authority to a bailiff to distrain the goods of the tenant, an indemnity against all costs and charges that he may be at on that account, applies only to cases where the distress is illegal on the ground that the landlord has no right to put in a distress (*d*). An indemnity against all costs in respect to any law expenses, actions that may arise, and all charges or expenses on that account, extends to the costs of defending an action wrongfully brought against the bailiff by the tenant (*e*).

<small>Express indemnity to bailiff.</small>

The landlord is responsible to the tenant for irregularities committed by the bailiff in carrying out his instructions; such, for instance, as selling the goods without notice of distress, or without appraisement (*f*). But the landlord is not liable for the wrongful act of his bailiff in seizing what his warrant does not authorize him to seize, unless the landlord ratifies the bailiff's act, with knowledge of the wrongful seizure (*g*), or chooses, without inquiry, to take the risk upon himself and to adopt the bailiff's acts (*h*).

<small>Landlord's liability to tenant for acts of bailiff.</small>

It is desirable, though not essential, that the arrears of rent should be formally demanded from the tenant before the distress is made. If the rent due, without any additional sum for expenses, is unconditionally

<small>Demand of rent.</small>

(*c*) 2 Ch. Pl. 503 (7th ed.); Woodfall, L. & T. 413.

(*d*) *Draper* v. *Thompson*, 4 C. & P. 84, 86.

(*e*) See *Ibbett* v. *De La Salle*, 6 H. & N. 233; 30 L. J., Ex. 44.

(*f*) *Haseler* v. *Lemoyne*, 5 C. B., N. S. 530; 28 L. J., C. P. 103. See *post*, p. 180, as to other irregularities.

(*g*) See *Moore* v. *Drinkwater*, 1 F. & F. 134.

(*h*) *Lewis* v. *Read*, 13 M. & W. 834; 14 L. J., Ex. 295; *Freeman* v. *Rosher*, 13 Q. B. 780; 18 L. J., Q. B. 340; *Haseler* v. *Lemoyne*, 5 C. B., N. S. 530; 28 L. J., C. P. 103. But see *Gauntlett* v. *King*, 3 C. B., N. S. 59.

154 TERMS OF TENANCY.

Effect of tender before seizure.

tendered to the landlord, or his agent or bailiff authorized to receive it (*k*), before seizure made, though after the warrant has been delivered to the bailiff, it is illegal to proceed with the distress (*l*). A sufficient tender before the distress renders the whole proceeding illegal: a sufficient tender after distress, but before the goods are impounded, renders the subsequent detainer illegal (*m*).

Entry.

In going to distrain, it is doubtful whether the landlord may lawfully gain access to the tenant's house by climbing over a fence (*n*). If the door of the house is shut, the landlord has authority by law to open it in the ordinary way in which other persons can do it, when it is left so as to be accessible to all who have occasion to go into the premises (*o*); as, for instance, by lifting a latch or pulling out a staple which serves to keep the door closed (*o*). It has been said that entry may be lawfully made through an open window (*p*); but it is illegal to open a window for the purpose of entering, whether such window is fastened with a hasp (*q*) or shut and not fastened (*r*). If the outer door is open, the person distraining may break open an inner door

---

(*k*) *Hatch* v. *Hale*, 15 Q. B. 10; 19 L. J., Q. B. 289.

(*l*) *Bennett* v. *Bayes*, 5 H. & N. 391; 29 L. J., Ex. 224. See *Branscomb* v. *Bridges*, 1 B. & C. 145; *Holland* v. *Bird*, 10 Bing. 15.

(*m*) See judgment in *Holland* v. *Bird*, 10 Bing., at p. 18. As to the effect of a tender after the goods are impounded, see *post*, p. 166.

(*n*) *Scott* v. *Buckley*, 16 L. T., N. S. 573. But see *Eldridge* v. *Stacey*, 15 C. B., N. S. 458; 12 W. R. 51; 9 L. T., N. S. 291.

(*o*) *Ryan* v. *Shilcock*, 7 Ex. 72, 76; 21 L. J., Ex. 55. See the observations of Cockburn, C. J., on the doctrine laid down in this case, in L. R., 2 Q. B. 594. See also *Curtis* v. *Hubbard*, 1 Hill's Rep. (New York) 336.

(*p*) Per Pollock, C. B., in *Nixon* v. *Freeman*, 5 H. & N., at p. 652; 29 L. J., Ex. 271. See *Gould* v. *Bradstock*, 4 Taunt. 562.

(*q*) *Hancock* v. *Austin*, 14 C. B., N. S. 634, 639; 32 L. J., C. P. 252.

(*r*) *Nash* v. *Lucas*, L. R., 2 Q. B. 590.

or lock (*s*). But the *outer* door (*t*) or window (*u*) of the tenant's house or stable (*x*) must not be forcibly broken open, or the landlord who has entered to distrain, and has sold the goods distrained, will be liable to an action of trespass, in which the tenant may recover the full value of such goods, although the proceeds of the sale have been applied in satisfaction of the rent (*y*).

If, however, a lawful entry has once been effected, but the person distraining is forcibly turned out of possession (*z*), or kept out of possession (*a*), there being no evidence of an abandonment of the goods (*b*), he is justified in breaking open the outer door in order to regain possession. But when a person has merely got his foot and arm between the door and the lintel, or by putting a pair of shears between the door and the lintel, has prevented the door from being closed, he has not such a possession as will entitle him to break open a door or window in order to gain admission to the house (*c*). It seems that after the person distraining has lawfully entered, he may break open the outer door in order to remove the goods distrained (*d*).

When outer door may be broken open.

It would appear that an actual entry upon the demised premises by the person distraining is not in all

Constructive entry.

(*s*) *Browning* v. *Dann*, Bull. N. P. 81; 2 Wms. Saund. 284, note.

(*t*) See *Semayne's Case*, 5 Co. R. 91; 1 Sm. L. C. 88 (6th ed.).

(*u*) *Attack* v. *Bramwell*, 3 B. & S. 520; 32 L. J., Q. B. 146. See *Hancock* v. *Austin*, 14 C. B., N. S. 634; 32 L. J., C. P. 252.

(*x*) *Brown* v. *Glenn*, 16 Q. B. 254; 20 L. J., Q. B. 205. As to the exception in the case of goods which have been fraudulently removed, see *ante*, p. 146.

(*y*) *Attack* v. *Bramwell*, 3 B. & S. 520; 32 L. J., Q. B. 146.

(*z*) *Eagleton* v. *Gutteridge*, 11 M. & W. 465, 469; 12 L. J., Ex., at p. 361; *Eldridge* v. *Stacey*, 15 C. B., N. S. 458.

(*a*) *Bannister* v. *Hyde*, 2 F. & E. 627; 29 L. J., Q. B. 141.

(*b*) See *post*, p. 163.

(*c*) *Boyd* v. *Profaze*, 16 L. T., N. S. 431.

(*d*) *Pugh* v. *Griffith*, 7 A. & E. 827.

cases necessary. Where the article seized is just inside the door, the tenant at the door, and the agent of the landlord in such a position as to be able in one moment to put her foot into the room, it will be taken that she is constructively in the room (e).

Seizure.

Entry having been made, the next step is to seize the goods. For this purpose, any distinct expression of an intention to distrain will suffice (f). It is not necessary that an actual formal seizure should be made; it is enough if the landlord takes sufficient means to prevent the articles on the premises from being taken away (e). A refusal by the landlord to allow the goods of the tenant to be taken away until the rent is paid, may amount to a seizure (g). A seizure of some goods as a distress, in the name of all the goods in the house, will operate as a valid seizure of all the goods in the house (h).

Requisites to seizure.

In making the seizure the following points should be observed:—

1. Must not be excessive.

That the goods distrained do not greatly exceed in saleable value (i) the amount of the arrears of rent and costs of the distress. When a landlord is about to make a distress he is not bound to calculate very nicely the value of the property seized; but he must take care that some proportion is kept between that and the sum for which he is entitled to take it (k).

(e) See judgment of Cockburn, C. J., in *Cramer* v. *Mott*, 39 L. J., Q. B., at p. 173.

(f) Bullen on Distress, 131. See *Swann* v. *Falmouth*, 8 B. & C. 456; *Hutchins* v. *Scott*, 2 M. & W. 809; *Thomas* v. *Harries*, 1 M. & Gr. 695; *Tennant* v. *Field*, 8 E. & B. 336; 27 L. J., Q. B. 33. See *Spice* v. *Webb*, 2 Jur. 943.

(g) *Wood* v. *Nunn*, 5 Bing. 10; 6 L. J., C. P. 198; *Cramer* v. *Mott*, 39 L. J., Q. B. 172; L. R., 5 Q. B. 357.

(h) *Dod* v. *Monger*, 6 Mod. 215.

(i) See *Wells* v. *Moody*, 7 C. & P. 59.

(k) Judgment of Bayley, J., in *Willoughby* v. *Backhouse*, 2 B. & C., at p. 823.

"Distresses shall be reasonable and not too great, and he that taketh great and unreasonable distresses shall be grievously amerced for the excess of such distresses." If goods are seized to an excessive amount,—as, for instance, if goods worth between 30*l*. and 40*l*. are distrained for the rent of ten guineas (*l*), or goods worth 260*l*. for the rent of 121*l*. 15*s*. 6*d*. (*m*), the landlord will be liable to an action for damages; and the tenant is entitled in such action to recover a verdict with nominal damages, although he fails to prove any actual damage, having had the use of the goods all the time (*n*). To determine whether a distress is excessive, it must be ascertained what the goods seized would have sold for at a broker's sale (*o*). An actual sale made under the distress, though not proved to be fraudulent or unfair, is not a conclusive test of value, and the tenant may therefore maintain an action, although the sale of the goods distrained (less the expenses) did not realize the amount of rent due (*p*). If only a single chattel is to be found on the premises, the person distraining will not be liable to an action for excessive distress, though the value of such chattel exceeds the amount of the rent due (*q*).

Stat. 52 Hen. 3, c. 4.
Distresses to be reasonable.

While avoiding an excessive seizure, however, the person distraining should take sufficient to cover the arrears of rent; for he cannot distrain twice for the same rent where he might have taken sufficient at first (*r*),

2. Sufficien must be taken.

(*l*) *Branscombe* v. *Bridges*, 3 Stark. 171.
(*m*) *Chandler* v. *Doulton*, 3 H. & C. 553; 34 L. J., Ex. 89.
(*n*) *Bayliss* v. *Fisher*, 7 Bing. 153; *Piggott* v. *Birtles*, 1 M. & W. 441; 5 L. J., Ex. 193; *Chandler* v. *Doulton*, 3 H. & C.

553; 34 L. J., Ex. 89.
(*o*) *Wells* v. *Moody*, 7 C. & P. 59.
(*p*) *Smith* v. *Ashforth*, 29 L. J., Ex. 259.
(*q*) *Avenell* v. *Croker*, Moo. & M. 172. See *Field* v. *Mitchell*, 6 Esp. 71.
(*r*) Judgment of Parke, B., in

158   TERMS OF TENANCY.

When second distress may be made for same rent.

unless, perhaps, where the value of the goods cannot be readily estimated. If a man *bonâ fide* mistake the value of the goods seized (which may be of uncertain or imaginary value, as pictures, jewels, racehorses, &c.), he may make a further seizure (*s*). The landlord may also distrain again if he is prevented by the unlawful act of the tenant from realizing the distress (*t*); as, for instance, if the tenant prevents a purchaser from taking away an article sold under the distress (*t*). If the landlord is induced to withdraw the distress by a false assurance by the tenant that a particular debt has been satisfied, the landlord, on the creditor's proceeding to judgment and execution, is entitled to a year's rent, under stat. 8 Ann. c. 14 (*u*).

Impounding.

After seizing the goods, the person distraining must impound them. In order to constitute an impounding it is not necessary that the whole of the goods distrained should be put together or removed from the premises (*x*).

Stat. 11 Geo. 2, c. 19, s. 10. Goods distrained may be secured and sold on premises.

It shall be lawful for any person lawfully taking any distress for any kind of rent, to impound or otherwise secure the distress so made, of what nature or kind soever it may be, in such place or on such part of the premises chargeable with the rent as shall be most convenient for the impounding and securing such distress; and to appraise, sell and dispose of the same upon the premises in like manner and under the like directions

Bagge v. *Mawby*, 8 Ex. 641; 22 L. J., Ex. 236; *Dawson* v. *Cropp*, 1 C. B. 961; 14 L. J., C. P. 281; *Lear* v. *Caldicott*, 4 Q. B. 123. See *Smith* v. *Goodwin*, 4 B. & Ad. 413.

(*s*) *Hutchins* v. *Chambers*, 1 Burr., at p. 589. See *Lingham* v. *Warren*, 2 B. & B. 36.

(*t*) *Lee* v. *Cooke*, 2 H. & N. 584; 3 H. & N. 203; 27 L. J., Ex. 337.

(*u*) *Wollaston* v. *Stafford*, 15 C. B. 278; *post*, p. 181.

(*x*) Per Lord Campbell, C. J., in *Johnson* v. *Upham*, 2 E. & E., at p. 255. See *Washborn* v. *Black*, 11 East, 405, note (*a*).

and restraints as any person taking a distress for rent may now do off the premises by virtue of (stats. 2 W. & M. c. 5 and 4 Geo. 2, c. 28); and it shall be lawful for any person to come and go to and from such place where any distress for rent shall be impounded, in order to view, appraise and buy, and also in order to carry off the same; and if any pound-breach or rescous shall be made of any goods or chattels, or stock distrained for rent, and impounded by virtue of this act, the person aggrieved thereby shall have the like remedy as in cases of pound-breach or rescous is given by the said statute.

Furniture may be secured in a room or rooms of the tenant's house, or, if the tenant gives permission, may be left in its ordinary position (*y*). Where such permission is not given, in common cases a person distraining in a dwelling-house must not take the whole of it in which to place the goods distrained, but must select one room for that purpose, or remove the goods out of the house (*z*). An action of trespass lies against a landlord who, on making a distress for rent, turns the tenant's wife out of possession and keeps the premises on which he has impounded his distress (*a*). It seems, however, that the whole house may be locked up, where it is absolutely necessary for the safe keeping of the goods distrained (*b*).

<small>Furniture.</small>

(Persons distraining sheaves or cocks of corn, or corn loose or in the straw, or hay in any barn or stack or

<small>Corn, straw or hay.</small>

(*y*) See *Cox* v. *Painter*, 7 C. & P. 767; *Washborn* v. *Black*, 11 East, 405, note (*a*); *Tennant* v. *Field*, 8 E. & B. 336; 27 L. J., Q. B. 33.

(*z*) Per Parke, B., in *Woods* v. *Durrant*, 16 M. & W., at p. 158;

16 L. J., Ex., at p. 316.

(*a*) *Etherton* v. *Popplewell*, 1 East, 139; *Smith* v. *Ashforth*, 29 L. J., Ex. 259.

(*b*) See 16 M. & W. 158; *Cox* v. *Painter*, 7 C. & P. 767.

Stat. 2 Will. & M. sess. 1, c. 5, s. 3. May be impounded in place where found.	otherwise upon any part of the land, may) lock up or detain the same in the place where the same shall be found, for a distress, until the same shall be replevied; and in default of replevying the same within (five days (sect. 2)), to sell the same after appraisement thereof; so as, nevertheless, such corn, grain or hay be not removed by the person distraining, to the damage of the owner thereof, out of the place where the same shall be found and seized, but be kept there (as impounded) until the same shall be replevied or sold.
Growing crops. Stat. 11 Geo. 2, c. 19, s. 8. When ripe, may be impounded in barns on farm.	The landlord, or his bailiff or other person empowered by him, (having distrained growing crops, may) lay up the same when ripe in the barns or other proper place on the premises demised; and in case there shall be no barn or proper place on the premises demised, then in any other barn or proper place which such landlord shall hire or otherwise procure for that purpose, and as near as may be to the premises, and in convenient time appraise, sell or otherwise dispose of the same towards satisfaction of the rent for which such distress shall have been taken, and of the charges of such distress, appraisement and sale, in the same manner as other goods and chattels may be seized, distrained and disposed of; and the appraisement ███ of to be taken when cut, gathered, cured and made, and not before.
Sect. 9. Notice of place where crops are deposited to be given to tenant.	Notice of the place where the goods and chattels so distrained shall be deposited shall, within one week after the depositing thereof in such place, be given to such tenant or left at the last place of his abode.
Cattle.	Cattle may be impounded in the byre or field where they are at the time of the distress (c). "No distress of
Stat. 1 & 2 Ph. & M. c. 12.	cattle shall be driven out of the hundred, rape, wapen-

(c) *Thomas* v. *Harries*, 1 M. & Gr. 695; *Castleman* v. *Hicks*, Car. & M. 266.

take or lathe where such distress shall be taken, except to a pound overt within the same shire, not above three miles distant from the place where the said distress is taken (*d*). No cattle or other goods distrained at one time shall be impounded in several places, whereby the owner of such distress shall be constrained to sue several replevies for the delivery of the said distress so taken at one time. *Cattle distrained not to be driven out of hundred, &c. where taken, except to pound in same shire not more than three miles distant.*

Every person who shall impound or cause to be impounded in any pound or receptacle of the like nature any animal, shall supply during such confinement a sufficient quantity of fit and wholesome food and water to such animal; and every such person who shall refuse or neglect to supply such animal with such food and water as aforesaid shall for. every such offence forfeit twenty shillings. *Stat. 12 & 13 Vict. c. 92, s. 5. Persons impounding animals to supply food and water.*

In case any animal shall at any time be impounded as aforesaid, and shall continue confined without fit and sufficient food and water for more than twelve successive hours, it shall be lawful for any person whomsoever from time to time, and as often as shall be necessary, to enter any pound or other receptacle of the like nature in which any such animal shall be so confined, and to supply such animal with fit and sufficient food and water during so long a time as such animal shall remain confined as aforesaid, without being liable to any action of trespass or other proceeding by any person whomsoever for such entry for the purposes aforesaid; and the reasonable cost of such food and water shall be paid by the owner of such animal, before such animal is removed, to the person who shall supply the same, and the said cost may be recovered (by summary proceedings before a justice of the peace). *Sect. 6. In default, any person may supply food and water.*

(*d*) See also stat. 3 Edw. 1, c. 16.

F.   M

162 TERMS OF TENANCY.

Stat. 17 & 18 Vict. c. 60, s. 1.

Person impounding animal and supplying food and water, may recover from the owner not exceeding double value of such food and water.

Every person who shall impound, as in the (above) act mentioned, any animal and shall supply such animal with food and water as therein mentioned, may recover from the owner of such animal not exceeding double the value of the food and water so supplied, in like manner as is by the last-mentioned act provided for the recovery of penalties under the same act. And every person who shall supply food and water shall be at liberty, if he shall so think fit, instead of proceeding for the recovery of the value thereof as last aforesaid, after the expiration of seven clear days from the time of impounding the same, to sell any such animal openly at any public market, after having given three days' public printed notice thereof, for the most money that can be got for the same, and to apply the produce in discharge of the value of such food and water so supplied as aforesaid, and the expenses of and attending such sale, rendering the overplus, if any, to the owner of such animal.

Power to sell animal after seven days' impounding.

Goods distrained must not be used.

The person distraining must not use the goods or work the cattle he has impounded. If he takes an animal out of the place where it was originally impounded for the purpose of making an unlawful use of it, the owner is justified in interfering and recovering possession of the animal (*e*). Milch cows which have been impounded may, however, be milked by the person distraining (*f*). If the condition of the pound is such that it is unfit to put cattle in at the time of the impounding the person distraining is responsible for injury thereby occasioned to the animals (*g*). But if

Injuries to goods impounded.

(*e*) *Smith* v. *Wright*, 6 H. & N. 821; 30 L. J., Ex. 313.
(*f*) See *Bagshawe* v. *Goward*, Cro. Jac., at p. 148.
(*g*) Per Bramwell, B, in *Bignell* v. *Clarke*, 5 H. & N., at p. 487; 29 L. J., Ex. 257; *Wilder* v. *Speer*, 8 A. & E. 547.

they die in the pound or escape without any default on the part of the person distraining, it seems that he may distrain again (*h*).

It is usual for the person distraining to leave a man in possession of the goods distrained; but the quitting possession of goods by the landlord after he has distrained them, is not necessarily an abandonment of the distress (*i*). Whether the landlord has or has not abandoned the distress, is a question of fact to be determined by a jury (*k*). An abandonment will not be inferred where the broker is forcibly expelled, and regains possession after an interval of three weeks (*k*); or where the man in possession, having quitted the house in which the goods are impounded in order to obtain refreshment, finds on his return the door locked against him by the tenant, and breaks it open for the purpose of re-entering (*l*); or where the person distraining, having permitted the goods of a stranger, who has had no notice of the distress, to be taken off the premises merely for a temporary purpose, they are subsequently restored by the voluntary act of the person who took them away (*m*).

Abandonment of distress.

Where goods distrained are removed by force, a rescue or poundbreach is committed. "Upon any poundbreach or rescue of goods distrained for rent, the person grieved thereby shall recover treble damages, and (a full and reasonable indemnity as to all costs, charges and expenses incurred in and about the ac-

Rescue or poundbreach. Stat. 2 Will. & M. sess. 1, c. 5, s. 4.

(*h*) *Vasper* v. *Eddowes*, Holt, N. P. 257; 1 Salk. 248.
(*i*) Per Wightman, J., in *Bannister* v. *Hyde*, 2 E. & E., at p. 631. See *Swann* v. *Falmouth*, 8 B. & C. 456.
(*k*) *Eldridge* v. *Stacey*, 15 C. B., N. S. 458, 459; 12 W. R. 51; 9 L. T., N. S. 291. But see *Russell* v. *Rider*, 6 C. & P. 416.
(*l*) *Bannister* v. *Hyde*, 2 E. & E. 627; 29 L. J., Q. B. 141.
(*m*) *Kerby* v. *Harding*, 6 Ex. 234; 20 L. J., Ex. 163.

tion (*n*)) against the offender or offenders in any such rescue or poundbreach, any or either of them, or against the owner of the goods distrained, in case the same be afterwards found to have come to his use or possession." The landlord may seize again the rescued goods wherever he may happen to find them, if he can do so without breach of the peace, and upon fresh pursuit (*o*). If he abandons the distress, the tenant may retake it without committing a rescue (*p*).

6. *Requisites to Sale under Distress.*

The goods distrained may either be sold or kept as a pledge until they are replevied or the arrears of rent with expenses are paid. If it is intended to sell the goods distrained, an inventory of them should be made, expressing clearly and with certainty what goods are taken (*q*), and at the foot of the inventory there should be written (*r*) a notice of the distress, stating the cause of taking (*s*), and also, if the goods are distrained under stat. 11 Geo. 2, c. 19, the place where they are lodged or deposited (*t*). The tenant is not bound by the state-

---

(*n*) Stat. 5 & 6 Vict. c. 97, s. 2.

(*o*) *Rich* v. *Woolley*, 7 Bing. 651, 661.

(*p*) *Dod* v. *Monger*, 6 Mod., at p. 216.

(*q*) *Kerby* v. *Harding*, 6 Ex. 234; 20 L. J., Ex. 163. See *Wakeman* v. *Lindsey*, 14 Q. B. 625; 19 L. J., Q. B. 166.

(*r*) *Wilson* v. *Nightingale*, 8 Q. B. 1034; 15 L. J., Q. B. 309.

(*s*) Stat. 2 Will. & M. sess. 1, c. 5, s. 2.

(*t*) Stat. 11 Geo. 2, c. 19, s. 9. The inventory and notice may be in the following forms:—

An inventory of the goods and chattels distrained by [A. B., of ——, by the authority and on behalf of] E. F., of ——, this —— day of ——, 18—, in and upon the house [farm] and premises in the occupation of C. D., situate at ——, in the parish of ——, in the county of ——, for £——, being the amount of [one half-year's] rent due to the said E. F. in respect of the same premises on the —— day of ——, 18—.

Goods in the Dwelling-house.

Kitchen.—One table [*describe similarly the furniture seized in each room*].

Cattle in the Fields.

Field called Thorncroft.—One

ment of the cause of taking contained in the notice, since he may distrain for one cause and afterwards, in a replevin or other action, may avow or justify for a different cause (*u*). The want of notice does not render a distress invalid, but the person distraining cannot proceed to sell the goods distrained (*x*). The omission to state in the notice that the goods are impounded does not make the impounding void (*y*).

The inventory and notice should either be given personally to the tenant (*z*) or be left at the chief mansion-house or other most notorious place on the premises

white milch cow, one bay horse, six Leicester ewes [*describe similarly the cattle seized in each field*].

Growing Crops.

Field called Holme.—About three acres of barley [*describe similarly the crops in each field*].

To Mr. C. D.

Take notice that [by the authority and on behalf of Mr. E. F., your landlord] I have this day distrained, on the premises above mentioned, the goods and chattels specified in the above inventory, for £ ——, being the amount of [one half-year's] rent due to [me, *or* the said E. F.] in respect of the same premises, on the —— day of ——, 18 —, [which goods are secured upon the said premises, *or, if removed*, are lodged or deposited at ——]. And unless you pay the said rent, together with the charges of distraining for the same, within five days from the service hereof, the said goods and chattels will be appraised and sold, according to law [*in a dis-tress of growing crops, after the word " same," say*, the said growing crops, when ripe, will be cut, gathered, cured and laid up in the barn or other proper place on the said premises, and in convenient time sold towards satisfaction of the said rent, and of the charges of such distress, according to law].

Dated, &c.   E. F.

[*or* A. B., bailiff of the said E. F.]

(*u*) *Gwinnet* v. *Phillips*, 3 T. R. 643; *Crowther* v. *Ramsbottom*, 7 T. R. 654, 658. Judgment in *Etherton* v. *Popplewell*, 1 East, at p. 142. See *Phillips* v. *Whitsed*, 2 E. & E. 804; 29 L. J., Q. B. 164; *Wootley* v. *Gregory*, 2 Y. & J. 536; *Trent* v. *Hunt*, 9 Ex. 14; 22 L. J., Ex. 318.

(*x*) *Trent* v. *Hunt*, 9 Ex. 14; 22 L. J., Ex. 318.

(*y*) *Tennant* v. *Field*, 8 E. & B. 336.

(*z*) *Walter* v. *Rumbal*, 1 Ld. Raym. 53.

charged with the rent in respect of which the distress is made.

Tender of rent and expenses before impounding.

After the goods have been seized, but before they are impounded, the tenant may tender the amount of rent actually due, and the expenses of the distress, either to the landlord (*b*) or his agent or bailiff (*c*), and after such tender it is illegal to proceed with the distress, or to detain the goods distrained (*d*). A man left by the bailiff in possession has, however, no implied authority to receive a tender of the rent (*e*).

Tender after impounding.

A tender after goods have been impounded will not render the subsequent detention of them illegal (*f*); but if the tender is made within five days after the seizure under the distress, and the landlord subsequently sells the goods, the tenant may maintain an action against him (*g*).

Tender on distress of growing crops.

Stat. 11 Geo. 2, c. 19, s. 9.

On payment or tender of rent and costs before crops are cut, distress to cease.

If after any distress for arrears of rent taken of corn, grass, hops, roots, fruits, pulse or other product which shall be growing, and at any time before the same shall be ripe and cut, cured or gathered, the tenant, his executors, administrators or assigns, shall pay or cause to be paid to the landlord, or to the steward or other person usually employed to receive the rent of such landlord, the whole rent which shall be then in arrear,

---

(*b*) *Smith* v. *Goodwin*, 4 B. & Ad. 413.

(*c*) *Hatch* v. *Hale*, 15 Q. B. 10; 19 L. J., Q. B. 289. See *Pilkington* v. *Hastings*, Cro. Eliz. 813; *Browne* v. *Powell*, 4 Bing. 230.

(*d*) *Vertue* v. *Beasley*, 1 Moo. & Rob. 21; *Evans* v. *Elliott*, 5 A. & E. 142; *Holland* v. *Bird*, 10 Bing. 15; *Loring* v. *Warburton*, E., B. & E. 507; 28 L. J., Q. B. 31.

(*e*) *Boulton* v. *Reynolds*, 2 E. & E. 369; 29 L. J., Q. B. 11.

(*f*) *Six Carpenters' Case*, 8 Co. R., at p. 147; *Ladd* v. *Thomas*, 12 A. & E. 117; *Tennant* v. *Field*, 8 E. & B. 336. See *West* v. *Nibbs*, 4 C. B. 172; 17 L. J., C. P. 150.

(*g*) *Johnson* v. *Upham*, 2 E. & E. 250; 28 L. J., Q. B. 252.

together with the full costs and charges of making such distress, then upon such payment or lawful tender thereof actually made, whereby the end of such distress will be fully answered, the same shall cease, and the corn, &c. so distrained shall be delivered up to the tenant, his executors, administrators or assigns.

In order to constitute a legal tender it is necessary that the sum actually due for rent and expenses of the distress should be unconditionally offered to the landlord (*h*).

Before proceeding to sell the goods distrained, "the person distraining shall, with the sheriff or under-sheriff of the county, or with the constable of the hundred, parish or place where such distress shall be taken, who are hereby required to be aiding and assisting therein, cause the goods and chattels so distrained to be appraised by two sworn appraisers, whom such sheriff, under-sheriff or constable are hereby empowered to swear to appraise the same truly, according to the best of their understandings." Though the rent distrained for does not exceed 20*l.*, two appraisers are necessary (*i*). If, however, the tenant expressly requests that appraisers may not be called in, and the goods are accordingly valued by the broker who made the seizure, the tenant cannot maintain an action for the irregularity (*k*). The appraisers must be reasonably competent, but need not be professional appraisers (*l*). The landlord or his bailiff must not appraise the

Appraisement.
Stat. 2 Will. & M. sess. 1, c. 5, s. 2.

(*h*) See *Finch* v. *Miller*, 5 C. B. 428; *Bowen* v. *Owen*, 11 Q. B. 130; 17 L. J., Q. B. 5.

(*i*) *Allen* v. *Flicker*, 10 A. & E. 640; but see *Fletcher* v. *Saunders*, 1 Moo. & Rob. 375; stat. 57 Geo. 3, c. 93, *Schedule; post*, p. 174.

(*k*) *Bishop* v. *Bryant*, 6 C. & P. 484.

(*l*) *Roden* v. *Eyton*, 6 C. B. 427; 18 L. J., C. P. 1.

goods (*m*). Before the appraisers make their appraisement (*n*), they must be sworn before the constable of the parish or place in which the distress is taken (*o*), who must attend with them at the time of the appraisement (*n*). The circumstance that the constable of the parish is not to be found at the time when he is wanted for this purpose does not authorize the interference of any other officer (*p*). The appraisement of growing crops distrained under stat. 11 Geo. 2, c. 19, s. 8, must not be taken before the crops are cut and gathered (*q*).

Having valued the goods, the appraisers usually indorse on a copy of the inventory a memorandum of their appraisement, which must be duly stamped (*r*). The duty on appraisements (*s*) is as follows:—

Stat. 33 & 34 Vict. c. 97, Schedule.

	£	s.	d.
Where the amount of the appraisement does not exceed £5	0	0	3

(*m*) *Andrews* v. *Russell*, Bull. N. P. 81 d; *Westwood* v. *Cowne*, 1 Stark. 172; *Lyon* v. *Weldon*, 2 Bing. 334.

(*n*) *Kenney* v. *May*, 1 Moo. & Rob. 56.

(*o*) *Avenell* v. *Croker*, M. & M. 172.

(*p*) Per Lord Tenterden, C. J., in *Avenell* v. *Croker*, M. & M., at p. 174.

(*q*) See *ante*, p. 160.

Form of Appraiser's Oath.

You, and each of you, shall well and truly appraise the goods and chattels specified in this inventory [*the constable must show the inventory*], according to the best of your understandings. So help you God.

Memorandum of Oath to be indorsed on the Inventory.

MEMORANDUM. On the ―― day of ――, 18 ―, G. H., of ――, and J. K., of ――, two sworn appraisers, were sworn upon the Holy Evangelists, by me, L. M., constable of the parish of ――, well and truly to appraise the goods and chattels specified in the within-written inventory, according to the best of their understandings.

As witness my hand,
L. M.

Present at the time of swearing the said G. H. and J. K. as above, and witness thereto, } N. O.

(*r*) *Form of Appraisement to be indorsed on Inventory.*

We, the undersigned G. H. and J. K., being duly sworn upon the Holy Evangelists by L. M., the

(*s*) See *post*, p. 169.

Where the amount of the appraisement—				£	s.	d.
Exceeds £5 and does not exceed £10				0	0	6
,,	10	,,	,, 20	0	1	0
,,	20	,,	,, 30	0	1	6
,,	30	,,	,, 40	0	2	0
,,	40	,,	,, 50	0	2	6
,,	50	,,	,, 100	0	5	0
,,	100	,,	,, 200	0	10	0
,,	200	,,	,, 500	0	15	0
,,	500	.	. . .	1	0	0

7. *Sale under the Distress.*

After five clear days, computed exclusively of the day of seizure (*t*), that is, five times twenty-four hours (*u*), have elapsed, provided the rent and costs of distress have not been paid or tendered, and the goods have not been replevied (*x*), the landlord may "lawfully sell the goods and chattels distrained for the best price that can be got for the same, towards satisfaction of the rent for which the said goods and chattels shall be distrained, and of the charges of such distress, appraisement and sale, leaving the overplus, if any (after payment of the rent and reasonable charges (*y*)), in the hands of the said sheriff, under-sheriff or constable, for the owner's use (and if the goods have been removed, returning the

Stat. 2 Will. & M. sess. 1, c. 5, s. 2.

constable of the parish of ——, well and truly to appraise the goods and chattels specified in the within-written inventory, according to the best of our understandings, having viewed the said goods and chattels, do appraise the same at the sum of —— pounds.

As witness our hands the —— day of —— 18 —.

G. H. } Sworn
J. K. } Appraisers.

(*s*) The same amount of duty was payable on appraisements made before 1871, under stat. 28 & 29 Vict. c. 96, s. 2.

(*t*) *Robinson* v. *Waddington*, 13 Q. B. 753; 18 L. J., Q. B. 250. See *Wallace* v. *King*, 1 H. Bl. 13.

(*u*) *Harper* v. *Taswell*, 6 C. & P. 166.

(*x*) See *post*, p. 176.

(*y*) *Lyon* v. *Tomkies*, 1 M. & W. 603.

surplus unsold to the premises from which the goods were taken (z)).

If the goods are not sold for the best price the tenant may bring an action against the landlord, and go into evidence to show that they were allowed to stand in the rain, and were improperly lotted (a); but goods sold at the appraised value are presumed to have been sold for the best price (b). It seems that there is no order required by law to be observed in the sale of goods under a distress. If the landlord distrains, among other goods, his tenant's cattle and beasts of the plough (c), it seems that he is not bound to sell the other goods first; and although it turns out after the sale (judging by the result) that there would have been sufficient to satisfy the rent and expenses without selling the cattle, the distress is not thereby proved to be illegal, if there was ground for supposing, from the appraisement of competent persons, made at the time of the seizure, that, without taking the cattle, the amount of the rent and expenses would not be realized (d). Where the goods of a lodger are distrained together with the goods of the tenant, and are sold first, after notice from the lodger, and the tenant's goods turn out to be sufficient to satisfy the rent and charges, the lodger is entitled to sue for an excessive distress (e).

It seems to be decided that a landlord who has distrained hay and straw prohibited by covenant from being carried off the premises, will render himself

(z) *Evans* v. *Wright*, 2 H. & N. 527; 27 L. J., Ex. 50.
(a) *Poynter* v. *Duckley*, 5 C. & P. 512.
(b) *Walter* v. *Rumbal*, 1 Ld. Raym., at p. 55.
(c) See *ante*, p. 143.
(d) *Jenner* v. *Yolland*, 6 Price, 3.
(e) *Wilkinson* v. *Ibbett*, 2 F. & F. 300.

liable to an action for not selling at the best price, if he sells such distress subject to a condition that the purchaser shall consume it on the premises, by reason whereof it produces less than the usual price (*f*).

The sale may, in general, be made either upon the demised premises, if the goods are impounded there, or at any other place. But corn, grain or hay (*g*) must not be " removed by the person or persons distraining, to the damage of the owner thereof, out of the place where the same shall be found and seized, but be kept there, as impounded, until the same shall be replevied or sold." Where sale may be made.
Stat. 2 Will. & M. sess. 1, c. 5, s. 3.
Corn, &c. not to be removed.

Until the goods distrained are sold, the property in them remains in the tenant (*h*), subject to the right of the landlord to detain or sell them. The person distraining does not acquire even the possession of the cattle or things distrained (*i*). Property in goods distrained.

Where the goods distrained are of small value, the appraisers sometimes take them at their own valuation, a receipt written at the foot of the inventory being considered a sufficient discharge (*k*). But this practice is so obviously unjust to the tenant that it should not be adopted in any case where the goods can be profitably disposed of by public auction. The *landlord* must not take the goods at the appraised value. If he does, the To whom sale may be made.

(*f*) *Ridgway* v. *Stafford*, 6 Ex. 404; 20 L. J., Ex. 226; *Roden* v. *Eyton*, 6 C. B. 427; 18 L. J., C. P. 1; *Jones* v. *Hamp*, cited in 10 M. & W. 710; 12 L. J., Ex. 322. See *Abbey* v. *Petch*, 8 M. & W. 419; 10 L. J., Ex. 455; *Frusher* v. *Lee*, 10 M. & W. 709; 12 L. J., Ex. 321.

(*g*) See *ante*, p. 159.

(*h*) *King* v. *England*, 4 B. & S. 782; 33 L. J., Q. B. 145, 146; *Turner* v. *Ford*, 15 M. & W. 212; 15 L. J., Ex. 215.

(*i*) *Rex* v. *Cotton*, Parker, at p. 121; *Turner* v. *Ford*, 15 M. & W. 212.

(*k*) See Bullen on Distress, 160.

transaction will not be considered as a sale, and the property in the goods will not be divested from the tenant or owner (*l*); unless they belong to the tenant, and are so taken with his consent (*m*).

When sale may be made.

If the sale is made before the expiration of five clear days, *and actual damage is thereby occasioned to the tenant*, he may maintain an action against the landlord (*n*); but the tenant is not entitled to a verdict unless he proves actual damage (*n*). It is lawful for the landlord, and those acting under him, to remain more than five days on the premises for the purpose of selling the goods distrained (*o*). If, however, the sale is not made, or the goods are not removed from the premises, within a reasonable time (*o*) after the expiration of the five days, the landlord will be liable to an action of trespass by the tenant (*p*). It must be left to the jury to say what is a reasonable time; in one case, where the distress was made on April 14th, and the sale on April 27th, the jury found that the sale was made within a reasonable time (*o*).

Postponement of sale.

The sale is often postponed at the request of the tenant (*q*), from whom the landlord should invariably obtain a written consent to his remaining on the premises (*r*).

(*l*) *King* v. *England*, 4 B. & S. 782; 33 L. J., Q. B. 145.

(*m*) See judgment of Blackburn, J., 33 L. J., Q. B., at p. 146.

(*n*) *Lucas* v. *Tarleton*, 3 H. & N. 116; 27 L. J., Ex. 246; *Rodgers* v. *Parker*, 18 C. B. 112; 25 L. J., C. P. 220; *post*, p. 181.

(*o*) *Pitt* v. *Shew*, 4 B. & A. 208.

(*p*) *Griffin* v. *Scott*, 2 Ld. Raym. 1424; *Winterbourne* v. *Morgan*, 11 East, 395.

(*q*) See *Harrison* v. *Barry*, 7 Price, 690; *Fisher* v. *Algar*, 2 C. & P. 374.

(*r*) *Form of Consent.*

To [Mr. A. B., bailiff of] Mr. E. F.

I hereby consent that you shall remain in possession of the goods and chattels which you have dis-

Standing corn and growing crops cannot legally be sold until they are ripe (*s*); but if no damage has been sustained by the premature sale, the tenant cannot recover even nominal damages (*t*).

Growing crops.

8. *Costs of Distress.*

No person whatsoever making any distress for rent where the sum demanded and due shall not exceed the sum of twenty pounds for such rent, nor any person whatsoever employed in any manner in making such distress, or doing any act whatsoever in the course of such distress, or for carrying the same into effect, shall receive out of the produce of the goods or chattels distrained upon and sold, or from the tenant distrained on, or from the landlord, or from any other person whatsoever, any other or more costs and charges for such distress, or any matter or thing done therein, than such as are fixed in the schedule hereunto annexed and appropriated to each act which shall have been done in the course of such distress; and no person whatsoever shall make any charge whatsoever for any act, matter or thing mentioned in the said schedule, unless such act shall have been really done.

Costs of distress.
Stat. 57 Geo. 3, c. 93, s. 1.
Costs of distresses under 20l. not to exceed specified scale.

trained for rent upon the premises in my occupation, and shall keep the said goods and chattels in the place where they are now impounded for the space of —— days from the date hereof, in order to enable me to discharge the said rent and costs of the distress. And I hereby agree that the expenses of keeping possession of the said goods and chattels for the space aforesaid shall be deemed to be part of the charges of the said distress, and shall be recoverable as such. Witness my hand this —— day of ——, 18—.

C. D.

(*s*) Stat. 11 Geo. 2, c. 19, s. 8; *ante*, p. 160; *Owen* v. *Legh*, 3 B. & A. 470.

(*t*) *Rodgers* v. *Parker*, 18 C. B. 112; 25 L. J., C. P. 220; *Proudlove* v. *Twemlow*, 1 Cr. & M. 326.

	s.	d.
Schedule. Levying distress	3	0
Man in possession, per day	2	6
Appraisement, whether by one broker or more, 6d. in the pound on the value of the goods.		
Stamp, the lawful amount thereof.		
All expenses of advertisements, if any such	10	0
Catalogues, sale and commission, and delivery of goods, 1s. in the pound on the net produce of the sale.		

Sect. 2.
Remedy for excessive charges.

If any person shall in any manner levy, take or receive any other or greater costs and charges than are mentioned in the said schedule, or make any charge whatsoever for any act, matter or thing mentioned in the said schedule, and not really done, it shall be lawful for the party aggrieved by such practices to apply to (a justice of the peace, who may order) treble the amount of the moneys so unlawfully taken to be paid by the person so having acted to the party who shall have preferred his complaint thereof, together with full costs.

Stat. 1 & 2 Ph. & M. c. 12, s. 2.
Charge for impounding in public pound.

No person shall take for keeping in pound, impounding or poundage of any manner of distress above the sum of fourpence for any one whole distress that shall be so impounded; and where less hath been used, there to take less; upon the pain of five pounds, to be paid to the party grieved, over and beside such money as he shall take above the sum of fourpence.

This section only applies to cases where the goods distrained are taken to a public pound (x). The costs of a distress for arrears of rent exceeding 20l., where the distress is impounded on the premises, are not regulated by statute (y).

(x) Per Lord Denman, C. J., in *Child* v. *Chamberlain*, 5 B. & Ad., at p. 1051.

(y) See *Child* v. *Chamberlain*, 5 B. & Ad. 1049.

Every broker or other person who shall make and levy any distress whatsoever, shall give a copy of his charges, and of all the costs and charges of any distress whatsoever, signed by him, to the person or persons on whose goods and chattels any distress shall be levied, although the amount of the rent demanded shall exceed the sum of twenty pounds.

<small>Stat. 57 Geo. 3, c. 93, s. 6. Broker to give copy of charges to person on whose goods he has distrained.</small>

A landlord who does not personally interfere in making a distress, is not liable for the neglect of the broker to deliver a copy of his charges pursuant to this section (z).

9. *Remedies for Illegal Distresses.*

A distress is *illegal* in the following cases:—Where no rent for which a distress can be made is due and in arrear (a); where no tenancy exists between the owner of the goods and the person distraining (b); where a valid tender of the rent due has been made before seizure (c); where the distress is made before sunrise or after sunset (d); where an unlawful entry is made (e); where goods are seized which are privileged from distress (f), or which are not upon the demised premises (g); where a second distress is vexatiously made for rent previously distrained for (h).

<small>Instances of illegal distress.</small>

In these cases the tenant may lawfully rescue the goods, or take them out of the hands of the person dis-

<small>Rescue.</small>

(z) *Hart* v. *Leach*, 1 M. & W. 560.

(a) See *Lockier* v. *Paterson*, 1 C. & K. 271; *ante*, p. 131; *post*, p. 178.

(b) See *Yates* v. *Tearle*, 6 Q. B. 282; 13 L. J., Q. B. 289.

(c) *Ante*, p. 154. A tender of rent and expenses after seizure, but before impounding, renders the subsequent detention of the goods illegal, *ante*, p. 166.

(d) *Ante*, p. 150.

(e) *Attack* v. *Bramwell*, 3 B. & S. 520; 32 L. J., Q. B. 146; *ante*, p. 155.

(f) *Ante*, pp. 138—144.

(g) *Ante*, p. 144.

(h) *Ante*, p. 157.

training, at any time before they are impounded (*i*), provided this can be done without occasioning a breach of the peace.

Replevin.

The tenant may obtain restitution of goods wrongfully taken out of his possession under an *illegal* distress by suing out a replevin, which he may do at any time before the goods distrained are sold, although they may have been removed from the demised premises or appraised (*k*). This remedy is not applicable to cases where fixtures, deeds, or animals *feræ naturæ* (*l*), are wrongfully distrained, or to irregular or excessive distresses. If the chattels distrained have been delivered to the plaintiff on the replevin, as is the usual practice, the damages recoverable by him are generally confined to the expenses of the replevin bond (*m*). He cannot in this form of action recover substantial damages for the wrongful taking, and after judgment in replevin he is precluded from bringing any other action in respect of the same distress (*n*).

Proceedings in replevin.
Stat. 19 & 20 Vict. c. 108, s. 63.
Registrar of County Court to grant replevins.

The registrar of the County Court of the district in which any distress subject to replevin shall be taken shall be empowered, subject to the regulations hereinafter contained, to approve of replevin bonds and to grant replevins, and to issue all necessary process in relation thereto, and such process shall be executed by the high bailiff.

Sect. 64.

Such registrar shall, at the instance of the party

(*i*) Per Bramwell, B., in *Keen* v. *Priest*, 4 H. & N., at p. 240.

(*k*) *Jacob* v. *King*, 5 Taunt. 451.

(*l*) *Niblet* v. *Smith*, 4 T. R. 504; *Darby* v. *Harris*, 10 L. J., Q. B., at p. 295; Bac. Abr. *Replevin* (F); Woodfall, L. & T. 789.

(*m*) Roscoe's Evidence, 683 (11th ed.).

(*n*) *Phillips.* v. *Berryman*, 3 Dougl. 286; 1 Selw. N. P. 679. See *Pease* v. *Chaytor*, 1 B. & S. 658; 31 L. J., M. C. 1; 3 B. & S. 620; 32 L. J., M. C. 121; Woodfall, L. & T. 796.

whose goods shall have been distrained, cause the same to be replevied to such party, on his giving one or other of such securities as are mentioned in the next two succeeding sections. *On security being given.*

If the replevisor shall wish to commence proceedings in any superior Court, he shall, at the time of replevying, give security, to be approved of by the registrar, for such an amount as such registrar shall deem sufficient to cover the alleged rent in respect of which the distress shall have been made and the probable costs of the cause in a superior Court, conditioned to commence an action of replevin against the distrainor in such superior Court as shall be named in the security, within one week from the date thereof, and to prosecute such action with effect and without delay, and, unless judgment thereon be obtained by default, to prove before such superior Court that he had good ground for believing either that the title to some corporeal or incorporeal hereditament, or to some toll, market, fair or franchise was in question, or that such rent exceeded twenty pounds, and to make return of the goods, if a return thereof shall be adjudged. *Sect. 65. Conditions of security to commence action in superior Court.*

If the replevisor shall wish to commence proceedings in a County Court (these Courts have jurisdiction to try actions of replevin although title may be in question (*o*)), he shall, at the time of replevying, give security (at the cost of the party giving it, and in the form of a bond, with sureties to the other party, or intended party in the action (sect. 70)), to be approved of by the registrar, for such an amount as such registrar shall deem sufficient to cover the alleged rent in respect of which the distress *Sect. 66. Conditions of security to commence action in County Court.*

(*o*) *Reg.* v. *Raines*, 1 E. & B. 855; 22 L. J., Q. B. 223; *Fordham* v. *Akers*, 4 B. & S. 578; 33 L. J., Q. B. 67.

shall have been made and the probable costs of the cause in the County Court, conditioned to commence an action of replevin against the distrainer in the County Court of the district in which the distress shall have been taken, within one month from the date of the security, and to prosecute such action with effect and without delay, and to make return of the goods, if a return thereof shall be adjudged.

<small>Sect. 71.
Security may be by deposit with memorandum.</small>

Where by this act a party is required to give security he may, in lieu thereof, deposit with the registrar, if the security is required to be given in a County Court, or with a master of the superior Court, if the security is required to be given in such Court, a sum equal in amount to the sum for which he would be required to give security, together with a memorandum, to be approved of by such registrar or master, and to be signed by such party, his attorney or agent, setting forth the conditions on which such money is deposited, and the registrar or master shall give to the party paying a written acknowledgment of such payment, and the judge may order such sum to be paid out to such party as to him shall seem just.

Security having been duly given, the registrar will issue his warrant to the bailiff directing him to replevy and deliver the goods and chattels to the replevisor, and the bailiff will execute such warrant accordingly, and make a return to that effect (*p*). After goods taken in distress for rent have been replevied, the person distraining has no lien on them at law or in equity, but is left to his remedy on the replevin bond (*q*).

<small>Remedy for distress where no rent is due.</small>

If a distress and sale " shall be made for rent pretended to be in arrear and due, where no rent is in arrear or

---

(*p*) Woodfall, L. & T. 806.   (*q*) *Bradyll* v. *Ball*, 1 Bro. C. C. 427.

due to the person distraining or to him in whose name or right such distress shall be taken, then the owner of such goods or chattels distrained and sold, his executors or administrators, may, by action of trespass, or upon the case, to be brought against the person so distraining, his executors or administrators, recover double the value of the goods or chattels so distrained and sold, together with full costs of suit."

Stat. 2 Will. & M. sess. 1, c. 5, s. 5.
Owner may recover double value of goods sold.

In other cases of illegal distress for rent the tenant may, by action, recover from the person on whose behalf the distress is made the full value of the goods and chattels distrained, without deducting the arrears of rent (*r*), unless there are circumstances of mitigation which the jury ought to take into consideration (*s*). The fact that the tenant has had part satisfaction by the return of the goods, may be used in mitigation of damages (*s*).

Remedy in other cases of illegal distress.

On complaint made to any of the (police) magistrates by any person who shall, within the metropolitan police district, have occupied any house or lodging by the week or month, or whereof the rent does not exceed fifteen pounds by the year, that his goods have been taken from him by an unlawful distress, or that the landlord, or his broker, has been guilty of any irregularity or excess in respect of such distress, such magistrate (may) summon the party complained against; and if upon the hearing of the matter it shall appear to the magistrate that such distress was improperly taken, or unfairly disposed of, or that the charges made by the party having distrained are contrary to law, or that the

Remedy for wrongful distresses in metropolitan police district.
Stat. 2 & 3 Vict. c. 71, s. 89.

(*r*) *Keen* v. *Priest*, 4 H. & N. 236; 28 L. J., Ex. 157; *Attack* v. *Bramwell*, 3 B. & S. 520; 32 L. J., Q. B. 146. See *Edmondson* v. *Nuttall*, 17 C. B., N. S. 280; 34 L. J., C. P. 102.

(*s*) Per Willes, J., in *Edmondson* v. *Nuttall*, 34 L. J., C. P., at p. 104; *Harvey* v. *Pocock*, 11 M. & W. 740; 12 L. J., Ex. 434.

proceeds of the sale of such distress have not been duly accounted for to the owner thereof, it shall be lawful for the magistrate to order the distress so taken, if not sold, to be returned to the tenant on payment of the rent at such time as the magistrate shall appoint, or if the distress shall have been sold, to order payment to the tenant of the value thereof, deducting thereout the rent, such value to be determined by the magistrate, and such landlord, or party complained against, in default of compliance with any such order, shall forfeit to the party aggrieved the value of such distress, not being greater than fifteen pounds, such value to be determined by the magistrate.

10. *Remedy for Irregular Distresses.*

<small>Instances of irregular distress.</small>

A distress made for rent justly due is *irregular* in the following cases:—Where the goods distrained are sold without a proper notice, or without a regular appraisement (*u*); or before the expiration of five days from the notice (*x*); also where, owing to the neglect or improper conduct of the person distraining, the goods distrained are not sold for the best price that can be got for the same (*y*); or where the surplus produce of the sale, after paying the rent and costs, is not left in the hands of the sheriff, under-sheriff or constable for the owner's use (*z*).

<small>Remedy. Stat. 11 Geo. 2, c. 19, s. 19.</small>

Where any distress shall be made for any kind of rent justly due, and any irregularity or unlawful act shall be afterwards done by the party distraining, or by his

---

(*u*) *Biggins* v. *Goode*, 2 Cr. & J. 364; *Knight* v. *Egerton*, 7 Ex. 407. See *Knotts* v. *Curtis*, 5 C. & P. 322.

(*x*) See *ante*, p. 169; *Wallace* v. *King*, 1 H. Bl. 13; *Lucas* v. *Tarleton*, 3 H. & N. 116.

(*y*) *Ante*, p. 170.

(*z*) *Ante*, p. 169. As to actions for excessive distresses, see *ante*, p. 156.

agents, the distress itself shall not be deemed to be unlawful, nor the party making it be therefore deemed a trespasser *ab initio*; but the party aggrieved by such unlawful act or irregularity may recover full satisfaction for the special damage he shall have sustained thereby, and no more, in any action of trespass, or on the case. Where the plaintiff shall recover in such action, he shall be paid his full costs of suit.

<small>Distress not to be rendered unlawful by irregularity. Person aggrieved may recover special damage only.</small>

No tenant shall recover in any action for any such unlawful act or irregularity as aforesaid, if tender of amends hath been made by the party distraining, or his agent, before such action brought.

<small>Sect. 20. Tenant not to recover if tender of amends made before action.</small>

Without proof of actual damage, the plaintiff in an action for an irregular distress is not entitled even to a verdict for nominal damages (*a*). The measure of damages in the action is the value of the goods distrained, after deducting the amount of rent due (*b*).

(b) *Remedy on Execution against Tenant.*

No goods or chattels whatsoever (by whomsoever owned (*c*)), being in or upon any messuage, lands or tenements, which shall be leased for life, term of years, at will or otherwise, shall be liable to be taken by virtue of any execution (issued by a third person, and not by the landlord himself (*d*)), unless the party, at whose suit the said execution is sued out, shall before the removal of such goods from off the said premises, by virtue of such execution, pay to the landlord of the said pre-

<small>Stat. 8 Anne, c. 14, s. 1. Goods not to be removed under execution until one year's rent is paid to landlord.</small>

(*a*) *Rodgers* v. *Parker*, 18 C. B. 112; 25 L. J., C. P. 220; *Lucas* v. *Tarleton*, 3 H. & N. 116; 27 L. J., Ex. 246; but see *ante*, p. 157, note (*n*).

(*b*) *Whitworth* v. *Maden*, 2 C. & K. 517; *Diggins* v. *Goode*, 2 Cr. & J. 364; *Knight* v. *Egerton*, 7 Ex. 407.

(*c*) *Forster* v. *Cookson*, 1 Q. B. 419; 10 L. J., Q. B. 167.

(*d*) *Taylor* v. *Lanyon*, 6 Bing. 536, 544.

mises or his bailiff, all such sums of money as shall be due for rent (*e*), for the said premises (under an existing tenancy (*f*), at a rent certain (*g*)), at the time of the taking such goods or chattels by virtue of such execution (rent accruing after the taking and during the continuance of the sheriff in possession cannot be claimed under this statute (*h*)): Provided the said arrears of rent do not amount to more than one year's (full (*i*)) rent; and in case the said arrears shall exceed one year's rent, then the said party at whose suit such execution is sued out, paying the said landlord or his bailiff one year's rent, may proceed to execute his judgment, as he might have done before the making of this act; and the sheriff or other officer is hereby empowered and required to levy and pay to the plaintiff as well the money so paid for rent as the execution money (*k*).

Stat. 7 & 8 Vict. c. 96, s. 67.
Landlord of weekly tenant to claim four weeks' arrears only.

No landlord of any tenement let at a weekly rent shall have any claim or lien upon any goods taken in execution under the process of any court of law for more than four weeks' arrears of rent; and if such tenement shall be let for any other term less than a year, the landlord shall not have any claim or lien on such goods for more than the arrears of rent accruing during four such terms or times of payment.

Duty of sheriff.

The sheriff must first levy for the rent and then for the execution (*l*). He infringes the statute, and renders

(*e*) See *Yates* v. *Ratledge*, 5 H. & N. 249; 29 L. J., Ex. 117.

(*f*) *Hodgson* v. *Gascoigne*, 5 B. & A. 88.

(*g*) *Riseley* v. *Ryle*, 11 M. & W. 16; 12 L. J., Ex. 322. See 10 M. & W. 101; 11 L. J., Ex. 385.

(*h*) *Hoskins* v. *Knight*, 1 M. & S. 245; *Reynolds* v. *Barford*, 7 M. & Gr. 449; 13 L. J., C. P. 177.

(*i*) *Williams* v. *Lewsey*, 8 Bing. 28.

(*k*) This enactment does not apply to goods taken in execution under the warrant of a County Court. See *post*, p. 184.

(*l*) *Colyer* v. *Speer*, 2 B. & B. 67, 70.

himself liable to an action by the landlord, if, after notice of rent in arrear, he removes any of the goods without retaining that rent (*m*). He is not bound to find out what rent is due to the landlord; the latter ought to inform him (*n*). It appears, however, that express *notice* to the sheriff is not necessary, and that he will be liable if he sells and removes the goods, without retaining the rent, knowing that it is due (*o*). There is no ground for an action against the sheriff unless there has been an actual or constructive removal of the goods (*p*). Neither the removal of the goods from the premises, nor a *bonâ fide* sale of them, will prevent the landlord from putting in his claim, so long as the money produced by such sale remains in the hands of the sheriff (*q*). An application may be made to a judge for an order to compel the sheriff to pay the arrears of rent out of the proceeds of the levy in his hands (*r*). The law casts on the sheriff the responsibility of ascertaining that the rent is really

(*m*) Judgment in *Colyer* v. *Speer*, 2 B. & B., at p. 69.

(*n*) *Smith* v. *Russell*, 3 Taunt. 400; *Gawler* v. *Chaplin*, 2 Ex. 503; 18 L. J., Ex. 42; *Colyer* v. *Speer*, 2 Br. & B., at p. 69. Notice may be given by the landlord in the following form:—
To the sheriff of the county of ——, and to his officer.

Take notice, that there is owing to me from my tenant, C. D., of ——, the sum of £ ——, for [one year's] rent, due on the —— day of —— last, in respect of the house [*or* farm] at ——, in the county of ——, in his occupation; and I require you not to remove the goods seized by you in execution in the said house [*or* upon the said farm] until the said arrears of rent have been paid.

Dated this —— day of ——, 18 —.

E. F.

(*o*) See per Parke, B., in *Riseley* v. *Ryle*, 11 M. & W., at p. 20; 12 L. J., Ex., at p. 324; *Andrews* v. *Dixon*, 3 B. & A. 645; *Arnitt* v. *Garnett*, 3 B. & A. 440.

(*p*) *Smallman* v. *Pollard*, 6 M. & Gr. 1001; 13 L. J., C. P. 116.

(*q*) *Arnitt* v. *Garnett*, 3 B. & A. 440.

(*r*) *Arnitt* v. *Garnett*, 3 B. & A. 440; *Yates* v. *Ratledge*, 5 H. & N. 249, 252; 29 L. J., Ex. 117.

due, and he has a right to see the lease (s); but he is not called upon by law to advance money to pay the rent. Such advance must be made by the execution creditor, and if he neglects to make it, after notice of the rent being due, the sheriff cannot be called upon to sell the goods, let their value be what it will. Until the rent is paid, there are no goods out of which the sheriff is bound to levy, that is, which he is bound to sell (t).

It seems that if, under an execution against a tenant, the sheriff takes fixtures belonging to the landlord, the Court of Chancery will interfere to prevent him from so doing, although it is not alleged that the removal of such fixtures will occasion irreparable damage (u).

Stat. 14 & 15 Vict. c. 25, s. 2. Growing crops seized and sold under execution to be liable to rent subsequently accruing.

Growing crops of the tenant of any farm seized and sold by any sheriff by virtue of any writ of execution, so long as the same shall remain on the farm or lands, shall, in default of sufficient distress of the goods and chattels of the tenant, be liable to the rent which may become due after any such seizure and sale, and to the remedies by distress for recovery of such rent, notwithstanding any bargain and sale or assignment which may have been made of such growing crops by any such sheriff.

Stat. 19 & 20 Vict. c. 108, s. 75. Where goods are seized under warrant of county court, landlord

Sect. 1 of the act of 8 Anne, c. 14, shall not apply to goods taken in execution under the warrant of a county court; but the landlord of any tenement in which any such goods shall be so taken may claim the rent thereof at any time within five clear days from the date of such

(s) *Augusticn* v. *Challis*, 1 Ex. 279, 280; 17 L. J., Ex. 73.
(t) Per Lord Denman, C. J., in *Cocker* v. *Musgrove*, 9 Q. B., at p. 235; 15 L. J., Q. B. 365; see

White v. *Binstead*, 13 C. B., at p. 307; 22 L. J., C. P. 115.
(u) *Richardson* v. *Ardley*, 38 L. J., Ch. 508, 509.

taking, or before the removal of the goods, by delivering to the officer making the levy any writing signed by himself or his agent which shall state the amount of rent claimed to be in arrear, and the time for and in respect of which such rent is due; and if such claim be made, the officer making the levy shall, in addition thereto, distrain for the rent so claimed and the costs of such distress, and shall not within five days next after such distress sell any part of the goods taken, unless they be of a perishable nature, or upon the request in writing of the party whose goods shall have been taken; and the bailiff shall afterwards sell such of the goods under the execution and distress as shall satisfy, first, the costs of the sale, next the claim of such landlord, not exceeding the rent of four weeks where the tenement is let by the week; the rent of two terms of payment where the tenement is let for any other term less than a year; and the rent of one year in any other case; and, lastly, the amount for which the warrant issued: and if any replevin be made of the goods so taken, the bailiff shall, notwithstanding, sell such portion thereof as will satisfy the costs of and incident to the sale under the execution and the amount for which the warrant issued; and in either event the overplus of the sale, if any, and the residue of the goods shall be returned to the defendant.

may claim certain arrears of rent.

Such arrears not to exceed, in weekly tenancy, rent of four weeks; in tenancy for less than a year, rent of two terms of payment; and in any other case, one year's rent.

(c) *Remedy on Bankruptcy of Tenant.*

Upon the bankruptcy of the tenant the landlord should distrain for his rent (*x*). He may do this at any time while the tenant's goods remain on the premises,

(*x*) See *Gethin* v. *Wilks*, 2 Dowl. 189.

notwithstanding the messenger is in possession (*y*), and even after the goods have been sold by the assignees (*z*). If the landlord permits the goods to be removed from the premises without distraining, he can only be considered as a common creditor, and must come in *pro ratâ* (*a*).

Stat. 32 & 33 Vict. c. 71, s. 34.

Distress levied after commencement of bankruptcy to be available for one year's rent only.

The landlord, or other person to whom any rent is due from the bankrupt, may at any time, either before or after the commencement of the bankruptcy, distrain upon the goods or effects of the bankrupt for the rent due to him from the bankrupt (*b*), with this limitation, that if such distress for rent be levied after the commencement of the bankruptcy (*c*), it shall be available only for one year's rent accrued due prior to the date of the order of adjudication; but the landlord or other person to whom the rent may be due from the bankrupt may prove under the bankruptcy for the overplus due for which the distress may not have been available.

(*y*) *Ex parte Grove*, 1 Atk. 104; *Briggs* v. *Sowry*, 8 M. & W. 729.

(*z*) *Ex parte Plummer*, 1 Atk. 103.

(*a*) *Ex parte Descharmes*, 1 Atk. 103.

(*b*) See *Brocklehurst* v. *Lame*, 7 E. & B. 176; 26 L. J., Q. B. 107.

(*c*) See *Ex parte Bayly*, 22 L. J., Bank. 26; *Paull* v. *Best*, 3 B. & S. 537; 32 L. J., Q. B. 96. The bankruptcy of a debtor shall be deemed to commence at the time of the act of bankruptcy being completed on which the order is made adjudging him to be bankrupt; or if the bankrupt is proved to have committed more acts of bankruptcy than one, to commence at the time of the first of the acts of bankruptcy that may be proved to have been committed by the bankrupt within twelve months next preceding the order of adjudication; but the bankruptcy shall not relate to any prior act of bankruptcy, unless it be that at the time of committing such prior act the bankrupt was indebted to some creditor or creditors in a sum or sums sufficient to support a petition in bankruptcy, and unless such debt or debts are still remaining due at the time of the adjudication. (Sect. 11.)

When any rent or other payment falls due at stated periods, and the order of adjudication is made at any time other than one of such periods, the person entitled to such rent or payment may prove for a proportionate part thereof up to the day of the adjudication, as if such rent or payment grew due from day to day (*d*).

_{Sect. 35.}
_{Landlord may prove for proportionate part of the rent.}

The trustee under a liquidation shall have the same powers and perform the same duties as a trustee under a bankruptcy, and the property of the debtor shall be distributed in the same manner as in a bankruptcy; and, with the modification hereinafter mentioned (*e*), all the provisions of this act shall, so far as the same are applicable, apply to the case of a liquidation by arrangement, in the same manner as if the word "bankrupt" included a debtor whose affairs are under liquidation, and the word "bankruptcy" included liquidation by arrangement; and in construing such provisions the appointment of the trustee under a liquidation shall, according to circumstances, be deemed to be equivalent to and a substitute for the presentation of a petition in bankruptcy, or the service of such petition, or an order of adjudication in bankruptcy.

_{Sect. 125 (7). Provisions of act to apply to liquidation by arrangement.}

(d) *Remedy by Action.*

All actions of debt for rent upon an indenture of demise, all actions of covenant or debt upon any bond or other specialty, shall be commenced and sued within twenty years (*f*) after the cause of such actions (*g*), but not after.

_{Stat. 3 & 4 Will. 4, c. 42, s. 3. If lease is by deed action to be brought within twenty years.}

(*d*) See *ante*, p. 127.
(*e*) Relating to provisions with reference to the close of the bankruptcy, discharge of the bankrupt, &c., see sect. 125 (9).
(*f*) *Paget* v. *Foley*, 2 Bing., N. C. 679; *Sims* v. *Thomas*, 12 A. & E. 536; *Grant* v. *Ellis*, 9 M. & W. 113.
(*g*) Except in case of the disability or absence beyond seas of the person entitled to such action,

Stat. 3 & 4 Will. 4, c. 27, s. 42.	No arrears of rent shall be recovered by any action but within six years next after the same shall have become due, or next after an acknowledgment of the same in writing shall have been given to the person entitled thereto or his agent, signed by the person by whom the same was payable or his agent.
If lease not by deed, within six years.	
Actions for rent where lease is not by deed.	Where the lease is not by deed, the action may be either for rent on the special contract (*h*) or for use and occupation.
Action for use and occupation.	Where premises have been entered upon and occupied (*i*) by one person as tenant to another, under a contract, express or implied, to pay for the occupation (*k*), "it shall be lawful for the landlord, where the agreement is not by deed, to recover a reasonable satisfaction for the lands, tenements or hereditaments held or occupied by the defendant, in an action on the case, for the use and occupation of what was so held or enjoyed; and if in evidence on the trial of such action any parol demise or any agreement (not being by deed), whereon a certain rent was reserved, shall appear, the plaintiff shall not therefore be nonsuited, but may make use thereof as an evidence of the *quantum* of the damages to be recovered." Under this form of action the measure of damages recoverable is the rent, where a rent has been agreed upon; and where no rent has been agreed upon, such
Stat. 11 Geo. 2, c. 19, s. 14. Where agreement is not by deed, landlord may recover reasonable satisfaction.	

or in case an acknowledgment has been made either in writing, signed by the person liable by virtue of such indenture, or his agent, or by part payment, or part satisfaction. See sects. 4, 5.

(*h*) For the evidence in this action, see Roscoe's Evidence, 447 (11th ed.).

(*i*) See *Edge* v. *Strafford*, 1 Cr. & J. 391; *How* v. *Kennett*, 3 A. & E. 659; *Lowe* v. *Ross*, 5 Ex. 553; 19 L. J., Ex. 318; *Towne* v. *D'Heinriche*, 13 C. B. 892; 22 L. J., C. P. 219. See *Smith* v. *Twoart*, 2 M. & Gr. 841.

(*k*) See judgment of Bayley, J., in *Hall* v. *Burgess*, 5 B. & C., at p. 333; *Smith* v. *Eldridge*, 15 C. B. 236.

sum as the jury may find the occupation to be worth (*l*).

If the lease is by deed, the action may be either for rent on the indenture or on a covenant for payment of rent (*m*).

Actions for rent where lease is by deed.

Sect. II.—*Repairs.*

	PAGE
(1) Where there is no express agreement	189
Obligations of tenants at will, or from year to year	189
„ tenants for years or life	190
„ landlord	190
(2) Where there is an express agreement	191
Construction of general covenant to repair	191
„ covenant to put into repair	193
„ covenant to keep in repair	193
„ conditional covenant to repair	195
„ special agreements to repair	195
Measure of damages for breach of covenant	197

---

(1) *Where there is no express Agreement.*

A tenant from year to year of a house is bound to keep it wind and water-tight (*n*), to use it in a tenant-like manner (*o*), and to make fair and tenantable repairs, such as putting in windows or doors that have been broken by him (*p*). He must not *commit* any waste (*p*), but he cannot be compelled to replace doors, windows or stairs worn out with age (*q*), or to

Obligations of tenants at will, or from year to year.

(*l*) *Mayor of Thetford* v. *Tyler*, 8 Q. B., at p. 100. For the evidence in this action, see Roscoe's Evidence, 162 (11th ed.).

(*m*) For the evidence in these actions, see Roscoe's Evidence, 425, 447 (11th ed.).

(*n*) *Auworth* v. *Johnson*, 5 C. & P. 239; *Leach* v. *Thomas*, 7 C. & P. 327.

(*o*) *Horsefall* v. *Mather*, Holt, N. P. 7.

(*p*) Per Lord Kenyon, C. J., in *Ferguson* v. ———, 2 Esp. 590.

(*q*) *Auworth* v. *Johnson*, 5 C. & P. 239. See *Torriano* v. *Young*, 6 C. & P. 8; *Martin* v. *Gilham*, 7 A. & E. 540.

re-roof the house, renew the main timbers, or execute other general or substantial repairs (*s*).

Obligations of tenants for years or life.

Tenants for terms of years, or for life, are under a more extensive obligation to repair, since it appears that they are liable for permissive waste (*t*).

Stat. 14 Geo. 3, c. 78, s. 86. No action maintainable for accidental fires.

No action, suit or process whatsoever shall be maintained against any person in whose house, chamber, stable, barn or other building, or on whose estate any fire shall accidentally (*i. e.*, as the result of chance, and not of negligence or want of reasonable care (*u*)) begin; nor shall any recompense be made by such person for any damage suffered thereby, any law, usage or custom to the contrary notwithstanding: provided that no contract or agreement made between landlord or tenant shall be hereby defeated or made void (*x*).

Obligations of landlord.

Where there is no stipulation on the subject, a person who agrees to take a house, must take it as it stands, and cannot compel the lessor to put it into a condition fit for habitation (*y*). As between the landlord and tenant of premises let from year to year, there is no obligation upon the former to do substantial repairs during the continuance of the lease, unless there is an express agreement to that effect (*z*). If the demised premises are burnt down during the lease, the landlord is not bound to rebuild them (*a*), even

---

(*s*) *Ferguson* v. ———, 2 Esp. 590; *Horsefall* v. *Mather*, Holt, N. P. 7; *Leach* v. *Thomas*, 7 C. & P. 327.

(*t*) See judgment in *Yellowley* v. *Gower*, 11 Ex., at p. 294; *Harnett* v. *Maitland*, 16 M. & W. 257; 16 L. J., Ex. 134; *Smith*, L. & T. 267; *post*, p. 200.

(*u*) *Filliter* v. *Phippard*, 11 Q. B. 347; 17 L. J., Q. B. 89.

See *Canterbury* v. *Reg.*, 12 L. J., Ch. 281, 284.

(*x*) *Post*, p. 192.

(*y*) *Chappell* v. *Gregory*, 34 Beav. 250. See *post*, p. 201.

(*z*) *Gott* v. *Gandy*, 2 E. & B. 847; 23 L. J., Q. B. 1. See *Arden* v. *Pullen*, 10 M. & W. 321.

(*a*) *Bayne* v. *Walker*, 3 Dow, 233.

REPAIRS. 191

though he has received insurance money (*b*), or covenanted for quiet enjoyment by the tenant (*c*). Where the lessee's covenant to repair contains an express exception of damage by fire and tempest, it seems that the landlord is not bound to repair in either of the excepted cases (*d*).

It has been said, that a landlord who lets a house in a dangerous state is not liable to the tenant's customers or guests for accidents happening during the term (*e*); but it has since been held, that a landlord who lets or relets premises in such a state as to constitute a nuisance, is responsible for such nuisance, notwithstanding the tenancy; and that the continuance of a tenancy from year to year is equivalent to a reletting (*f*). But where a tenant, having a long lease of premises, so uses them as to create a nuisance, the landlord having no power or right of interference, incurs no responsibility (*g*).

(2) *Where there is an express Agreement.*

Under a *general covenant to repair* a house, the tenant must keep it in substantial repair, according to the age and nature of the building (*h*). It is perfectly well settled, that a general covenant to repair must be construed to have reference to the condition of the premises at the time when the covenant begins to ope-

<small>Construction of general covenant to repair.</small>

(*b*) *Leeds* v. *Cheetham*, 1 Sim. 146; *Lofft* v. *Dennis*, 1 E. & E. 474; 28 L. J., Q. B. 168.

(*c*) See *Brown* v. *Quilter*, 2 Ambl., at p. 620.

(*d*) Judgment of Lord Kenyon, C. J., in *Weigall* v. *Waters*, 6 T. R., at p. 488.

(*e*) Per Erle, C. J., in *Robbins* v. *Jones*, 15 C. B., N. S., at p. 240.

(*f*) *Gandy* v. *Jubber*, 5 B. & S. 78; 33 L. J., Q. B. 151. But see 5 B. & S. 485. See *Rich* v. *Basterfield*, 4 C. B. 783; 16 L. J., C. P. 273.

(*g*) Judgment of Crompton, J., in *Gandy* v. *Jubber*, 5 B. & S., at p. 78; 33 L. J., Q. B., at p. 154.

(*h*) *Harris* v. *Jones*, 1 Moo. & Rob. 173.

rate (*i*). If the house demised is an old one, the tenant is only bound to keep it up as an old house, and is not obliged to give the landlord the benefit of new work (*k*). It is not meant, in fact, that the old building is to be restored in a renewed form at the end of the term, so as to make the value of it greater than it was at the commencement of the term. Diminution in value, resulting from the natural operation of time and the elements, falls upon the landlord; but the tenant must take care that the premises do not suffer more damage than the operation of these causes would effect, and he is bound, by seasonable applications of labour, to keep the house as nearly as possible in the same condition as when it was demised (*l*). He is liable for repairs only, and not for alterations, such as laying a new floor on an improved plan (*m*). An agreement to keep a piece of ornamental water in good and substantial repair is performed by keeping the water from bursting its banks and maintaining the sluices in working order (*n*).

Unless the covenant by the tenant to repair contains an express exception of damage by fire or other casualty, he will be bound to rebuild or repair the demised premises if they should be burned down (*o*), or otherwise destroyed (*p*) or injured during the term. Although the lease contains a covenant by the tenant to insure the premises in a specified sum, he is still

---

(*i*) Per Parke, B., in *Walker* v. *Hatton*, 11 L. J., Ex., at p. 365; 10 M. & W., at p. 258.

(*k*) Per Tindal, C. J., in *Harris* v. *Jones*, 1 Moo. & Rob., at p. 175.

(*l*) See summing up of Tindal, C. J., in *Gutteridge* v. *Munyard*, 1 Moo. & Rob., at p. 336.

(*m*) *Saward* v. *Leggatt*, 7 C. & P. 613.

(*n*) *Bird* v. *Elwes*, 37 L. J., Ex. 91, 95; L. R., 3 Ex. 225.

(*o*) *Bullock* v. *Dommitt*, 6 T. R. 650; *Digby* v. *Atkinson*, 4 Camp. 275. See *Clark* v. *Glasgow Ass. Co.*, 1 Macqueen, 668; *Gregg* v. *Coates*, 23 Beav. 33.

(*p*) *Brecknock Co.* v. *Pritchard*, 6 T. R. 750.

liable on the covenant to repair, and his responsibility is not limited to the sum named in the covenant to insure (*q*).

Under a covenant to *put into habitable repair*, the tenant must, if necessary, place the demised premises in a better state than that in which he found them (*r*). He is not bound to make a new house, but regard being had to the state of the premises at the time of the agreement and to their situation, and to the class of persons who are likely to inhabit them, he is to put them into a condition fit for a tenant to inhabit (*r*). A covenant "forthwith" to put premises into complete repair is not construed as referring to any specific time; it is for a jury to say, upon a reasonable construction, whether it has been performed (*s*). A covenant to put in repair can only be broken once for all, and therefore if a breach has been committed in the time of the lessee, and damages recovered from him by the lessor in respect of such breach, the assignee of the lessee will not be liable (*t*). Covenant to put into repair.

A covenant to *keep premises in good repair* binds the lessee to put them into good repair with reference to their age and class, to maintain them in that state, and in that state to deliver them up at the end of the term (*u*). He must have them constantly in repair, and if at any time during the term they are out of repair, he is guilty of a breach of covenant, which is the proper subject of an action before the expiration of the lease (*x*). Covenant to keep in repair.

(*q*) *Digby* v. *Atkinson*, 4 Camp. 275, 278.
(*r*) *Belcher* v. *M'Intosh*, 8 C. & P. 720.
(*s*) *Doe* v. *Sutton*, 9 C. & P. 706.
(*t*) *Conard* v. *Gregory*, 36 L. J., C. P. 1, 9; L. R., 2 C. P. 153.
(*u*) *Payne* v. *Haine*, 16 M. & W. 541; *Burdett* v. *Withers*, 7 A. & E. 136; *Woolcock* v. *Dew*, 1 F. & F. 337.
(*x*) *Luxmore* v. *Robson*, 1 B. & A. 584, 585.

F.

As this covenant is a continuing one, the recovery of damages upon it in a previous action is no bar to a subsequent action against the tenant or his assignee, so long as the premises are out of repair, but the fact may be used in mitigation of damages (*y*). It is a breach of this covenant to pull down the demised premises either wholly or partially, or to open a doorway in a wall (*z*), unless by the terms of the lease it is implied that additions and improvements are to be made (*a*). A tenant who has covenanted to *substantially repair, uphold and maintain* a house, is bound to paint the inside woodwork, &c. (*b*).

Where there is a general covenant by the lessee to *repair and keep and leave in repair*, it will be inferred that he undertakes to repair buildings which may be erected during the term (*c*). On the other hand, a particular covenant to repair the demised buildings will be construed as referring only to existing buildings (*d*).

Covenants on the part of the tenant to *repair and keep in repair* the demised premises during the term, and *to repair specified defects within a certain time after notice*, are considered separate and independent covenants, if they severally make a complete sentence, or are found in different parts of the same deed (*e*);

(*y*) *Coward* v. *Gregory*, 36 L. J., C. P. 1; L. R., 2 C. P. 153.

(*z*) *Gange* v. *Lockwood*, 2 F. & F. 115; *Doe* v. *Jackson*, 2 Stark. 293; *Doe* v. *Bird*, 6 C. & P. 195.

(*a*) See *Doe* v. *Jones*, 4 B. & Ad. 126.

(*b*) *Monk* v. *Noyes*, 1 C. & P. 265. See *Scales* v. *Lawrence*, 2 F. & F. 289.

(*c*) *Douse* v. *Earle*, 3 Lev. 264; 2 Ventr. 126; judgment of Channell, B., in *Cornish* v. *Cleife*, 34 L. J., Ex., at p. 22.

(*d*) See *Cornish* v. *Cleife*, 3 H. & C. 446; 34 L. J., Ex. 19, 22.

(*e*) Judgment in *Horsefall* v. *Testar*, 7 Taunt., at p. 388; *Roe* v. *Paine*, 2 Camp. 520; *Baylis* v. *Le Gros*, 4 C. B., N. S. 537, 554. See *Doe* v. *Lewis*, 5 A. &

but if the whole stands in the same sentence it may be held to be one entire covenant (*f*).

A covenant by the lessee to repair is sometimes made conditional on the performance of some act by the lessor; as, for instance, on his first putting the premises into repair. Under this covenant the lessee is not liable for the non-repair of any part of the premises until the lessor has entirely performed his condition (*g*). A covenant by the tenant to repair, " having or taking sufficient house-bote, hedge-bote, &c. for the doing thereof, without committing any waste or spoil," is an absolute covenant to repair (*h*).

Conditional covenants to repair.

The liability of the lessee upon a covenant to repair commences only from the execution of the lease by the lessor. He is not liable for breaches of this covenant committed before the time of the execution of the lease, although the *habendum* of the lease states the premises to be held from a day prior to its execution (*i*).

COVENANT *by lessee to keep in repair the premises and all erections, buildings and improvements erected thereon during the term, and yield up the same in good repair.* The lessee cannot remove a veranda erected by him, the lower part of which is attached to posts fixed in the ground (*k*).

Construction of special agreements relating to repairs.

COVENANT *by lessee of a farm well and substantially*

E. 277; *Few* v. *Perkins*, 36 L. J., Ex. 54; L. R., 2 Ex. 92.

(*f*) *Horsefall* v. *Testar*, 7 Taunt. 385, 388.

(*g*) *Neale* v. *Ratcliffe*, 15 Q. B. 916; 20 L. J., Q. B. 130; *Cannock* v. *Jones*, 3 Ex. 233; 18 L. J., Ex. 204. See *Counter* v. *Macpherson*, 5 Moore, P. C. C. 83;

Conard v. *Gregory*, 36 L. J., C. P. 1, 10; L. R., 2 C. P. 153.

(*h*) *Dean and Chapter of Bristol* v. *Jones*, 1 E. & E. 484; 28 L. J., Q. B. 201.

(*i*) *Shaw* v. *Kay*, 1 Ex. 412; 17 L. J., Ex. 17; *ante*, p. 80.

(*k*) *Penry* v. *Brown*, 2 Stark. 403.

to repair and keep in good substantial repair, and so well and substantially repaired to yield up at the end of the term. The tenant is bound to give up the premises in as good a state of repair as they were in when he took possession, and they must be inferred to have been then in a tenantable state (*l*).

AGREEMENT *by tenant to leave a farm in as good condition as he found it.* Is an agreement to leave it in tenantable repair if he found it so (*m*).

COVENANT *by lessee of coal mine at the end of the term to yield up the works and mines, and all ways and roads, in such good repair, order and condition, that the works may be continued and carried on by the lessor.* Does not extend to moveable chattels, such as iron tram-plates fastened to wooden sleepers not let into the ground (*n*).

COVENANT *by lessee of farm to repair and leave in good repair all buildings to be erected thereon during the term.* Extends to a farm-house erected during the term, partly on the land demised and partly on the waste adjoining belonging to the lessor (*o*).

COVENANT *by lessor of a house to repair and keep in repair all the external parts of the demised premises.* A partition wall dividing the demised house from an adjoining house is an external part of the premises within this covenant (*p*).

(*l*) *Brown* v. *Trumper*, 26 Beav. 11, 15.
(*m*) *Winn* v. *White*, 2 W. Bl. 840.
(*n*) *Beaufort* v. *Bates*, 3 De G.,
F. & J. 381; 31 L. J., Ch. 481.
(*o*) *White* v. *Wakley*, 26 Beav. 17; 28 L. J., Ch. 77.
(*p*) *Green* v. *Eales*, 2 Q. B. 225; 11 L. J., Q. B. 63.

COVENANT *by lessor that, in case the demised premises shall be burned down, he will "rebuild and replace" the same in the same state as they were in before the fire.* The lessor is only bound to restore the premises to the state in which they were when he let them, and is not obliged to rebuild an additional story subsequently erected by the tenant(*q*).

Where the lessor is liable to repair the interior of the demised premises, the lessee cannot charge him for breach of repairs without notice, for he may not know that repairs are necessary(*r*).

A landlord cannot lawfully enter upon his tenant's premises to execute repairs, unless some express stipulation to that effect has been made (*s*). A provision in a lease that the landlord may enter the demised house "at convenient times" to view the state of repair, is not contravened by his being excluded from some of the rooms, if he has given no notice of his coming (*t*).

The damages recoverable in an action for non-repair of premises, held by the defendant under a lease which has several years to run, are not the amount which would be required to put the premises into repair, but the amount to which the saleable value of the reversion is injured by the non-repair of the premises (*u*). If a tenant, who is bound to repair, leaves the premises at the end of the term out of repair, the landlord may recover, in an action against him, in addition to the amount of the actual expense of the repairs, a com-

Measure of damages for breach of covenant.

(*q*) *Loader* v. *Kemp*, 2 C. & P. 375.
(*r*) *Makin* v. *Watkinson*, 40 L. J., Ex. 33; L. R., 6 Ex. 25; see per Mansfield, C. J., in *Moore* v. *Clark*, 5 Taunt., at p. 96.
(*s*) *Barker* v. *Barker*, 3 C. & P. 557.
(*t*) *Doe* v. *Bird*, 6 C. & P. 195.
(*u*) *Smith* v. *Peat*, 9 Ex. 161; 23 L. J., Ex. 84. See *Doe* v. *Rowlands*, 9 C. & P. 734.

pensation for the loss of the use of the premises while they were undergoing repair (*x*). Where a lessee has left the demised premises out of repair, a jury is not compelled to give only nominal damages, although before the end of the term the lessor has verbally agreed with another person to grant him a lease for a term of years, under the provisions of which agreement the premises are to be pulled down (*y*).

Sect. III.—*Waste*.

		PAGE
(1)	Voluntary	198
(2)	Permissive	199
(3)	Remedies for	200

(1) *Voluntary Waste*.

There are two kinds of waste,—voluntary or actual, and permissive (*a*). A tenant commits voluntary waste by acts of destruction, such as pulling down houses, or removing wainscots, doors or windows (*a*); or cutting down, destroying or topping timber-trees, or trees affording shelter to a house, or fruit trees in a garden (*a*); or destroying a quickset hedge of whitethorn (*a*); or ploughing up strawberry beds in full bearing (*b*); or opening new mines or quarries (*c*). Under a lease of land by an owner in fee, not mentioning mines, the lessee may work and take the profits of mines which are open at the time of making the

1. Acts of destruction.

(*x*) *Woods* v. *Pope*, 6 C. & P. 782.

(*y*) *Rawlings* v. *Morgan*, 18 C. B., N. S. 776; 34 L. J., C. P. 185.

(*a*) Co. Lit. 53 a.

(*b*) *Watherell* v. *Howells*, 1 Camp. 227.

(*c*) Co. Lit. 53 b.

lease (*d*). Under a lease of land, with the mines therein, where there is a mine open, the lessee cannot work or open unopened mines (*d*). The lessee may dig for gravel or clay for the reparation of the house demised, and for the same purpose may take convenient timber-trees (*e*). Waste can only be committed of the thing demised; hence, cutting down trees excepted out of a demise is not waste (*f*).

Waste may also be committed by changing the nature of the thing demised (*g*); as, for instance, by demolishing an old building and erecting in place of it new buildings of greater value (*h*); or converting a corn-mill into a fulling-mill (*i*); or turning ancient meadow or pasture into arable land (*j*); or arable land into wood, or *è converso* (*k*). Every lessee of land is liable for all waste done on the land in lease, by whomsoever it may be committed, for it is presumed in law that the lessee may withstand it (*l*).

2. Changing nature of the demised premises.

(2) *Permissive Waste.*

Permissive waste consists in suffering houses to fall into decay through want of necessary repairs (*m*); but if a house was uncovered when the tenant came in, it is no waste in him to suffer it to fall down (*n*). It is not

(*d*) Co. Lit. 54 b; judgment in *Clegg* v. *Rowland*, 35 L. J., Ch., at p. 398; L. R., 2 Eq., at p. 165.

(*e*) Co. Lit. 53 b; *Simmons* v. *Norton*, 7 Bing. 640.

(*f*) *Goodright* v. *Vivian*, 8 East, 190, 192.

(*g*) *Darcy* v. *Askwith*, Hob. 234.

(*h*) *Cole* v. *Greene*, 1 Lev. 309; *Cole* v. *Forth*, 1 Mod. 94; *London* v. *Greyme*, Cro. Jac. 182.

(*i*) Judgment in *London* v. *Greyme*, Cro. Jac. 182.

(*j*) Co. Lit. 53 b; judgment in *Simmons* v. *Norton*, 7 Bing., at pp. 647—649.

(*k*) Co. Lit. 53 b.

(*l*) 2 Wms. Saund. 259 b, note (*f*). See *Attersol* v. *Stevens*, 1 Taunt., at p. 196.

(*m*) See *Herne* v. *Benbow*, 4 Taunt. 764.

(*n*) Co. Lit. 53 a.

waste at common law, either wilful or permissive, to leave land uncultivated (o).

Tenants for life or for years (p) are responsible for permissive waste, but tenants at will (q) or from year to year (r) are exempt from this liability.

(3) *Remedy for Waste.*

1. Action at law.

The remedy for waste is by an action on the case in the nature of waste. The landlord may claim a writ of injunction against the repetition or continuance of the injury, or the committal of any injury of a like kind, relating to the same property (s).

2. Injunction of Court of Chancery.

If an act of voluntary waste, likely to be a lasting damage to the estate is in contemplation by the tenant, the landlord may obtain an injunction from the Court of Chancery to prevent it.

SECT. IV.—*Mode of using Premises.*

(1) Where there is no express agreement 200
    Illegal purposes 200
    Fitness of premises for use intended 201
(2) Where there is an express agreement 202
    Construction of contracts—
    Relating to exercise of trades 202
       " trading with particular persons 205
       " working of mines, &c. 206

---

(1) *Where there is no express Agreement.*

Illegal purposes.

No legal demand can arise out of a contract based upon an illegal or immoral consideration. Hence, rent

---

(o) Per Parke, B., in *Hutton* v. *Warren*, at p. 472.

(p) *Harnett* v. *Maitland*, 16 M. & W. 257; 16 L. J., Ex. 134; judgment in *Yellowley* v. *Gower*, 11 Ex., at p. 294.

(q) *Harnett* v. *Maitland*, 16 M. & W. 257; 16 L. J., Ex. 134.

(r) *Torriano* v. *Young*, 6 C. & P. 8.

(s) Stat. 17 & 18 Vict. c. 125, ss. 79—82.

or damages for breaches of covenant are not recoverable under leases of houses used for purposes of prostitution; provided the lessor is aware that the premises are so used (*t*). As every right or obligation arising out of the contract is tainted by the immorality of the transaction, the lessee cannot recover from his assignee, under a covenant in the assignment for indemnity in respect of all the lessee's covenants, a sum which the lessor has compelled the lessee to pay for dilapidations (*u*). Rent reserved upon a lease of premises used for the purpose of boiling oil and tar, contrary to the provisions of the Building Act, cannot be recovered (*x*).

In an action for breach of a contract to let premises, the defendant may justify such breach by proving that the plaintiff intended to use the premises for an illegal purpose, although at the time of refusing to perform the contract he did not assign or act upon such intended use, as a reason for his refusal (*y*). After the lessee has entered into possession under a lease, however, the lessor cannot avoid such lease, on the ground that it was obtained by the fraudulent misrepresentations of the lessee as to matters collateral to the lease; as, for instance, that he intended to use the demised premises for a respectable business, whereas he used them for an immoral purpose (*z*).

There is no contract implied by law on the part of the lessor of an unfurnished house, that it is in a rea- <small>Fitness of premises for use intended.</small>

(*t*) *Girardy* v. *Richardson*, 1 Esp. 13; *Crisp* v. *Churchill*, 1 B. & P. 340; *Jennings* v. *Throgmorton*, Ry. & M. 251; *Appleton* v. *Campbell*, 2 C. & P. 347.

(*u*) *Smith* v. *White*, 35 L. J., Ch. 454; L. R., 1 Eq. 626.

(*x*) *Gas Light Co.* v. *Turner*, 6 Bing. N. C. 324.

(*y*) *Cowan* v. *Milbourn*, 36 L. J., Ex. 124; L. R., 2 Ex. 230.

(*z*) *Feret* v. *Hill*, 15 C. B. 207; 23 L. J., C. P. 186.

1. On demise of unfurnished house.

sonably fit state for occupation, although it is let for the purpose of immediate habitation (*a*). The owner of a house is not bound to disclose to an intended lessee that it is in a ruinous state and dangerous to occupy, unless he knows that the intended lessee is influenced by his belief of the soundness of the house in agreeing to take it (*b*). In the absence of express warranty or active deceit, no action will lie against the owner for not making this disclosure (*b*).

2. On demise of furnished house.

It has been held, that upon the demise of a furnished house, since the bargain is not so much for the house as the furniture, there is an implied condition that it shall be reasonably fit for immediate habitation (*c*). It is a breach of this condition, whether express or implied, if the house, or any of the rooms, are infested and overrun with bugs; but to justify the tenant in quitting without notice, it must appear that the nuisance existed to a serious and substantial extent, and was such as he could not reasonably be expected either to endure or to extirpate (*d*).

3. On demise of land.

On a demise of land, or the vesture of land, there is no implied obligation on the part of the lessor, that it shall be fit for the purpose for which it is taken (*e*).

(2) *Where there is an express Agreement.*

Construction of contracts relating to exercise of trades.

Contracts whereby a person is restricted generally, and without reference to place, from exercising his trade

---

(*a*) *Hart* v. *Windsor*, 12 M. & W. 68; 13 L. J., Ex. 129.

(*b*) *Keates* v. *Cadogan*, 10 C. B. 591; 20 L. J., C. P. 76. See judgment in *Hart* v. *Windsor*, 12 M. & W., at p. 87.

(*c*) *Smith* v. *Marrable*, 11 M. & W. 5; 12 L. J., Ex. 223. See judgment in *Sutton* v. *Temple*, 13 L. J., Ex., at p. 22; *Hart* v. *Windsor*, 13 L. J., Ex., at p. 136.

(*d*) *Campbell* v. *Wenlock*, 4 F. & F. 716.

(*e*) *Sutton* v. *Temple*, 12 M. & W. 52; 13 L. J., Ex. 17.

for a special time are void (*f*). Covenants restraining a lessee or lessor from carrying on a specified trade within a particular area are valid, provided they are reasonable, having regard to the subject-matter of the contract (*g*); *i. e.* if the restriction is such only as to afford a fair protection to the interests of the party in favour of whom it is given, and is not so large as to interfere with the interests of the public (*h*).

COVENANT *not to exercise any trade or business.* The word "trade" is applicable only to a business conducted by buying and selling, and does not extend to the keeping of a private lunatic asylum (*i*). The occupation of a schoolmaster is a business within the meaning of this covenant (*k*). The covenantee does not waive the benefit of the covenant by permitting another house held under the like covenant to be used as a school (*l*). The partial exercise of a trade on the demised premises will operate as a breach of a covenant not to carry on such trade (*m*). Under a covenant not to use premises for certain purposes, there is a new breach every day during the time the premises are so used (*n*).

<small>Construction of covenants prohibiting exercise of trades on demised premises.</small>

COVENANT *not to carry on any noisome or offensive*

(*f*) *Ward* v. *Byrne*, 5 M. & W. 548; 9 L. J., Ex. 14; *Hinde* v. *Gray*, 1 M. & Gr. 195, 203.

(*g*) See *Leather Cloth Co.* v. *Lorsont*, 39 L. J., Ch. 86, 90; L. R., 9 Eq. 345; *Mitchell* v. *Reynolds*, 1 P. Wms. 181; *Hitchcock* v. *Coker*, 6 A. & E. 438; 6 L. J., Ex. 266.

(*h*) Per Tindal, C. J., in *Horner* v. *Graves*, 7 Bing., at p. 743.

(*i*) *Doe* v. *Bird*, 2 A. & E. 161.

(*k*) *Doe* v. *Keeling*, 1 M. & S. 95, 99; *Kemp* v. *Sober*, 1 Sim., N. S. 517; 20 L. J., Ch. 602. See *Wickenden* v. *Webster*, 6 E. & B. 387; 25 L. J., Q. B. 264.

(*l*) *Kemp* v. *Sober*, 1 Sim., N. S. 517; 20 L. J., Ch. 602.

(*m*) *Doe* v. *Spry*, 1 B. & A. 617, 619. See *Doe* v. *Elsam*, M. & M. 180.

(*n*) Judgment in *Doe* v. *Woodbridge*, 9 B. & C., at p. 378.

trade. Carrying on a dangerous trade is not a breach of this covenant (*o*). In construing this covenant, it is particularly worthy of consideration, whether the trade complained of was carried on upon the premises at the time of the demise (*p*).

COVENANT *not to do any act, &c. upon the demised premises which may lead to the damage, annoyance or disturbance of the lessor, or any of his tenants, or any part of the neighbourhood; followed by proviso for re-entry upon the carrying on of certain specified trades (not including that of a licensed victualler),* " *or any other trade or business that may be, or grow, or lead to be offensive, or any annoyance or disturbance*" *to any of the lessor's tenants.* The opening of a public-house upon the premises is not a breach of the covenant or proviso (*q*).

COVENANT *not to carry on the business of a common brewer or retailer of beer.* Carrying on the business of a retail brewer is not a breach (*r*).

COVENANT *not to use a house as a public-house for the sale of beer, &c.* Is not broken by the tenant's taking out an excise licence for the sale of beer not to be drunk on the premises (*s*).

COVENANT *in deed executed in* 1854, *not to carry on the trade or calling of hotel or tavern keeper, publican or beershop keeper, or seller by retail*

(*o*) *Hickman* v. *Isaacs*, 4 L. T., N. S. 285.

(*p*) *Gutteridge* v. *Munyard*, 7 C. & P. 129.

(*q*) *Jones* v. *Thorne*, 1 B. & C. 715. See *Macher* v. *Foundling Hospital*, 1 V. & B. 188.

(*r*) *Simons* v. *Farren*, 1 Bing. N. C. 126; 4 L. J., C. P. 41.

(*s*) *Pease* v. *Coates*, 36 L. J., Ch. 57; L. R., 2 Eq. 688. See *London and N. W. Ry. Co.* v. *Garnett*, 39 L. J., Ch. 25; L. R., 9 Eq. 26.

of wine, beer, spirits or spirituous liquors. Is not broken by a grocer's selling, across the counter, wine and spirits by retail, in bottles only, such wines and spirits not to be consumed on the premises, under a licence granted under stat. 24 & 25 Vict. c. 21, s. 2 (*t*).

COVENANT *not to exercise the trade of a butcher.* Is broken by selling raw meat by retail upon the premises, although no beasts are slaughtered there (*u*).

COVENANT *to use house as a private dwelling-house only.* It seems that conversion into a shop may be effected by user, without any structural alterations of the house (*x*).

AGREEMENT *to take land for ninety years, with liberty to build thereon erections necessary for carrying on the business of a glass manufacturer, the lessee not to use the premises for any other purpose than a glass manufactory.* Does not warrant the insertion in a lease, prepared in pursuance of the agreement, of an affirmative covenant by the lessee, that he will carry on the business of a glass manufacturer on the premises during the term (*y*).

Agreements intended to compel the lessees of public-houses to purchase beer of the lessors, are held to be injurious to the public welfare (*z*). It is incumbent on

Construction of covenants relating to trading with particular persons.

(*t*) *Jones* v. *Bone*, 39 L. J., Ch. 405; L. R., 9 Eq. 674.
(*u*) *Doe* v. *Spry*, 1 B. & A. 617. See *Doe* v. *Elsam*, M. & M. 189.
(*x*) *Wilkinson* v. *Rogers*, 2 De G., J. & S. 62.

(*y*) *Doe* v. *Guest*, 15 M. & W. 160.
(*z*) *Cooper* v. *Twibill*, 3 Camp. 286, note (*a*); *Holcombe* v. *Henson*, 2 Camp. 391. See *Doe* v. *Reid*, 10 B. & C. 849; *Weaver* v. *Sessions*, 6 Taunt. 154.

the plaintiff suing for breaches of a covenant of this nature, to show that the beer delivered by him was good marketable beer (*a*).

Where a lessor agrees to supply to the lessee the whole of the chlorine still waste as it comes from the still, at a given rate, and not to use, or injure, or part with any of the still waste, except to the lessee, the lessee is bound to take the whole of the waste which, during his occupancy, comes from the still (*b*).

Construction of covenants relating to working of mines, &c.

COVENANT *to work coal mine as long as it is fairly workable.* The lessee is not bound to work the mine at a dead loss (*c*).

COVENANT *in indenture demising all mines which had been or during the demise should be open, to work the mines in a proper and workmanlike manner.* The lessee is not liable under this covenant, if the mines have not been worked at all (*d*).

COVENANT *to work furnaces effectually, unless prevented by inevitable accident or want of materials, or unless the ironstone should be insufficient in quantity or quality, or would not by itself, or with a proper mixture and process, make good common pig-iron.* It is not necessary that the ingredients for the mixture should be procurable on the demised premises (*e*).

(*a*) *Thornton* v. *Sherratt*, 8 Taunt. 529, 530.
(*b*) *Bealey* v. *Stuart*, 7 H. & N. 753; 31 L. J., Ex. 281.
(*c*) *Jones* v. *Shears*, 7 C. & P. 346. See *Phillips* v. *Jones*, 9 Sim. 519; *Griffiths* v. *Rigby*, 1 H. & N. 237; 25 L. J., Ex. 284.
(*d*) *Quarrington* v. *Arthur*, 10 M. & W. 335.
(*e*) *Foley* v. *Addenbrooke*, 13 M. & W. 174; 14 L. J., Ex. 169.

Sect. V.—*Cultivation of Land.*

	PAGE
(1) Where there is no express agreement	207
Obligation of tenant as to husbandlike cultivation	207
„ „ expenditure of produce on premises	208
(2) Where there is an express agreement	209
Provisions in case of execution, &c.	209
Construction of covenants relating to course of husbandry	210
„ „ „ hay and straw, &c.	212
„ „ „ manure	213

(1) *Where there is no express Agreement.*

Every tenant is bound to cultivate his farm in a husbandlike manner according to the custom of the country, and to consume the produce upon it. This is an engagement which arises out of the letting, and which the tenant cannot dispense with unless by special agreement (*f*). What is to be considered as a good and husbandlike mode of cultivation must vary exceedingly according to soil, climate and situation; therefore the "custom of the country," with reference to good husbandry, must be applied to the approved habits of husbandry in the neighbourhood under circumstances of a like nature. Evidence that an estate had been managed according to the custom of the country, would be always a medium of proof that it had been treated in a good and husbandlike manner (*g*). In an action against a tenant for treating the demised farm contrary to good husbandry and the custom of the country, it is not incumbent on the landlord to prove a definite known custom or course of husbandry; it is sufficient to show what is *the prevalent course of good management;* and

_{Obligation of tenant as to husbandlike cultivation.}

(*f*) Per Gibbs, C. J., in *Brown v. Crump*, 1 Marsh. 567; *Powley v. Walker*, 5 T. R. 373. Judgment in *Onslow v. ——*, 16 Ves. 173; *Hallifax v. Chambers*, 4 M. & W. 662.

(*g*) Per Lord Ellenborough, C.J., in *Legh v. Hewitt*, 4 East, at pp. 159, 160.

by proving that the estate was not so managed, the landlord will prove that it was treated contrary to good husbandry and the custom of the country (*h*). The fact that a tenant has half his farm under tillage at the same time, while no other farmer in the neighbourhood tills more than a third, is clear proof of mismanagement contrary to the custom of the country in good husbandry (*i*). Out of the bare relation of landlord and tenant, no obligation arises to make a certain quantity of fallow, and to spread a certain quantity of manure every year thereon (*k*).

As to expenditure of produce on premises.

The tenant must not carry dung and compost off the demised premises (*l*), or remove anything except according to the custom of the country (*m*). It has been said that the tenant may carry hay and straw off the premises, if the practice is not contrary to the custom of the country, or prohibited by the lease or agreement under which he holds (*n*). The custom of the country relating to cultivation will be excluded by an express covenant or agreement inconsistent with it (*o*).

Stat. 56 Geo. 3, c. 50, s. 7. Sheriff not to sell clover, &c. sown with corn.

No sheriff shall, by virtue of any process whatsoever, sell or dispose of any clover, rye-grass, or any artificial grass whatsoever, which shall be newly sown, and be growing under any crop of standing corn.

(*h*) Judgment of Lawrence, J., in *Legh* v. *Hewitt*, 4 East, at p. 161. See *Dalby* v. *Hirst*, 1 B. & B. 224.

(*i*) *Legh* v. *Hewitt*, 4 East, 154, 160.

(*k*) *Brown* v. *Crump*, 1 Marsh. 567. See judgment in *Granger* v. *Collins*, 6 M. & W., at p. 461.

(*l*) *Powley* v. *Walker*, 5 T. R. 373; *Gough* v. *Howard*, Peake Add. Cas. 197.

(*m*) *Onslow* v. ———, 16 Ves. 173.

(*n*) *Gough* v. *Howard*, Peake Add. Cas. 197. But see *Brown* v. *Crump*, 1 Marsh. at p. 569.

(*o*) *Hutton* v. *Warren*, 1 M. & W. 466. See *Webb* v. *Plummer*, 2 B. & A. 746; *Roberts* v. *Barker*, 1 Cr. & M. 808; *Clarke* v. *Roystone*, 13 M. & W. 752. *Post*, Chap. VI., Sect. 3.

(2) *Where there is an express Agreement.*

No sheriff shall, by virtue of any process of any court of law (except process at the suit of the crown (*p*)), carry off or sell, or dispose of for the purpose of being carried off from any lands let to farm, straw, chaff, colder, turnips, or manure in any case, nor hay, grass or grasses, nor tares or vetches, nor any roots or vegetables being produce of such lands, in any case where, according to any covenant or written agreement, such hay, &c., ought not to be taken off such lands, or which, by the tenor or effect of such covenants or agreements, ought to be used or expended thereon, and of which covenants or agreements such sheriff shall have received a written notice before he shall have proceeded to sale. *Provisions in case of execution, &c. Stat. 56 Geo. 3, c. 50, s. 1. Sheriff not to sell off straw, &c., in any case, or hay, &c. contrary to covenants.*

The tenant against whose goods any process shall issue, shall, on having knowledge of such process, give a written notice to the sheriff or other officer executing the same of such covenants or agreements, and of the name and residence of the landlord; and such sheriff or other officer shall forthwith send a notice by post to the landlord (as to whose name and residence he is to make due inquiry before any sale of any crops (sect. 5)), and also to the known steward or agent of such landlord, stating the fact of possession having been taken of any produce hereinbefore mentioned; and such sheriff or other officer shall, in the absence or silence of such landlord or his agent, delay the sale of such produce until the latest day he lawfully can appoint. *Sect. 2. Tenant to give notice of covenants to sheriff. Sheriff to give notice of seizure to landlord.*

Such sheriff may dispose of any produce hereinbefore mentioned to any person who shall agree in writing, in cases where no covenant or written agreement shall be shown, to use and expend the same on such lands in *Sect. 3. Sheriff may dispose of produce to person agreeing to expend it on land.*

(*p*) *Rex* v. *Osbourne*, 6 Price, 94.

such manner as shall accord with the custom of the country; and in cases where any covenant or written agreement shall be shown, according to such covenant or written agreement; and after such sale it shall be lawful for such person to use all such necessary barns, buildings, yards and fields for the purposes of consuming such produce, as such sheriff shall assign and such tenant would have been entitled to for the like purpose.

Sect. 11.
Assignee not to use produce in any other manner than tenant might have done.

No assignee of any bankrupt, nor any assignee under any bill of sale, nor any purchaser of the goods or crop of any person employed in husbandry on any lands let to farm (*q*), shall take, use or dispose of any hay or other produce, or any manure or other dressings intended for such lands and being thereon, in any other manner than such bankrupt or other person so employed in husbandry ought to have taken, used or disposed of the same.

Construction of agreements relating to course of husbandry.

COVENANT *not to sow land with wheat more than once in four years, nor with more than two crops of any kind of grain whatsoever during the same period of four years.* Applies to any four years of the term, however taken, and not to each successive four years from the commencement (*r*).

COVENANT *to cultivate, on the four-course system, according to the custom of the country.* Means only so far as is universally obligatory by the custom of the country (*s*). A jury may find that the tenant ploughed as much as he was *bound* to do by the custom (*s*).

(*q*) This section applies to an ordinary sale by the tenant himself. *Wilmot* v. *Rose*, 3 E. & B. 563; 23 L. J., Q. B. 281.

(*r*) *Fleming* v. *Snook*, 5 Beav. 250.

(*s*) *Newson* v. *Smythies*, 1 F. & F. 477, 479. As to the mean-

AGREEMENT *to manage and quit premises agreeably to the manner in which the same have been managed and quitted by the former tenants.* A tenant, without notice, is not bound by the terms upon which the former tenants held. The only rule by which, according to the agreement, he is to be guided, is the condition of the estate and the mode in which it was managed at the time of his taking possession (*t*).

COVENANT *to manage pasture in a husbandlike manner.* Is equivalent to a covenant not to convert it into arable land (*u*).

COVENANT *to permit the landlord in the last year of the term to sow clover among the tenant's barley.* The landlord must use due diligence to ascertain for himself when the tenant sows his barley (*x*).

COVENANT *at the end of the lease to leave the turnip or fallow breaks once ploughed for the incoming tenant.* The words turnip or fallow breaks mean the land which would, in the natural course of good husbandry, be ploughed and left fallow for the purpose of being planted with turnips (*y*).

COVENANT *to pay additional rent for pasture land which lessee should ear, plough, break up, dig, use or convert to tillage, or for brick earth, or for any other purpose whatsoever.* It seems

ing of a covenant to farm on the four-course system, see *Rankin* v. *Lay*, 2 De G., F. & J. 65.

(*t*) *Liebenrood* v. *Vines*, 1 Mer. 15, 18. See *Hood* v. *Kendall*, 17 C. B. 260.

(*u*) Per Lord Eldon, in *Drury* v. *Molins*, 6 Ves. 328. See *Hills* v. *Rowland*, 4 De G., M. & G. 430; 22 L. J., Ch. 964.

(*x*) *Hughes* v. *Riehman*, Cowp. 125.

(*y*) *Hunter* v. *Miller*, 9 L. T., N. S. 159.

that whether the use of the land as a race-course and ground for training horses is a breach of the covenant is a question of fact for a jury (z). Laying down the land to permanent grass again will not protect the lessee, who has once ploughed it up, from future accruing additional rent (a).

Construction of agreements relating to hay and straw.

COVENANT *not to remove from the farm, during the last year of the term, any of the hay, &c., which shall grow on the farm.* The lessee is prohibited from removing hay, &c. which is on the farm in the last year of the term, at whatever time during the term it may have grown (b).

AGREEMENT *that tenant shall not sell any straw or manure grown or produced on the farm without the licence of the landlord, under certain penalties, recoverable as additional rent.* Extends to straw sold by the tenant after the determination of the tenancy (c).

AGREEMENT *that tenant shall consume the hay on the premises, or for every load of hay removed shall bring two loads of manure.* The bringing on the manure is not a condition precedent to the carrying off the hay as between the landlord and tenant, but after the tenant has quitted possession of the premises, the succeeding tenant may refuse to permit the hay to be removed until the manure is brought on (d).

AGREEMENT *that " value" of straw or hay sold off is to be returned in manure on the land.* The

---

(z) *Aldridge* v. *Howard*, 4 M. & Gr. 921.

(a) *Birch* v. *Stephenson*, 3 Taunt. 469, 478.

(b) *Gale* v. *Bates*, 3 H. & C. 84; 33 L. J., Ex. 235.

(c) *Massey* v. *Goodall*, 17 Q. B. 310; 20 L. J., Q. B 526.

(d) *Smith* v. *Chance*, 2 B. & A. 753, 755.

Court of Exchequer was equally divided upon the question whether the market value of the straw is to be returned in manure, or so much manure only is to be spent upon the land as the hay or straw would have produced (*e*).

AGREEMENT *that tenant shall be paid "a fair price" for straw left on the premises at the end of his tenancy, not containing any stipulation as to payment for manure.* The tenant is to be paid for the straw at a fodder price only, *i. e.*, one-half the market price (*f*).

AGREEMENT *by tenant to pay an additional rent for every ton of hay, &c., sold off or removed from the premises.* Hay of very bad quality and unfit to be eaten by cattle is within the meaning of this agreement (*g*).

COVENANT *that lessee shall not sell or carry away from the demised premises any hay, straw or manure grown or produced thereon without the consent of the lessor, under the increased rent of 10l. for every ton so sold or carried away, but that the lessee will consume the hay and straw by his cattle.* The lessee is entitled to sell the hay and straw on payment of the increased rent (*h*).

CONDITION *not to sell or convey away any dung, &c., from a farm.* Extends to manure made on the

Construction of agreements relating to manure.

(*e*) *Lowndes* v. *Fountain*, 11 Ex. 487. The opinion of Parke, B., was in favour of the latter construction.

(*f*) *Clarke* v. *Westrope*, 18 C. B. 765; 25 L. J., C. P. 287. As to the meaning of a "fair valuation," see *Cumberland* v. *Bowes*, 15 C. B. 348; 24 L. J., C. P. 46.

(*g*) *Fielden* v. *Tattersall*, 7 L. T., N. S. 718.

(*h*) *Legh* v. *Lillie*, 6 H. & N. 165; 30 L. J., Ex. 25.

farm by cows sold by the tenant and provided with provender by the buyer (*i*).

COVENANT *to manure land with two sets of muck within the space of six of the last years of the term, the last set of muck to be laid upon the premises within three years of the expiration of the term.* The tenant may lay on both sets of muck within the three last years of the term (*k*).

COVENANT, *by outgoing tenant, to leave the manure on the farm and sell it to the incoming tenant at a valuation.* The effect of this covenant is to give the outgoing tenant a right of onstand for his manure upon the farm, and he has such a continuing possession of it and property in it, in the meantime, as enable him to maintain an action of trespass if the incoming tenant take it before the valuation has been made (*l*).

SECT. VI.—*Fences.*

	PAGE
(1) Liability to repair where there is no express agreement	.. 214
Obligation of tenants for life or years	.. 214
„ „ from year to year or at will	.. 215
(2) Ownership of fences	.. 215
General presumption	.. 216
Obligation to keep up boundaries ..	.. 216

(1) *Liability to repair, where there is no express Agreement.*

Obligation of tenants for life or years.

It is so notoriously the duty of the actual occupier of lands to repair the fences, and so little the duty of the

(*i*) *Hindle* v. *Pollitt*, 6 M. & W. 529.
(*k*) *Pornall* v. *Moores*, 5 B. &

A. 416, 418.
(*l*) *Beaty* v. *Gibbons*, 16 East, 116, 118.

landlord, who is not in possession, that, without any agreement to that effect, the landlord may maintain an action against his tenant for not so doing, upon the ground of the injury done to the inheritance (*m*). It would seem, however, that a tenant at will or from year to year, since he is not liable for mere permissive waste, is not bound to make good the decay of the fences (*n*). The general rule of law is, that a man is only bound to take care that his cattle do not wander from his own land and trespass upon the lands of others. He is under no legal obligation, therefore, to keep up fences between adjoining closes of which he is owner; and even where adjoining lands, which have once belonged to different persons, one of whom was bound to repair the fences between the two, afterwards become the property of the same person, the pre-existing obligation to repair the fences is destroyed by unity of ownership. And where the person who has so become the owner of the entirety afterwards parts with one of the two closes, the obligation to repair the fences will not revive, unless express words are introduced into the conveyance for that purpose (*o*).

Obligation of tenants from year to year or at will.

Where two persons have adjoining fields, and there is no hedge between them, each must take care that his beasts do not trespass upon his neighbour's land (*p*).

(2) *Ownership of Fences, &c.*

There is no rule as to a certain width which the owner of a ditch is entitled to have. No man making

(*m*) Judgment of Ld. Kenyon, C. J., in *Cheetham* v. *Hampson*, 4 T. R., at p. 319. See *Whitfield* v. *Weedon*, 2 Chit. 685.

(*n*) See cases cited, *ante*, p. 200; also *Gandy* v. *Jubber*, 5 B. & S. 78; 33 L. J., Q. B. 151.

(*o*) Per Bayley, J., in *Boyle* v. *Tamlyn*, 6 B. & C., at p. 337. See observations on this case in *Barber* v. *Whiteley*, 34 L. J., Q. B., at p. 216.

(*p*) 2 Rol. Abr. 565, pl. 7. See *Churchill* v. *Evans*, 1 Taunt. 529.

a ditch can cut into his neighbour's soil; but usually he cuts it to the very extremity of his own land. He is, of course, bound to throw the soil which he digs out upon his own land, and often he plants a hedge on the top of it. If he afterwards cuts beyond the edge of the ditch, which is the extremity of his land, he cuts into his neighbour's soil, and is a trespasser (*q*). Hence, where two adjacent fields are separated by a hedge and a ditch, the hedge *primâ facie* belongs to the owner of the field in which the ditch is not (*r*). If there are two ditches, one on each side of the hedge, the ownership of the hedge must be proved by showing acts of ownership (*r*).

General presumption.

The common use of a wall separating adjoining lands belonging to different owners, is presumptive evidence that the wall belongs to the owners of those adjoining lands as tenants in common; for the law will presume that the acts of enjoyment were lawful (*s*).

Obligation of tenant to keep up boundaries.

Among other obligations resulting from the relation of landlord and tenant, a tenant contracts an obligation to keep his landlord's property distinct from his own property during the term, and at the end of the term to leave it clearly distinct, and not in any way confounded with his own. If he has put his landlord's property and his own together, for his own convenience, in order to make the most of it during his tenancy, he is bound at the end of the term to render up specifically the landlord's land; and if the tenant has so confounded the boundaries that the landlord's land cannot be ascertained, the Court of Chancery will inquire what was

. (*q*) Per Lawrence, J., in *Vowles* v. *Miller*, 3 Taunt., at p. 138.

(*r*) Per Bayley, J., in *Guy* v. *West*, cited 2 Selw. N. P. 1244;

Noye v. *Reed*, 1 Man. & Ry. 63.

(*s*) *Cubitt* v. *Porter*, 8 B. & C. 257, 259, note (*b*), 266. See *Matts* v. *Hawkins*, 5 Taunt. 20.

the value of the landlord's estate, valued fairly, but to the utmost, as against the tenant (*t*).

Sect. VII.—*Trees.*

	PAGE
(1) Where there is no express agreement	217
Property in trees as between landlord and tenant	217
„ „ „ and third persons	217
„ bushes, &c.	218
Estovers	218
Windfalls	218
(2) Where there is an express agreement	218
Construction of agreements relating to trees	218

(1) *Where there is no express Agreement.*

The general property in timber-trees is in the landlord (*u*). Oak, ash and elm, which are timber-trees everywhere, by the general rule of the realm, become timber at twenty years' growth (*x*). By the custom of the country, in some places, trees are considered as timber which, generally speaking, are not so (*y*). When a particular kind of wood is admitted to be timber by the custom of the country, the rule of law applicable to timber-trees in general attaches upon it, so as to give it the properties and privileges of timber at twenty years' growth (*z*). *Property in trees as between landlord and tenant.*

The landlord of a tenant from year to year, although there is no reservation of the timber on the premises, may bring an action of trespass against a third person for carrying it away after it has been cut down (*a*). *Property in trees as between landlord and third persons.*

(*t*) Judgment of Ld. Eldon, in *Att.-Gen.* v. *Fullerton*, 2 V. & B., at p. 264. See *Att.-Gen.* v. *Stephens*, 6 De G., M. & G. 111; 25 L. J., Ch. 888.

(*u*) *Berriman* v. *Peacock*, 9 Bing. 384, 387.

(*x*) Judgment of Ld. Ellenborough, C. J., in *Aubrey* v. *Fisher*, 10 East, at p. 455; Co.

Lit. 53 a. See *Whitty* v. *Dillon*, 2 F. & F. 67.

(*y*) See *Chandos* v. *Talbot*, 2 P. W., at p. 606; *Aubrey* v. *Fisher*, 10 East, 446; Co. Lit. 53 a.

(*z*) *Aubrey* v. *Fisher*, 10 East, 446.

(*a*) *Ward* v. *Andrews*, 2 Chit. 636.

Where a tree grows near the land of two persons, so that the roots derive nourishment from the soil of both, the property in the tree is to be ascertained by showing where it was first sown or planted (*b*).

Property in bushes.
The property in bushes is in the tenant, but if he exceeds his right, as by grubbing up or destroying fences, he may be liable to an action of waste (*c*).

Estovers.
Every tenant, except a tenant at will, may take sufficient wood to repair the walls, pales, fences, hedges and ditches as he found them; but he cannot make new fences, &c. He may also take wood to burn in the house, or for repairing the house, and for making and repairing implements of husbandry (*d*); but not for sale (*e*). If he cuts down growing wood to burn when he has a sufficient quantity of dead wood, he will be guilty of waste (*d*). In felling timber for repairs, he is bound to confine himself to such trees as are adapted for that purpose, and to employ them accordingly (*f*).

Windfalls.
Windfalls of decayed timber-trees belong to the tenant for life or years, and windfalls of trees which are not timber, may, in the absence of express exception, be claimed by him (*g*). But windfalls of sound timber-trees, as between lessee and lessor, belong to the lessor (*g*).

(2) *Where there is an express Agreement.*

Construction of agreements relating to trees.
COVENANT *in a lease of a farm and quarries of stone thereon, with liberty to work the quarries, and*

(*b*) *Holder* v. *Coates*, M. & M. 112. See *Dixon* v. *Geldard*, Dixon's Law of the Farm, 81.
(*c*) *Berriman* v. *Peacock*, 9 Bing. 384, 387.
(*d*) Co. Lit. 53 b.
(*e*) Co. Lit. 53 b. See *Cour-town* v. *Ward*, 1 Sch. & Lef. 8.
(*f*) *Simmons* v. *Norton*, 7 Bing. 640, 649.
(*g*) Craig on Trees, 123. See *Herlakenden's Case*, 4 Co. R. 62; *Channon* v. *Patch*, 5 B. & C. 897.

containing an exception of trees, not to commit waste by cutting down timber-trees, saplings, or any other wood or underwood. Cutting down wood and underwood necessary to be cut down in order to work a quarry on the demised premises is not a breach of the covenant (*h*).

COVENANT *that tenant shall not during the term cut down any of the coppice of less than ten years' growth or at any unseasonable time of the year. At the end of the term the landlord agrees to pay to the tenant the value of all such growth of coppice and underwood as shall be then standing and growing.* The landlord is bound to pay the tenant for the value of all the coppice of less than ten years' growth left standing on the demised premises at the end of the term, though no special consideration appears on the face of the deed for the landlord's agreeing to make a compensation to the tenant for the value of the part of the coppice which the tenant was not entitled to cut (*i*).

COVENANT *to deliver timber growing on the premises sufficient for the repairs thereof.* The timber must be sufficient in quality as well as quantity (*j*).

COVENANT *to deliver up at the end of the term all the trees standing in the orchard at the time of the demise, "reasonable use and wear only excepted."* If the trees in the orchard are too crowded, the removal of such as are past bearing must be considered as a reasonable use of the orchard and trees (*k*).

(*h*) *Doe* v. *Price*, 8 C. B. 894; 19 L. J., C. P. 121.
(*i*) *Love* v. *Pares*, 13 East, 80.
(*j*) *Snell* v. *Snell*, 4 B. & C. 741, 749.
(*k*) *Doe* v. *Crouch*, 2 Camp. 449, 450.

COVENANT *not to fell, stub up, lop, or top timber-trees excepted out of the demise.* ' The executor of the lessor is entitled to sue for a breach of this covenant committed in the lifetime of the testator (*l*).

COVENANT *not to remove or grub up or destroy trees.* Removing trees from one part of the premises to another, or taking away trees, though the lessee plants a greater quantity than he takes away (those taken away not being dead) will constitute breaches of this covenant (*m*).

SECT. VIII.—*Insurance.*

PAGE
Construction of general covenant to insure 220
    ,,   covenant to insure in names of specified persons .. 221
Statutory provisions in case of fire 222

Construction of general covenant to insure and keep insured.

Under a *general covenant to insure and keep insured* the demised premises, the lessee must keep them insured during the whole term (*n*); the covenant is broken if they are uninsured at any time (*o*), although no inconvenience or loss may be occasioned to the landlord (*p*). The insurance must be made within a reasonable time after the execution of the lease, and if any delay occurs, the *onus* of showing that such delay is reasonable will rest on the tenant (*q*). The insurance must extend to the whole of the premises specified in the covenant, since a breach will be committed if any por-

---

(*l*) *Raymond* v. *Fitch*, 2 Cr. M. & R. 588. As to the construction of exceptions of timber, see *ante*, p. 78.

(*m*) *Doe* v. *Bird*, 6 C. & P. 195.

(*n*) See *Heckman* v. *Isaac*, 6 L. T., N. S. 383.

(*o*) See judgment in *Doe* v. *Peck*, 1 B. & Ad., at p. 438.

(*p*) *Doe* v. *Shewin*, 3 Camp. 134, 137. See *Wilson* v. *Wilson*, 14 C. B. 616; 23 L. J., C. P. 137; *Price* v. *Worwood*, 4 H. & N. 512; 28 L. J., Ex. 329; *Doe* v. *Laming*, 4 Camp. 73.

(*q*) *Doe* v. *Ulph*, 13 Q. B. 204; 18 L. J., Q. B. 106.

tion remains uninsured (r). Though no fire occurred during the period for which premises remained uninsured, a jury may give more than nominal damages to the landlord in respect of the possibility of loss to which he has been exposed (s).

A covenant to insure, which does not specify in what sort of office such insurance is to be effected, is not void for uncertainty (t); but express provision is frequently made, both as to the office in which the insurance is to be effected and the persons in whose names it is to be taken out. These particulars must be carefully observed by the tenant. A covenant to insure and keep insured *in the joint names of the lessee and lessor* will be broken by an insurance in the name of the lessee only (u); but if the conduct of the lessor has been such as to induce a reasonable and cautious man to believe that he would do all that was necessary or required of him by insuring in his own name, the lessor cannot recover for a forfeiture (x). Although this covenant is not literally performed by an insurance in the name of the lessor only, it is substantially performed for the benefit of the lessor, and he cannot recover for a breach of the covenant; the stipulation for the insurance in the name of the lessee being for the exclusive benefit of the latter (y). A covenant to insure *in the names of three lessors*, is broken by an insurance effected by the lessee in their names jointly with his own (z).

<small>Construction of covenants to insure in names of specified persons.</small>

(r) *Penniall* v. *Harborne*, 11 Q. B. 368; 17 L. J., Q. B. 94.

(s) *Hey* v. *Wyche*, 12 L. J., Q. B. 83, 85; 2 G. & D. 569.

(t) *Doe* v. *Shewin*, 3 Camp. 134.

(u) *Doe* v. *Gladwin*, 6 Q. B. 953; 14 L. J., Q. B. 189. See *Doe* v. *Rowe*, Ry. & M. 343.

(x) *Doe* v. *Rowe*, Ry. & M. 343, 346. As to relief against forfeiture for breach of a covenant to insure, see *post*, p. 289.

(y) *Havens* v. *Middleton*, 10 Hare, 641; 22 L. J., Ch. 746.

(z) *Penniall* v. *Harborne*, 11 Q. B. 368; 17 L. J., Q. B. 94.

So long as the terms of a covenant to insure are not complied with, there is a continuing breach, and the receipt of rent by the landlord will only operate as a waiver of breaches committed before the time when such rent was received (*a*).

<small>Statutory provisions in case of fire.
Stat. 22 & 23 Vict. c. 35, s. 7.
Lessor to have benefit of insurance not in conformity with covenant.</small>

The person entitled to the benefit of a covenant on the part of a lessee (for years or life (sect. 9)), to insure against loss or damage by fire, shall, on loss or damage by fire happening, have the same advantage from any then subsisting insurance relating to the building covenanted to be insured, effected by the lessee in respect of his interest under the lease, or by any person claiming under him, but not effected in conformity with the covenant, as he would have from an insurance effected in conformity with the covenant.

<small>Stat. 14 Geo. 3, c. 78, s. 83.
Insurance offices, on request of persons interested in property burnt, or on suspicion of fraud or arson, to lay out insurance money in rebuilding.</small>

The governors or directors of the several insurance offices for insuring houses or other buildings against loss by fire are authorized and required, upon the request (to be distinctly made before the office has settled with the insurer (*b*)), of any person interested in or entitled unto any house or other buildings (*c*), which may hereafter be burnt down, demolished or damaged by fire; or upon any grounds of suspicion that the owner, occupier or other person who shall have insured such house or other buildings, have been guilty of fraud, or of wilfully setting their house, or other buildings, on fire, to cause the insurance money to be laid out, as far as the same will go, towards rebuilding, reinstating or repairing such

---

(*a*) *Doe* v. *Gladwin*, 6 Q. B. 953; 14 L. J., Q. B. 189.

(*b*) *Simpson* v. *Scottish Union Insurance Co.*, 1 Hem. & M. 618; 32 L. J., Ch. 329.

(*c*) Trade fixtures put up by a tenant are not within these words, although the tenant has covenanted to deliver up the fixtures at the determination of the tenancy. *Ex parte Gorely*, 34 L. J., Bk. 1; 13 W. R. 60.

house, or other buildings so burnt down, demolished or damaged by fire; unless the party claiming such insurance money shall, within sixty days next after his claim is adjusted, give a sufficient security to the governors or directors of the insurance office where such house, or other buildings, are insured, that the same insurance money shall be laid out as aforesaid; or unless the said insurance money shall be, in that time, settled and disposed of, to and amongst all the contending parties to the satisfaction of such governors or directors of such insurance office respectively (*d*).

SECT. IX.— *Taxes.*

	PAGE
(1) Where there is no express agreement	223
Taxes which fall on the landlord	223
(2) Where there is an express agreement	225
Agreements relating to property tax	225
Payment of tithe rent-charge	225
Construction of agreements relating to payment of taxes	226

(1) *Where there is no express Agreement.*

As a general rule, taxes and rates are payable in the first instance by the tenant. In the following cases he may obtain repayment by deducting the amount from his next payment of rent:—Where he has paid the landlord's share of the property tax (*e*), or the landlord's proportion of the land tax or sewer's rate; or rent-charge in lieu of tithes (*f*). One-half of the cattle plague rate may also be deducted from the growing

Taxes which fall on landlord.

(*d*) This section is of universal application, and not limited in its operation to the metropolitan district. See *Ex parte Gorely*, 34 L. J., Bk. 1; 13 W. R. 60. It seems to follow that a covenant to insure premises, not situate within the limits mentioned in the above act, will run with the land. See *Vernon* v. *Smith*, 5 B. & A. 1, 5.

(*e*) See *ante*, pp. 119, 120.
(*f*) *Ante*, p. 120.

rent due to the owner of the premises in respect of which the rate is levied (*g*).

<small>Stat. 32 & 33 Vict. c. 41, s. 1.
Tenant for shorter term than three months may deduct poor rates paid by him from rent.</small>

The occupier of any rateable hereditament let to him for a term not exceeding three months, shall be entitled to deduct the amount paid by him in respect of any poor rate assessed upon such hereditament from the rent due or accruing due to the owner, and every such payment shall be a valid discharge of the rent to the extent of the rate so paid.

<small>Sect. 2.
Such tenant not to be compelled to pay at one time more than one quarter's rate.</small>

No such occupier shall be compelled to pay to the overseers at one time, or within four weeks, a greater amount of the rate than would be due for one quarter of the year.

<small>Sect. 8.
Where owner who is liable to pay poor rates neglects to do so, tenant may pay and deduct from rent.</small>

Where an owner who has undertaken, whether by agreement with the occupier or with the overseers (*h*), to pay the poor rates, or has otherwise become liable to pay the same (*i*), omits or neglects to pay any such rate, the occupier may pay the same, and deduct the amount from the rent due or accruing due to the owner, and the receipt for such rate shall be a valid discharge of the rent to the extent of the rate so paid.

(*g*) Stat. 32 & 33 Vict. c. 70, s. 89.

(*h*) In case the rateable value of any hereditament does not exceed twenty pounds if situate in the metropolis, or thirteen pounds if situate in any parish wholly or partly within the borough of Liverpool, or ten pounds if situate in any parish wholly or partly within the city of Manchester or the borough of Birmingham, or eight pounds if situate elsewhere, and the owner is willing to enter into an agreement in writing with the overseers to become liable to them for the poor rates, for any term not less than one year, and to pay the poor rates whether the hereditament is occupied or not, the overseers may, subject to the control of the vestry, agree with the owner to receive the rates from him, and to allow to him a commission not exceeding twenty-five per cent. on the amount thereof (sect. 3).

(*i*) The vestry of any parish may order that the owners of all rateable hereditaments to which section three of this Act extends, situate within such parish, shall be rated to the poor rate instead of the occupiers. Provided that this clause shall not be applicable to any rateable hereditament in which a dwelling-house shall not be included (sect. 4).

(2) *Where there is an express Agreement.*

No covenant or agreement between landlord and tenant, or any other persons, touching the payment of taxes and assessments, to be charged on their respective premises, shall be deemed to extend to the duties charged thereon under this act, nor to be binding contrary to the intent and meaning of this act; but all such duties shall be charged upon and paid by the respective occupiers, subject to such deductions and repayments as are by this act authorized and allowed; and all such deductions and repayments shall be made and allowed accordingly, notwithstanding such covenants or agreements.

Agreements relating to property tax.
Stat. 5 & 6 Vict. c. 35, s. 73.
Agreements contrary to meaning of act not to be binding.

All contracts, covenants and agreements made or entered into or to be made or entered into for payment of any rent in full, without allowing such deduction (for the property tax), shall be utterly void (so far as regards such non-allowance of the deduction (*k*). A provision for reducing the rent if the property tax shall be repealed is, however, valid (*l*)).

Sect. 103.
Agreements for payment of rent without deducting property tax to be void.

If any occupying tenant of land shall quit, leaving unpaid any tithe rent-charge charged upon such land, which he was by the terms of his tenancy legally, or equitably, liable to pay, and the tithe owner shall give notice of proceeding by distress upon the land for recovery thereof, it shall be lawful for the landlord, or the succeeding tenant or occupier, to pay such tithe rent-charge, and any expenses incident thereto, and to recover the amount he may so pay, over against such

Payment of tithe rent-charge.
Stat. 14 & 15 Vict. c. 25, s. 4.
Landlord or succeeding tenant may pay tithe rent-charge left unpaid by preceding tenant, and

---

(*k*) *Gaskell* v. *King*, 11 East, 165; *Readshaw* v. *Balders*, 4 Taunt. 57; *Fuller* v. *Abbot*, Ib. 105; *Tinckler* v. *Prentice*, Ib. 549. See *Festing* v. *Taylor*, 3 B. & S. 217, 235; 31 L. J., Q. B. 36; 32 L. J., Q. B. 41.

(*l*) *Colbron* v. *Travers*, 12 C. B., N. S. 181; 31 L. J., C. P. 257.

F.   Q

Construction of agreements relating to payment of taxes.

AGREEMENT, *by tenant, to pay all taxes, &c.* The words comprehend the land tax, although not specially mentioned (*m*).

COVENANT, *by lessee, to pay all taxes, charges, rates, tithes, or rent-charge in lieu of tithe, dues, and duties whatsoever now, or at any time during the demise, imposed upon the demised premises.* Does not relate solely to rates payable by the landlord, but includes all rates imposed on the lessee in respect of his occupation, and all future rates which may be imposed on the land (*n*).

COVENANT, *by lessor, to pay all taxes on the land demised.* Does not include poor rates (*o*).

COVENANT *to pay parliamentary taxes.* Includes the land tax (*p*) and all taxes directly imposed by parliament; but not a county rate (*q*), or sewer's rate (*r*), or an assessment levied under an act for repairing a bridge, to the repair of which the owners of land are liable *ratione tenuræ* (*s*).

(*m*) *Amfield* v. *White*, Ry. & M. 246.

(*n*) *Hurst* v. *Hurst*, 4 Ex. 571; 19 L. J., Ex. 410.

(*o*) *Theed* v. *Starkey*, 8 Mod. 314.

(*p*) *Manning* v. *Lunn*, 2 C. & K. 13. See *Christ's Hospital* v. *Harrild*, 3 Sc. N. R. 126; 2 M. & Gr. 707.

(*q*) See *Palmer* v. *Earith*, 14 M. & W., at p. 430.

(*r*) *Palmer* v. *Earith*, 14 M. & W. 428; 14 L. J., Ex. 256. See *Brewster* v. *Kitchel*, 2 Salk. 616.

(*s*) *Baker* v. *Greenhill*, 3 Q. B. 148.

COVENANT *to pay parochial taxes and assessments.* Apparently includes a county rate (*t*).

COVENANT, *by lessee, to pay all such parliamentary, parochial and county, district and occasional levies, rates, assessments, taxes, charges, impositions, contributions, burdens, duties and services whatsoever as during the term shall be imposed upon the premises.* The lessee will be liable for the expense of executing drainage works done by the authority of " The Metropolis Local Management Act, 1855 "(*u*).

COVENANT, *by tenant of a house, to pay all taxes, rates, duties and assessments whatsoever which during the demise shall be imposed on the tenant or landlord of the premises demised in respect thereof, whether parliamentary, parochial or otherwise.* Extends to a payment which the landlord has been obliged to make, under the Metropolis Local Management Acts, for the paving of the street (*x*). But if under a local improvement act the landlord's duty in the first instance is not to pay money but to pave the street, with a provision that, on default of the landlord, the council may pave and charge the landlord with the expenses thereof, or, by way of additional remedy, charge the occupier, who may deduct sums so paid from his rent; a tenant who has entered into a covenant similar to that above mentioned will not be liable to

---

(*t*) *Reg.* v. *Aylesbury,* 9 Q. B. 261.
(*u*) *Sweet* v. *Seager,* 2 C. B., N. S. 119.
(*x*) *Thompson* v. *Lapworth,* 37 L. J., C. P. 74 ; L. R., 3 C. P. 149. See *Payne* v. *Burridge,* 12 M. & W. 727 ; 13 L. J., Ex. 190.

repay to the landlord the amount of expenses (*y*).

AGREEMENT *to demise a farm at the yearly rent of 40l. payable quarterly, free of all outgoings.* The landlord is entitled to a net rent payable free of land tax and tithe commutation rent-charge (*z*).

COVENANT, *by landlord, to pay land tax.* The landlord is only liable to pay land tax in proportion to the rent reserved to him, and not according to the rent upon which the premises are taxed (*a*).

COVENANT *to pay a yearly rent of 60l. clear of all rates and assessments, sewer's rate and land tax excepted.* Where the tenant, by building on the land, has increased its rateable value, he is only entitled to deduct the proportion of the sewer's rate and land tax payable upon the original rent (*b*).

COVENANT, *by lessor, to pay all taxes now chargeable on the demised premises, and by lessee to pay all fresh taxes which shall hereafter be charged on the premises.* The lessor must pay the taxes chargeable on the premises at the time of making the lease, but the lessee must pay all fresh taxes, and also all such additions to the amount of the taxes formerly chargeable, as are occasioned by the improved value of the premises (*c*).

(*y*) *Tidswell* v. *Whitworth*, 36 L. J., C. P. 103; L. R., 2 C. P. 326.

(*z*) *Parish* v. *Sleeman*, 1 De G., F. & J. 326; 29 L. J., Ch. 96.

(*a*) *Yaw* v. *Leman*, 1 Wils. 21; *Whitfield* v. *Brandwood*, 2 Stark. 440; *Watson* v. *Home*, 7 B. & C. 285. See *Ward* v. *Const*, 10 B. & C. 635.

(*b*) *Smith* v. *Humble*, 15 C. B. 321; *Hyde* v. *Hill*, 3 T. R. 377.

(*c*) *Watson* v. *Atkins*, 3 B. & A. 647. See *Graham* v. *Wade*,

Sect. X.— *Quiet Enjoyment.*

	PAGE
(1) Where there is no express agreement	229
Implied contract for quiet enjoyment	229
What constitutes an eviction	230
(2) Where there is an express agreement	232
Construction of restricted covenant for quiet enjoyment	232
„ general covenant „ „ ..	233
„ special covenants „ „ ..	233
Damages for breach of covenant „ „ ..	234

---

(1) Where there is no express Agreement.

A contract for quiet enjoyment is implied under a parol demise of a tenement (*d*). An action of covenant will lie against the lessor upon the word "demise" in a lease by deed, for that word imports a covenant in law on the part of the lessor that he has good title, and that the lessee shall quietly enjoy during the term (*e*). But this implied covenant ceases with the estate of the lessor; hence if, under a lease made by a tenant for life (not containing any express covenant for quiet enjoyment) the lessee is evicted by the remainderman after the death of the lessor, the lessee cannot maintain an action upon an implied covenant for quiet enjoyment against the executor of the tenant for life (*f*). A person who lets premises agrees to give possession, and not merely to give a chance of a lawsuit (*g*). If he does not give possession the lessee may recover damages against

Implied contract for quiet enjoyment.

---

16 East, 29; *Hurst* v. *Hurst*, 4 Ex. 571; 19 L. J., Ex. 410.

(*d*) *Bandy* v. *Cartwright*, 8 Ex. 913; 22 L. J., Ex. 285; *Hall* v. *City of London Brewery Co.*, 2 B. & S. 737; 31 L. J., Q. B. 257. See *Granger* v. *Collins*, 6 M. & W. 458; *Messent* v. *Reynolds*, 3 C. B. 194; 15 L. J., C. P. 226.

(*e*) Per Littledale, J., in *Burnett* v. *Lynch*, 5 B. & C., at p. 609; *Iggulden* v. *May*, 9 Ves., at p. 330.

(*f*) *Adams* v. *Gibney*, 6 Bing. 656. See *Penfold* v. *Abbot*, 32 L. J., Q. B. 67; 11 W. R. 169; 7 L. T., N. S. 384.

(*g*) Judgment in *Coe* v. *Clay*, 5 Bing. 440.

him, and is not obliged to bring ejectment against an occupier who wrongfully refuses to quit (*h*). One of the necessary consequences of the implied agreement on the part of every landlord for his tenant's quiet enjoyment is that the landlord, if himself a lessee, shall, by paying over to the superior landlord the rent received from the under-tenant, protect such under-tenant from the superior landlord's distress (*i*).

The covenant implied in the word "demise" will be qualified and restrained by an express covenant for quiet enjoyment (*k*). Hence, the lessee, upon an eviction by a paramount title, cannot recover under the implied covenant if the lease contains an express covenant for quiet enjoyment against the lessor and those who claim under him (*l*). The implied indemnity is also limited to the wrongful entry of the lessor or of persons claiming under or paramount to him (*m*). No action will lie upon it for an eviction of the tenant by a stranger (*n*).

What constitutes an eviction.

To constitute an eviction of a tenant by his landlord which will operate as a suspension of rent, it is not necessary that there should be an actual physical expulsion from any part of the premises; any act of a permanent character done by the landlord or by his authority, with the intention of depriving the tenant of the enjoyment of the premises as demised, or any part of them, will operate as an eviction (*o*). Whether such intention does or does not exist is a question for a

(*h*) *Coe* v. *Clay*, 5 Bing. 440; *Jinks* v. *Edwards*, 11 Ex. 775. See *Drury* v. *Macnamara*, 5 E. & B. 612; 25 L. J., Q. B. 5.

(*i*) See judgment in *Hancock* v. *Caffyn*, 8 Bing., at p. 366. See *Upton* v. *Fergusson*, 3 Moo. & Sc. 88.

(*k*) *Line* v. *Stephenson*, 4 Bing. N. C. 678; 5 Bing. N. C. 183.

(*l*) *Merrill* v. *Frame*, 4 Taunt. 329.

(*m*) Smith L. & T. 285.

(*n*) See *Andrew's Case*, Cro. Eliz. 214.

(*o*) *Upton* v. *Townend*, 17 C. B. 30; 25 L. J., C. P. 44.

jury (p). Where a tenant from year to year quits at the end of the current year without notice, and before the expiration of the next half-year the landlord lets the premises to another tenant, who occupies them, such letting constitutes an eviction of the previous tenant (q), and the landlord is not entitled to recover rent from him for the period which elapsed from the time when he quitted the premises to the time when the landlord relet them (r), or for any subsequent period during which they may be unoccupied (s). The landlord who relets should give notice to the former tenant that he lets the premises solely on such tenant's account (s). If while a tenant is in the possession of premises, the landlord enters and uses any part of them, he thereby deprives himself of his claim to rent (t). So also if after a tenant has left a house unoccupied, the landlord enters and is in profitable occupation of the house, he cannot recover rent from the tenant after such occupation; but this result will not be produced by merely putting a person into the house to take care of it and prevent depredations (u). The landlord of apartments deserted by the tenant may recover rent, although he has put up a bill in the window for the purpose of letting them (x), or has lighted fires in the rooms and made some use of such fires (t).

(p) *Upton* v. *Townend*, 17 C. B. 30; 25 L. J., C. P. 44; *Henderson* v. *Mears*, 28 L. J., Q. B. 305; 7 W. R. 554. See *Wheeler* v. *Stevenson*, 6 H. & N. 155; 30 L. J., Ex. 46.

(q) Judgment of Holroyd, J., in *Hall* v. *Burgess*, 5 B. & C., at p. 333.

(r) *Hall* v. *Burgess*, 5 B. & C. 332.

(s) *Walls* v. *Atcheson*, 3 Bing. 462.

(t) *Griffith* v. *Hodges*, 1 C. & P. 419, 420.

(u) *Bird* v. *Defonvielle*, 2 C. & K. 415.

(x) *Redpath* v. *Roberts*, 3 Esp. 225.

(2) *Where there is an express Agreement.*

<small>Construction of restricted covenant for quiet enjoyment.</small>

The ordinary *covenant, by the lessor, for quiet enjoyment as against any person claiming by, from or under him*, is broken by an eviction of the tenant by the lessor's widow entitled under a conveyance taken by the lessor to the use of himself and his wife (*y*); also by an eviction by a person claiming under a prior appointment by the covenantor and another person (*z*); but a distress for arrears of land tax due from the lessor at the time of the demise will not operate as a breach (*a*). The lessee of a house and garden, forming part of a large area of building ground, is not entitled under this covenant to restrain the lessor or persons claiming under him from building on the adjoining land so as to obstruct the free access of light and air to the garden (*b*). When contained in a lease of the exclusive right of shooting and sporting over a farm, this covenant does not hinder the tenant of the farm from using the land in the ordinary way, or from destroying furze and underwood in the reasonable use of the land as a farm; and the lessor will not be liable for wrongful acts committed by such tenant contrary to the reservation of his landlord (*c*). Under a covenant in the form above mentioned contained in a lease of a stream of water, excepting so much as should be sufficient for the supply of persons with whom the lessor should have already contracted, diversions occasioned by contracts made previously to the demise will not constitute breaches (*d*).

(*y*) *Butler* v. *Swinnerton*, Cro. Jac. 657.

(*z*) *Calvert* v. *Sebright*, 15 Beav. 156.

(*a*) *Stanley* v. *Hayes*, 3 Q. B. 105.

(*b*) *Potts* v. *Smith*, 38 L. J., Ch. 58; L. R., 6 Eq. 311.

(*c*) *Jeffryes* v. *Evans*, 34 L. J., C. P. 261, 264; 19 C. B., N. S. 246. See *Newton* v. *Wilmot*, 8 M. & W. 711; *post*, p. 261.

(*d*) *Blatchford* v. *Plymouth*, 3 Bing. N. C. 691.

Where the covenant provides that the lessee shall quietly hold and enjoy the premises *for and during the said term*, the last words must be taken to refer to the term which the lessor assumed to grant by the lease, and not to the term which he actually had power to grant (e).

A *general covenant for quiet enjoyment* extends only to the acts of persons claiming under a lawful title (f); for the law will never adjudge that a lessor covenants against the wrongful acts of strangers, except his covenant is express to that purpose (g). The construction, however, is different where an individual is named; for there the covenantor is presumed to know the person against whose acts he is content to covenant, and may therefore be reasonably expected to stipulate against any disturbance from him, whether by lawful title or otherwise (h).

Construction of general covenant for quiet enjoyment.

Under a general covenant for quiet enjoyment contained in the lease of a coal mine, the working of ironstone lying between the surface and the demised coal in such a manner as to interrupt the lessee in his occupation of the mine, will constitute a breach (i).

COVENANT, *by lessor, in an underlease, that lessee shall hold the premises without any lawful eviction, &c. by the lessor, or any persons whomsoever claiming by, from, under or in trust for her, or by or through her acts,* MEANS, *right, &c.* An eviction of the underlessee by the original lessor

Construction of special covenants for quiet enjoyment.

(e) *Evans* v. *Vaughan,* 4 B. & C. 261, 268.
(f) *Dudley* v. *Folliott,* 3 T. R. 584.
(g) *Wotton* v. *Hele,* 2 Wms. Saund. 178, note (8).
(h) Judgment of Ld. Ellenborough, C. J., in *Nash* v. *Palmer,* 5 M. & S., at p. 380; *Fowle* v. *Welsh,* 1 B. & C. 29.
(i) *Shaw* v. *Stenton,* 2 H. & N. 858; 27 L. J., Ex. 253.

for a forfeiture incurred by the use of the premises as a shop, contrary to a covenant in the original lease, of which the underlessee had not been informed, is not an eviction by *means* of the lessor within the meaning of the covenant (*l*).

COVENANT *that the tenant, paying the rent and performing the covenants, shall quietly enjoy.* The payment of rent is not a condition precedent to the performance of the covenant for quiet enjoyment (*m*).

CLAUSE *in a deed whereby the lessor "for himself, his heirs and assigns, the premises unto (the lessee), his executors, administrators and assigns under the rents, covenants, &c. before expressed, against all persons whatsoever lawfully claiming the same, shall and will, during the term, warrant and defend."* The clause operates as an express covenant for quiet enjoyment during the whole term granted by the lease (*n*).

Damages for breach of covenant. Upon the breach of a covenant for quiet enjoyment in a lease, which turns out to be void, and under which the lessee has entered, the lessee is entitled to recover the value of the term and the costs of defending an action of ejectment, and also the sum recovered as mesne profits by the plaintiff in such action (*n*). The same rule applies where the lessee has not actually entered, but has only an *interesse termini* (*o*), and where he has accepted a new lease of the premises from the person entitled to them, the difference in value between the two

---

(*l*) *Spencer* v. *Marriott*, 1 B. & C. 457. See *Woodhouse* v. *Jenkins*, 9 Bing. 431.
(*m*) *Dawson* v. *Dyer*, 5 B. & Ad. 584.
(*n*) *Williams* v. *Burrell*, 1 C. B. 402; 14 L. J., C. P. 99.
(*o*) See *ante*, p. 107.

leases may be used as a test of the amount of damages to which he is entitled (*p*).

Sect. XI.—*Underleases.*

	PAGE
(1) Right to underlet	235
Where there is no express agreement	235
Where there is an express agreement	236
(2) What constitutes an underlease	236
Underleases distinguished from assignments	236
(3) Rights and liabilities of underlessee	237
As against original lessor	237
,, underlessor	238
,, co-lessees	239

(1) *Right to underlet.*

A lessee for years or from year to year, unless restrained by express agreement, may, without the consent of his lessor, grant underleases for any number of years less than the term for which he holds the premises. A demise by a tenant from year to year to another, also to hold from year to year, is, in legal operation, a demise from year to year during the continuance of the original demise to the intermediate landlord (*q*). *[Where there is no express agreement. Tenant for years or from year to year.]*

There cannot, strictly speaking, be a tenant to a tenant at will, since, if the latter leases, the will is determined (*r*). But though a tenant at will cannot, as against his landlord, constitute another person tenant at will, he can make a tenant at will as against himself (*s*). One tenant at sufferance cannot make another (*t*). *[Tenant at will. Tenant at sufferance.]*

(*p*) *Lock* v. *Furze,* 34 L. J., C. P. 201; 35 L. J., C. P. 141; 19 C. B., N. S. 96; L. R., 1 C. P. 441.

(*q*) Per Parke, B., in *Oxley* v. *James,* 13 L. J., Ex., at p. 359; 13 M. & W. 209; *Pike* v. *Eyre,* 9 B. & C. 909.

(*r*) Judgment of Buller, J., in *Birch* v. *Wright,* 1 T. R., at p. 382. See *post,* p. 240, n (*r*).

(*s*) Per Patteson, J., in *Doe* v. *Carter,* 9 Q. B., at p. 865.

(*t*) Judgment of Ld. Ellen-

236 TERMS OF TENANCY.

Where there is an express agreement. There is nothing unreasonable in a covenant not to sublet without licence, although contained in a building lease (*u*).

Construction of express covenants relating to underletting. COVENANT, *by lessee, not to grant any underlease for any term whatsoever, or let, assign, transfer, set over or otherwise part with the messuage and premises without the special licence of the lessor.* Extends only to such underletting as a licence might be expected to be applied for, and therefore letting lodgings is not a breach of the covenant (*w*).

COVENANT *not to assign, transfer, set over or otherwise do or put away the lease or premises.* Does not extend to an underlease for part of the term (*x*).

PROVISO *not to assign or otherwise part with the premises or any part thereof for the whole or any part of the term.* The words include an underlease (*y*).

COVENANT *not to let, set or demise the premises for all or any part of the term.* An assignment will be a breach (*z*).

(2) *What constitutes an Underlease.*

Underleases distinguished from assignments. The term granted by an underlease must, in general (*a*), be shorter than that which the underlessor

borough, C. J., in *Thunder* v. *Belcher*, 3 East, at p. 451. See *Shopland* v. *Ryder*, Cro. Jac. 55.
(*u*) *Haberdashers' Co.* v. *Isaac*, 3 Jur., N. S. 64.
(*w*) *Doe* v. *Laming*, 4 Camp. 77. But see *Roe* v. *Sales*, 1 M. & S. 297; and observations of Parke, B., in *Greenslade* v. *Tapscott*, 1

Cr. M. & R., at p. 59.
(*x*) *Crusoe* v. *Bugby*, 2 W. Bl. 766; *Church* v. *Brown*, 15 Ves., at p. 265.
(*y*) *Doe* v. *Worsley*, 1 Camp. 20.
(*z*) *Greenaway* v. *Adams*, 12 Ves. 395.
(*a*) See *ante*, p. 136, note (*t*).

himself possesses. A grant by a man by deed of the whole of his interest in premises, or of a greater interest in them than he actually possesses (*b*), will operate as an absolute conveyance or assignment, whatever may be the form of words used, and though the deed reserves rent, and contains a power of re-entry on non-payment of rent (*c*). In some recent cases it has, however, been held, that where the parties intend to create the relation of landlord and tenant, a parol demise for all the residue of the interest of the lessor, since it cannot operate as an assignment, may be construed a lease, and that the lessor may maintain an action of use and occupation, or of debt for the rent thereby reserved, though he cannot distrain for it (*d*).

(3) *Rights and Liabilities of Underlessee.*

The underlessee is not personally liable for the rent reserved in the original lease, but any goods belonging to him which are upon the demised premises may be distrained for arrears of rent due by the original lessee (*e*). At law the underlessee is not directly liable for breaches of the covenants in the original lease (*f*), but he may be

As against original lessor. As to rent.

As to covenants in original lease.

(*b*) *Hicks* v. *Downing*, 1 Ld. Raym. 99; *Wollaston* v. *Hakewill*, 3 M. & Gr. 297; 10 L. J., C. P., pp. 308, 309. See *Baker* v. *Gostling*, 1 Bing. N. C. 19.

(*c*) *Smith* v. *Mapleback*, 1 T. R. 441; *Palmer* v. *Edwards*, 1 Dougl. 187 (note); *Parmenter* v. *Webber*, 8 Taunt. 593; *Thorn* v. *Woolcombe*, 3 B. & Ad. 586; *Pluck* v. *Digges*, 5 Bligh, N. S. 31; *Beardmore* v. *Wilson*, 38 L. J., C. P. 91; L. R., 4 C. P. 57.

(*d*) *Baker* v. *Gostling*, 1 Bing.

N. C. 19; *Williams* v. *Hayward*, 1 E. & E. 1040; *Pollock* v. *Stacy*, 9 Q. B. 1033; 16 L. J., Q. B. 132. See observations of Bovill, C. J., in *Beardmore* v. *Wilson*, 38 L. J., C. P., at p. 92; L. R., 4 C. P., at p. 58. See also *Poultney* v. *Holmes*, 1 Stra. 405; *Precce* v. *Corrie*, 5 Bing. 24.

(*e*) See *ante*, pp. 137, 170, note (*e*).

(*f*) *Berney* v. *Moore*, 2 Ridg. P. C., at p. 323.

evicted by the original lessor for a forfeiture incurred by such breaches, and, in that case, it would seem that, in the absence of fraudulent misrepresentation or concealment, he will have no remedy against his immediate lessor (*g*). The original lessor may obtain an injunction from the Court of Chancery to restrain the underlessee from committing breaches of the covenants in the original lease (*h*). It is the duty of a person contracting for an underlease from year to year (*i*), or for any longer term, to inform himself of the covenants contained in the original lease; and if he enters and takes possession of the property, he will be considered as having full notice of, and will be bound by such covenants (*j*). Where a person takes an underlease from the assignee of a lease, the underlessee, without notice, is bound by the covenants contained in the assignment (*k*).

<small>Underlessee considered to have notice of covenants in original lease.</small>

Covenants to repair in a lease and an underlease granted at different periods, though in terms the same, are in effect substantially different (*l*), because the underlessee is only bound to put the premises in the same condition as he found them in at the time of the lease to him (*l*). Where an underlease contains a covenant to repair identical in language with a covenant contained in the original lease, and the original lessor has sued the lessee on his covenant to repair, the latter may recover from his underlessee the damages obtained by

<small>Liability of underlessee to underlessor. As to repairs.</small>

(*g*) See *Spencer* v. *Marriott*, 1 B. & C. 457, 459; *Hayward* v. *Parke*, 16 C. B. 295; 24 L. J., C. P. 217. But see *Van* v. *Corpe*, 3 My. & K. 269.

(*h*) See *Clements* v. *Welles*, 35 L. J., Ch. 265; L. R., 1 Eq. 200.

(*i*) *Wilson* v. *Hart*, 35 L. J., Ch. 569; L. R., 1 Ch. 463.

(*j*) *Cosser* v. *Collinge*, 3 My. & K. 283; *Flight* v. *Barton*, Ib. 282; *Clements* v. *Welles*, 35 L. J., Ch. 265; L. R., 1 Eq. 200.

(*k*) *Clements* v. *Welles*, 35 L. J., Ch. 265, 267; L. R., 1 Eq. 200.

(*l*) *Walker* v. *Hatton*, 10 M. & W. 249, 257; 11 L. J., Ex. 361.

the original lessor, but not the costs incurred by defending the action (*m*). Premises held under a lease containing a clause of re-entry for want of repairs were underlet, and the underlessee undertook to repair within three months after notice; the original lessor having threatened to insist on the forfeiture if the premises were not repaired, and the underlessee not having repaired at the expiration of three months after notice to do so, the original lessee entered and repaired: it was held that he might recover from the underlessee the sum expended in such repairs (*n*). An undertenant may deduct from his rent compulsory payments made by him of arrears of rent due from the original tenant to the original landlord (*o*). Where underlessees hold separate portions of premises at distinct rents, the whole of the premises being held under one original lease at an entire rent; and one of the underlessees under threat of a distress by the owner of the reversion on the original lease pays the whole rent, an action is not maintainable by him to recover from the other underlessee, as money paid to his use, the proportion of the rent due from him (*p*).

As to rent.

Liability of underlessees as between themselves.

Sect. XII.—*Assignments.*

	PAGE
(1) Voluntary	240
(a) Right to assign	240
Where there is no express agreement	240
Where there is an express agreement	240
Construction of covenant not to assign	241
Operation of licence	242

(*m*) *Walker* v. *Hatton*, 10 M. & W. 249, 257; 11 L. J., Ex. 361; *Penley* v. *Watts*, 7 M. & W. 601; 10 L. J., Ex. 229.

(*n*) *Colley* v. *Streeton*, 2 B. & C. 273.

(*o*) *Ante*, p. 121.

(*p*) *Hunter* v. *Hunt*, 1 C. B. 300.

	PAGE
(1) Voluntary—*continued*.	
(b) Mode of making assignment	244
Statutory requisites	244
(c) Rights and liabilities of assignee	245
As against lessor	245
In what cases covenants run with land	246
Effect of re-assignment	249
Continued liability of lessee	250
As against lessee	250
Covenants to indemnify lessee	250
Rights of assignee as to title	251
(d) Grant by landlord of his reversion	252
(2) Involuntary	253
(a) On death	253
Of lessor	253
Of lessee	254
(b) On bankruptcy of lessee	256
(c) On conviction of lessee for felony	258

(1) *Voluntary Assignments.*

(a) *Right to assign.*

Where there is no express agreement.

The right to assign, unless expressly restrained, is incident to the estate of every tenant (*q*), except a tenant by sufferance. An assignment by a tenant at will determines the tenancy if the lessor has notice, but not otherwise (*r*).

Where there is an express agreement.

The lessor, either by proviso or covenant, may restrain the lessee from assigning; and if the lessor grants the term subject to a condition that it shall cease if the lessee assigns, an assignment by the lessee will be void. But where the restraint is by covenant only, the lessee by assigning will commit a breach of covenant, but the assignment itself will not be void (*s*). A proviso against assignment without licence contained in a lease to the lessee, his executors, administrators AND ASSIGNS, is not

(*q*) See *Church* v. *Brown*, 15 Ves., at p. 264. As to assignments of leases to which lunatics are entitled, see stat. 16 & 17 Vict. c. 70, s. 127.

(*r*) *Pinhorn* v. *Souster*, 8 Ex.

763; 22 L. J., Ex. 266; *Carpenter* v. *Colins*, Yelv. 73. See *post*, Chap. V., Sect. 1, (b).

(*s*) See remarks of Holroyd, J., in *Paul* v. *Nurse*, 8 B. & C., at p. 488.

repugnant; for the assigns mentioned in the proviso must be understood to be such as the lessee may lawfully have, *i. e.* assigns by licence (*t*).

A covenant not to assign or otherwise part with the demised premises or any part thereof without the licence of the lessor does not extend to an involuntary assignment, upon the death (*u*) or bankruptcy of the lessee (*x*); or under a *bonâ fide* execution against him (*y*); or to a railway company under the Lands Clauses Consolidation Act (*z*); but if the tenant gives a warrant of attorney for the express purpose of having the lease taken in execution (*a*), or executes a deed assigning his property for the benefit of his creditors (*b*), he will commit a breach of the covenant. A trustee in bankruptcy (*x*), and perhaps also an executor or administrator where not named in the covenant, may dispose of the lease as assets, notwithstanding a proviso or covenant that the lessee shall not alien (*u*). It seems that the covenant will not be broken by a bequest of the term by the lessee (*c*). Depositing the lease with a creditor as security for an advance of money (*d*), or a mere parting with the possession,—no transfer of the lease being executed so as to make the

Construction of covenant not to assign.

(*t*) *Weatherall* v. *Geering*, 12 Ves. 504, 511.
(*u*) See *Seers* v. *Hind*, 1 Ves. jun., at p. 295; *Roe* v. *Harrison*, 2 T. R. 425.
(*x*) *Doe* v. *Bevan*, 3 M. & S. 353, 358, 360. See *Weatherall* v. *Geering*, 12 Ves. 504; *Doe* v. *Smith*, 5 Taunt. 795.
(*y*) *Doe* v. *Carter*, 8 T. R. 57.
(*z*) *Slipper* v. *Tottenham and Hampstead Junction Ry. Co.*, 36 L. J., Ch. 841; L. R, 4 Eq. 112.

(*a*) *Doe* v. *Carter*, 8 T. R. 300.
(*b*) *Holland* v. *Cole*, 1 H. & C. 67; 31 L. J., Ex. 481.
(*c*) Per Bayley, J., in *Doe* v. *Bevan*, 3 M. & S., at p. 361; *Crusoe* v. *Bugby*, 3 Wils, at p. 237. But see *Knight* v. *Mory*, Cro. Eliz. 60; *Barry* v. *Stanton*, Ib. 330.
(*d*) *Doe* v. *Laming*, Ry. & M. 36; *Doe* v. *Hogg*, 4 D. & R. 226. See *Doe* v. *Bevan*, 3 M. & S. 353.

F.

242   TERMS OF TENANCY.

possessor an assignee bound by the covenants running with the land,—will not occasion a forfeiture for breach of this covenant (*e*). An assignment which is void in law as an act of bankruptcy, will not give rise to a forfeiture under a clause of re-entry on the lessee's assigning without the licence of the lessor (*f*).

Licence to assign.

The licence of the landlord may be by parol, unless required by the terms of the covenant to be in writing (*g*). It should expressly forbid the lessee from parting with the possession until a complete transfer of the legal interest has been effected. The practice of letting a purchaser into possession before the legal estate is transferred, is, however, so common, that, if it is intended to forbid it, such intention must be clearly expressed (*h*). A covenant by the lessor not to withhold his licence to assign unreasonably or vexatiously, is broken by his refusing his licence to assign to an unobjectionable person, in order thereby to obtain a surrender of the lease for the purpose of rebuilding (*i*). Upon an agreement to assign a lease containing a covenant not to

---

(*e*) *West* v. *Dobb*, 38 L. J., Q. B. 289; L. R., 4 Q. B. 634.

(*f*) *Doe* v. *Powell*, 5 B. & C. 308.

(*g*) See *Roe* v. *Harrison*, 2 T. R. 425; *Richardson* v. *Evans*, 3 Madd. 218. Where the licence is indorsed on the assignment, it may be in the following form:—

I do hereby consent to the within-written assignment.

—— February, 187—.   E. F.

If the licence is not indorsed on the assignment, the following form may be used (no stamp is requisite):—

I do hereby consent to the assignment by C. D. of all his estate in the premises demised by an indenture of lease, dated the —— day of —— 18—, unto P. Q. of ——, his executors and administrators; on condition, nevertheless, that the said C. D. shall not part with the possession of the said premises, or any part thereof, until the whole of his estate and interest therein shall be legally and effectually vested in the said P. Q.

—— February, 187—.   E. F.

Witness, N. O.

(*h*) *West* v. *Dobb*, 38 L. J., Q. B. 289, 292; L. R., 4 Q. B. 634.

(*i*) *Lehmann* v. *M'Arthur*, 15 W. R. 551; L. R., 3 Eq. 746.

assign without the licence of the lessor, it is the duty of the vendor, and not of the purchaser, to procure the lessor's licence for the assignment (*k*).

Where any licence to do any act which without such licence would create a forfeiture, or give a right to re-enter under a condition or power reserved in any lease shall, after the passing of this act, be given to any lessee or his assigns, every such licence shall, unless otherwise expressed, extend only to the permission actually given, or to any specific breach of any proviso or covenant made or to be made, or to the actual assignment, underlease or other matter thereby specifically authorized to be done, but not so as to prevent any proceeding for any subsequent breach (unless otherwise specified in such licence); and all rights under covenants and powers of forfeiture and re-entry in the lease contained shall remain in full force and virtue, and shall be available as against any subsequent breach of covenant or condition, assignment, underlease or other matter not specifically authorized or made dispunishable by such licence, in the same manner as if no such licence had been given; and the condition or right of re-entry shall remain in all respects as if such licence had not been given, except in respect of the particular matter authorized to be done. Stat. 22 & 23 Vict. c. 35, s. 1. Effect of licence restricted to breach of covenant authorized.

Where in any lease there shall be a power or condition of re-entry on assigning or underletting or doing any other specified act without licence, and a licence at any time after the passing of this act shall be given to one of several lessees or co-owners to assign or underlet his share or interest, or to do any other act prohibited to be done without licence; or shall be given to any lessee or owner, or any one of several lessees or owners, Sect. 2. Licence to one of several co-lessees;

(*k*) *Lloyd* v. *Crispe*, 5 Taunt. 249; *Mason* v. *Corder*, 7 Taunt. 9.

or relating to part only of property, not to destroy condition of re-entry on breach of covenant by other co-lessees or in respect of remaining property.

to assign or underlet part only of the property, or to do any other such act as aforesaid in respect of part only of such property, such licence shall not operate to destroy or extinguish the right of re-entry in case of any breach of the covenant or condition by the co-lessee or co-lessees or owner or owners of the other shares or interests in the property, or by the lessee or owner of the rest of the property (as the case may be) in respect of such shares or interests or remaining property, but such right of re-entry shall remain in full force in respect of the shares or interests or property not the subject of such licence.

(b) *Mode of making Assignment.*

Statutory requisites.
Stat. 29 Car. 2, c. 3, s. 3.
Assignments to be in writing.

No leases, estates or interests, either of freehold or terms of years, or any uncertain interest, not being copyhold or customary interest, shall be assigned unless it be by deed or note in writing, signed by the party so assigning or (his) agent thereunto lawfully authorized by writing, or by act or operation of law.

Stat. 8 & 9 Vict. c. 106, s. 3.
Assignments void at law unless made by deed.

An assignment of a chattel interest, not being copyhold, in any tenements or hereditaments shall be void at law, unless made by deed (*o*).

(*o*) For the stamp duty on an assignment of a lease, upon a sale, see *ante*, p. 98, note (*f*). The duty on an assignment by way of security is as follows (stat. 33 & 34 Vict. c. 97):—

				£	*s.*	*d.*
(1.) Being the only or principal or primary security for the payment or repayment of money not exceeding 25*l*.				0	0	8
Exceeding 25*l*. and not exceeding 50*l*.			..	0	1	3
,,	50*l*.	,,	100*l*. ..	0	2	6
,,	100*l*.	,,	150*l*. ..	0	3	9
,,	150*l*.	,,	200*l*. ..	0	5	0
,,	200*l*.	,,	250*l*. ..	0	6	3
,,	250*l*.	,,	300*l*. ..	0	7	6
,,	300*l*. For every 100*l*. and also for any fractional part of 100*l*. of such amount		..	0	2	6

ASSIGNMENTS.

Any person shall have power to assign personal property, now by law assignable, including chattels real, directly to himself and another person or other persons or corporation, by the like means as he might assign the same to another.

<small>Stat. 22 & 23 Vict. c. 35, s. 21.
Assignor may assign directly to himself and another person.</small>

(c) *Rights and Liabilities of Assignee.*

A mere deposit of a lease by way of equitable mortgage does not render the person with whom it is deposited liable at law (*p*) or, perhaps, in equity (*q*) for the rent or upon the covenants. An agreement to take an assignment of a lease, followed by possession on the part of the equitable assignee, does not entitle the lessor to sue him on the covenants in the lease (*r*).

<small>1. As against the lessor.</small>

A person who has accepted a valid assignment from the lessee, although he has not taken possession of the premises (*s*), becomes liable for rent subsequently accruing, and for breaches committed subsequently to the assignment (*t*), of such of the lessee's covenants as run with the land. On the other hand, he is entitled to sue the lessor for breaches, committed subsequently

---

(2.) Being a collateral, or auxiliary, or additional, or substituted security, or by way of further assurance for the above-mentioned purpose where the principal or primary security is duly stamped:

For every 100*l.* and also for any fractional part of 100*l.* of the amount secured .. .. .. £ *s. d.* 0 0 6

(*p*) *Doe* v. *Roe*, 5 Esp. 105.
(*q*) *Moores* v. *Choat*, 8 Sim. 508; *Robinson* v. *Rosher*, 1 Y. & C. C. C. 7. See *Lucas* v. *Comerford*, 1 Ves. 235; *Williams* v. *Evans*, 23 Beav. 239.
(*r*) *Cox* v. *Bishop*, 8 De G., M. & G. 815; 26 L. J., Ch. 389. But see *Close* v. *Wilberforce*, 1 Beav. 112.
(*s*) *Williams* v. *Bosanquet*, 1 B. & B. 238; *Burton* v. *Barclay*, 7 Bing. 745, 761.
(*t*) *St. Saviour's, Southwark* v. *Smith*, 1 W. Bl. 351. See *Hawkins* v. *Sherman*, 3 C. & P. 459.

to the assignment (*u*), of such of the lessor's covenants as run with the land. The doctrine of covenants running with the land applies only to covenants which are annexed to the estate by the indenture which creates the estate, and it seems that there is no case in which a mere assignment of a parol tenancy has been held to pass to the assignees the right to enforce collateral stipulations, unless the landlord has consented to the substitution of the assignee in the place of the original tenant, so as to create a new contract between them upon the terms of the previous tenancy (*x*). The assignee of part of the demised premises is liable to an action on every covenant running with the land and affecting such part (*y*). He is not chargeable as assignee of the land for the entire rent (*z*), but after an assignment by the lessee of his interest in part of the demised land, the lessor may distrain upon that part for the rent which has accrued due for the whole (*z*).

Where covenants run with land.
1. Where "assigns" are not mentioned.

In the following cases the burden and benefit of covenants pass with the land to the assignee:—Where a covenant in a demise of corporeal or incorporeal (*a*) hereditaments relates to a thing *in esse*, parcel of the demise, the thing to be done by force of the covenant is *quodammodo* annexed and appurtenant to the thing

---

(*u*) *Lewes* v. *Ridge*, Cro. Eliz. 863.

(*x*) See judgment of Lush, J., in *Elliott* v. *Johnson*, 36 L. J., Q. B., at p. 50; L. R., 2 Q. B., at p. 127.

(*y*) Judgment of Tindal, C. J., in *Wollaston* v. *Hakewill*, 3 M. & Gr., at p. 322; 10 L. J., C. P., at p. 309; Com. Dig. tit. Covenant (C.) 3; *Congham* v. *King*, Cro. Car. 221; judgment in *Stevenson* v. *Lambard*, 2 East, at p. 580.

(*z*) *Curtis* v. *Spitty*, 1 Bing. N. C., at p. 760.

(*a*) *Hooper* v. *Clark*, 36 L. J., Q. B. 79; L. R., 2 Q. B. 200; *Martyn* v. *Williams*, 1 H. & N. 817; 26 L. J., Ex. 117.

demised, and shall go with the land, and bind the assignee, although he be not bound by express words (*b*). Of this kind are the following covenants:—Covenant by lessee to repair houses already built (*c*); to leave houses already built in repair (*d*); to pay rent (*e*) or to render services in the nature of rent (*f*); to allow deductions out of rent (*g*); not to plough more than a certain quantity of land (*h*); to reside upon the demised premises during the demise (*i*); to use a house as a private dwelling-house only (*j*); to insure against fire premises in London situate within the limits mentioned in stat. 14 Geo. 3, c. 78 (*k*); (in a mining licence), to pay compensation for damage done to the surface (*l*); covenant by lessor for quiet enjoyment (*m*); and to supply the houses demised with water (*n*).

Where a covenant relates to a thing not *in esse* at the time of the demise, yet if it directly touches or concerns the thing demised (*o*), *and the word assigns is used*

2. Where "assigns" are mentioned.

(*b*) *Spencer's Case*, 5 Co. R. 16.
(*c*) *Dean and Chapter of Windsor's Case*, 5 Co. R. 24; *Wakefield* v. *Brown*, 9 Q. B. 209, 223; 15 L. J., Q. B. 373.
(*d*) *Matures* v. *Westwood*, Cro. Eliz. 599; *Martyn* v. *Clue*, 18 Q. B. 661; 22 L. J., Q. B. 147.
(*e*) *Stevenson* v. *Lambard*, 2 East, 575, 580; *Parker* v. *Webb*, 3 Salk. 5; *Williams* v. *Bosanquet*, 1 Br. & B. 238.
(*f*) *Vyryan* v. *Arthur*, 1 B. & C. 410; see 2 My. & K. 541; 34 L. J., Ch. 84.
(*g*) *Baylye* v. *Offord*, Cro. Car. 137.
(*h*) *Cockson* v. *Cock*, Cro. Jac. 125.
(*i*) *Tatem* v. *Chaplin*, 2 H. Bl. 133.

(*j*) *Wilkinson* v. *Rogers*, 2 De G., J. & S. 62; 12 W. R. 119.
(*k*) *Vernon* v. *Smith*, 5 B. & A. 1; see *ante*, p. 223, note (*d*).
(*l*) *Norval* v. *Pascoe*, 34 L. J., Ch. 82; 12 W. R. 973.
(*m*) *Noke* v. *Awder*, Cro. Eliz. 373, 436; *Campbell* v. *Lewis*, 3 B. & A. 392.
(*n*) *Jourdain* v. *Wilson*, 4 B. & A. 266; 2 Platt on Leases, 402.
(*o*) *Spencer's Case*, 5 Co. R. 16a; *Thomas* v. *Hayward*, 38 L. J., Ex. 175, 176; L. R., 4 Ex. 311; *Mayor of Congleton* v. *Pattison*, 10 East, at p. 135; *Doughty* v. *Bowman*, 11 Q. B. 444, 454; 17 L. J., Q. B. 111. But see *Minshull* v. *Oakes*, 2 H. & N. 793; 27 L. J., Ex. 194.

in the covenant, the assignee will be bound by, or may take advantage of it. The following covenants belong to this class:—Covenant to build a wall (*q*), or a house (*r*), on the demised premises; (in a mining lease) to build a smelting mill on waste land not demised (*s*); to convey upon a railway, for making which land is demised, all coal got in a certain colliery (*t*); (in a demise of the right to kill game) to leave the land at the end of the term as well stocked with game as at the time of the demise (*u*); not to assign without the consent in writing of the lessor (*x*).

Covenants which will not run with land. If the thing to be done under the covenant be merely collateral to the land, and do not touch or concern the thing demised in any sort (*y*), the assignee shall not be charged (*z*). Hence the following covenants will not run with the land:—Covenant to build a house, not touching or concerning the land demised (*s*), upon land of the lessor which is not parcel of the demise (*z*); to pay a collateral sum to the lessor or to a stranger (*a*); (in a lease of ground, with liberty for the lessee to erect a mill) not to hire persons to work in the mill who were settled in other parishes without a certificate of the settlement of such persons (*b*); covenant by lessor to give the lessee an offer of pre-emption

---

(*q*) *Spencer's Case*, 5 Co. R., at p. 16 a.

(*r*) *Doughty* v. *Bowman*, 11 Q. B. 444; 17 L. J., Q. B. 111.

(*s*) *Sampson* v. *Easterby*, 9 B. & C. 505, 516; 6 Bing. 644.

(*t*) *Hemingway* v. *Fernandes*, 13 Sim. 228.

(*u*) *Hooper* v. *Clark*, 36 L. J., Q. B. 79; L. R., 2 Q. B. 200.

(*x*) *Williams* v. *Earle*, 37 L. J., Q. B. 231; L. R., 3 Q. B. 739; as explained by Blackburn, J., in *West* v. *Dobb*, 38 L. J., Q. B., at p. 291.

(*y*) See judgments in *Thomas* v. *Hayward*, 38 L. J., Ex., at p. 176; L. R., 4 Ex. 311.

(*z*) *Spencer's Case*, 5 Co. R., at p. 16 a.

(*a*) *Mayho* v. *Buckhurst*, Cro. Jac. 438.

(*b*) *Mayor of Congleton* v. *Pattison*, 10 East, 130.

of an adjoining piece of ground (*c*); (in the lease of a beershop) not to build or keep any house for sale of spirits or beer within half-a-mile of the demised premises (*d*); condition for re-entry if the lessee or his assigns, or any occupier of the land demised, should at any time during the term be lawfully convicted of committing any offence against the game laws (*e*).

The assignee may rid himself of all future liability *to the lessor* in respect of the rent (*f*), and covenants in the original lease, by re-assigning the lease to any person. He may do this without giving notice to the lessor, or obtaining his leave (*g*); and, notwithstanding a covenant in the original lease, that the lessee, his executors or administrators, should not assign without the licence of the lessor (*h*). There is no fraud in the assignee of a lease re-assigning his interest with a view to get rid of the lease; hence he may re-assign it to a beggar (*i*), or a married woman (*k*), or a person leaving the kingdom (*l*), for the express purpose of relieving himself of liability under the covenants. It is not even necessary that the person to whom the re-assignment is made should take possession of the premises (*i*), or assent to the lease (*i*). In one case it was held that a re-assignment of a lease might be lawfully made to a pri-

Effect of re-assignment.

(*c*) *Collison* v. *Lettsom*, 6 Taunt. 224, 229.

(*d*) *Thomas* v. *Hayward*, 38 L. J., Ex. 175; L. R., 4 Ex. 311.

(*e*) *Stevens* v. *Copp*, 38 L. J., Ex. 31; L. R., 4 Ex. 20.

(*f*) *Paul* v. *Nurse*, 8 B. & C. 486; *Odell* v. *Wake*, 3 Camp. 394; *Chancellor* v. *Poole*, 2 Dougl. 764.

(*g*) *Valliant* v. *Dodemede*, 2 Atk. 546; *Le Keux* v. *Nash*, 2 Stra. 1221; *Onslow* v. *Corrie*, 2 Madd. 330.

(*h*) *Paul* v. *Nurse*, 8 B. & C. 486.

(*i*) *Taylor* v. *Shum*, 1 B. & P. 21, 23. See *Odell* v. *Wake*, 3 Camp. 394.

(*k*) *Barnfather* v. *Jordan*, 2 Dougl. 452.

(*l*) Per Eyre, C. J., in *Taylor* v. *Shum*, 1 B. & P., at p. 23.

soner in the Fleet, who was paid a sum of money to accept of the assignment (*m*).

Continued liability of lessee.

A *lessee* cannot, by assigning his lease, rid himself of liability under the covenants. The effect of an assignment is to make the lessee a surety to the lessor for the assignee; who, as between himself and the lessor, is the principal bound whilst he is assignee to pay the rent and perform the covenants (*n*). If the lessor, tacitly or expressly, accepts the assignee as his tenant, it appears that an action of *debt* for rent will not lie against the lessee (*o*); but if the lease contains an express covenant by the lessee, an action on such covenant may be brought against him or his executor (*p*) at any time during the term, notwithstanding the lessee has assigned his interest and parted with the possession of the premises, and the lessor has received rent from the assignee (*q*). The lessor may sue either the lessee or his assignee, or both at the same time, but he can only have execution against one of them (*p*).

2. Rights and liabilities of assignee as against lessee.

To protect themselves from this continued liability, lessees, on assigning their leases, are entitled to require the assignees to indemnify them against future payment of rent and performance of covenants (*r*). Even executors, who cannot be compelled to enter into the ordinary covenants for title, may require a covenant of

---

(*m*) *Valliant* v. *Dodemede*, 2 Atk. 546.

(*n*) See per Ld. Denman in *Wolveridge* v. *Steward*, 1 Cr. & M., at p. 659. Per Parke, B., in *Humble* v. *Langston*, 7 M. & W., at p. 530; 10 L. J., Ex., at p. 445.

(*o*) Judgment in *Auriol* v. *Mills*, 4 T. R., at p. 98. See *Wadham* v. *Marlowe*, 8 East,

814, note (*c*).

(*p*) *Brett* v. *Cumberland*, Cro. Jac. 521. See *Bachelour* v. *Gage*, Cro. Car. 188.

(*q*) *Barnard* v. *Godscall*, Cro. Jac. 309. See *Auriol* v. *Mills*, 4 T. R., at p. 98; *Staines* v. *Morris*, 1 V. & B., at p. 11; *Orgill* v. *Kemshead*, 4 Taunt. 642.

indemnity from their assignees (*r*). Upon a covenant of indemnity, contained in the assignment, the assignee will be liable to the lessee during the residue of the term, and he cannot relieve himself from this liability by re-assigning the lease. An assignee who has covenanted to indemnify the lessee against the covenants in the lease may, on re-assigning the lease, require a similar covenant from his assignee (*s*).

During the continuance of the interest of each successive assignee there is a duty on his part to pay the rent and perform the covenants (*t*). If the lessee in his capacity of a surety as between himself and the assignee for the payment of rent and performance of covenants (*u*), has paid the rent or discharged the obligation, he has his remedy over against the principal (*x*); and he has the same remedy over against each subsequent assignee, in respect of breaches committed during the continuance of the interest of each of them; for the lessee is in effect a surety for each of them to the lessor (*y*). The assignee is liable for a breach of any covenant running with the land, incurred in his own time, though the action is not commenced until after he has assigned the premises (*z*).

Unless there is an express stipulation to the contrary, Rights as to title.

(*r*) *Staines* v. *Morris*, 1 V. & B. 8. As to the construction of covenants of indemnity, see *Crossfield* v. *Morrison*, 7 C. B. 286; 18 L. J., C. P. 135.

(*s*) See *Staines* v. *Morris*, 1 V. & B. 8, 13.

(*t*) See *Wolveridge* v. *Steward*, 1 Cr. & M., at p. 659; *Mule* v. *Garrett*, 39 L. J., Ex. 69; L. R., 5 Ex. 132.

(*u*) Per Parke, B., in *Humble* v. *Langston*, 7 M. & W., at p. 530; 10 L. J., Ex., at p. 445; *supra*, p. 250.

(*x*) *Burnett* v. *Lynch*, 5 B. & C. 589. See judgment in *Wolveridge* v. *Steward*, 1 Cr. & M., at pp. 659, 660.

(*y*) Judgment in *Mule* v. *Garrett*, 39 L. J., Ex., at p. 73; *Wolveridge* v. *Steward*, 1 Cr. & M., at p. 660.

(*z*) *Burnett* v. *Lynch*, 5 B. & C. 589; *Harley* v. *King*, 2 Cr. M. & R. 18.

every contract for the sale of a lease contains an implied undertaking, available at law as well as in equity, to make out the lessor's title to demise as well as that of the vendor to the lease itself (*b*). But upon the sale of an agreement for a lease, there is no implied contract that the lessor has power to grant the lease (*c*).

(d) *Grant by the Landlord of his Reversion.*

Stat. 32 Hen. 8, c. 34, s. 1. Grantees of reversion to have same remedies against lessees as lessors had.

Upon a grant by deed (*d*) by a landlord of his reversion, the grantees "and the heirs, executors, successors and assigns of every of them, shall have like advantages against the lessees, their executors, administrators and assigns, by entry for non-payment of rent, or for doing of waste or other forfeiture; and the same remedies by action for not performing of other conditions, covenants or agreements (running with the land (*e*)) contained in the indentures of their said leases as the said lessors themselves, or their heirs or successors had."

Sect. 2. Lessees to have same remedy against grantees of reversion as they might have had against lessors.

All lessees of hereditaments for term of years, life or lives, their executors, administrators and assigns, shall have like remedy against all persons and bodies politic, their heirs, successors and assigns, who shall have any gift or grant of the reversion of the same hereditaments or any parcel thereof, for any condition, covenant or agreement contained in the indentures of their leases, as the same lessees might have had against the said lessors, their heirs and successors.

(*b*) Judgment of Ld. Denman, C. J., in *Souter* v. *Drake*, 5 B. & Ad., at p. 1002; *Purvis* v. *Rayer*, 9 Price, 488.

(*c*) *Kintrea* v. *Perston*, 1 H. & N. 357; 25 L. J., Ex. 287.

(*d*) *Standen* v. *Christmas*, 10 Q. B. 135; 16 L. J., Q. B. 265.

(*e*) *Webb* v. *Russell*, 3 T. R. 393, 402.

Where the reversion upon a lease is severed, and the rent is legally apportioned, the assignee of each part of the reversion shall, in respect of the apportioned rent allotted or belonging to him, be entitled to the benefit of all conditions or powers of re-entry for non-payment of the original rent, in like manner as if such conditions or powers had been reserved to him as incident to his part of the reversion in respect of the apportioned rent allotted or belonging to him. *Stat. 22 & 23 Vict. c. 35, s. 3. Where reversion is severed, assignees of each part to have benefit of all conditions of re-entry for non-payment of rent.*

All grants or conveyances, of any manors or rents, or of the reversion or remainder of any messuages or lands, shall be good and effectual without any attornment of the tenants of any such manors or of the land out of which such rent shall be issuing, or upon whose estates any such reversions or remainders shall be expectant or depending. *Stat. 4 Anne, c. 16, s. 9. Conveyances to be good without attornment of tenant.*

No such tenant shall be prejudiced or damaged by payment of any rent to any such grantor, or by breach of any condition for nonpayment of rent, before notice shall be given to him of such grant by the grantee. *Sect. 10. Tenant not to be prejudiced by payment of rent to grantor before notice of grant.*

(2) *Involuntary Assignments.*

(a) *On Death.*

Arrears of rent accrued and payable in the lifetime of the landlord go to his executor or administrator as part of his personal estate (*f*). Executors may sue upon any covenant with the testator which has been broken in his lifetime (*g*). But where the covenant runs with the land and descends to the heir, though there may have been a formal breach in the ancestor's *1. Of lessor.*

(*f*) See 1 Williams on Exors. 733; *Dollen* v. *Batt*, 4 C. B., N. S. 760; 27 L. J., C. P. 281.
(*g*) *Raymond* v. *Fitch*, 2 Cr. M. & R. 588, 598; 5 L. J., Ex. 45; *Ricketts* v. *Weaver*, 12 M. & W. 718; 13 L. J., Ex. 195.

lifetime, yet if the substantial damage has taken place since his death, the heir is the proper plaintiff (*h*).

2. Of lessee. Upon the death of a tenant from year to year (*i*), or for a term of years, the lease vests in his executor or administrator. Even where a term of years is specifically bequeathed, it will, in the first instance, vest in the executor, by virtue of his office, for the usual purposes to which the testator's assets are applied, and the legatee has no right to enter without the executor's special assent (*j*). The executor or administrator cannot, generally speaking, refuse the lease, though it be worth nothing, for he must renounce the executorship *in toto* or not at all (*k*); but if the value of the land is less than the rent, and there is a deficiency of assets, he may waive the lease (*l*). He is liable, to the extent of the assets, for arrears of rent accruing and breaches of covenant committed during the life of the tenant (*m*). Although the executor or administrator does not enter into possession of the demised premises, he may be sued as assignee of the lease for rent due and breaches of covenant committed subsequently to the death of the lessee (*n*). But he may, by proper pleading, discharge himself from personal liability, by alleging that he is no otherwise assignee than by being executor or administrator of the lessee, and that he has never entered or taken possession of the demised premises; and he may also discharge himself from all liability as executor, by

(*h*) *Kingdon* v. *Nottle*, 1 M. & S. 355. See 2 Cr. M. & R. 598.
(*i*) *Doe* v. *Porter*, 3 T. R. 13; *James* v. *Dean*, 15 Ves., at p. 241.
(*j*) 1 Williams on Exors. 601.
(*k*) Per Denman, C. J., in *Rubery* v. *Stevens*, 4 B. & Ad., at p. 244.
(*l*) 2 Williams on Exors. 1591.
(*m*) 2 Williams on Exors. 1587 (5th ed.).
(*n*) *Wollaston* v. *Hakewill*, 3 M. & Gr. 297, 320; 10 L. J., C. P. 303.

alleging that the term is of no value, and that he has fully administered all the assets which have come to his hands (*o*). If the executor or administrator enters upon the demised premises, he becomes personally liable, so long as he continues in possession, for so much of the rent accruing due after the testator's death as the premises are worth (*p*), *i.e.* the amount of rent for which they could have been let (*q*).

When an executor is sued for use and occupation in his own right, he must show that his occupation is as executor, and that he entered in that character; that he has no assets, and that the value of the land is not equal to the rent. Where the land yields some profit, but less than the rent, he may tender the amount of profit and plead a tender, or he may pay it into Court (*r*). The executor is liable to the same extent as any other assignee for any breaches of the covenants in the lease committed since the death of the tenant (*s*). But by assigning the term the executor or administrator may free himself from liability for subsequent rent and breaches of covenant (*t*).

Where an executor or administrator, liable as such to the rents, covenants or agreements contained in any lease or agreement for a lease granted or assigned to the testator or intestate whose estate is being adminis- *Stat.* 22 & 23 Vict. c. 35, s. 27. Executor or administrator in certain cases

---

(*o*) *Wollaston* v. *Hakewill*, 3 M. & Gr., at p. 321; 10 L. J., C. P., at p. 308.

(*p*) See 1 Wms. Saund. 112, note (*c*); *Rubery* v. *Stevens*, 4 B. & Ad. 241, 245; *Hopwood* v. *Whaley*, 6 C. B. 744; 18 L. J., C. P. 43; *Hornidge* v. *Wilson*, 11 A. & E. 645.

(*q*) *Hopwood* v. *Whaley*, 6 C. B. 744; 18 L. J., C. P. 43.

(*r*) *Patten* v. *Reid*, 6 L. T., N. S. 281.

(*s*) *Tremeere* v. *Morison*, 1 Bing. N. C. 89, 97; *Sleap* v. *Newman*, 12 C. B., N. S. 116. See *Buckworth* v. *Simpson*, 1 Cr. M. & R. 834.

(*t*) *Taylor* v. *Shum*, 1 B. & P. 21. See *Collins* v. *Crouch*, 13 Q. B. 542; 18 L. J., Q. B. 209; *ante*, p. 249.

tered, shall have satisfied all such liabilities under the said lease or agreement for a lease as may have accrued due and been claimed up to the time of the assignment hereafter mentioned, and shall have set apart a sufficient fund to answer any future claim that may be made in respect of any fixed and ascertained sum covenanted or agreed by the lessee to be laid out on the property demised or agreed to be demised, although the period for laying out the same may not have arrived, and shall have assigned the lease or agreement for a lease to a purchaser thereof, he shall be at liberty to distribute the residuary personal estate of the deceased to and amongst the parties entitled thereto respectively, without appropriating any part, or any further part (as the case may be), of the personal estate of the deceased to meet any future liability under the said lease or agreement for a lease; and the executor or administrator so distributing the residuary estate shall not, after having assigned the said lease or agreement for a lease, and having, where necessary, set apart such sufficient fund as aforesaid, be personally liable in respect of any subsequent claim under the said lease or agreement for a lease; but nothing herein contained shall prejudice the right of the lessor, or those claiming under him, to follow the assets of the deceased into the hands of the person or persons amongst whom the said assets may have been distributed.

Marginal note: not to be personally liable upon lease after he has assigned it.

(b) *On Bankruptcy.*

Until a trustee is appointed the registrar shall be the trustee for the purposes of this act, and immediately upon the order of adjudication being made, the property of the bankrupt (*u*) shall vest in the registrar. On the

Marginal notes: Stat. 32 & 33 Vict. c. 71, s. 17. Property of bankrupt to vest in trustee.

(*u*) See sect. 15.

appointment of a trustee, the property shall forthwith pass to and vest in the trustee appointed.

An option to call on the landlord to grant a lease passes, on the bankruptcy of the tenant, to the trustee, and may be assigned over by him (*x*). A proviso or covenant against assignment will not prevent the lease containing it from passing to the trustee in bankruptcy, or hinder him from disposing of it (*y*).

When any property of the bankrupt acquired by the trustee under this act consists of land of any tenure burdened with onerous covenants, or of any other property that is unsaleable, or not readily saleable by reason of its binding the possessor thereof to the performance of any onerous act, or to the payment of any sum of money, the trustee, notwithstanding he has endeavoured to sell, or has taken possession of such property or exercised any act of ownership in relation thereto, may, by writing under his hand, disclaim such property, and upon the execution of such disclaimer the property disclaimed shall, if the same is a lease, be deemed to have been surrendered on the date (of the order of adjudication). Any person interested in any disclaimed property may apply to the Court, and the Court may, upon such application, order possession of the disclaimed property to be delivered up to him, or make such other order as to the possession thereof as may be just. *Stat. 32 & 33 Vict. c. 71, s. 23. Trustee may disclaim onerous lease.*

The trustee shall not be entitled to disclaim any property in pursuance of this act in cases where an application in writing has been made to him by any person interested in such property, requiring such trustee to decide whether he will disclaim or not, and *Sect. 24. Trustee not to disclaim after period not less than twenty-eight days from application by person interested.*

(*x*) *Buckland* v. *Papillon*, 36 L. J., Ch. 81; L. R., 2 Ch. 67.
(*y*) *Doe* v. *Smith*, 5 Taunt.
795; *Doe* v. *Bevan*, 3 M. & S. 353. See *Wadham* v. *Marlowe*, 8 East, 314, note.

the trustee has for a period of not less than twenty-eight days after the receipt of such application or such further time as may be allowed by the Court, declined or neglected to give notice whether he disclaims the same or not.

(c) *On Conviction of Lessee for Treason or Felony.*

<small>Stat. 33 & 34 Vict. c. 23, s. 10.
Property of convict to vest in administrator.</small>

Upon the appointment of any administrator all the real and personal property, including *choses in action*, to which the convict named in such appointment was, at the time of his conviction, or shall afterwards, while he shall continue subject to the operation of this act, become or be entitled, shall vest in such administrator for all the estate and interest of such convict therein.

<small>Sect. 12.</small>

The administrator shall have absolute power to let, mortgage, sell, convey and transfer any part of such property as to him shall seem fit.

<small>Sect. 14.</small>

The administrator may cause payment or satisfaction to be made out of such property of any debt or liability of such convict which may be established in due course of law, or may otherwise be proved to his satisfaction.

SECT. XIII.—*Live Stock.*

<small>Rights and liabilities of lessee and lessor.</small>

Upon a lease of a stock of live cattle, the lessee has the use and profits of them during the term; and the lessor has only a possibility of property in case the cattle all outlive the term (z). If any of the cattle die during the term, the property in them vests absolutely in the lessee, and the lessor cannot claim to have them replaced after the term; hence, he has no reversion to

(z) Bac. Abr. (A.) 7.

grant over to another, either during the term or after, until the lessee has re-delivered the cattle to him (z). All the young produced by the cattle during the term belong to the lessee (z).

A covenant by the lessee of sheep or cattle, on behalf of himself and his assigns, at the end of the lease to deliver cattle or goods of the same value as those let to him, or to pay a certain price, is a personal contract only, and will not bind a person to whom the lessee has assigned the sheep or cattle (a).

SECT. XIV.—*Game.*

Rights and liabilities of lessee and lessor	259
Statutory provisions	259
Construction of demise or reservation of right of shooting, &c.	260
„ special agreements relating to game	261

Rights and Liabilities of Lessee and Lessor.

Nothing in this act contained shall authorize any person holding any land to kill or take the game, or to permit any other person to kill or take the game upon such land, in any case where, by deed, grant, lease or any written or parol demise or contract, a right of entry upon such land for the purpose of killing or taking the game shall be reserved by or given to any grantor, lessor or other person whatsoever. Statutory provisions. Stat. 1 & 2 Will. 4, c. 32, s. 8. Act not to affect agreements relating to game.

Where the landlord shall have reserved to himself the right of killing the game upon any land, it shall be lawful for him to authorize any other person or persons, who shall have obtained an annual game cer- Sect. 11. Landlord to whom game is reserved may authorize other persons to pursue and kill it.

(z) Bac. Abr. (A.) 7.   (a) *Spencer's Case*, 5 Co. R. 16 a.

tificate, to enter upon such land for the purpose of pursuing and killing game thereon.

Sect. 12. Where game belongs to landlord, occupier to be subject to penalty for pursuing or killing it.

Where the right of killing the game upon any land shall be specially reserved by or granted to, or shall belong to, the landlord, or any person whatsoever other than the occupier of such land, then, if the occupier of such land shall pursue, kill or take any game upon such land, or shall give permission to any other person so to do, without the authority of the landlord or other person having the right of killing the game upon such land, such occupier shall, on conviction thereof before two justices of the peace, forfeit and pay for such pursuit such sum of money not exceeding two pounds, and for every head of game so killed or taken such sum of money not exceeding one pound, as to the convicting justices shall seem meet, together with the costs of the conviction.

Construction of demise or reservation of right of shooting, &c.

Under a *demise or reservation of the exclusive right of hunting, shooting, fishing and sporting* over a farm, the person entitled to shoot over the farm must not trample fields of standing crops at a time when it is not usual or reasonable to do so (*b*). He has no right to bring rabbits or other game on to the farm; and he is liable for damage done to the crops by rabbits so brought on without the leave of the occupier (*b*). The reservation includes whatever is ordinarily known as "hunting, shooting, fishing and sporting," and under it the tenant of the land is not entitled to shoot rabbits (*c*). He may, however, use the land in the ordinary and reasonable way; but must not resort to expedients for

(*b*) *Hilton* v. *Green*, 2 F. & F. 821; *Birkbeck* v. *Paget*, 31 Beav. 403. As to contracts by landlord to kill hares and rabbits, see *Barrow* v. *Ashburnham*, 4 L. J., K. B. 146.

(*c*) *Jeffryes* v. *Evans*, 34 L. J., C. P. 261, 263; 19 C. B., N. S. 246.

driving the game away (c). The destruction of furze and underwood in such reasonable use of the land, is no eviction from the right of shooting (c). It seems that a grant of leave to hunt over premises does not give the grantee the liberty of shooting over them (d).

> EXCEPTION *of liberty for each tenant on his farm to kill rabbits with ferrets only* (*in a demise of a house and land with sole licence of shooting and sporting over lands, plantations and coverts of the lessor*). The exception extends not only to farms existing at the time of the demise, but also to plantations, &c., which are subsequently let as farms (e).

Construction of special agreements relating to game.

> GRANT *to a person, his heirs and assigns, of free liberty, with servants or otherwise, to come into and upon lands and there to hawk, hunt, fish and fowl.* Is a grant of a licence of profit, and not of a mere personal licence of pleasure; therefore it authorizes the grantee, his heirs and assigns, to hawk, &c., by his servants in his absence (f).

> GRANT *to lessee of right of sporting over land demised and other lands,* " *in common with the lessor, his heirs and assigns, and any friend of his or them.*" The exercise of the privilege is not confined to a single friend at a time (g).

(c) *Jeffryes* v. *Evans*, 34 L. J., C. P. 261, 264; 19 C. B., N. S. 246.

(d) See judgment of Gibb, C. J., in *Moore* v. *Plymouth*, 7 Taunt., at p. 627.

(e) *Newton* v. *Wilmot*, 8 M. & W. 711.

(f) *Wickham* v. *Hawker*, 7 M. & W. 63; *Ewart* v. *Graham*, 29 L. J., Ex. 88; 7 H. L. C. 331.

(g) *Gardiner* v. *Colyer*, 12 W. R. 979.

CHAP. V.

DETERMINATION OF THE TENANCY.

	PAGE
SECT. I. MODES APPLICABLE TO PARTICULAR KINDS OF TENANCY..	262
(1) Determination of tenancy at sufferance	262
(2) Determination of tenancy at will	263
Express	263
Implied	263
(3) Determination of tenancy from year to year	265
(a) When determinable	265
(b) Notice to quit	265
Length of notice	265
When to be given	266
Form of notice	269
By whom given	270
To whom given	271
Mode of service	271
Waiver of notice	272
(c) Verbal disclaimer	274
(4) Determination of tenancies for optional terms of years..	275
(5) Determination of tenancies for life	275
II. MODES GENERALLY APPLICABLE	277
(1) Merger	277
(2) Surrender ..	278
Express	278
Implied	279
(3) Forfeiture..	283
(a) Where there is no express proviso for re-entry	283
(b) Where there is an express proviso	284
Demand of rent	284
(c) Waiver of forfeiture	286
(d) Relief against forfeiture	288

SECT. I.—*Modes applicable to particular kinds of Tenancy.*

(1) *Determination of Tenancy at Sufferance.*

TENANCY at sufferance may be determined at any time by landlord or tenant without any demand of possession or notice to quit (*a*).

(*a*) *Doe* v. *Turner,* 7 M. & W., at p. 235; *Doe* v. *Lawder,* 1 Stark. 308; *Doe* v. *Murrell,* 8 C. & P. 134; *Doe* v. *Maisey,* 8 B. &

(2) *Determination of Tenancy at Will.*

Every lease at will must in law be at the will of both parties, and therefore when the lease is made, to have and to hold at the will of the lessor, the law implies it to be at the will of the lessee also (*b*). The landlord may determine a tenancy at will, expressly, by stating his will to be that the tenant shall leave (*c*); or by demanding possession (*d*); or sending for the keys (*e*). Anything which amounts to a demand of possession, although not expressed in precise and formal language, will indicate the landlord's will to determine the tenancy (*f*); hence a letter from the agent of the landlord to the agent of the tenant, stating that unless the tenant pays what he owes, the landlord will take immediate measures to recover possession of the property, is a sufficient manifestation that the tenancy is to determine (*f*). By words spoken off the demised premises the will is not determined until the lessee has notice (*g*).

1. Express determination. By landlord.

The tenant may expressly determine the tenancy by declaring that he will no longer hold possession of the premises, and quitting them accordingly; but the mere declaration will not produce this effect (*h*).

By tenant.

The landlord may impliedly determine a tenancy at will by acts showing an intention that it should no longer exist; as, for instance, by making a lease of the premises to another, to commence presently (*i*); or by

2. Implied determination. By landlord.

C. 767; see *Wallis* v. *Delmar*, 29 L. J., Ex. 276.
 (*b*) Co. Lit. 55 a.
 (*c*) *Pollen* v. *Brewer*, 7 C. B., N. S. 371, 373.
 (*d*) *Doe* v. *Jones*, 10 B. & C. 718, 721.
 (*e*) *Pollen* v. *Brewer*, 7 C. B., N. S. 371.
 (*f*) Judgment of Tindal, C. J., in *Doe* v. *Price*, 9 Bing., at p. 358. See *Locke* v. *Matthews*, 13 C. B., N. S. 753; 11 W. R. 343.
 (*g*) Co. Lit. 55 b.
 (*h*) Co. Lit. 55 b, note 373.
 (*i*) *Dinsdale* v. *Iles*, 2 Lev. 88.

entering upon the land, without the tenant's consent, to cut and carry away trees or stone (*k*), provided such trees and stone are not excepted from the demise (*l*); or by agreeing to sell the freehold to the tenant (*m*). It seems that the bankruptcy of the landlord will operate as a determination of a tenancy at will, if the tenant has knowledge thereof (*n*). Where the act by which the intention of the landlord to determine the tenancy is manifested is done on the demised premises, it is presumed that the tenant is there and knows of it; but if the act relied upon be done off the premises, it is requisite that the landlord should give the tenant notice that he determines the tenancy (*o*).

By tenant.   The tenant may impliedly determine the tenancy at will by granting an underlease (*p*), or assigning the premises (provided the landlord has notice) (*q*); or by committing waste (*r*). The general doctrine is that the death of either landlord or tenant will operate as a determination of the will (*s*); but it would rather seem that a tenancy at will may continue after the death of one of the parties, unless the heir, or legal representative, does something to manifest his intention to determine the tenancy (*t*).

(*k*) *Doe* v. *Turner*, 7 M. & W. 226; 9 M. & W. 643.

(*l*) Co. Lit. 55 b.

(*m*) See judgment of Lord Eldon, C., in *Daniels* v. *Davison*, 16 Ves., at p. 252.

(*n*) *Doe* v. *Thomas*, 6 Ex. 854; 20 L. J., Ex. 367.

(*o*) Per Parke, B., in *Pinhorn* v. *Souster*, 8 Ex., at p. 770. See *Ball* v. *Cullimore*, 2 Cr., M. & R. 120.

(*p*) Judgment in *Birch* v. *Wright*, 1 T. R., at p. 382.

(*q*) *Pinhorn* v. *Souster*, 8 Ex. 763, 772; 22 L. J., Ex. 266; *Carpenter* v. *Colins*, Yelv. 73.

(*r*) Co. Lit. 57 a.

(*s*) Judgment in *James* v. *Dean*, 11 Ves., at p. 391; Co. Lit. 57 b. See *Doe* v. *Rock*, Car. & M. 549, 553; 11 L. J., C. P. 194.

(*t*) Judgment in *Morton* v. *Woods*, 38 L. J., Q. B., at p. 87; L. R., 4 Q. B , at p. 306.

(3) Determination of Tenancy from Year to Year.

(a) *When determinable.*

A tenancy from year to year may be determined at the end of the first or any subsequent year (*u*); unless, in creating the tenancy, the parties use expressions showing that they contemplate a tenancy for two years at least (*x*). A tenancy "for one year certain, and so on from year to year," cannot be determined before the end of the second year (*y*).

(b) *Notice to quit.*

Where no express stipulation is made between the parties as to the length of notice required to be given, it seems that this may be regulated by custom (*z*); but there must be strong evidence of such custom (*a*).

Length of notice.
1. Where there is no express agreement.

If no such custom exists, it is a general presumption of law, that if an estate from year to year is created, and nothing is said about determining it, the notice intended is half-a-year's notice, expiring at the end of some current year of the tenancy (*b*).

There is some uncertainty as to the length of the notice required to determine a quarterly, monthly, or weekly tenancy. It does not appear to have ever been decided, that in the case of an ordinary monthly or

---

(*u*) Doe v. *Smaridge*, 7 Q. B. 957; 14 L. J., Q. B. 327. See *Thompson* v. *Maberly*, 2 Camp. 573.

(*x*) Doe v. *Smaridge*, 7 Q. B., at p. 959. See *Denn* v. *Cartwright*, 4 East, 29; Doe v. *Mainby*, 10 Q. B. 473; 16 L. J., Q. B. 303.

(*y*) Doe v. *Green*, 9 A. & E. 658; *Reg.* v. *Chawton*, 1 Q. B. 247. See *Jones* v. *Nixon*, 1 H. & C. 48; 31 L. J., Ex. 505.

(*z*) Roe v. *Wilkinson*, cited in note 228 to Co. Lit. 270 b. See Roe v. *Charnock*, Peake, N. P. C. 4; also judgment in Doe v. *Snowdon*, 2 W. Bl., at p. 1225.

(*a*) Roe v. *Charnock*, Peake, at p. 5.

(*b*) Judgment of Erle, C. J., in *Bridges* v. *Potts*, 33 L. J., C. P., at p. 343; 17 C. B., N. S., at p. 332.

weekly tenancy, a month's or week's notice to quit must be given. A tenant who enters upon a fresh week may be bound to continue until the expiration of that week, or to pay the week's rent; but that is a very different thing from giving a week's notice to quit (*c*). A weekly tenancy cannot, however, be determined without some notice (*d*), and the safest course is to give a notice corresponding to the letting, *i. e.*, a week's notice in a weekly letting, and a month's notice in a monthly letting (*e*).

2. Where there is an express agreement.

The parties to the tenancy may alter the notice necessary to determine it; thus, they may agree that a three months' notice, or even a week's notice, shall be sufficient (*f*), and they may also stipulate that the notice shall expire at any period of the year (*g*). Where there is no express or implied stipulation, the notice agreed upon between the parties must be given so as to expire at the end of some current year of the tenancy (*h*). Thus, an agreement by a tenant from year to year to quit at a quarter's notice, means a quarter's notice expiring at the end of some year of the tenancy (*h*).

Period with reference to which notice must be given.

The implied condition as to the notice expiring at the end of some year of the tenancy renders it important that the time of commencement of the tenancy should be correctly ascertained. The question at what

(*c*) Per Parke, B., in *Huffell* v. *Armitstead*, 7 C. & P., at p. 58. But see *Doe* v. *Hazell*, 1 Esp. 94; *Doe* v. *Ruffan*, 6 Esp. 4.

(*d*) *Jones* v. *Mills*, 10 C. B., N. S. 788, 796; 31 L. J., C. P. 66.

(*e*) See per Williams, J., in *Jones* v. *Mills*, 10 C. B., N. S., at p. 798.

(*f*) Judgment of Erle, C. J., in *Bridges* v. *Potts*, 33 L. J., C. P., at p. 343.

(*g*) See *Bridges* v. *Potts*, 17 C. B., N. S. 333; 33 L. J., C. P. 338, 343; *Doe* v. *Grafton*, 18 Q. B. 496; 21 L. J., Q. B. 276; *Collett* v. *Curling*, 10 Q. B. 785; 16 L. J., Q. B. 390.

(*h*) *Doe* v. *Donovan*, 1 Taunt. 555; 2 Camp. 78; *Kemp* v. *Derrett*, 3 Camp. 510. See *Bridges* v. *Potts*, 17 C. B., N. S. 333; 33 L. J., C. P. 338.

period a tenancy began is a matter for the decision of a jury, upon a consideration of all the facts (*i*). If the tenant alleges that a notice to quit given to him does not correspond with the time at which his tenancy commenced, it is incumbent on him to prove the true time of commencement (*k*).

When a tenant, on being applied to respecting the commencement of his holding, informs the person making the inquiry that it begins on a certain day, and notice to quit on that day is given at a subsequent time, the tenant will not be allowed to set up a holding from a different day (*l*). It makes no difference whether the information so given proceeds from mistake or design (*l*). The mere notice to quit, at a certain time, given by the landlord, is not, in itself, evidence of a holding from that time (*m*); but if it be served personally on the tenant, and he make no objection at the time, this is *primâ facie* evidence from which a jury may find that the tenancy commenced at the period specified in the notice (*n*). The tenant, however, is not precluded from afterwards insisting on the insufficiency of the notice (*o*). Admissions by tenant.

Where a tenant continues in possession after the expiration of his lease without having entered into any new contract, he holds upon the former terms as to the time of quitting (*p*). If he assigns his interest, the Where tenant keeps possession after expiration of lease.

(*i*) *Walker* v. *Godè*, 6 H. & N. 594; *ante*, p. 56.
(*k*) *Doe* v. *Wrightman*, 4 Esp., at p. 7.
(*l*) *Doe* v. *Lambley*, 2 Esp. 635.
(*m*) Per Lord Ellenborough, C. J., in *Doe* v. *Forster*, 13 East, at p. 406.
(*n*) *Doe* v. *Forster*, 13 East, 405; *Thomas* v. *Thomas*, 2 Camp. 647; *Doe* v. *Biggs*, 2 Taunt. 109.
(*o*) *Oakapple* v. *Copous*, 4 T. R. 361.
(*p*) See judgment in *Doe* v. *Bell*, 5 T. R., at p. 472; *Roe* v. *Ward*, 1 H. Bl. 96; *Doe* v. *Weller*, 7 T. R. 478. See *Doe* v. *Dobell*, 1 Q. B. 806; *Humphreys* v. *Franks*, 18 C. B. 323.

tenancy of the assignee will also be held to commence on the same day as the original lease (*q*).

Where tenant enters under void lease.

A void lease or agreement, under which a tenant has entered and paid rent, will regulate the terms on which the tenancy subsists, as to the time of the year when the tenant is to quit (*r*). If the void lease or agreement contains no express stipulation on this subject, the tenancy from year to year will be determinable by notice to quit expiring at the time of the original entry of the tenant (*s*).

Where tenant enters on different parts of demised premises at different times.

In cases where the incoming tenant enters upon different parts of the demised premises at different times, it is sufficient to give half-a-year's notice to quit before the substantial time of entry (*t*); *i.e.* the time of entry on the principal part of the premises. In these cases, the question of what is the principal and what the accessory, must depend upon the relative value and importance of the premises let together, and is a matter for the decision of a jury (*u*).

Where tenant enters between two quarter days.

Where a tenant from year to year, having entered in the middle of a quarter, pays rent to the next quarter-day, and thenceforth from quarter to quarter, his tenancy is held to commence on the quarter-day after his entry (*x*). Where he has not paid rent for the fraction of a quarter, the period of his entry is taken to be the time of commencement of his tenancy (*y*).

(*q*) *Doe* v. *Samuel,* 5 Esp. 173. But see *Doe* v. *Lines,* 11 Q. B. 402.

(*r*) *Doe* v. *Bell,* 5 T. R. 471.

(*s*) See judgment of Coltman, J., in *Berrey* v. *Lindley,* 11 L. J., C. P., at p. 32; 3 M. & Gr. 498.

(*t*) See judgment of Lord Ellenborough, C. J., in *Doe* v. *Watkins,* 7 East, at p. 555; *Doe* v. *Snowden,* 2 W. Bl. 1224; *Doe* v. *Spence,* 6 East, 120, 122; *Doe* v. *Hughes,* 7 M. & W. 139; *Doe* v. *Rhodes,* 11 M. & W. 600.

(*u*) *Doe* v. *Howard,* 11 East, 498, 501.

(*x*) *Doe* v. *Johnson,* 6 Esp. 10; *Doe* v. *Stapleton,* 3 C. & P. 275.

(*y*) *Doe* v. *Matthews,* 11 C. B. 675.

Where any doubt exists as to the period at which the current year of the tenancy expires, the notice to quit may be expressed in general terms, requiring the tenant to quit at the end of the current year of his tenancy, which shall expire next after the end of one half-year from the date of the notice (*z*). It is not essential that a notice to quit should be in writing (*a*), or that it should state to whom possession is to be delivered up (*b*). It must, however, be expressed with reasonable certainty, not giving an option to the tenant to quit or to do something else (*c*). A notice to quit on one of two days is good, if served six months before the day on which the tenancy commenced (*d*). An error in the description of the premises will not invalidate the notice if the person to whom it is given has not been misled by it (*e*), and a mistake in the christian name of the tenant will not be fatal if the notice is kept by him without objection (*f*). A notice to quit a part only of premises leased together is void (*g*).

Form of notice.

(*z*) Doe v. *Butler*, 2 Esp. 589; Doe v. *Steel*, 3 Camp., at p. 117; Doe v. *Smith*, 5 A. & E. 350; Doe v. *Timothy*, 2 C. & K. 351.

(*a*) Doe v. *Crick*, 5 Esp. 196; *Bird* v. *Defonvielle*, 2 C. & K. 415; *Roe* v. *Pierce*, 2 Camp. 96.

(*b*) Doe v. *Foster*, 3 C. B. 215.

(*c*) See Doe v. *Goldwin*, 2 Q. B. 146. But see *Roberts* v. *Hayward*, 3 C. & P. 432.

(*d*) Doe v. *Wrightman*, 4 Esp., at p. 6.

(*e*) Doe d. *Cox*, 4 Esp. 185; Doe v. *Wilkinson*, 12 A. & E. 743.

(*f*) Doe v. *Spiller*, 6 Esp. 70.

(*g*) Doe v. *Archer*, 14 East, 245. A notice to quit, given by, or on behalf of, the landlord, may be in the following form, the words between brackets being used when the notice is by an agent:—

To Mr. C. D.

I hereby [*as agent for and on behalf of Mr. E. F., your landlord*] give you notice to quit and deliver up possession of the premises, situate at ——, in the county of ——, which you now hold of me [*him*], on the —— day of —— next, or at the expiration of the year of your tenancy thereof, which shall expire next after the end of one half-year from the date of this

By whom notice may be given.

The notice may in all cases be given by either landlord or tenant. The notion, thrown out by Lord Mansfield, of a tenancy from year to year, in which the lessor binds himself not to give notice to quit, has been long exploded (*h*). It may be stipulated, that, upon a particular event, the lessee may quit without notice (*i*).

Agents.

A notice to quit, given by the landlord, must be such as the tenant may safely act on at the time of receiving it (*k*); that is one which is in fact, and which the tenant has reason to believe to be then binding on the landlord (*l*). A notice to quit given without authority will not be made valid by the subsequent adoption or ratification of the landlord (*k*). It is not essential to the validity of a notice to quit given by a general agent, that his agency should appear on the face of the document (*l*). There is, however, a distinction in this respect between a general agent and one having a special or limited authority (*l*), and in the case of the latter, it would appear, that a notice is bad, if it does not state that it is given by authority or in the name of the principal (*m*).

notice. Dated the —— day of ——, 18—. E. F.
[*R. S., agent for the said E. F.*]

A notice to quit, given by, or on behalf of, the tenant, may be in the following form, the words between brackets being used when the notice is by an agent:—

To Mr. E. F.

I hereby [*as agent for and on behalf of Mr. C. D., your tenant*] give you notice that on the —— day of —— next I shall [*he will*] quit and deliver up possession of the premises situate at ——, in the county of ——, which I [*he*] now hold [*holds*] of you as tenant thereof. Dated the —— day of ——, 18—. C. D.
[*R. S., agent for the said C. D.*]

(*h*) Per Lawrence, J., in *Doe* v. *Browne*, 8 East, at p. 167.

(*i*) *Bethell* v. *Blencowe*, 3 M. & Gr. 119.

(*k*) *Doe* v. *Goldwin*, 2 Q. B. 143; 10 L. J., Q. B. 275, 277; *Doe* v. *Walters*, 10 B. & C. 626.

(*l*) Judgment in *Jones* v. *Phipps*, 37 L. J., Q. B., at p. 201; L. R., 3 Q. B., at p. 572.

(*m*) *Doe* v. *Goldwin*, 2 Q. B. 143; 10 L. J., Q. B. 275. See judgment in *Jones* v. *Phipps*, 37

A *cestui que trust*, who has been permitted for many years by the trustees to have the entire management of the trust estates (*n*), and a receiver appointed by the Court of Chancery, with a general authority to let lands to tenants from year to year (*o*), are deemed general agents, and may give valid notices to quit in their own names. A notice to quit, signed by one of two joint tenants on behalf of the other, is sufficient to put an end to a tenancy from year to year as to both (*p*). An assignee of the reversion may avail himself of a notice to quit given by the preceding owner (*q*).

Cestui que trust.
Receiver.
Joint tenant.

A notice to quit proceeding from the landlord must be served upon the original tenant (*r*). Since there is no privity of contract between the landlord and an under-tenant, the landlord cannot entitle himself to recover against such under-tenant by giving a notice to quit in his own name (*r*).

To whom given.

It is not necessary that the notice should be directed to the tenant if it can be proved to have been delivered to him in proper time (*s*). It may be either served upon him personally, or upon his attorney (*t*); or it may be left with his wife (*u*) or servant at his dwelling-house (*x*), but in this case an explanation of the nature of the notice should be given at the time when it is

Mode of service.

L. J., Q. B., at p. 201; L. R., 3 Q. B., at p. 572.

(*n*) *Jones* v. *Phipps*, 37 L. J., Q. B. 198; L. R., 3 Q. B. 567.

(*o*) *Wilkinson* v. *Colley*, 5 Burr. 2694; *Doe* v. *Read*, 12 East, 57.

(*p*) *Doe* v. *Summersett*, 1 B. & Ad. 135; *Doe* v. *Hulme*, 2 Man. & Ry. 434; *Doe* v. *Hughes*, 7 M. & W. 139, 141.

(*q*) *Doe* v. *Forwood*, 3 Q. B. 627.

(*r*) *Pleasant* v. *Benson*, 14 East, 234.

(*s*) *Doe* v. *Wrightman*, 4 Esp. 5.

(*t*) See *Doe* v. *Ongley*, 10 C. B. 25; 20 L. J., C. P. 26.

(*u*) *Pulteney* v. *Shelton*, 5 Ves. 260, note (*a*).

(*x*) *Jones* v. *Marsh*, 4 T. R. 464.

served (*z*). The service of a notice upon the demised premises on one of two tenants, holding under a joint demise, is presumptive evidence that the notice reached the other (*a*). A notice put under the door of the tenant's house will be valid, if it can be proved to have come to the tenant's hands half a year before the expiration of the current year of the tenancy (*b*). Where a corporation is the tenant, the notice to quit may be served on one of its officers (*c*).

If the notice proceeds from the tenant, it should be given to his immediate landlord or to the attorney or agent of such landlord authorized to receive such notices, and not to a mere collector of rents (*d*). When a notice is sent by post to the landlord or his agent, it seems that the day on which the letter is delivered will be considered as the time at which the notice is given (*e*). It is sufficient if the notice sent by post can be proved to have reached the office of the person on whom it is served at any time during the last day on which service can be made, although after business hours (*f*). At the time of service of a notice to quit, a memorandum of the fact of such service should be indorsed upon a duplicate of the notice (*g*).

Waiver of notice to quit.

If, after the expiration of a notice to quit, the parties

(*z*) See *Doe* v. *Lucas*, 5 Esp. 153; *Smith* v. *Clark*, 9 Dowl. 202.

(*a*) *Doe* v. *Watkins*, 7 East, 551. See *Doe* v. *Crick*, 5 Esp. 196.

(*b*) *Alford* v. *Vickery*, Car. & M. 280. See *Doe* v. *Hall*, 5 M. & Gr. 795.

(*c*) *Doe* v. *Woodman*, 8 East, 228.

(*d*) *Pearse* v. *Boulter*, 2 F. & F. 133.

(*e*) See *Reg.* v. *Slawstone*, 18 Q. B. 388; *Reg.* v. *Recorder of Richmond*, E. B. & E. 253.

(*f*) See *Papillon* v. *Brunton*, 5 H. & N. 518, 522; 29 L. J., Ex. 265.

(*g*) See *Doe* v. *Turford*, 3 B. & Ad. 890; *Doe* v. *Somerton*, 7 Q. B. 58; 14 L. J., Q. B. 210.

by their acts unmistakably acknowledge a subsisting tenancy between them, the notice will be deemed to be waived (*h*). A second notice to quit is considered as such an acknowledgment (*i*), unless, under the circumstances of the case, the person to whom it is given would not understand it as waiving the former notice (*k*).

Second notice to quit.

A landlord may waive a notice to quit by accepting, either personally (*l*), or by an agent specially authorized to receive it (*m*), rent (*l*) due for the occupation of premises after the expiration of the notice (*n*); or by distraining for rent accruing thereafter (*o*). A mere demand of rent, due after the expiration of the notice (*p*), or a holding over or accidental detention of the key by the tenant after that event (*q*), does not necessarily operate as a waiver of the notice.

Acceptance of rent.

Holding over.

When a valid (*r*) notice to quit is given by landlord or tenant, the party to whom it is given is entitled to count upon it, and it cannot be withdrawn without the consent of both parties. If such consent is given, there is a new agreement between the parties, and a new tenancy is created which exists only under that new agreement; consequently a guarantor of the rent under the original tenancy is not liable for rent which became due after

(*h*) See *Doe* v. *Palmer*, 16 East, 53, 56.

(*i*) Per Lord Ellenborough, in *Doe* v. *Palmer*, 16 East, at p. 56.

(*k*) See judgment in *Doe* v. *Humphreys*, 2 East, at p. 240; *Doe* v. *Steele*, 3 Camp. 117.

(*l*) *Goodright* v. *Cordwent*, 6 T. R. 219.

(*m*) See *Doe* v. *Calvert*, 2 Camp. 387.

(*n*) See *Doe* v. *Batten*, Cowp. 243.

(*o*) *Zouch* v. *Willingale*, 1 H. Bl. 311. The landlord cannot distrain for such rent, unless a new tenancy has been created; *ante*, pp. 111, 131.

(*p*) *Blyth* v. *Dennett*, 13 C. B. 178; 22 L. J., C. P. 79.

(*q*) *Jenner* v. *Clegg*, 1 Moo. & Rob. 213, 215; *Gray* v. *Bompas*, 11 C. B., N. S. 520. See *Jones* v. *Shears*, 4 A. & E. 832.

(*r*) See *Doe* v. *Milward*, 3 M. & W. 328.

F.   T

the time when the notice would have expired (*s*). An agreement by the landlord, at the request of the tenant, to suspend the exercise of his rights under the notice to quit, will not operate as a waiver of the notice, or as a licence to the tenant to be on the premises otherwise than subject to the landlord's right of acting on such notice if necessary (*t*).

(b) *By verbal Disclaimer.*

What amounts to a disclaimer.

If a tenant from year to year, verbally or in writing, unequivocally denies the title of his landlord, and renounces his character of tenant, either by setting up title in another, or by claiming title in himself (*u*), the tenancy may be determined by the landlord without any notice to quit (*w*). It seems that whether a particular expression does or does not amount to a disclaimer, is a question for the decision of a jury (*x*). An omission to acknowledge the landlord as such, by requesting further information, will not be enough; nor will a mere refusal to pay rent. A refusal to deliver possession, or a declaration by the tenant that he will continue to hold possession, cannot have that effect, at a time when the landlord has no right to claim it (*y*).

(*s*) *Tayleur* v. *Wildin*, 37 L. J., Ex. 173, 174; L. R., 3 Ex. 303, 305; *Blyth* v. *Dennett*, 13 C. B. 178; 22 L. J., C. P. 79.

(*t*) *Whiteacre* v. *Symonds*, 10 East, at p. 16.

(*u*) Per Tindal, C. J., in *Doe* v. *Cooper*, 1 M. & Gr., at p. 139. See *Jones* v. *Mills*, 10 C. B., N. S. 788; 31 L. J., C. P. 66; *Doe* v. *Cawdor*, 1 Cr., M. & R. 398; *Hunt* v. *Allgood*, 10 C. B., N. S. 253; 30 L. J., C. P. 313.

(*w*) *Doe* v. *Whittick*, Gow, 195;

judgment in *Doe* v. *Pasquali*, Peake, N. P. C., at p. 197; *Doe* v. *Frowd*, 4 Bing. 557; *Doe* v. *Grubb*, 10 B. & C. 816; *Doe* v. *Rollings*, 4 C. B. 188; 17 L. J., C. P. 268; *Doe* v. *Thompson*, 5 A. & E. 532; *Doe* v. *Evans*, 9 M. & W. 48; *Doe* v. *Gower*, 17 Q. B. 589; 21 L. J., Q. B. 57.

(*x*) See *Doe* v. *Long*, 9 C. & P. 773.

(*y*) See judgment in *Doe* v. *Stanion*, 1 M. & W., at p. 703.

(4) *Determination of Tenancies for optional Terms of Years.*

If a lease is made determinable at certain specified periods, and nothing is said as to the person by whom the option is to be exercised, the lessee only can exercise it (z); but a lease which is made determinable "if the parties think fit," is determinable only by consent of both parties (a). A proviso whereby the option to determine a lease is given to either of the parties, his executors or administrators, extends to the devisee of the lessor, who is entitled to the rent and reversion (b). Where the proviso requires notice to be given in writing of the intention to exercise the option to determine the lease, such notice will be good though given in the form of a notice to quit (c). The notice will be invalid if it varies from the terms of the proviso as to the time at which the option is to be exercised (d).

<small>By whom option may be exercised.</small>

(5) *Determination of Tenancies for Life.*

Any person who shall have any claim to any remainder, reversion or expectancy in or to any estate after the death of any person whatsoever, upon affidavit

<small>Statutory provision for production of persons on</small>

(z) *Price* v. *Dyer*, 17 Ves., at p. 363; *Dann* v. *Spurrier*, 3 B. & P. 399; 7 Ves. 231; *Doe* v. *Dixon*, 9 East, 15.

(a) *Fowell* v. *Tranter*, 3 H. & C. 458; 34 L. J., Ex. 6.

(b) *Roe* v. *Hayley*, 12 East, 464.

(c) *Giddens* v. *Dodd*, 3 Drew. 485; 25 L. J., Ch. 451. Notice may be given by the lessee in the following form:—
To Mr. E. F.
I hereby give you notice that I am desirous of putting an end to the term granted by an indenture of lease dated the —— day of ——, 18 —, and made between [yourself] of the one part and [myself] of the other part, at the end of the first [seven] years of the said term, in pursuance of a proviso contained in the said lease. Dated the —— day of ——, 18 —.
C. D.

(d) See *Cadby* v. *Martinez*, 11 A. & E. 720.

made in the Court of Chancery by the person so claiming such estate, of his title, and that he hath cause to believe that such person is dead, and that his death is concealed by (any) guardian, trustee, husband or any other person, may, once a year, if the person aggrieved shall think fit, move the Lord Chancellor to order; and (he is) hereby authorized and required to order such guardian, &c. concealing or suspected to conceal such person, at such time and place as the said court shall direct, on personal or other due service of such order, to produce to such person and persons, not exceeding two, as shall in such order be named by the party prosecuting such order, such person aforesaid; and if such guardian, &c. shall refuse or neglect to produce such person on whose life any such estate doth depend according to the directions of the said order, the Court of Chancery is hereby authorized and required to order such guardian, &c. to produce such person in the Court of Chancery or otherwise, before commissioners to be appointed by the said Court, at such time and place as the Court shall direct, two of which commissioners shall be nominated by the party prosecuting such order at his costs; and in case such guardian, &c. shall refuse or neglect to produce such person in the Court of Chancery, or before such commissioners, the said person shall be taken to be dead, and it shall be lawful for any person claiming any interest in remainder or reversion or otherwise after the death of such person, to enter upon such lands, tenements and hereditaments, as if such person were actually dead (*f*).

Marginal notes:
whose lives estates are held.
Stat. 6 Anne, c. 18, s. 1 (*e*). Persons claiming in remainder after death of any person may obtain production of *cestui que vie*.
If *cestui que vie* not produced, to be taken to be dead.

(*e*) See also stat. 19 Car. 2, c. 6.

(*f*) See sect. 2, as to the mode of procedure when *cestui que vie* is beyond seas.

If it shall afterwards appear upon proof, in any action to be brought, that such person for whose life any such estate is holden, (was) alive at the time of such order made, it shall be lawful for (any) person having any estate or interest determinable upon such life, to re-enter upon the said lands, &c. and to maintain an action against those who since the said order received the profits of such lands, &c., or their executors or administrators, and therein to recover full damages for the profits of the same received. Sect. 3. If *cestui que vie* be afterwards proved to be alive, tenant for life may re-enter.

Every person having any estate determinable upon any life or lives, who after the determination of such particular estates, without the express consent of him who shall be immediately entitled after the determination of such particular estates, shall continue in possession of any manors, messuages, lands, tenements or hereditaments, shall be adjudged to be trespassers, and every person, his executors and administrators, who shall be entitled to any such manors, messuages, &c., upon or after the determination of such particular estates, shall recover in damages against every such person so holding over as aforesaid, and against his executors or administrators, the full value of the profits received during such wrongful possession as aforesaid. Sect. 5. Tenants for the life of another holding over, to be deemed trespassers.

SECT. II.—*Modes of determination generally applicable.*

(1) *Merger.*

Merger occurs where a greater and a less estate coincide and meet in one and the same person, without any intermediate estate (*g*); as, for instance, when When it occurs.

(*g*) See *Burton* v. *Barclay*, 7 Bing. 745, 756.

tenant for years obtains the fee (*h*). If a tenant for years acquires a life interest in the estate *pur autre vie*, the two being concurrent, one only can exist, and the other is merged; but there is no inconsistency or incompatibility in a man's having, not two concurrent, but two *successive* estates. If a lease for years be granted to a tenant *pur autre vie*, to commence when his life estate ceases, he will be tenant of the freehold, so long as *cestui que vie* lives, but amenable to the reversioner for every duty to which that tenancy is subject; and he will be tenant for the term when *cestui que vie* dies, and still amenable to the reversioner for all the duties of that tenancy. He will never stand in the character, which the law of merger is intended to prevent, of reversioner to himself (*i*). Merger will not take place where the two estates are held in different rights, and the tenant has not acquired the freehold by his own act (*j*). The fact that the reversion is for a less number of years than the estate in possession, will not prevent the latter from merging in the former (*k*).

(2) *Surrender.*

Express. To constitute a valid express surrender, it is essential that it should be made to and accepted by the owner in his own right of the immediate estate in reversion or remainder (*l*). Any form of words, whereby such an intent and agreement of the parties may appear, will be sufficient to work a surrender; and the law will direct the operation and construction of the words ac-

---

(*h*) 2 Black. Com. 177; judgment in *Doe* v. *Walker*, 5 B. & C., at p. 120.

(*i*) Judgment in *Doe* v. *Walker*, 5 B. & C., at p. 121.

(*j*) *Jones* v. *Davies*, 5 H. & N. 766; 29 L. J., Ex. 374; 7 H. & N. 507; 31 L. J., Ex. 116.

(*k*) Bac. Abr. (S. 2) 211.

(*l*) See Bac. Abr. (S. 1) 209.

cordingly, without the precise or formal mention of the word *surrender* (m).

No leases, estates or interests, either of freehold or terms of years, or any uncertain interest not being copyhold or customary interest, in any messuages, manors, lands, tenements or hereditaments, shall be assigned, granted or surrendered, unless it be by deed or note in writing, signed by the party so assigning, granting or surrendering the same, or their agents thereunto lawfully authorized by writing, or by act or operation of law. Stat. 29 Car. 2, c. 3, s. 3. Leases to be surrendered by writing.

A surrender in writing of an interest in any tenements or hereditaments, not being a copyhold interest, and not being an interest which might by law have been created without writing, shall be void at law, unless made by deed. Stat. 8 & 9 Vict. c. 106, s. 3. Surrenders to be by deed.

A surrender may be implied by operation of law from any thing which amounts to an agreement on the part of the tenant to abandon, and on the part of the landlord to resume possession of the premises (n). The following circumstances have been held to amount to a surrender by operation of law:—Delivery by the tenant to the landlord, and acceptance by the landlord of the keys of the demised house, with the intention that there shall be a transfer of possession (o). In this case, however, there must be clear evidence of the acceptance *Implied.*

1. Delivery of keys.

(m) Bac .Abr. (S. 1) 209. See *Smith* v. *Mapleback*, 1 T. R. 441; *Doe* v. *Stagg*, 5 Bing. N. C. 564. The stamp duty on a surrender, not chargeable with duty as a conveyance on sale or mortgage, is ten shillings. (Stat. 33 & 34 Vict. c. 97, Schedule.)

(n) Per Erle, C. J., in *Phenè* v. *Popplewell*, 12 C. B., N. S., at p, 340.

(o) *Dodd* v. *Acklom*, 6 M. & Gr. 672; 13 L. J., C. P. 11; *Phenè* v. *Popplewell*, 12 C. B., N. S. 334; 31 L. J., C. P. 235. See *Whitehead* v. *Clifford*, 5 Taunt. 518; *Grimman* v. *Legge*, 8 B. & C. 324.

of the key by the landlord (*p*). The mere fact that he has not sent back the key which the tenant has left at his office, is not evidence from which a surrender can be implied (*p*). A parol license to quit will not of itself operate as a surrender of the tenant's interest; but when the tenant gives up possession in pursuance of such a license, and the landlord accepts possession, the license, coupled with the fact of the change of possession, is a surrender by act and operation of law, and the landlord cannot recover any rent which becomes due after his acceptance of the possession (*q*).

2. Acceptance of new lease.

Acceptance by the lessee of a new lease, from the lessor, to begin during the continuance of the old lease (*r*). The surrender in this case is the act of the law, and will prevail in spite of the intention of the parties (*s*). A new lease will operate as a surrender, although for a shorter term than the prior lease; and a new valid lease by parol will constitute a surrender of a prior lease by deed (*r*). But where the new lease does not pass an interest according to the contract, the acceptance of it will not amount to a surrender of the former lease (*t*). Hence, the acceptance of a void lease (*t*), or the execution of a mere agreement for a new lease (*u*), will not operate as a surrender.

(*p*) *Cannan* v. *Hartley*, 9 C. B. 634; 19 L. J., C. P. 323. See *Brown* v. *Burtinshaw*, 7 D. & R. 603.

(*q*) Per Bayley, J., in *Grimman* v. *Legge*, 8 B. & C., at p. 325.

(*r*) See judgment of Tindal, C. J., in *Dodd* v. *Acklom*, 6 M. & Gr. 679; 13 L. J., C. P., at p. 13; *Fulmerstone* v. *Steward*, Plowd. 106, 107 a; *Ive* v. *Sams*, Cro.

Eliz., at p. 522; *Davison* v. *Stanley*, 4 Burr. 2210; *M'Donnell* v. *Pope*, 9 Hare, 705.

(*s*) *Lyon* v. *Reed*, 13 M. & W. 285; 13 L. J., Ex. 377, 382.

(*t*) See *Doe* v. *Courtenay*, 11 Q. B. 702; 17 L. J., Q. B. 151; *Doe* v. *Poole*, 11 Q. B. 713; 17 L. J., Q. B. 143.

(*u*) *Foquet* v. *Moor*, 7 Ex. 870; 22 L. J., Ex. 35. See *Graham* v. *Whichelo*, 1 Cr. & M. 188; judg-

MODES OF DETERMINATION GENERALLY APPLICABLE. 281

The grant of a new lease, by the landlord, to a third person, with the assent of the tenant, who gives up his own possession (*x*); or the acceptance by the landlord, with the assent of a tenant from year to year, of another person as tenant, who takes possession (*y*). Where an under-tenant is in possession, the acceptance of such under-tenant as tenant by the lessor may be proved by his having accepted the key from the original lessee, or by his acceptance of rent from the under-tenant, or by some act tantamount to it (*z*). Receipts for rent received by a landlord from a third person are strong evidence of a change of tenancy with the consent of the landlord, amounting to a surrender by operation of law (*a*).

3. Acceptance by landlord of third person as tenant with consent of prior tenant.

The creation of a new relation in regard to the demised property, wholly inconsistent with that of landlord and tenant (*b*), as, for instance, where the tenant becomes the servant of the landlord, accounting to him for all the profits of the demised premises, and being allowed fixed daily wages (*b*).

4. Creation of inconsistent relation.

The mere cancelling of a lease is not a surrender by operation of law of the term thereby granted (*c*), or *primâ facie* evidence of a surrender by deed (*d*).

Though a surrender operates between the parties as an extinguishment of the interest which is surrendered,

Operation of surrender on rights of third persons.

ment of Holroyd, J., in *Hamerton* v. *Stead*, 3 B. & C., at p. 482.
(*x*) *Davison* v. *Gent*, 1 H. & N. 744; 26 L. J., Ex. 122; *Walker* v. *Richardson*, 2 M. & W. 882; *M'Donnell* v. *Pope*, 9 Hare, 705. See *Rex* v. *Banbury*, 1 A. & E. 136; *Nickells* v. *Atherstone*, 10 Q. B. 944; 16 L. J., Q. B. 371; *Reeve* v. *Bird*, 1 Cr., M. & R. 31; *Hamerton* v. *Stead*, 3 B. & C. 478.
(*y*) *Thomas* v. *Cook*, 2 B. & A. 119; *Stone* v. *Whiting*, 2 Stark.

235. See *Harding* v. *Crethorn*, 1 Esp. 57; *Cadle* v. *Moody*, 30 L. J., Ex. 385.
(*z*) Per Lord Kenyon, C. J., in *Harding* v. *Crethorn*, 1 Esp. 57.
(*a*) *Lawrance* v. *Faux*, 2 F. & F. 435.
(*b*) *Peter* v. *Kendal*, 6 B. & C. 703, 710.
(*c*) *Roe* v. *Archbishop of York*, 6 East, 86.
(*d*) *Doe* v. *Thomas*, 9 B. & C. 268. See *Ward* v. *Lumley*, 5 H. & N. 87; 29 L. J., Ex. 322.

it does not so operate as to third persons who, at the time of the surrender, had rights which such extinguishment would destroy. As to them the surrender operates only as a grant subject to their right, and the interest surrendered still has, for the preservation of their right, continuance (e).

<small>Stat. 4 Geo. 2, c. 28, s. 6. Surrender for purpose of renewal to be valid without surrender of underleases.</small>

In case any lease shall be duly surrendered, in order to be renewed, and a new lease executed by the chief landlord, the same new lease shall, without a surrender of the underleases, be as valid as if all the underleases derived thereout had been likewise surrendered before the taking of such new lease; and every person in whom any estate for life or lives, or for years, shall from time to time be vested by virtue of such new lease, his executors and administrators, shall be entitled to the rents, covenants and duties, and have like remedy for recovery thereof, and the under-lessees shall hold the messuages, lands and tenements in the respective underleases comprised, as if the original leases, out of which the respective underleases are derived, had been still kept on foot and continued, and the chief landlord shall have the same remedy, by distress or entry upon the messuages, &c., comprised in any such underlease, for the rents and duties reserved by such new lease so far as the same exceed not the rents and duties reserved in the lease out of which such underlease was derived, as they would have had in case such former lease had been continued, or the underleases had been renewed under such new lease.

<small>Stat. 8 & 9 Vict. c. 106, s. 9. When reversion on a lease is surrendered</small>

When the reversion expectant on a lease shall be surrendered or merge, the estate which shall for the time being confer, as against the tenant under the same lease, the next vested right to the same tenements or

(e) Judgment in *Doe* v. *Pyke*, *Benson*, 4 East, 234, 238; Co. 5 M. & S., at p. 154; *Pleasant* v. Lit. 338 b.

hereditaments, shall, to the extent and for the purpose of preserving such incidents to and obligations on the same reversion, as, but for the surrender or merger thereof, would have subsisted, be deemed the reversion expectant on the same lease. *or merged, the next vested estate to be deemed the reversion.*

(3) *Forfeiture.*

(a) *Where there is no express Proviso for Re-entry.*

Any act of the lessee by which he disaffirms or impugns the title of his lessor occasions a forfeiture of his lease; for to every lease the law tacitly annexes a condition, that if the lessee do anything that may affect the interest of his lessor, the lease shall be void, and the lessor may re-enter (*f*). A lessee may thus incur a forfeiture where he sues out a writ, or resorts to a remedy, which claims or supposes a right to the freehold (*f*), or where, in an action by his lessor grounded upon the lease, he resists the demand under the grant of a higher interest in the land (*f*); or where he acknowledges the fee to be in a stranger (*f*). The mere payment of rent, by a tenant *for a term of years*, to a third person (*g*), or a verbal denial by such tenant of the landlord's title (*h*), will not operate as a forfeiture of the lease. *Disclaimer by matter of record, &c.*

Forfeitures are also incurred by the breach of express or conventionary conditions annexed by the lessor to his grant (*i*). In a lease for years, no precise form of words is necessary to make a condition; it is sufficient if it appear that the words used were intended to have *On breach of conditions annexed to grant.*

(*f*) Bac. Abr. (T. 2) 219.
(*g*) *Doe* v. *Parker*, Gow, 180.
(*h*) *Doe* v. *Wells*, 10 A. & E. 427.
(*i*) Bac. Abr. (T. 2) 220.

that effect (*j*); hence, a clause in a lease whereby it is stipulated and conditioned that the lessee shall not assign, creates a condition, for the breach of which the lessor may maintain an ejectment (*k*).

(b) *Where there is an express Proviso for Re-entry.*

By whom lease may be determined under proviso for re-entry. The construction of a proviso for re-entry by the lessor on non-performance by the lessee of the covenants, and of a proviso that upon such non-performance the term shall cease and become void, is that the lease shall be voidable only at the option of the lessor; for the lessee who has been guilty of a wrongful act cannot avail himself of that wrongful act to insist that thereby the lease has become void to all intents and purposes (*l*), and the tenancy will therefore continue until some act is done by the lessor showing his intention to determine it (*m*).

Demand of rent. Before advantage can be taken of a proviso for re-entry for non-payment of rent, a formal demand of rent must be made; unless such demand has been either expressly dispensed with in the proviso or condition (*n*), or one half-year's rent is in arrear, and no sufficient distress can be found on the premises (*o*). The demand must be of the sum due for rent for the last term of

---

(*j*) Judgment of Bayley, J., in *Doe* v. *Watt*, 8 B. & C., at p. 315.

(*k*) *Doe* v. *Watt*, 8 B. & C. 308. See *Simpson* v. *Titterell*, Cro. Eliz. 242; *Pembroke* v. *Berkeley*, *ib.* 384; *Harrington* v. *Wise*, *ib.* 486; Co. Lit. 203 b.

(*l*) Judgment of Bayley, J., in *Doe* v. *Bancks*, 4 B. & A. 406; *Arnsby* v. *Woodward*, 6 B. & C. 519; *Dakin* v. *Cope*, 2 Russ. 170; *Doe* v. *Birch*, 1 M. & W. 402.

(*m*) See judgment of Denman, C. J., in *Roberts* v. *Davey*, 4 B. & Ad., at p. 671; *Hartshorne* v. *Watson*, 4 Bing. N. C. 178.

(*n*) *Doe* v. *Masters*, 2 B. & C. 490.

(*o*) Stat. 15 & 16 Vict. c. 76, s. 210; *post*, p. 285.

payment (*p*), and must be made at a convenient time before sunset on the last day of payment (*q*). The demand must be made upon the land; if there is a house on the premises, at the front door of such house (*r*); or if the premises consist of lands and woods, upon the lands (*s*); or if they consist of woods only, at the gate of the wood, or at some highway leading through it, or other most notorious place (*t*). It is not material whether the tenant is there or not (*u*). If tender of the rent is made to him who is to receive it upon any part of the land, at any time on the last day of payment, the tender will save the condition (*t*).

Where "one half-year's rent shall be in arrear (*x*), and the landlord, to whom the same is due, hath right by law to re-enter for the non-payment thereof (*y*), such landlord may, without any formal demand or re-entry, serve a writ in ejectment for the recovery of the demised premises, or in case the same cannot be legally served, or no tenant be in actual possession of the premises, such landlord may affix a copy thereof upon the door of any demised messuage, or in case such action in ejectment shall not be for the recovery of any messuage, then upon some notorious place of the lands, tenements or hereditaments comprised in such writ in ejectment, and such affixing shall be deemed legal service thereof, which service or affixing such writ in ejectment shall stand in the place of a demand and re-entry; and in case of judgment against the defendant for non-appear-

Stat. 15 & 16 Vict. c. 76, s. 210.
Where one half-year's rent is in arrear and landlord has right to re-enter, he may, instead of formal demand, serve writ in ejectment.

(*p*) See *Doe* v. *Paul*, 3 C. & P. 613; *Fabian* v. *Winston*, Cro. Eliz. 209.
(*q*) Co. Lit. 202 a.
(*r*) Co. Lit. 201 b.
(*s*) Poph. 58.
(*t*) Co. Lit. 202 a.

(*u*) Co. Lit. 201 b.
(*x*) See *Cotesworth* v. *Spokes*, 10 C. B., N. S. 103; 30 L. J., C. P. 220.
(*y*) See *Doe* v. *Roe*, 7 C. B. 134.

ance, if it shall be made to appear to the court where the said action is depending, by affidavit (*z*), or be proved upon the trial in case the defendant appears, that half-a-year's rent was due before the said writ was served, and (that the premises were locked up (*a*), or) that no sufficient distress was to be found on the demised premises, countervailing the arrears then due, and that the lessor had power to re-enter, in such case the lessor shall recover judgment and execution, in the same manner as if the rent in arrear had been legally demanded, and a re-entry made."

(c) *Waiver of Forfeiture.*

If a landlord, when he is in a position to take advantage of a forfeiture, elects not to take advantage of it, and so declares to the person against whom he has power to enforce it, and at a later period acknowledges the continuance of the tenancy, he thereby waives such forfeiture (*b*). Mere knowledge and acquiescence in an act constituting a forfeiture, does not amount to a waiver; there must be some act affirming the tenancy (*c*). The following circumstances have been held to operate as waivers of forfeitures:—Acceptance by the landlord from the tenant of rent due after the forfeiture (*d*); or an action (*e*) or distress (*f*) by the landlord for such rent. No words of the landlord

Acts amounting to waiver.
1. *Receipt of rent.*

(*z*) See *Cross* v. *Jordan*, 8 Ex. 149; 22 L. J., Ex. 70.

(*a*) *Hammond* v. *Mather*, 3 F. & F. 151. See *Doe* v. *Dyson*, M. & M. 77.

(*b*) Per Erle, C. J., in *Ward* v. *Day*, 5 B. & S., at p. 364; 33 L. J., Q. B., at p. 255.

(*c*) Per Heath, J., in *Doe* v. *Allen*, 3 Taunt., at p. 81.

(*d*) *Arnsby* v. *Woodward*, 6 B. & C. 519; *Doe* v. *Rees*, 4 Bing. N. C. 384; *Doe* v. *Pritchard*, 5 B. & Ad. 765.

(*e*) *Dendy* v. *Nicholl*, 4 C. B., N. S. 376; 27 L. J., C. P. 220.

(*f*) *Doe* v. *Peck*, 1 B. & Ad. 428.

at the time of his receiving the money can prevent this legal effect (*g*). A forfeiture will not be waived by acceptance by the landlord of rent due *before* the forfeiture was incurred (*h*), or after he has commenced an action of ejectment against the tenant (*i*).

An absolute and unqualified demand of rent due after the forfeiture, made by a person having sufficient authority (*j*).

2. Demand of rent.

An agreement by the landlord to grant a new term after the expiration by effluxion of time of a term in respect of which a forfeiture has been incurred (*k*).

3. Agreement to grant new lease after expiration of forfeited lease.

Advice given by the landlord after the forfeiture, to a third person to purchase the lease of the lessee (*l*). Advice to a person having an interest in premises, to "take to" them, will not waive a forfeiture (*l*).

4. Advice to purchase lease.

Where the breach of covenant causing a forfeiture is continuous (*m*), the receipt of rent, or other acknowledgment of tenancy by the landlord, will not preclude him from taking advantage of a forfeiture incurred subsequently to such acknowledgment (*n*).

Continuous breach.

Where any actual waiver of the benefit of any covenant or condition in any lease on the part of any lessor, or his heirs, executors, administrators or assigns, shall be proved to have taken place after the passing of this act, in any one particular instance, such actual waiver shall not be deemed to extend to any instance or any

Stat. 23 & 24 Vict. c. 38, s. 6. Effect of waiver restricted to breach to which it specially relates.

(*g*) *Croft* v. *Lumley*, 5 E. & B. 648; 25 L. J., Q. B. 223; 6 H. L. C. 672; 27 L. J., Q. B. 321.
(*h*) See *Price* v. *Worwood*, 4 H. & N. 512; 28 L. J., Ex. 329.
(*i*) See *Jones* v. *Carter*, 15 M. & W. 718.
(*j*) Per Parke, B., in *Doe* v. *Birch*, 1 M. & W., at p. 408.

(*k*) *Ward* v. *Day*, 5 B. & S. 359; 33 L. J., Q. B. 254.
(*l*) *Doe* v. *Eykins*, 1 C. & P. 154; Ry. & M. 29, 30.
(*m*) *Ante*, pp. 194, 222.
(*n*) *Doe* v. *Woodbridge*, 9 B. & C. 376; *Doe* v. *Jones*, 5 Ex. 498; 19 L. J., Ex. 405.

breach of covenant or condition, other than that to which such waiver shall specially relate, or to be a general waiver of the benefit of any such covenant or condition, unless an intention to that effect shall appear.

(d) *Relief against Forfeiture.*

For non-payment of rent.

Courts of equity will relieve the tenant from forfeiture for nonpayment of rent within six months after execution executed (*o*), on payment by him of the rent, together with full costs.

Stat. 15 & 16 Vict. c. 76, s. 211.

Lessee proceeding for relief in equity not to have injunction against proceedings at law unless he pays into Court rent and costs.

In case the lessee, his assignee, or other person claiming any right, title or interest, in law or equity, to the said lease, shall, within the time aforesaid, proceed for relief in any Court of equity, such person shall not have or continue any injunction against the proceedings at law on such ejectment, unless he shall, within forty days next after a full and perfect answer shall be made by the claimant in such ejectment, bring into Court, and lodge with the proper officer, such sum and sums of money as the landlord shall in his answer swear to be due and in arrear over and above all just allowances, and also the costs taxed in the said suit, there to remain till the hearing of the cause, or to be paid out to the landlord on good security, subject to the decree of the Court; and in case such proceedings for relief in equity shall be taken within the time aforesaid, and after execution is executed, the landlord shall be accountable only for so much, and no more, as he shall really and *bonâ fide*, without fraud, deceit or wilful neglect make of the demised premises from the time of his entering into the actual possession thereof; and if what shall be so

(*o*) Stat. 15 & 16 Vict. c. 76, s. 210.

made by the landlord happen to be less than the rent reserved on the said lease, then the said lessee or his assignee, before he shall be restored to his possession, shall pay such landlord what the money so by him made fell short of the reserved rent for the time such lessor or landlord held the said lands.

If the tenant or his assignee shall, at any time before the trial in such ejectment, pay or tender to the landlord, his executors or administrators, or his or their attorney in that cause, or pay into the Court, where the same cause is depending, all the rent and arrears, together with the costs, all further proceedings on the said ejectment shall cease and be discontinued; and if such lessee, his executors, administrators or assigns, shall, upon such proceedings as aforesaid, be relieved in equity, he and they shall have, hold and enjoy the demised lands, according to the lease thereof made, without any new lease. *Sect. 212. If tenant, before trial, tenders to landlord or pays into Court rent and costs, proceedings to cease.*

A Court of equity shall have power to relieve against a forfeiture for breach of a covenant or condition to insure against loss or damage by fire, where no loss or damage by fire has happened, and the breach has, in the opinion of the Court, been committed through accident or mistake, or otherwise without fraud or gross negligence, and there is an insurance on foot at the time of the application to the Court in conformity with the covenant to insure, upon such terms as to the Court may seem fit. *Stat. 22 & 23 Vict. c. 35, s. 4. Relief against forfeiture for breach of covenant to insure.*

The Court, where relief shall be granted, shall direct a record of such relief having been granted to be made by indorsement on the lease or otherwise. *Sect. 5. Record of relief to be indorsed on lease.*

The Court shall not have power, under this act, to relieve the same person more than once in respect of the *Sect. 6. Relief to be* same covenant or condition; nor shall it have power to grant any relief under this act where a forfeiture under the covenant in respect of which relief is sought shall have been already waived out of Court in favour of the person seeking the relief.

granted only once to same person in respect of same covenant.

Stat. 23 & 24 Vict. c. 126, s. 1.
Courts of law may relieve on ejectment for forfeiture for non-payment of rent;

In the case of any ejectment for a forfeiture brought for non-payment of rent, the Court or a judge shall have power, upon rule or summons, to give relief in a summary manner, but subject to appeal as hereinafter mentioned (see sects. 4—11), up to and within the like time after execution executed, and subject to the same terms and conditions in all respects as to payment of rent, costs, and otherwise, as in the Court of Chancery; and if the lessee, his executors, administrators or assigns shall, upon such proceeding, be relieved, he and they shall hold the demised lands according to the lease thereof made, without any new lease.

Sect. 2.
or on ejectment for forfeiture for non-insurance.

In the case of any ejectment for a forfeiture for breach of a covenant or condition to insure against loss or damage by fire, the Court or a judge shall have power, upon rule or summons, to give relief in a summary manner, but subject to appeal as hereinafter mentioned (see sects. 4—11), in all cases in which such relief may now be obtained in the Court of Chancery under the provisions of (stat. 22 & 23 Vict. c. 35), and upon such terms as would be imposed in such Court.

Sect. 3.

Where such relief shall be granted, the Court or a judge shall direct a minute thereof to be made by indorsement on the lease, or otherwise.

Cases in which Courts of Chancery will not relieve against forfeiture.

Courts of equity will not relieve against forfeiture for breach of the following covenants, unless by unavoidable accident (*p*), fraud, surprise, or ignorance

(*p*) See *Dargent v. Thomson*, 9 Jur., N. S. 1192; 4 Giff. 473.

not wilful, persons have been prevented from executing them literally;—Covenant not to assign or underlet without consent (*q*); not to permit a way over land (*r*); to repair (*s*).

(*q*) *Hill* v. *Barclay,* 18 Ves., at p. 63.
(*r*) *Descarlett* v. *Dennett,* 9 Mod. 22.

(*s*) *Hill* v. *Barclay,* 18 Ves. 56; *Gregory* v. *Wilson,* 9 Hare, 683. But see *Bamford* v. *Creasy,* 3 Giff. 675.

CHAP. VI.

TERMS OF QUITTING.

	PAGE
SECT. I. FIXTURES	292
(1) What articles are fixtures	292
(2) Ownership of fixtures where there is no express agreement	293
Fixtures put up by landlord	293
,, ,, tenant	293
Ornamental fixtures	294
Trade fixtures	294
Agricultural fixtures	295
Time of removal	296
(3) Ownership under express agreements	297
II. EMBLEMENTS	298
(1) In what cases they may be claimed	298
(2) Provision as to tenants of landlords entitled for uncertain interests	299
III. AWAY-GOING CROPS	300
IV. COMPENSATION FOR TILLAGES, &C.	300
V. DELIVERY OF POSSESSION	301
(1) Tenant's obligation to give possession	301
(2) Landlord's remedies for recovering possession	302
(a) Indirect	302
Action for double value	302
Action or distress for double rent	304
(b) Direct	305
Entry	305
Proceedings before justices	306
In case of houses at rents not exceeding 20*l.* a-year	306
In case of deserted premises	310
Proceedings in county court	310
Action of ejectment	313

SECT. I.—*Fixtures.*

(1) *What Articles are Fixtures.*

To affix a chattel to land, so as to make it a fixture, it is not sufficient that it has been laid upon the land and brought into contact with it; something more is required than mere juxtaposition; as, that the soil shall have been displaced for the purpose of receiving the article, or that the chattel should be cemented or otherwise fastened to some fabric previously attached to the ground (*a*). Hence, articles standing merely by their own weight (*b*), such as wooden erections resting upon, but not attached to, blocks of wood (*c*), or brick pillars (*d*), or a foundation of brick and stone (*e*), are not fixtures. Machines screwed to the floor to steady them are not thereby made fixtures (*f*). A greenhouse resting on a brick wall, to which the upper frame is attached in the usual way, by a course of mortar, is a fixture as between landlord and tenant (*g*).

(2) Ownership of Fixtures where there is no express Agreement.

Fixtures erected before the commencement of the tenancy, or put up by the landlord during the tenancy for a permanent purpose and for the better enjoyment of his estate, though in the ordinary case of landlord and tenant they would be removable by the latter during the term, become part of the freehold (*h*). Fixtures erected before commencement of tenancy or by landlord during tenancy.

The general rule is, that where a lessee having annexed a personal chattel to the freehold during his term Fixtures put up by tenant during tenancy.

(*a*) Amos & Ferard on Fixtures, p. 2, cited by Mellor, J., in *Turner* v. *Cameron*, 39 L. J., Q. B., at p. 130.
(*b*) See *Mather* v. *Fraser*, 2 K. & J. 536; 25 L. J., Ch. 361.
(*c*) *Culling* v. *Tuffnal*, Bull. N. P. 34.
(*d*) See *Rex* v. *Londonthorpe*, 6 T. R. 377.
(*e*) *Wansbrough* v. *Maton*, 4 A. & E. 884; *Wiltshear* v. *Cottrell*, 1 E. & B. 674. See *Rex* v. *Otley*,

1 B. & Ad. 161; *Dean* v. *Allalley*, 3 Esp. 11.
(*f*) Per Lord Lyndhurst, C. B., in *Trappes* v. *Harter*, 2 Cr. & M., at p. 177; *Hellawell* v. *Eastwood*, 6 Ex. 295; 20 L. J., Ex. 154.
(*g*) *Jenkins* v. *Gething*, 2 J. & H. 520. See *Buckland* v. *Butterfield*, 2 B. & B. 54.
(*h*) *Walmsley* v. *Milne*, 7 C. B., N. S. 115; 29 L. J., C. P. 97; *Mather* v. *Fraser*, 2 K. & J. 536; 25 L. J., Ch. 361.

afterwards takes it away, it is waste (*i*). In the progress of time, however, this rule has been relaxed, and many exceptions have been grafted upon it (*i*). In the following cases articles affixed by the tenant during his tenancy may be claimed by him, provided they can be removed without doing substantial injury to the freehold:—

1. Ornamental fixtures, &c.

Articles of ornament and domestic utility; such as ornamental chimney-pieces (*j*), stoves and grates (*k*), wainscots fastened with screws (*k*), cornices (*l*), beds fastened to the wall or ceiling (*m*), chimney-glasses and pier-glasses (*n*), ovens, coppers and pumps slightly affixed to the freehold (*o*). A tenant who is not a nurseryman by trade cannot remove or sell any trees (*p*), shrubs (*q*), or flowers (*r*), which he may have planted upon the demised premises.

2. Trade fixtures.

Machinery and utensils of a chattel nature (*s*); such as salt-pans (*t*), vats, &c. for soap-boiling (*u*), engines for working collieries (*x*); also buildings of a temporary description erected by the tenant for the purpose of carrying on his business (*y*). Buildings of a permanent

(*i*) Per Dallas, C. J., in *Buckland* v. *Butterfield*, 2 Br. & B., at p. 58.

(*j*) *Leach* v. *Thomas*, 7 C. & P. 327. See judgment in *Lawton* v. *Salmon*, 1 H. Bl., at p. 260, note; *Bishop* v. *Elliott*, 11 Ex. 113, 119; 24 L. J., Ex. 229.

(*k*) Per Tindal, C.J., in *Grymes* v. *Boweren*, 6 Bing., at p. 439. See *Birch* v. *Dawson*, 2 A. & E. 37.

(*l*) *Avery* v. *Cheslyn*, 3 A. & E. 75.

(*m*) *Ex parte Quincey*, 1 Atk., at p. 478.

(*n*) *Beck* v. *Rebow*, 1 P. Wms. 94.

(*o*) *Grymes* v. *Boweren*, 6 Bing. 437; *Winn* v. *Ingilby*, 5 B. & A. 625.

(*p*) *Wyndham* v. *Way*, 4 Taunt. 316.

(*q*) *Empson* v. *Soden*, 4 B. & Ad. 655.

(*r*) Per Littledale, J., in *Empson* v. *Soden*, 4 B. & Ad., at p. 657.

(*s*) See *Fisher* v. *Dixon*, 12 Cl. & F. 312, 325, 331.

(*t*) *Lawton* v. *Salmon*, 1 H. Bl. 259, note (*d*).

(*u*) *Poole's Case*, 1 Salk. 368.

(*x*) *Lawton* v. *Lawton*, 3 Atk. 13; *Dudley* v. *Warde*, Ambl. 114.

(*y*) *Lawton* v. *Lawton*, 3 Atk. 13, 15; *Lawton* v. *Salmon*, 1 H.

character, although used as accessories to trade fixtures, are not removable by the tenant (z). Nurserymen may remove trees and shrubs grown for sale (a), and, perhaps, also hothouses erected by them (b). It seems that a custom of the neighbourhood, as to the removal of articles erected by a tenant, may be taken as an explanation of their nature and character (c).

Farm buildings, machinery, &c. erected by agricultural tenants, and affixed to the soil (d), before 24th July, 1851, cannot be removed by them (e), unless there is an express agreement to that effect. "If any tenant of a farm or lands shall, after the passing of this act (24 July, 1851), with the consent in writing (f) of the landlord for the time being, at his own cost and expense, erect any farm building, either detached or otherwise, or put up any other building, engine or machinery, either for agricultural purposes or for the purposes of trade and agriculture, which shall not have been erected or put up in pursuance of some obligation in that behalf, then all such buildings, engines and machinery shall be the property of the tenant, and shall be removable by him, notwithstanding the same may

3. Agricultural fixtures.

Stat. 14 & 15 Vict. c. 25, s. 3.

Buildings, &c. erected by tenant for agricultural purposes, with consent of landlord, to be removable unless landlord shall choose to purchase them.

Bl. 259, note; *Penton* v. *Robart*, 4 Esp. 33. See *Climie* v. *Wood*, 37 L. J., Ex. 158; L. R., 3 Ex. 257.

(z) *Whitehead* v. *Bennett*, 27 L. J., Ch. 474. See *Thresher* v. *East London Waterworks Co.*, 2 B. & C. 608.

(a) *Wardell* v. *Usher*, 3 Sc. N. R. 508.

(b) Per Lord Kenyon, C. J., in *Penton* v. *Robart*, 2 East, at p. 90; but see 2 B. & B., at p. 58; Amos & Ferard on Fixtures, 70, 343.

(c) Judgment in *Davis* v. *Jones*,

2 B. & A., at p. 168; *Trappes* v. *Harter*, 3 Tyr. 603; *Culling* v. *Tuffnal*, Bull. N. P. 34.

(d) See *ante*, p. 292.

(e) *Elwes* v. *Maw*, 3 East, 38.

(f) The consent may be in the following form:—

To Mr. C. D.

I do hereby consent to the erection by you, at your own cost and expense, of [*an engine or boiler*] in or upon [describe the exact situation] upon the premises now held by you as my tenant.

Dated the —— day of ——, 18—.

E. F.

consist of separate buildings, or that the same or any part thereof may be built in or permanently fixed to the soil, so as the tenant making any such removal do not in anywise injure the land or buildings belonging to the landlord, or otherwise do put the same in like condition, or as good condition, as the same were in before the erection of anything so removed: Provided nevertheless, that no tenant shall, under the provision last aforesaid, be entitled to remove any such thing as aforesaid without first giving to the landlord or his agent one month's previous notice in writing of his intention so to do (*g*); and thereupon it shall be lawful for the landlord, or his agent on his authority, to elect to purchase the matters and things so proposed to be removed, or any of them, and the right to remove the same shall thereby cease, and the same shall belong to the landlord; and the value thereof shall be ascertained and determined by two referees, one to be chosen by each party, or by an umpire to be named by such referees, and shall be paid or allowed in account by the landlord who shall have so elected to purchase the same."

The tenant must remove his fixtures during the continuance of his original term (*h*), or during such further period of possession by him as he holds the premises under a right still to consider himself as tenant (*i*). In

---

(*g*) The notice may be in the following form:—

To Mr. E. F.

I hereby give you notice that I intend, after the lapse of one month from your receipt of this notice, to remove from the premises which I now hold of you as tenant, the [*engine and boiler*] erected by me thereon.

Dated the —— day of ——, 18—.

C. D.

(*h*) *Lyde* v. *Russell*, 1 B. & Ad. 394, 395; *Minshall* v. *Lloyd*, 2 M. & W. 450. See *Poole's Case*, 1 Salk. 368.

(*i*) *Weeton* v. *Woodcock*, 7 M. & W. 14, 19; *Penton* v. *Robart*, 2 East, 88; *Leader* v. *Homewood*, 5 C. B., N. S. 546; 27 L. J., C. P. 316.

whatever way a lease may be determined, the tenant has no right to remove his fixtures after the landlord has entered (*k*), unless there is an express agreement that they shall be removed, in which case a reasonable time after the expiration of the lease will be allowed for their removal (*l*). A licence by the landlord to take away fixtures, if not under seal, will not be a valid grant of such privilege as against a new tenant in possession not a party to the licence (*m*).

(3) *Ownership under express Agreements.*

A tenant who has covenanted to yield up in repair at the expiration of the term the demised premises, and all buildings and improvements erected thereon during the term (*n*); or to keep and leave in repair all erections and improvements (*o*) made during the term, will be unable to remove any fixtures erected by him, even for purposes of trade (*p*). Under a covenant by a tenant to deliver up the demised premises, together with all locks, &c., " and other fixtures and articles in the nature of fixtures, which shall at any time during the said term be fixed or fastened to the said demised premises, or be thereto belonging," the tenant may remove fixtures of the description known

(*k*) *Pugh* v. *Arton*, 38 L. J., Ch. 619; L. R., 8 Eq. 626.

(*l*) See *Stansfield* v. *Mayor of Portsmouth*, 4 C. B., N. S. 120; 27 L. J., C. P. 124; *Sumner* v. *Bromilow*, 34 L. J., Q. B. 130.

(*m*) *Roffey* v. *Henderson*, 17 Q. B. 574; 21 L. J., Q. B. 49.

(*n*) *Penry* v. *Brown*, 2 Stark. 403; *Naylor* v. *Collinge*, 1 Taunt. 19; *Foley* v. *Addenbrooke*, 13 M. & W. 174; 14 L. J., Ex. 169.

See *Dumergue* v. *Rumsey*, 2 H. & C. 777; 33 L. J., Ex. 88; *Wilson* v. *Whateley*, 1 J. & H. 436; *Heap* v. *Barton*, 12 C. B. 274; 21 L. J., C. P. 153.

(*o*) *Martyr* v. *Bradley*, 9 Bing. 24.

(*p*) See *Burt* v. *Haslett*, 18 C. B. 162, 893; 25 L. J., C. P. 201, 295; *Mansfield* v. *Blackburne*, 6 Bing. N. C. 426.

as trade and tenant's fixtures (*r*). The mere removal and sale by a tenant, during the term, of fixtures, which he does not immediately replace, but which can be replaced before the end of the term, is not of itself a breach of his covenant to repair and uphold the demised premises, and to deliver up the same at the end of the term, together with all things affixed thereto (*s*).

Sect. II.—*Emblements.*

(1) *In what Cases they may be claimed.*

Tenants for life, at will (*t*), or for other uncertain interests not determinable on the death or cesser of the estate of a landlord entitled for his life or for any other uncertain interest (*u*), on the determination of the tenancy otherwise than by the tenant's own act (*x*), are entitled to such crops then growing upon the land as ordinarily repay the labour by which they are produced within the year in which that labour is bestowed (*y*). Grain crops (*z*), hemp, flax (*t*), teazles (*a*), potatoes (*b*) and hops (*c*), may be claimed as emblements; but permanent or natural profits of the earth, such as fruit trees or grass (*d*), do not come within that designation.

(*r*) *Bishop* v. *Elliott*, 11 Ex. 113, 229; 24 L. J., Ex. 229. See *Sumner* v. *Bromilow*, 34 L. J., Q. B. 130; *Wilde* v. *Waters*, 16 C. B. 637; 24 L. J., C. P. 193.

(*s*) *Doe* v. *Davis*, 15 Jur. 155.

(*t*) Co. Lit. 55 a. As to tenants from year to year, see 4 Bing. 207; 5 B. & Ad. 114.

(*u*) See *post*, p. 299.

(*x*) *Bulwer* v. *Bulwer*, 2 B. & A. 470, 471; *Davis* v. *Eyton*, 7 Bing. 154.

(*y*) *Graves* v. *Weld*, 5 B. & Ad. 105.

(*z*) 1 Rol. Abr. 728 (A.) 22.

(*a*) *Kingsbury* v. *Collins*, 4 Bing. 202.

(*b*) Judgment of Bayley, J., in *Evans* v. *Roberts*, 5 B. & C., at p. 832.

(*c*) Judgment in *Graves* v. *Weld*, 5 B. & Ad., at p. 119; *Latham* v. *Atwood*, Cro. Car. 515.

(*d*) 2 Black. Com. 123.

A person entitled to emblements may enter upon the lands after the determination of his tenancy for the purpose of cutting and carrying away the crops (*e*).

(2) *Provision as to Tenants of Landlords entitled for uncertain Interests.*

Where the tenancy of any farm or lands (*f*) held by a tenant at rack-rent shall determine by the death or cesser of the estate of any landlord entitled for his life, or for any other uncertain interest, instead of claims to emblements, the tenant shall continue to occupy such farm or lands until the expiration of the then current year of his tenancy, and shall then quit, upon the terms of his holding, in the same manner as if such tenancy were then determined by effluxion of time or other lawful means during the continuance of his landlord's estate; and the succeeding landlord shall be entitled to recover (either by action or distress (*f*)) and receive of the tenant in the same manner as his predecessor or such tenant's lessor could have done, if he had been living or had continued the lessor, a fair proportion of the rent for the period which may have elapsed from the day of the death or cesser of the estate of such predecessor or lessor to the time of the tenant so quitting, and the succeeding landlord and the tenant respectively shall, as between themselves and as against each other, be entitled to all the benefits and advantages, and be subject to the terms, conditions and restrictions, to which the preceding landlord and such tenant respectively would have been entitled and subject in case the tenancy had determined in manner aforesaid at the

Stat. 14 & 15 Vict. c. 25, s. 1.

Tenants at rack-rent of landlord entitled for life or other uncertain estate to be entitled, instead of emblements, to hold farm till end of current year.

Succeeding landlord may recover proportion of rent.

Succeeding landlord and tenant to hold upon terms of former tenancy.

(*e*) *Kingsbury* v. *Collins,* 4 Bing. 202. See *Hayling* v. *Okey,* 8 Ex. 531, 545; 22 L. J., Ex. 139.

(*f*) *Haines* v. *Welch,* 38 L. J., C. P. 118; L. R., 4 C. P. 91.

No notice to quit required to determine holding.

expiration of such current year: Provided always, that no notice to quit shall be necessary or required by or from either party to determine any such holding therein.

SECT. III.—*Away-going Crops.*

To induce tenants for fixed terms to sow their lands during the last year of tenancy it is frequently provided, by express stipulation or by the custom of the country (*h*), either that the outgoing tenant shall be permitted, after he has quitted the premises, to reap all or part of the crops he has sown, and to deposit them in the barns of the farm; or that he shall receive payment for the away-going crops from the incoming tenant or from the landlord.

If there is any condition in the lease necessarily repugnant to or inconsistent with such a custom the custom is excluded (*i*); but if the lease contains no stipulations as to the mode of quitting, the off-going tenant is entitled to his away-going crop according to the custom of the country, although the terms of *holding* may be inconsistent with such a custom (*i*).

SECT. IV.—*Compensation for Tillages, &c.*

By express stipulation in the lease there is sometimes also given to a tenant a right, on quitting his farm, to remuneration for tillage and fallows which are not ex-

---

(*h*) *Wigglesworth* v. *Dallison*, 1 Smith's L. C. (6th ed.) 539. See *Caldecott* v. *Smythies*, 7 C. & P. 808.

(*i*) Judgment in *Holding* v. *Pigott*, 7 Bing., at p. 474.

hausted at the time (*k*). If no such stipulation is made, a right to remuneration may be conferred by the usage or general practice of the neighbourhood (*l*), which, if consistent with the agreement between the parties as to the mode of quitting, will be considered as engrafted upon the lease, and forming part of it, as fully as if it were expressly stated (*m*).

The usage or practice is not to be treated as a custom strictly so called, and need not be immemorial (*n*).

Primâ facie the landlord is bound to pay the outgoing tenant for tillages, and the incoming tenant does not render himself liable to do so by the mere fact of entering upon the land, unless a new contract has been entered into with him (*o*). Where there is a custom that the incoming tenant shall pay for the fallows, and shall be repaid upon his leaving the premises, there is an implied contract on the part of the landlord that if there be no incoming tenant the landlord will pay the outgoing tenant according to the custom (*p*).

SECT. V.—*Delivery of Possession.*

(1) *Tenant's Obligation to give Possession.*

Upon a demise of a house or premises there is implied an undertaking by the tenant that he will deliver

(*k*) See *Whittaker* v. *Barker*, 1 Cr. & M. 113; *Newson* v. *Smythies*, 3 H. & N. 840; 28 L. J., Ex. 97. See *Brocklington* v. *Saunders*, 13 W. R., Q. B. 46.

(*l*) *Dalby* v. *Hirst*, 1 B. & B., at pp. 228, 230.

(*m*) *Hutton* v. *Warren*, 1 M. & W. 466; *Wigglesworth* v. *Dallison*, 1 Smith's L. C. (6th ed.) 539; *Senior* v. *Armytage*, Holt, N. P. 197; *Caldecott* v. *Smythies*, 7 C. & P. 808. See *Webb* v. *Plummer*, 2 B. & A. 746; *Clarke* v. *Roystone*, 13 M. & W. 752.

(*n*) *Dalby* v. *Hirst*, 1 B. & B. 224.

(*o*) *Codd* v. *Brown*, 15 L. T., N. S. 536. See *Sucksmith* v. *Wilson*, 4 F. & F. 1083.

(*p*) *Favisll* v. *Gaskoin*, 7 Ex. 273.

up possession to the landlord at the expiration of the term (*q*). If the premises are then in the occupation of an under-tenant, the landlord may refuse to accept the possession (*r*), and may recover from the original tenant rent for the period after the expiration of the term during which the under-tenant remains in possession (*s*), and also the costs of an action of ejectment brought against such under-tenant in order to obtain possession (*t*). Where premises are let to two persons for a term of years, and at the end of such term one of them holds over with the assent of the other, both will be liable for the time during which the one holds over (*u*). But one tenant cannot bind his co-tenant by holding over without his assent (*x*).

(2) *Landlord's Remedies for recovering Possession.*

(a) *Indirect.*

<small>Action for double value. Stat. 4 Geo. 2, c. 28, s. 1.

Tenant holding over after determination of tenancy and notice in writing given by landlord, to</small>

In case any tenant for any term of life or years (a weekly tenant is not within the statute (*y*)), or other person who shall come into possession of any lands, tenements or hereditaments under, or by collusion with, such tenant, shall wilfully (not *bonâ fide* by mistake, or under a fair claim of right (*z*)) hold over any lands, tenements or hereditaments (the statute does not apply

---

(*q*) Judgment of Cockburn, C. J., in *Henderson* v. *Squire*, 38 L. J., Q. B., at p. 75; L. R., 4 Q. B., at p. 173; *Harding* v. *Crethorne*, 1 Esp. 57.

(*r*) Per Lord Kenyon, C. J., in *Harding* v. *Crethorne*, 1 Esp. 57.

(*s*) *Ibbs* v. *Richardson*, 9 A. & E. 849.

(*t*) *Henderson* v. *Squire*, 38 L. J., Q. B. 73; L. R., 4 Q. B. 170.

(*u*) *Christy* v. *Tancred*, 9 M. & W. 438; see 7 M. & W. 127; *Tancred* v. *Christy*, 12 M. & W. 316.

(*x*) *Draper* v. *Crofts*, 15 M. & W. 166; 15 L. J., Ex. 92.

(*y*) *Lloyd* v. *Rosbee*, 2 Camp. 453.

(*z*) *Wright* v. *Smith*, 5 Esp. 203; judgment in *Soulsby* v. *Neving*, 9 East, at p. 313; *Swinfen* v. *Bacon*, 6 H. & N. 184; 30 L. J., Ex. 33; aff. 6 H. & N. 846; 30 L. J., Ex. 368.

to the letting of a supply of steam-power (*a*)) after the determination of such term and after demand made and notice in writing given (either before (*b*) or after (*c*) the expiration of the tenancy. In the case of a tenant from year to year a valid notice to quit will suffice (*d*)) for delivering the possession thereof, by his landlord, or the person to whom the remainder or reversion of such lands, &c. shall belong, (or) his agent thereunto lawfully authorized, such person so holding over shall, during the time he shall so hold over, or keep the person entitled out of possession of the said lands, &c. as aforesaid, pay to the person so kept out of possession, (his) executors, administrators or assigns, at the rate of

pay double value.

(*a*) *Robinson* v. *Learoyd*, 7 M. & W. 48.

(*b*) *Cutting* v. *Derby*, 2 W. Bl. 1075; *Messenger* v. *Armstrong*, 1 T. R. 53.

(*c*) *Cobb* v. *Stokes*, 8 East, 358. But the landlord must not have done any act in the meantime to recognize the person to whom the notice is given as continuing his tenant. Per Lord Ellenborough, p. 361.

(*d*) *Hirst* v. *Horn*, 6 M. & W. 393. See *Page* v. *More*, 15 Q. B. 684. The notice, when given before the expiration of the tenancy, may be in the following form:—

To Mr. C. D.

I hereby demand of you that you deliver up possession of the house (lands) and premises, with the appurtenances, situate at ——, in the parish of ——, in the county of ——, on the —— day of —— next, being the day on which your term therein will determine. And I give you notice, that in case you hold over the said premises after the determination of such term, you will be required to pay at the rate of double the yearly value of the said premises for so long a time as the same shall be detained by you.

Dated this —— day of ——, 18—.

E. F.

If given after the tenancy has expired, the notice may be in the following form:—

To Mr. C. D.

I hereby demand of you that you immediately deliver up possession of the house (lands) and premises, with the appurtenances, situate at ——, in the parish of ——, in the county of ——. And I give you notice, that in case you hold over the said premises after the service of this demand and notice, you will be required to pay at the rate of double the yearly value of the said premises for so long a time as the same shall be detained by you.

Dated this —— day of ——, 18—.

E. F.

double the yearly value of the lands, &c. so detained, for so long time as the same are detained (calculated from the determination of the tenancy, if the notice was given before such determination (*e*), or if the notice was given after such determination, then from the time of the giving of such notice (*f*)), to be recovered (by the landlord or reversioner (*g*)) in any of his Majesty's Courts of record (or in a County Court (*h*)); against the recovering of which said penalty there shall be no relief in equity.

The landlord cannot distrain for double value (*i*); and if he demands possession in the middle of a quarter or other term of payment, he cannot recover the rent for the antecedent fraction of such quarter or other term of payment (*k*). Acceptance of rent before an action is brought by the landlord for the double value may operate as a waiver of the landlord's claim to the double value, but if rent is accepted after such action has been brought, it becomes a question whether it has been received in part satisfaction of the double value, or as a waiver of it (*l*).

Action for double rent. Stat. 11 Geo. 2, c. 19, s. 18.

In case any tenant (*m*) (having the power of determining his tenancy by notice (*n*)) shall give notice (either verbal (*o*) or written) of his intention to quit

---

(*e*) *Soulsby* v. *Neving*, 9 East, 310.

(*f*) *Cobb* v. *Stokes*, 8 East, 358.

(*g*) *Blatchford* v. *Cole*, 5 C. B., N. S. 514; 28 L. J., C. P. 140.

(*h*) *Wickham* v. *Lee*, 12 Q. B. 521; 18 L. J., Q. B. 21.

(*i*) Judgment of Wilmot, J., in *Timmins* v. *Rowlison*, 1 W. Bl., at p. 535.

(*k*) *Cobb* v. *Stokes*, 8 East, 358.

(*l*) Judgment of Lord Ellenborough, in *Ryall* v. *Rich*, 10 East, at p. 52. See *Doe* v. *Batten*, 1 Cowp. 243, 246.

(*m*) See *Sullivan* v. *Bishop*, 2 C. & P. 359.

(*n*) *Johnstone* v. *Hudlestone*, 4 B. & C. 922, 931.

(*o*) *Timmins* v. *Rowlison*, 1 W. Bl. 533. It will be observed, that the landlord's notice for *double value* (*ante*, p. 303) must be in writing. Wilmot, J., explains that the reason of the dif-

the premises by him holden, at a (fixed (*p*)) time mentioned in such notice, and shall not accordingly deliver up the possession thereof at the time in such notice contained, the said tenant, his executors or administrators, shall from thenceforward pay to the landlord double the rent or sum which he should otherwise have paid, to be levied (by distress (*q*)), sued for and recovered at the same time and in the same manner as the single rent before the giving such notice could be levied, sued for or recovered; and such double rent shall continue to be paid during all the time such tenant shall continue in possession as aforesaid. *Tenant holding over after expiration of notice to quit given by him, to pay double rent.*

Double rent ceases to be payable on the tenant's quitting possession, and he may do this at any time without giving a new notice to quit (*r*).

(b) *Direct Remedies for recovering Possession.*

Where at the time of the expiration or determination of the tenancy there is no person in possession of the premises,—the tenant having wholly abandoned them without any intention of returning,—the landlord may enter and take possession (*s*). *Entry. 1. On abandoned premises.*

If the tenancy of a house is determined, and the tenant and his family have gone away, and the house is locked up—no one being in possession—the landlord is justified in breaking in and obtaining possession, although some articles of furniture may remain (*t*). *2. On locked-up premises, where no one is in possession.*

---

ference is, that "landlords can usually write and tenants cannot." 1 W. Bl. 535.

(*p*) *Furrance* v. *Elkington*, 2 Camp. 591, 592.

(*q*) See n. (*o*), ante, p. 304.

(*r*) *Booth* v. *Macfarlane*, 1 B. & Ad. 904, 906.

(*s*) *Lacey* v. *Lear*, Peake's Add. Cas. 210. See *Wildbor* v. *Rainforth*, 8 B. & C. 4, 6.

(*t*) *Hillary* v. *Gay*, 6 C. & P. 284; *Taunton* v. *Costar*, 7 T. R. 431; *Turner* v. *Meymott*, 1 Bing. 158.

3. Where tenant is in possession.

Even where the tenant is in possession the landlord, after the expiration of the tenancy, may enter peaceably on the premises. He may also acquire lawful possession by entering forcibly (*t*), and, after requesting the tenant to leave the premises, may, in case of his refusing or neglecting to do so, expel him, using, however, only so much force as may be necessary for that purpose. In this case he will not be liable to an action of trespass, or to damages for the expulsion of the tenant (*u*), but he may subject himself to an indictment for a forcible entry (*x*).

Proceedings before justices.
Stat. 1 & 2 Vict. c. 74, s. 1.
If tenant at rent not exceeding 20*l*. a year upon expiration or determination of his interest refuses or neglects to deliver up possession, landlord may serve him with notice of his intention to proceed under this act.

When the term or interest of the tenant of any house, land or other corporeal hereditaments held by him at will or for any term not exceeding seven years, either without being liable to the payment of any rent, or at a rent not exceeding the rate of 20*l*. a year, and upon which no fine shall have been reserved or made payable, shall have ended or shall have been duly determined by a legal notice to quit or otherwise, and such tenant, or, if such tenant do not actually occupy the premises, or only occupy a part thereof, any person by whom the same or any part thereof shall be then actually occupied, shall neglect or refuse to quit and deliver up possession of the premises or of such part thereof respectively, it shall be lawful for the landlord of the said premises, or his agent, to cause the person so neglecting or refusing to quit and deliver up possession, to be served, in the manner hereinafter mentioned, with a written notice in

---

(*t*) *Harvey* v. *Bridges*, 14 M. & W. 437, 442; 14 L. J., Ex. 272; *Pollen* v. *Brewer*, 7 C. B., N. S. 371.

(*u*) *Davison* v. *Wilson*, 11 Q. B. 890; 17 L. J., Q. B. 196; *Burling* v. *Read*, 11 Q. B. 904; 19 L. J., Q. B. 291. But see *Newton* v. *Harland*, 1 M. & Gr. 644.

(*x*) See Archbold's Pleading and Evidence in Criminal Cases, p. 736 (15th ed.).

the form set forth in the schedule to this act (*y*), signed by the said landlord or his agent, of his intention to proceed to recover possession under the authority and according to the mode prescribed in this act; and if the tenant or occupier shall not thereupon appear at the time and place appointed, and show to the satisfaction of the justices hereinafter mentioned reasonable cause why possession should not be given under the provisions of this act, and shall still neglect or refuse to deliver up possession of the premises, or of such part thereof of which he is then in possession, to the said landlord or his agent, it shall be lawful for such landlord or agent to give to such justices proof of the holding and of the end or other determination of the tenancy, with the time or manner thereof, and where the title of the landlord has accrued since the letting of the premises, the right by which he claims the possession, and upon proof of service of the notice, and of the neglect or refusal of

If tenant does not appear before justices and show cause why possession should not be delivered up, on proof by landlord of certain facts, justices may issue warrant directing constables to give possession of premises to landlord.

(*y*) *Form of Notice.*

I, [owner, *or* agent to the owner, *as the case may be*], do hereby give you notice, that unless peaceable possession of the tenement [*shortly describing it*] situate , which was held of me, *or* of the said [*as the case may be*], under a tenancy from year to year, *or* [*as the case may be*], which expired [*or* was determined] by notice to quit from the said , *or otherwise* [*as the case may be*], on the day of , and which tenement is now held over and detained from the said , be given to [the owner or agent], on or before the expiration of seven clear days from the service of this notice, I, , shall on next, the day of , at of the clock on the same day, at , apply to her Majesty's justices of the peace acting for the district of [*being the district, division or place in which the said tenement, or any part thereof, is situate*], in petty sessions assembled, to issue their warrant directing the constables of the said district to enter and take possession of the said tenement and to eject any person therefrom.

Dated this .

(Signed) , .
[owner *or* agent].

To Mr. .

the tenant or occupier, as the case may be (where the tenancy and its determination and the tenant's refusal to quit are proved, the jurisdiction of the justices is not ousted by the tenant's setting up the title of a third person (*z*)), it shall be lawful for the justices acting for the district, division or place within which the said premises, or any part thereof, shall be situate, in petty sessions assembled, or any two of them, to issue a warrant under their hands and seals to the constables and peace officers of the district, division or place within which the said premises or any part thereof shall be situate, commanding them, within a period to be therein named, not less than twenty-one nor more than thirty clear days from the date of such warrant, to enter, by force if needful, into the premises, and give possession of the same to such landlord or agent. Entry upon any such warrant shall not be made on a Sunday, Good Friday or Christmas Day, or at any time except between the hours of nine in the morning and four in the afternoon. Nothing herein contained shall be deemed to protect any person on whose application and to whom any such warrant shall be granted from any action which may be brought against him by any such tenant or occupier, for or in respect of such entry and taking possession, where such person had not at the time of granting the same lawful right to the possession of the same premises. Nothing herein contained shall affect any rights to which any person may be entitled as outgoing tenant by the custom of the country or otherwise.

Sect. 2. Notice of application to be

Notice of application intended to be made under this act may be served either personally or by leaving the

(*z*) *Rees* v. *Daries*, 4 C. B., N. S. 56.

same with some person being in and apparently residing at the place of abode of the persons so holding over as aforesaid, and the person serving the same shall read over the same to the person served or with whom the same shall be left as aforesaid, and explain the purport and intent thereof. If the person so holding over cannot be found, and the place of abode of such person shall either not be known, or admission thereto cannot be obtained for serving such summons, the posting up of the summons on some conspicuous part of the premises so held over shall be deemed to be good service upon such person. *served either personally or by reading it over and leaving it with some person at the tenant's house; or, if this cannot be done, by posting it up on a conspicuous part of the premises.*

In every case in which the person to whom any such warrant shall be granted had not, at the time of granting the same, lawful right to the possession of the premises, the obtaining of any such warrant as aforesaid shall be deemed a trespass by him against the tenant or occupier of the premises, although no entry shall be made by virtue of the warrant; and in case any such tenant or occupier will become bound with two sureties, to be approved of by the said justices (in a bond to be made to the said landlord or his agent, at the costs of such landlord or agent, and approved of and signed by the justices (sect. 4)) in such sum as to them shall seem reasonable, regard being had to the value of the premises and to the probable costs of an action, to sue the person to whom such warrant was granted with effect and without delay, and to pay all the costs of the proceeding in such action in case a verdict shall pass for the defendant, or the plaintiff shall discontinue or not prosecute his action, or become nonsuit therein, execution of the warrant shall be delayed until judgment shall have been given in such action of trespass; and if upon the trial of such action of trespass a verdict shall pass for the plaintiff, such verdict and judgment there- *Sect. 3. Execution of warrant may be stayed on bond given by tenant conditioned to prosecute action of trespass against landlord.*

upon shall supersede the warrant so granted; and the plaintiff shall be entitled to (such full and reasonable indemnity as to all costs, charges and expenses as shall be taxed by the proper officer in that behalf (stat. 5 & 6 Vict. c. 97, s. 2)).

<small>In case of deserted premises. Stat. 11 Geo. 2, c. 19, s. 16. If tenant, owing half-year's rent, desert the demised premises, so that no sufficient distress can be found, landlord may request two justices to come and view the same.</small>

If any tenant holding any lands, tenements, or hereditaments at a rack-rent, or where the rent reserved shall be full three-fourths of the yearly value of the demised premises, who shall be in arrear for one (half-year's (a)) rent, shall desert the demised premises (b), and leave the same uncultivated or unoccupied, so as no sufficient distress can be had to countervail the arrears of rent, it shall be lawful for two or more justices of the peace of the county, riding, division or place, having no interest in the demised premises, at the request (the request or complaint need not be on oath (c)) of the landlord or his bailiff to go upon and view the

<small>And to affix on premises notice of time at which they will take second view.</small>

same, and to affix or cause to be affixed on the most notorious part of the premises notice in writing what day, at the distance of fourteen (clear (d)) days at least, they will return to take a second view thereof; and if

<small>If tenant at such second view do not appear and pay rent and there is no sufficient distress, justices to put landlord in possession and demise to be thenceforth void.</small>

upon such second view the tenant, or some person on his behalf, shall not appear and pay the rent in arrear, or there shall not be sufficient distress upon the premises, then the said justices may put the landlord into the possession of the said demised premises, and the lease thereof to such tenant as to any demise therein contained only, shall from thenceforth become void. An appeal may be made from the decision of the justices to the judge of assize (sect. 17).

<small>By proceedings</small>

When the term and interest of the tenant of any cor-

(a) Stat. 57 Geo. 3, c. 52.
(b) See *Ex parte Pilton*, 1 B. & A. 369.
(c) *Basten v. Carew*, 3 B. & C. 649.
(d) *Creak v. Justices of Brighton*, 1 F. & F. 110.

poreal hereditament, where neither the value of the premises nor the rent payable in respect thereof shall have exceeded 50*l.* by the year, and upon which no fine shall have been paid, shall have expired, or shall have been determined either by the landlord or the tenant by a legal notice to quit, and such tenant, or any person holding under him, shall neglect or refuse to deliver up possession accordingly, the landlord may enter a plaint at his option either against such tenant or against such person so neglecting or refusing, in the County Court of the district in which the premises lie for the recovery of the same, and thereupon a summons shall issue to such tenant or such person so neglecting or refusing; and if the defendant shall not, at the time named in the summons, show good cause to the contrary, then, on proof of his still neglecting or refusing to deliver up possession of the premises, and of the yearly value and rent of the premises, and of the holding, and of the expiration or other determination of the tenancy, with the time and manner thereof, and of the title of the plaintiff if such title has accrued since the letting of the premises, and of the service of the summons if the defendant shall not appear thereto, the judge may order that possession of the premises mentioned in the plaint be given by the defendant to the plaintiff, either forthwith, or on or before such day as the judge shall think fit to name; and if such order be not obeyed, the registrar, whether such order can be proved to have been served or not, shall, at the instance of the plaintiff, issue a warrant authorizing and requiring the high bailiff of the court to give possession of such premises to the plaintiff.

in the County Court. Stat. 19 & 20 Vict. c. 108, s. 50. Where neither rent nor value of premises exceeds 50l. a year, and tenancy has expired or been determined by notice to quit, and tenant refuses to quit, landlord may enter plaint in County Court. Thereupon summons to issue and on proof by landlord of certain facts, judge may order possession of premises to be given to landlord.

When the rent of any corporeal hereditament, where neither the value of the premises, nor the rent payable in respect thereof exceeds 50*l.* by the year,

Sect. 52. Where neither rent nor value of premises

TERMS OF QUITTING.

exceeds 50l. a year, and rent is in arrear for one half-year, and landlord has right to re-enter for non-payment of rent, he may, without formal demand or re-entry, enter plaint in County Court.

Thereupon summons to issue. If tenant, within five days, pays rent and costs action to cease.

If he does not, on proof of certain facts, judge may order possession to be given to landlord.

shall for one half-year be in arrear, and the landlord shall have right by law to re-enter for the non-payment thereof, he may, without any formal demand or re-entry, enter a plaint in the County Court of the district in which the premises lie for the recovery of the premises, and thereupon a summons shall issue to the tenant, the service whereof shall stand in lieu of a demand and re-entry; and if the tenant shall, five clear days before the return-day of such summons, pay into Court all the rent in arrear and the costs, the said action shall cease; but if he shall not make such payment, and shall not at the time named in the summons show good cause why the premises should not be recovered, then on proof of the yearly value and rent of the premises, and of the fact that one half-year's rent was in arrear before the plaint was entered, and that no sufficient distress was then to be found on the premises to countervail such arrear, and of the landlord's power to re-enter, and of the rent being still in arrear, and of the title of the plaintiff if such title has accrued since the letting of the premises, and of the service of the summons if the defendant shall not appear thereto, the judge may order that possession of the premises mentioned in the plaint be given by the defendant to the plaintiff on or before such day, not being less than four weeks from the day of hearing, as the judge shall

Unless tenant shall pay rent and costs.

think fit to name, unless within that period all the rent in arrear and the costs be paid into Court; and if such order be not obeyed, and such rent and costs be not so paid, the registrar shall, whether such order can be proved to have been served or not, at the instance of the plaintiff, issue a warrant requiring the high bailiff of the Court to give possession of such premises to the plaintiff, and the plaintiff shall from the time of the execution of such warrant hold the premises discharged of the tenancy, and the defendant, and all persons claiming by, through or under him, shall, so long as the order of the Court remains unreversed, be barred from all relief in equity or otherwise.

Where the term or interest of any tenant holding under a lease or agreement in writing any lands, tenements or hereditaments for any term of years certain, or from year to year, shall have expired or been determined either by the landlord or tenant by regular notice to quit, and such tenant or any one holding or claiming under him shall refuse to deliver up possession accordingly after lawful demand in writing made and signed by the landlord or his agent, and served personally upon or left at the dwelling-house or usual place of abode of such tenant or person, and the landlord shall thereupon proceed by action of ejectment for the recovery of possession, it shall be lawful for him, at the foot of the writ in ejectment, to address a notice to such tenant or person requiring him to find such bail, if ordered by the Court or a judge, and for such purposes as are hereinafter next specified; and upon the appearance of the party or an affidavit of service of the writ and notice, it shall be lawful for the landlord producing the lease or agreement, or some counterpart or duplicate thereof, and proving the execution of the same by affidavit, and upon affidavit that the premises have been actually enjoyed under such lease or agreement, and that the interest of the tenant has expired, or been determined by regular notice to quit, as the case may be, and that possession has been lawfully demanded in manner aforesaid, to move the Court, or apply by summons to a judge at chambers, for a rule or summons for such tenant or person to show cause, within a time

Stat. 15 & 16 Vict. c. 76, s. 213.

Where interest of tenant for term of years, or from year to year, has expired or been determined by notice to quit, and he refuses to quit after demand in writing made by landlord and served upon tenant, landlord, proceeding by action of ejectment, may address notice to tenant at foot of writ in ejectment requiring him to find bail.

On proof of certain facts, landlord may obtain rule or summons for

tenant to give bail.

to be fixed by the Court or judge on a consideration of the situation of the premises, why such tenant or person should not enter into a recognizance by himself and two sufficient sureties in a reasonable sum, conditioned to pay the costs and damages, which shall be recovered by the claimants in the action; and it shall be lawful for the Court or judge upon cause shown, or upon affidavit of the service of the rule or summons in case

Such rule may be made absolute.

no cause shall be shown, to make the same absolute in the whole or in part, and to order such tenant or person, within a time to be fixed, upon a consideration of all the circumstances, to find such bail, with such conditions and in such manner as shall be specified in the said rule or summons, or such part of the same so

On neglect or refusal of tenant, judgment may be signed for landlord.

made absolute; and in case the party shall neglect or refuse so to do, and shall lay no ground to induce the Court or judge to enlarge the time for obeying the same, then the lessor or landlord filing an affidavit that such rule or order has been made and served and not complied with, shall be at liberty to sign judgment for recovery of possession and costs of suit.

Sect. 214.
Upon trial of ejectment between landlord and tenant, jury to find verdict for mesne profits to time of verdict, or other specified day.

Wherever it shall appear on the trial of any ejectment, at the suit of a landlord against a tenant, that such tenant or his attorney has been served with due notice of trial, the judge before whom such cause shall come on to be tried shall, whether the defendant shall appear upon such trial or not, permit the claimant on the trial, after proof of his right, to recover possession of the whole or of any part of the premises mentioned in the writ in ejectment, to go into evidence of the mesne profits thereof which shall or might have accrued from the day of the expiration or determination of the tenant's interest in the same down to the time of the verdict given in the cause, or to some preceding day to be specially mentioned therein, and the jury on the trial finding for the claimant, shall in such case give their verdict upon the whole matter, both as to the recovery of the whole or any part of the premises, and also as to the amount of the damages to be paid for such mesne profits; and in such case the landlord shall have judgment within the time hereinbefore provided, not only for the recovery of possession and costs, but also for the mesne profits found by the jury.

Nothing herein contained shall be construed to prejudice or affect any other right of action or remedy which landlords may possess in any of the cases hereinbefore provided for, otherwise than hereinbefore expressly enacted. *Sect. 218. Landlords to retain all previous remedies.*

Every tenant to whom any writ in ejectment shall be delivered, or to whose knowledge it shall come, shall forthwith give notice thereof to his landlord, or his bailiff or receiver, under penalty of forfeiting the value of three years' improved or rack-rent of the premises (e) demised or holden in the possession of such tenant, to the person of whom he holds, to be recovered by action in any Court of common law having jurisdiction for the amount. *Sect. 209. Tenant who knows of writ in ejectment, to give notice thereof to landlord.*

All actions of ejectment where neither the value of the lands, tenements or hereditaments, nor the rent payable in respect thereof, shall exceed the sum of 20*l*. by the year, may be brought in the County Court of the district in which the lands, tenements or hereditaments are situate. *Stat. 30 & 31 Vict. c. 142, s. 11. Actions of ejectment, where value of lands, &c. shall not exceed 20l. a year, may be brought in County Court.*

(e) *Crocker* v. *Fothergill*, 2 B. & A. 652.

APPENDIX.

FORMS OF LEASES.

I. *Short Statutory Form.*

WHENEVER any party to any deed, made according to the forms set forth in the first schedule to this act, or to any other deed which shall be expressed to be made in pursuance of this act, shall employ in such deed respectively any of the forms of words contained in column 1 of the second schedule hereto annexed, and distinguished by any number therein, such deed shall be taken to have the same effect, and be construed, as if such party had inserted in such deed the form of words contained in column 2 of the same schedule, and distinguished by the same number as is annexed to the form of words employed by such party; but it shall not be necessary in any such deed to insert any such number. Stat. 8 & 9 Vict. c. 124, s. 1. Where words contained in column 1 of the second schedule are employed, the deed is to have the same effect as if the words contained in column 2 had been used.

Every such deed, unless any exception be specially made therein, shall be held and construed to include all outhouses, buildings, barns, stables, yards, gardens, cellars, ancient and other lights, paths, passages, ways, waters, watercourses, liberties, privileges, easements, profits, commodities, emoluments, hereditaments and appurtenances whatsoever to the lands and tenements therein comprised belonging or in anywise appertaining. Sect. 2. Deed to include outhouses, appurtenances, &c.

In taxing any bill for preparing and executing any deed under this act, the taxing officer is hereby required, in estimating the proper sum to be charged for such transaction, to consider not the length of such deed, but only the skill and labour employed, and responsibility incurred in the preparation thereof. Sect. 3. Remuneration to be according to skill, labour and responsibility, and not according to length of deed.

Sect. 4.
Deed not taking effect by this act to be as valid as if act had not been made.

Any deed or part of a deed, which shall fail to take effect by virtue of this act, shall nevertheless be as valid and effectual, and shall bind the parties thereto, so far as the rules of law and equity will permit, as if this act had not been made.

Sect. 5.
Construction of words.

In the construction and for the purposes of this act and the schedules hereto annexed, unless there be something in the subject or context repugnant to such construction, the word "lands" shall extend to all tenements and hereditaments of freehold tenure, and to such customary lands as will pass by deed, or deed and surrender, and not by surrender alone, or any undivided part or share therein respectively; and every word importing the singular number only, shall extend and be applied to several persons or things, as well as one person or thing, and the converse; and every word importing the masculine gender only, shall extend and be applied to a female as well as a male; and the word "party" shall mean and include any body politic or corporate, or collegiate, as well as an individual.

Sect. 6.
Schedules to part of act.

The schedules, and the directions and forms therein contained, shall be deemed and taken to be parts of this act.

Sect. 7.

This act shall commence and take effect from and after the first day of October (1845).

Sect. 8.

This act shall not extend to Scotland.

Schedules to which this Act refers.

The FIRST SCHEDULE.

This indenture, made the   day of   , one thousand eight hundred and forty   . [*or other year*], in pursuance of an Act to facilitate the granting of certain leases, Between [*here insert the names of the parties, and recitals, if any*]: Witnesseth, that the said [*lessor*] or [*lessors*] doth, *or* do demise unto the said [*lessee*] or [*lessees*], his [*or* their] executors, administrators and assigns, All, &c. [*parcels*], From the   day of   for the term of   thence ensuing: Yielding therefor during the said term the rent of [*state the rent and mode of payment, and insert the cove-*

nants in the form contained in column 1 *of the Second Schedule*].

In witness whereof the said parties hereto have hereunto set their hands and seals.

The SECOND SCHEDULE.

Directions as to the forms in this Schedule.

1. Parties who use any of the forms in the first column of this Schedule, may substitute for the words "lessee" or "lessor," any name or names; and in every such case corresponding substitutions shall be taken to be made in the corresponding forms in the second column.

2. Such parties may substitute the feminine gender for the masculine, or the plural number for the singular, in the forms in the first column of this Schedule; and corresponding changes shall be taken to be made in the corresponding forms in the second column.

3. Such parties may fill up the blank spaces left in the forms 4 and 5 in the first column of this Schedule so employed by them, with any words or figures, and the words or figures so introduced shall be taken to be inserted in the corresponding blank spaces left in the forms embodied.

4. Such parties may introduce into or annex to any of the forms in the first column any express exceptions from, or express qualifications thereof respectively; and the like exceptions or qualifications shall be taken to be made from or in the corresponding forms in the second column.

5. Where the premises demised shall be of freehold tenure, the covenants 1 to 10 shall be taken to be made with, and the proviso 11 to apply to, the heirs and assigns of the lessor, and where the premises demised shall be of leasehold tenure, the covenants and proviso shall be taken to be made with and apply to the lessor, his executors, administrators and assigns.

Column 1.	Column 2.
1. That the said [*lessee*] covenants with the said [*lessor*] to pay rent.	1. And the said [*lessee*] doth hereby for himself, his heirs, executors, administrators and assigns, covenant with the said [*lessor*], that he the said [*lessee*], his executors, administrators and assigns, will during the said term pay unto the said [*lessor*] the rent hereby reserved, in manner hereinbefore mentioned, without any deduction whatsoever.
2. And to pay taxes;	2. And also will pay all taxes, rates, duties and assessments whatsoever, whether parochial, parliamentary, or otherwise, now charged or hereafter to be charged upon the said demised premises, or upon the said [*lessor*], on account thereof (excepting land tax, and excepting, in Ireland, tithe rent-charge, and such portion of the poor rate as the [*lessor*] is or may be liable to pay; and excepting also all taxes, rates, duties and assessments whatsoever, or any portion thereof, which the [*lessee*] is or may be by law exempted from).
3. And to repair;	3. And also will, during the said term, well and sufficiently repair, maintain, pave, empty, cleanse, amend, and keep the said demised premises, with the appurtenances, in good and substantial repair, together with all chimney-pieces, windows, doors, fastenings, water-closets, cisterns, partitions, fixed presses, shelves, pipes, pumps, pails, rails, locks and keys, and all other fixtures and things, which at any time during the said term shall be erected and made, when, where, and so often as need shall be.

FORMS OF LEASES.

Column 1.

4. And to paint outside every year;

5. And to paint and paper inside every year;

6. And to insure from fire in the joint names of the said [*lessor*] and the said [*lessee*];

to show receipts;

and to rebuild in case of fire.

Column 2.

4. And also that the said [*lessee*], his executors, administrators and assigns, will in every year in the said term, paint all the outside woodwork and ironwork belonging to the said premises, with two coats of proper oil colours, in a workmanlike manner.

5. And also that the said [*lessee*], his executors, administrators and assigns, will in every year paint the inside wood, iron and other works now or usually painted, with two coats of proper oil colours, in a workmanlike manner; and also re-paper with paper of a quality as at present, such parts of the premises as are now papered; and also wash, stop, whiten or colour such parts of the said premises as are now plastered.

6. And also that the said [*lessee*], his executors, administrators and assigns, will forthwith insure the said premises hereby demised to the full value thereof in some respectable insurance office, in the joint names of the said [*lessor*], his executors, administrators and assigns, and the said [*lessee*], his executors, administrators or assigns, and keep the same so insured during the said term; and will, upon the request of the said [*lessor*], or his agent, show the receipt for the last premium paid for such insurance for every current year; and as often as the said premises hereby demised shall be burnt down or damaged by fire, all and every the sums or sum of money which shall be recovered or received by the said [*lessee*],

Column 1. | *Column 2.*

his executors, administrators or assigns, for or in respect of such insurance, shall be laid out and expended by him in building or repairing the said demised premises, or such parts thereof as shall be burnt down or damaged by fire as aforesaid.

7. And that the said [*lessor*] may enter and view state of repair, and that the said [*lessee*] will repair according to notice.

7. And it is hereby agreed, that it shall be lawful for the said [*lessor*], and his agents, at all seasonable times during the said term, to enter the said demised premises to take a schedule of the fixtures and things made and erected thereupon, and to examine the condition of the said premises; and further, that all wants of reparation, which upon such views shall be found, and for the amendment of which notice in writing shall be left at the premises, the said [*lessee*], his executors, administrators and assigns, will, within three calendar months next after every such notice, well and sufficiently repair and make good accordingly.

8. That the said [*lessee*] will not use premises as a shop.

8. And also that the said [*lessee*], his executors, administrators and assigns, will not convert, use or occupy the said premises or any part thereof, into or as a shop, warehouse or other place for carrying on any trade or business whatsoever, or suffer the said premises to be used for any such purpose, or otherwise than as a private dwelling-house, without the consent in writing of the said [*lessor*].

9. And will not assign without leave.

9. And also that the said [*lessee*] shall not nor will during the said term assign, transfer or set over, or other-

Column 1.	Column 2.
	wise by any act or deed procure the said premises, or any of them, to be assigned, transferred or set over, unto any person or persons whomsoever, without the consent in writing of the said [*lessor*], his executors, administrators or assigns, first had and obtained.
10. And that he will leave premises in good repair.	10. And further, that the said [*lessee*] will, at the expiration or other sooner determination of the said term, peaceably surrender and yield up unto the said [*lessor*] the said premises hereby demised, with the appurtenances, together with all buildings, erections and fixtures now or hereafter to be built or erected thereon, in good and substantial repair and condition in all respects, reasonable wear and tear, and damage by fire, only excepted.
11. Proviso for re-entry by the said [*lessor*], on non-payment of rent or non-performance of covenants.	11. Provided always, and it is expressly agreed, that if the rent hereby reserved, or any part thereof, shall be unpaid for fifteen days after any of the days on which the same ought to have been paid (although no formal demand shall have been made thereof), or in case of the breach or non-performance of any of the covenants and agreements herein contained on the part of the said [*lessee*], his executors, administrators and assigns, then and in either of such cases it shall be lawful for the said [*lessor*], at any time thereafter, into and upon the said demised premises, or any part thereof, in the name of the whole to re-enter, and the same to have again, re-possess and enjoy as of his or their former estate, anything herein-

Column 1.	Column 2.
	after contained to the contrary notwithstanding.
12. The said [*lessor*] covenants with the said [*lessee*] for quiet enjoyment.	12. And the [*lessor*] doth hereby, for himself, his heirs, executors, administrators and assigns, covenant with the said [*lessee*], his executors, administrators and assigns, that he and they paying the rent hereby reserved, and performing the covenants hereinbefore on his and their part contained, shall and may peaceably possess and enjoy the said demised premises for the term hereby granted, without any interruption or disturbance from the said [*lessor*], his executors, administrators or assigns, or any other person or persons lawfully claiming by, from or under him, them or any of them.

II. *Lease in the Statutory Form* (a).

THIS INDENTURE, made the   day of   , one thousand eight hundred and seventy   , in pursuance of an Act to facilitate the granting of certain leases, BETWEEN E. F. of   [builder], of the one part, and C. D. of   [merchant's clerk] of the other part; WITNESSETH that the said E. F. DOTH demise unto the said C. D., his executors, administrators and assigns, ALL that dwelling-house [known as No. 3, Albert Street, Liverpool, in the county of Lancaster], WITH all the easements and appurtenances to the said dwelling-house belonging or therewith held or enjoyed, FROM the   day of   18   (*b*), for the term of [two]

(*a*) Suitable for small houses, where a very short deed is required. The obvious disadvantage of the abbreviated covenants is, that the lessee, unless he refers to the Act, cannot ascertain the extent or nature of his obligations.

(*b*) See *ante*, p. 79.

years thence ensuing [*or* on a tenancy from year to year *or* from quarter to quarter], YIELDING therefor during the said term [*or* tenancy] the rent of £   by equal [quarterly] payments on the 25th March, 24th June, 29th September and 25th December in each year, the first of such payments to be made on the   day of   , 18 . AND THAT the said C. D. covenants with the said E. F. to pay rent; and to pay taxes; and to repair; and that the said E. F. may enter and view state of repair, and that the said C. D. will repair according to notice; that the said C. D. will not use premises as a shop; and will not assign without leave; and that he will leave premises in good repair. The said E. F. covenants with the said C. D. for quiet enjoyment. Covenants by lessee.
Covenant by lessor.

In witness whereof the said parties hereto have hereunto set their hands and seals (*c*).

III. *Lease of a House* (*d*).

THIS INDENTURE, made the   day of   18 , BETWEEN E. F. of   ,   , of the one part, and C. D. of   ,   , of the other part, WITNESSETH that the said E. F. DOTH demise unto the said C. D., his executors, administrators and assigns, ALL [*insert description of parcels* (*e*)], WITH all the easements and appurtenances to the said messuage belonging or therewith held or enjoyed (*f*), TO HAVE AND TO HOLD the said messuage and premises hereby demised, with the appurtenances, UNTO the said C. D., his executors, administrators and assigns, from the   day of   , 18 (*g*), for the term of   years thence ensuing (*h*): YIELDING therefor during the said term the yearly rent of £   by equal [half-yearly] payments on the   day of   and the   day of   in each

(*c*) As to the execution of leases by deed, see *ante*, p. 102.
(*d*) This form, and the next, are adapted from that given in stat. 8 & 9 Vict. c. 124.

(*e*) See *ante*, p. 74.
(*f*) Insert here the exceptions, if any.
(*g*) See *ante*, p. 79.
(*h*) Or "from year to year."

APPENDIX.

Covenants by lessee.
To pay rent.

To pay taxes.

To repair.

To paint external wood-work, &c.

To paint inside wood-work, &c.

To insure.

year, the first of such payments to be made on the   day of   18   . AND the said C. D. doth hereby for himself, his heirs, executors, administrators and assigns, covenant with the said E. F., his heirs (*i*) and assigns, that he the said C. D., his executors, administrators and assigns, will during the said term pay unto the said E. F., his heirs or assigns, the rent hereby reserved in manner hereinbefore mentioned, without any deduction whatsoever. AND ALSO will pay all taxes, rates, duties and assessments whatsoever, whether parochial, parliamentary or otherwise, now charged or hereafter to be charged upon the said demised premises or upon the said E. F., his heirs or assigns, on account thereof [excepting land tax and property tax (*k*)]. AND ALSO will during this demise well and sufficiently repair, maintain, pave, empty, cleanse, amend and keep the said demised premises, with the appurtenances, in good and substantial repair, together with all chimney-pieces, windows, doors, fastenings, water-closets, cisterns, partitions, fixed presses, shelves, pipes, pumps, pales, rails, locks and keys, and all other fixtures and things which at any time during the said term shall be erected and made, when, where and so often as need shall be (damage by fire excepted). AND ALSO will in every   year   in the said term paint all the outside wood-work and iron-work belonging to the said premises with two coats of proper oil colours in a workmanlike manner. AND ALSO will in every   year   paint the inside wood, iron and other works now or usually painted with two coats of proper oil colours in a workmanlike manner ; and also re-paper with paper of a quality as at present such parts of the premises as are now papered ; and also wash, stop, whiten or colour such parts of the said premises as are now plastered. AND ALSO will forthwith insure the said premises hereby demised to the full value thereof in some respectable insurance office, in the joint names of the said E. F., his heirs or assigns, and of the said C. D., his executors, administrators or assigns, and keep the same so insured during the said term ; and will, upon the request of the said E. F., or his heirs or

(*i*) In an underlease substitute "executors, administrators." for "heirs" throughout the deed   (*k*) See *ante*, p. 223.

assigns, or of his or their agent, show the receipt for the last premium paid for such insurance for every current year; and as often as the said premises hereby demised shall be burnt down or damaged by fire, all and every the sums or sum of money which shall be recovered or received by the said C. D., his executors, administrators or assigns, for or in respect of such insurance shall be laid out and expended in building or repairing the said demised premises or such parts thereof as shall be burnt down or damaged by fire as aforesaid. AND it is hereby agreed that it shall be lawful for the said E. F., his heirs and assigns, and his and their agents, at all seasonable times during the said term to enter the said demised premises to take a schedule of the fixtures and things made and erected thereupon, and to examine the condition of the said premises; and further, that all wants of reparation which upon such views shall be found, and for the amendment of which notice in writing shall be left at the premises, the said C. D., his executors, administrators and assigns, will, within three calendar months next after every such notice, well and sufficiently repair and make good accordingly. AND ALSO that the said C. D., his executors, administrators and assigns, will not convert, use or occupy the said premises, or any part thereof into or as a shop, warehouse or other place for carrying on any trade or business whatsoever, or suffer the said premises to be used for any such purpose, or otherwise than as a private dwelling-house, without the previous consent in writing of the said E. F., his heirs or assigns. AND ALSO that the said C. D., his executors, administrators or assigns, shall not nor will during the said term assign, transfer or underlet, or otherwise by any act or deed procure the said premises, or any of them, to be assigned, transferred or underlet, unto any person or persons whomsoever without the previous consent in writing of the said E. F., his heirs or assigns. AND FURTHER, that the said C. D., his executors, administrators or assigns, will, at the expiration or other sooner determination of the said term, peaceably surrender and yield up unto the said E. F., his heirs or assigns, the said premises hereby demised, with the appurtenances, together with all buildings, erections and fixtures now or hereafter

Power to landlord to enter to take schedule of fixtures, and to view state of repair.

Premises not to be used as a shop, &c.

Lessee not to assign or underlet.

To yield up premises in repair.

to be built or erected thereon, in good and substantial repair and condition in all respects, reasonable wear and tear and damage by fire (*l*) or tempest only excepted. PROVIDED ALWAYS, and it is expressly agreed, that if the rent hereby reserved, or any part thereof, shall be unpaid for fifteen days after any of the days on which the same ought to have been paid (although no formal demand shall have been made thereof), or in case of the breach or non-performance of any of the covenants and agreements herein contained on the part of the said C. D., his executors, administrators and assigns, then and in either of such cases it shall be lawful for the said E. F., his heirs or assigns, at any time thereafter, into and upon the said demised premises, or any part thereof in the name of the whole, to re-enter, and the same to have again, repossess and enjoy as of his or their former estate, anything herein contained to the contrary notwithstanding. AND the said E. F. doth hereby, for himself, his heirs, executors, administrators and assigns, covenant with the said C. D., his executors, administrators and assigns, that he and they, paying the rent hereby reserved, and performing the covenants hereinbefore on his and their part contained, shall and may peaceably possess and enjoy the said demised premises for the term hereby granted, without any interruption or disturbance from the said E. F., his heirs or assigns, or any other person or persons lawfully claiming by, from or under him, them or any of them. IN WITNESS whereof the said parties to these presents have hereunto set their hands and seals the day and year first above written.

Proviso for re-entry.

Covenant by lessor for quiet enjoyment.

IV. *Lease of a Farm.*

THIS INDENTURE, made the   day of   18 , BETWEEN E. F. of   ,   , of the one part, and C. D. of   ,   , of the other part, WITNESSETH that the said E. F. DOTH demise unto the said C. D., his executors, administrators and assigns, ALL [*insert description of parcels* (*m*)], AND all the easements and appurtenances to the

(*l*) See *ante*, p. 192.   (*m*) See *ante*, p. 74.

same premises belonging or therewith held or enjoyed: EXCEPT all timber and timber-like trees [and all other trees and bushes whatsoever (n)]; ALSO all mines, minerals (o) [gravel pits] and quarries; ALSO the exclusive right of hunting, shooting, fishing and sporting over the said premises (p): TO HAVE AND TO HOLD the said messuage, lands and premises hereby demised, with the appurtenances, unto the said C. D., his executors, administrators and assigns, from the   day of   18 (q), for the term of   years thence ensuing, YIELDING therefor during the said term the yearly rent of £   , by equal [half-yearly] payments, on the   day of   , and the   day of   in each year, the first of such payments to be made on the   day of   18 . [AND ALSO YIELDING to the said E. F., his heirs or assigns, the further yearly rent of £   , by equal [half-yearly] payments, on the days aforesaid, for every acre, and so in proportion for every less quantity than an acre of the meadow or pasture land hereby demised, which the said C. D., his executors, administrators and assigns, shall during this demise plough up or convert into tillage without the previous consent in writing of the said E. F., his heirs or assigns, the first payment of the last-mentioned yearly rent to be made on such of the said days of payment as shall happen next after any such ploughing up or conversion into tillage.] AND the said C. D. doth hereby for himself, his heirs, executors, administrators and assigns, covenant with the said E. F., his heirs and assigns, that he the said C. D., his executors, administrators and assigns, will, during the said term, pay unto the said E. F., his heirs or assigns, the certain yearly rent hereby reserved [and also (if the same shall become payable) the said additional rent hereby reserved], in manner hereinbefore mentioned. AND ALSO will pay all taxes, rates, duties and assessments whatsoever, whether parochial, parliamentary or otherwise, now charged or hereafter to be charged upon the said demised premises, or upon the said E. F., his heirs or assigns, on account thereof (excepting sewers rate, land tax and property

Additional rent payable for land converted into tillage.

Covenants by lessee.
To pay rent.

To pay taxes.

(n) *Ante*, p. 218.
(o) *Ante*, p. 79.
(p) *Ante*, p. 260.
(q) Or "from year to year."

To repair.	tax (*r*)). AND ALSO will during this demise well and sufficiently repair, maintain and keep the said demised premises in good and substantial repair (damage by fire or tempest excepted), and will at the expiration, or other sooner determination of the said term, peaceably surrender and yield up unto the said E. F., his heirs or assigns, the said premises, together with all buildings, erections and fixtures now or hereafter to be built or erected thereon, in good and substantial repair and condition in all respects, reasonable wear and
Power for landlord to enter to view premises.	tear, and damage by fire or tempest, only excepted. AND it is hereby agreed that it shall be lawful for the said E. F., his heirs and assigns, and his and their agents, at all seasonable times during the said term, to enter the said demised premises to examine the condition of the said premises; and further, that all wants of reparation, which upon such views shall be found, and for the amendment of which notice in writing shall be left at the premises, the said C. D., his executors, administrators and assigns, will, within three calendar months next after every such notice, well and
Lessee not to assign.	sufficiently repair and make good accordingly. AND ALSO that the said C. D., his executors, administrators or assigns, shall not nor will during the said term assign, transfer or underlet, or otherwise by any act or deed procure the said premises or any of them to be assigned, transferred or underlet, unto any person or persons whomsoever, without the previous consent in writing of the said E. F., his heirs or assigns.
To cultivate meadow and pasture land in husbandlike manner.	AND ALSO that the said C. D., his executors, administrators and assigns, shall and will at all times during this demise manure and cultivate the meadow and pasture lands hereby demised according to the most approved mode of good husbandry, and shall not nor will plough up or convert into tillage any part of the said meadow or pasture lands, or mow
To manage arable land in regular course of husbandry.	any of the meadows more than once in any one year. AND ALSO shall and will manage the arable lands hereby demised in a regular course of good husbandry, so that every year one [fifth] part thereof shall be summer-fallowed and manured, and one other [fifth] part thereof sown with good clover or grass seeds; also that not more than two grain

(*r*) See *ante*, p. 223.

crops shall be taken in succession (s). AND ALSO shall and will consume upon the said premises all the hay, straw, turnips and fodder produced thereon, and every year spread on the said premises, or some part thereof, all the manure arising therefrom. AND ALSO shall and will leave upon the said demised premises all the manure which shall be produced thereon within the last year of the said term, without requiring any recompense for the same. PROVIDED ALWAYS, and it is expressly agreed, that if the rent hereby reserved, or any part thereof, shall be unpaid for [twenty-one] days after any of the days on which the same ought to have been paid (although no formal demand shall have been made thereof), or in case of the breach or non-performance of any of the covenants and agreements herein contained on the part of the said C. D., his executors, administrators and assigns, then and in either of such cases it shall be lawful for the said E. F., his heirs or assigns, at any time thereafter, into and upon the said demised premises, or any part thereof, in the name of the whole, to re-enter, and the same to have again, re-possess, and enjoy as of his or their former estate. AND the said E. F. doth hereby for himself, his heirs, executors, administrators and assigns, covenant with the said C. D., his executors, administrators and assigns, that he and they, paying the rent hereby reserved, and performing the covenants hereinbefore on his and their part contained, shall and may peaceably possess and enjoy the said demised premises for the term hereby granted without any interruption or disturbance from the said E. F., his heirs or assigns, or any other person or persons lawfully claiming by, from or under him, them or any of them.

Marginalia: To consume on premises all hay, &c. produced thereon. To leave on premises manure produced in last year of term. Proviso for re-entry. Covenant by lessor for quiet enjoyment.

In witness, &c.

(s) See agreement for letting farm in Dixon's Law of the Farm, Appendix, p. x.

INDEX.

ABANDONED PREMISES, entry of landlord upon, at expiration of lease, 305.
    proceedings before justices for recovery of, 310.

ABANDONMENT OF DISTRESS, quitting possession of goods does not necessarily operate as, 163.
    tenant may retake abandoned distress, 164.

ACCEPTANCE, of new lease, when implied surrender, 280.
    of third person as tenant, with consent of prior tenant, 281.
        undertenant as tenant by lessor, 281.
        assignee as tenant by lessor, 250.
        rent under void lease, 53.
            agreement for lease, 53.
        from tenant holding over, 54.
        when waiver of notice to quit, 273.
            forfeiture, 286.
            double value, 304.

ACKNOWLEDGMENT, of lease by married woman, 9.
    of antecedent tenancy, 137.
        when it authorizes distress, 137.
        does not require lease stamp, 97.

ACTION, for damages upon breach of agreement for lease, 65.
    for irregular distress, 180.
        excessive distress, 157.
        illegal distress, 176—179.
        waste, 200.
        rent on special contract, 188.
        use and occupation, 188.
        double value, 302.
            rent, 304.
    in county court for recovery of possession of premises, 310.
    of ejectment, 313, 315.

ADDITIONAL RENT,
    on breach of covenants, 118.
        distress for, 132.
    no stamp duty chargeable upon, 100.
    for improvements, 111.

ADHESIVE STAMP, when duty on lease may be denoted by, 101.
    penalty on not affixing before execution of instrument, 101.

ADMINISTRATORS, leases by, 30.
    when they may distrain, 135.
    liability of, for rent and upon covenants in lease, 254.

ADMINISTRATORS OF CONVICTS, convict's property vests in, 258.
    leases by, 14, 258.

ADMISSIONS, by tenant, evidence of time of commencement of tenancy, 267.

ADVANCE, RENT PAYABLE IN, mode of reservation of, 83.
    custom of country as to, 112.
    when it may be distrained for, 132.

ADVANCES, by tenant on account of rent not due, effect of, 114.

AGENTS, to execute leases by deed, how to be appointed, 31.
    leases by, 31.
        mode of execution of, 103.
    leases to, by principals, 44.
    payment of rent to, 115.
        effect of, as evidence of principal's title, 130.
    notice to quit given by, 270.

AGISTMENT, cattle at, may be distrained, 144.

AGREEMENT,
    for lease, 61–67.
        how distinguished from lease, 44—47.
        effect of occupation under, 51.
            and payment of rent under, 53.
        how to be made, 61.
        stamp duty upon, 66.
        in what cases parol agreements are enforceable, 62.
            part performance, 62.
            fraud, 64.
            agreement admitted and statute not insisted on, 64.
        rights of intended lessee under, 64.
            as to title, 64.
            as to covenants, 64.
        sums by way of rent reserved upon, 111, 131.

INDEX. 335

AGREEMENT—*continued.*
for lease—*continued.*
remedies for breach of, 65.
action for damages, 65.
suit for specific performance, 65.

AGRICULTURAL FIXTURES, when removable by tenant, 295.
form of consent of landlord to erection of, 295, *n.* (f).
notice by tenant of intention to remove, 296, *n.* (g).

ALIEN, leases by or to, 13.
enemies, leases by or to, 2.

ALTERATIONS in lease, after execution, effect of, 104.

AMBASSADOR, goods of, not distrainable, 143.

AMENDS, tender of, before action for irregular distress, 181.

ANIMALS. *See* CATTLE.
feræ naturæ cannot be distrained, 140.
impounded, to be supplied with food and water, 161.

APPORTIONMENT OF RENT,
in respect of estate, 126.
on grant or devise of part of reversion, 126.
severance of reversion, 126.
tenant's losing possession of part of premises, 126.
in respect of time, 127.
how made, 128.

APPRAISEMENT of distress, 167.
who may appraise, 167.
swearing appraisers, 168.
form of appraiser's oath, 168, *n.* (q).
memorandum of appraisement, 168.
form of, 168, *n.* (r).
stamp duty upon, 168.
action for selling goods distrained without, 180.

APPRAISERS, sale to, of goods distrained, 171.

APPURTENANCES, meaning of term, 76.
to a house, what may pass as, 76.
to land, what may pass as, 76.

ARCHBISHOPS, leases by, 18.
See CORPORATIONS, ECCLESIASTICAL.

ARREAR, when rent is in, 114, 132.

ASSIGNEE, under bill of sale, use and disposal of produce by, 210.
effect of acceptance of, as tenant by lessor, 250.

ASSIGNEE—*continued.*
    rights and liabilities of, 245.
        as against the lessor, 245.
            for rent, 245.
            upon covenants in lease, 245.
                covenants which run with land, 246.
            effect of re-assignment, 249.
                to whom it may be made, 249.
        as against lessee, 250.
            as to title, 251.

ASSIGNMENT OF LEASE, right to assign, where there is no express agreement, 240.
    construction of covenant not to assign, 241.
    licence to assign, 242.
    how distinguished from underlease, 236.
    mode of making, 244.
        statutory requisites, 244.
        assignor may assign directly to himself and another, 245.
    effect of, 245—252.
    sums by way of rent reserved upon, 112, 132.
    upon death of lessee, 254. *See* DEATH.
        bankruptcy of lessee, 256. *See* BANKRUPTCY.

ASSIGNS, effect of naming, in covenants, 85, 246, 247.
    covenants which run with land only when assigns are named, 247.

ATTESTATION of leases by deed, 103.
    under powers to lease, 34.

ATTORNEY, lease to, by client, 44.

ATTORNMENT of tenant, not necessary to conveyance, 117, 253.
    what amounts to, 129.

AUCTIONEER, goods in hands of, for sale, protected from distress, 139.

AWAY-GOING CROP, right to, 300.
    custom to leave in barns, effect of, 150.

BAIL, in ejectment, 313.

BAILIFF, to distrain, 152.
    warrant of distress, 152.
        form of, 152, *n.* (z).
    indemnity to, 152.
    landlord's liability for acts of, 153.
    to give copy of charges to tenant, 175.
    tender of rent to, 154, 166.
    of county court, notice to, that rent is due, 185.
    farm, his authority to let, 31.

INDEX.   337

BANKRUPTCY,
  of landlord,
    when it determines tenancy at will, 264.
  of tenant,
    remedy of landlord for rent upon, 185.
    distress after commencement of, 152, 186.
    when deemed to commence, 186, *n.* (c).
    trustee may dispose of lease containing covenant against assignment, 241.
                  option to call on landlord to grant lease, 257.
            disclaim onerous lease, 257.
    proviso for re-entry upon, 88.

BEER, agreements compelling lessees to purchase of lessors, 205.

BEQUEST, of leaseholds, executor's assent to, 254.
  not breach of covenant not to assign, 241.

BILL OF EXCHANGE, payment of rent by, 128, 132.

BISHOPS, leases by, 15, 18.

BOND, on replevin, 177.

BOUNDARIES, obligation of tenant to keep up, 216.

BROKER, to distrain, 152. *See* BAILIFF.

BUSHES, property in, 218.

CANCELLATION OF LEASE, does not operate as surrender, 281.

CARRIAGES, at livery, may be distrained, 140.

CARRIER, goods in hands of, for conveyance, not distrainable, 140.

CATTLE, kept to consume produce sold by sheriff to be consumed on land, not distrainable, 142.
  when distrainable, 143.
    feeding on common, 145.
    at agistment, 144.
    seen on demised premises, by landlord coming to distrain, 145.
  distress of, where to be impounded, 160.
    supply of food and water to, 161, 162.
    sale under, 170.
  leases of, 258.
    rights and liabilities of lessee and lessor, 258.
      to whom cattle dying during term belong, 258.
        young produced during term belong, 259.

CATTLE-PLAGUE RATE, one-half of, may be deducted from rent, 223.

CERTAINTY, as to commencement of lease, 79.
    as to duration of lease, 81.
        amount of rent, 83, 131.
    requisite in notice to quit, 269.

CESTUI QUE TRUST, lease by, to trustee, 44.
    when tenant at will to trustee, 52.
        merely agent of trustee, 52.
    notice to quit by, 271.

CESTUI QUE VIE, proceedings for production of, 275.

CHARITABLE USES, leases to trustees for, 22.

CHATTELS,
    leases of, 2.
        payments by way of rent reserved upon, 110.

CLOVER, growing under standing corn, not to be sold by sheriff, 208.

COAL, construction of covenants relating to, 122.

COLLATERAL COVENANTS, what are, 248.
    do not bind assignee, 248.

COLLEGES, leases by, 22.

COMMENCEMENT OF LEASE, from what periods leases may be made to commence, 79.
    construction of provisions as to, 80.
    certainty as to, 80.
    from year to year, how to be ascertained, 266.

COMMISSIONERS OF WOODS AND FORESTS, leases of crown lands vested in, 22.

COMMITTEES OF LUNATICS, leases by, 7, 8.
    renewal of leases by, 8.

COMMON, RIGHT OF, lease of, 69.

COMMON, TENANTS IN, to whom rent is payable upon lease by, 116.
    distress by, 137.

COMMONS, leases of, by lords of manors, 29.

COMPANY, goods of, not distrainable, after commencement of winding-up, 143.

COMPULSORY PAYMENTS, when tenant may deduct from rent, 121.

CONDITION, how created, 283.
    forfeiture for breach of, 283.

CONFIDENTIAL RELATION, leases to persons standing in, 43.

CONFIRMATION, of lease made during infancy, 5.
    of lease made by tenant in tail, 28.
        of wife's freeholds not made under statutes, 12.
    of leases by spiritual corporations sole, 17.
        under powers, 32, 33.

CONSENT, by tenant, to landlord's remaining on premises to sell distress, 172.
    form of, 172, *n.* (r).
    of landlord to erection of agricultural machinery or buildings, 295.
    form of, 295, *n.* (f).

CONSIDERATION,
    for a lease, 73.
        effect of mis-statement of, 95.

CONSTRUCTION, of terms of description, 75.
    of exceptions and reservations, 77.
        habendum, 79.
        reddendum, 83.
        powers of re-entry, 89—92.
            to resume possession of part of premises, 92, 93.
        stipulations as to time of payment of rent, 112.
        covenants generally, 86.
            relating to repairs, 191—197.
            against assignment, 241.
            prohibiting exercise of trades, 203.
            for quiet enjoyment, 232.
            relating to working of mines, 206.
                trading with particular persons, 205.
            to insure, 220.
        agreements relating to course of husbandry, 210—212.
                hay and straw, 212.
                manure, 213.
                trees, 218.
                payment of taxes, 226.
                underletting, 236.
                game, 261.

CONTINUOUS BREACH OF COVENANT, what is, 194, 222.
    effect of receipt of rent or other acknowledgment of tenancy, 287.

CONVICT, property of, vests in administrator, 258.
    leases of property of, by administrator, 14, 258.

COPARCENERS, distress by one of several, 136.

COPYHOLDS, leases of, 29.
    registration of, 105.

CORN,
    distress of, 138.
        where to be impounded, 159.
        not to be removed to damage of owner, 171.
        when to be sold, 173.
    sold by sheriff to be consumed on land, not liable to distress, 141.
    claimable as emblements, 298.

CORPORATIONS, service of notice to quit upon, 272.
    leases by or to, how to be made, 14.
    effect of entry and payment of rent under void lease by, 14.
    ecclesiastical, 15.
        enabling statutes, 15.
        leases by, not in pursuance of statutes, 17.
        restraining statutes, 18.
        renewal of leases by, 20.
        stamps upon leases by, 100.
        leases to, 21.
    municipal, leases by, 21.
    the crown, leases by, 22.

CORRESPONDENCE, leases by, 72, 101.

COSTS, of lease and counterpart, by whom to be borne, 106.
    of distress, 173.
        for rent under 20*l.*, 173.
            scale of charges, 174.
            remedy for excessive charges, 174.
        for rent above 20*l.*, 169, 174.
        bailiff to give copy of charges, 175.

COUNTERPART, by whom executed and kept, 102.
    costs of, by whom to be borne, 106.
    presumptive evidence of execution of lease, 102.
    denoting stamp, 102.

COUNTY COURT, registrar grants replevins, 176.
    action of replevin in, 177.
    proceedings in, for recovery of possession after expiration of tenancy, 310.
    when action of ejectment may be brought in, 315.
    suit in, to enforce performance of parol agreement for lease, 62.

COUNTY RATES, construction of covenants relating to, 226, 227.

COURSE OF HUSBANDRY, construction of agreements relating to, 210.

COVENANT, action of, for rent, 189.

COVENANTS, 84.
    construction of, generally, 86.

INDEX. 341

COVENANTS—*continued.*
  usual, 65, 85.
  dependent or independent, 87.
  joint or several, 87.
  collateral, 248.
  where they run with the land, 246—248.
    where "assigns" are not mentioned, 246.
                 are mentioned, 247.
  covenants which do not run with land, 248.
  implied, 74, 83, 229.
  express, 84.
    for payment of rent, 85.
      forms of, 320, 325, 326, 329.
    to repair, construction of, 191.
      forms of, 320, 325, 326, 330.
      no relief in equity for forfeiture on breach of, 291.
    to put into repair, construction of, 193.
    to leave in repair, construction of, 194.
      forms of, 323, 325, 327.
    conditional, to repair, construction of, 195.
    to repair after notice, 194.
      forms of, 322, 325, 327, 330.
    to paint, *form of,* 321, 326.
    prohibiting exercise of trades, 203.
      forms of, 322, 325, 327.
  relating to working of mines, 206.
            trading with particular persons, 205.
            cultivation of land, 210—214.
  to insure against fire, 220.
    forms of, 321, 326.
  to pay taxes, 226.
    forms of, 320, 325, 326, 329.
  for quiet enjoyment, 232.
    forms of, 324, 325, 328, 331.
  relating to underletting, 236.
  not to assign without licence, 241.
    forms of, 322, 325, 327, 330.
    no relief in equity on forfeiture for breach of, 291.
  to indemnify lessee on assignment of lease, 250.

CROPS, what, claimable as emblements, 298.
  growing, distress on, 138. *See* GROWING CROPS.
  away-going, 300.

CROWN, leases by, 22.
    where rent reserved upon, is payable, 115.
    no tenancy at sufferance against, 50.

CULTIVATION OF LAND,
    obligations of tenant, where there is no express agreement, 207.
        as to husbandlike cultivation, 207.
            implied obligation to cultivate according to custom, 207.
        as to expenditure of produce on demised premises, 208.
    obligations of tenant where there is an express agreement, 209.
        provisions in case of execution, 209.
        construction of agreements relating to course of husbandry, 210.
                                        hay and straw, 212.
                                        manure, 213.

CURTESY, TENANT BY, leases by, 10.

CUSTODY OF LAW, goods in, cannot be distrained, 141.

CUSTODY OF LEASE, who is entitled to, 105.

CUSTOM, evidence of, when admitted to explain lease, 70.
    as to rent becoming due in advance, 112.
    as to what trees are timber, 217.
    as to meaning of "Lady-day," 113.
    as to length of notice requisite to determine tenancy from year to year, 265.
    to leave away-going crops in barns, effect of, 150.
    as to removal of articles erected by tenant, 295.
        away-going crops, 300.
        compensation for tillages, 301.
    implied obligation of agricultural tenant to cultivate according to, 207.
    excluded by express agreement inconsistent with it, 208, 300.

DAMAGE FEASANT, cattle distrained, not distrainable for rent, 141.

DAMAGES, in replevin, 176.
    on action for illegal distress, 179.
        circumstances of mitigation, 179.
    on action for irregular distress, 181.
                use and occupation, 188.
                breach of covenant to repair, 197.
                        for quiet enjoyment, 234.
    court of chancery may award, 66.

DATE of lease by deed, 73.

DEAN AND CHAPTER, leases by, 18.

DEATH, of lessor, 253.
    of lessee, 254.
        liability of executor for rent and upon the covenants, 254.
    of landlord or tenant at will, effect of, 264.
    cestui que vie not produced, to be taken to be dead, 276.

DEDUCTIONS FROM RENT, property tax, 119.
   land tax, 120.
   sewers' rate, 120.
   tithe rent-charge, 120.
   rent due to original landlord, 121.
   other compulsory payments, 121.
   permitted by mistake, effect of, 122.

DEED, when leases must be made by, 68, 69.
   execution and attestation of leases by, 102, 103.

DELIVERY OF DEED, mode of, 103.

DEMAND, of rent before distress, 153.
   of rent not necessarily waiver of notice to quit, 273.
      due after forfeiture, when waiver of forfeiture, 287.
      under proviso for re-entry on non-payment of, 284.
         how and when to be made, 284.
         where to be made, 285.
         when writ in ejectment may stand in place of, 285.
   of possession, or double value, 303. *Form of*, 303, *n.* (d).

DEMISE, implied covenant for quiet enjoyment under, 74, 229.

DEPOSIT of lease as security, not a breach of covenant against assignment, 241.
   liability of depositee, 245.

DESERTED PREMISES, proceedings before justices for recovery of, 310.

DETERMINATION OF LEASE, when distress may be made after, 149.
   modes of, applicable to particular kinds of tenancy, 262—277.
      determination of tenancy by sufferance, 262.
         at will, 263.
         from year to year, 265.
         for optional term, 275.
         for life, 275.
   modes of, generally applicable, 277—291.
      merger, 277.
      surrender, 278.
      forfeiture, 283.

DIGNITIES cannot be granted for years, 2.

DISABILITY, restrictions arising from, 2.

DISCLAIMER,
   verbal, 274.
      what expressions amount to, 274.
   by matter of record, &c., 283.
   of onerous lease, by trustee of bankrupt, 257.

DISTRESS FOR RENT,
    requisites to, 131—144.
        certain and proper rent, 131, 175.
        remedy of tenant when no rent is due, 178.
        rent in arrear, 132.
        reversion in person distraining, 132—137, 175.
        who may distrain,
            mortgagor, under lease by him after mortgage, 116, 133.
                      before mortgage, 133.
            mortgagee, under lease by mortgagor after mortgage, 133.
                      before mortgage, 133.
            receivers, 134.
            husband, 134.
            executors and administrators, 135.
            joint-tenants, 136.
            tenants in common, 137.
                from year to year, 136.
                at will, 136.
        goods liable to be distrained, 137—144.
        goods on premises belonging to third persons, 137.
        corn or hay, 138. *See* CORN.
        growing crops, 138. *See* GROWING CROPS.
        property privileged from distress, 138—143.
            fixtures, 138.
            title deeds and keys, 139.
            things sent to trader, 139.
            wild animals, 140.
            things in actual use, 140.
            perishable goods, 141.
            goods in custody of law, 141.
            produce sold by sheriff subject to agreement to consume on land, 141.
            frames and materials entrusted to workmen, 142.
            goods of ambassador, 143.
            effects of company being wound up, 143.
        property conditionally privileged, 143.
            implements of trade, 143.
            cattle and sheep, 143.
        effect of seizing goods privileged from distress, 175.
    where to be made,
        general rule, 144.
            exceptions, 145—149.
                stock feeding on common, 145.
                cattle seen by landlord on premises, 145.
                fraudulent removal, 145.
    effect of seizing goods not upon the demised premises, 175.

DISTRESS FOR RENT—*continued.*
  when to be made, 149.
    distress after determination of lease, 149.
    time within which distress for rent-charge may be made, 150.
      rent may be made, 151.
    time of day at which distress must be made, 150.
    postponement of right to distrain, 150.
  amount for which it may be made, 151.
    six years' arrears only recoverable, 151.
    distress for more rent than is due, 151.
    distress after bankruptcy, 152, 186.
  mode of making, 152.
    warrant of distress, 152. *See* WARRANT.
      landlord's liability for acts of bailiff, 153.
    demand of rent, 153. *See* DEMAND.
    effect of tender of rent before seizure, 154. *See* TENDER.
      after seizure, but before impounding, 158, 166.
      after impounding, 166.
    how entry may be lawfully made, 154—156. *See* ENTRY.
    seizure, 156.
    impounding, 158—163. *See* IMPOUNDING.
      abandonment of distress, 163, 164.
      rescue or poundbreach, 163.
  requisites to sale under, 164.
    inventory and notice, 164, 180.
      forms of, 164, *n.* (t).
      how to be served, 165.
    appraisement, 167, 180. *See* APPRAISEMENT.
      form of, 168, *n.* (q).
      stamps upon, 168.
    sale under, 169—173. *See* SALE.
    costs of, 173. *See* COSTS.
  remedies for illegal, 175—180.
  remedy for irregular, 180.
    excessive, 157.
  when waiver of forfeiture, 286.
    notice to quit, 273.

DITCHES, ownership of, 215.

DOOR, outer, when it may be broken open to distrain, 146, 155.
  inner, may be broken open, if outer door is open, 154.

DOUBLE RENT,
  action or distress for, 304.
    when it ceases to be payable, 305.

DOUBLE VALUE,
 action for, 302.
  forms of notice by landlord, 303, *n*. (d).
  when acceptance of rent operates as waiver of, 304.
 no distress for, 131, *n*. (p).

DOWER, tenant in, leases by, 10.

DUCHY OF CORNWALL, leases of lands belonging to, 22.

DUCHY OF LANCASTER, leases of lands belonging to, 22.

DUPLICATE OF LEASE, 102.
 stamps upon, 102.

DURATION OF LEASES, certainty as to, 81.

ECCLESIASTICAL CORPORATIONS,
 leases by, 15—20.
  stamps upon, 100.
 leases to, 21. *See* CORPORATIONS, ECCLESIASTICAL.

EJECTMENT,
 action of, 313.
  may be brought before entry, 108.
  for non-payment of rent, 285.
  jury to find verdict for mesne profits, 314.
  tenant knowing of writ in, to give notice to landlord, 315.
  when it may be brought in county court, 315.

EMBLEMENTS, by what tenants claimable, 298.
 on what events, 298.
 of what crops, 298.
 entry to cut and carry away, 299.
 provision as to tenant at rack rent of landlord entitled for uncertain interest, 299.

ENDOWMENT OF SEE, leases of lands assigned as, 19.

ENROLMENT of leases by tenants in tail, where necessary, 27.

ENTRY,
 by tenant, effect of, 106—108.
  under agreement for lease, 51.
   void lease, 51.
   purchase agreement, 51.
   parol agreement for lease, 63.
  nature of lessee's interest until, 107.
  on different parts of premises at different times, 268.

INDEX. 347

ENTRY—*continued.*
  by tenant—*continued.*
    necessary to enable him to maintain trespass, 107.
                    landlord to maintain use and occupation against him, 108.
  by executor or administrator of tenant, effect of, 255.
  by landlord, to repair, 197.
    to distrain, 154—156.
        in case of fraudulent removal, 146.
        when outer door may be broken open, 146, 155.
        constructive entry, 155.
        effect of unlawful entry, 155, 175.
    at end of tenancy, to recover possession, 305.
        where premises are abandoned, 305.
                locked up, 305.
        tenant is in possession, 306.

EQUITY, courts of,
  application to, for specific performance of agreement for lease, 65.
               injunction against waste, 200.
               relief against forfeiture, 288.

ERROR in notice to quit, 269.

ESCROW, delivery of deed as, 103.

ESTOPPEL, leases by, 42, 43.
  on reservation of rent to stranger to reversion, 112.
  reversion by, sufficient to support distress, 132.
  tenant estopped from disputing title of landlord, 42.
        may show that it has expired, 42.

ESTOVERS, right to, 218.

EVICTION,
  of tenant by landlord, what acts constitute, 230.
    effect of, 126, 231.
    from part of premises, 126.
    by title paramount, apportionment of rent upon, 126.

EVIDENCE, extrinsic or verbal, when admissible to explain lease, 69—71.
  terms upon which unstamped instruments are received in, 94.

EXCEPTION, how it differs from reservation, 77.
  construction of, 77.
  timber, 78.
    form of, 329.
  minerals, 79.
    form of, 329.
  liberty to tenant to kill rabbits, 261. *See* RESERVATION.

EXCESSIVE DISTRESS, what seizure is excessive, 157.
    tenant's remedy for, 157.
EXECUTION AGAINST TENANT, landlord's remedy for rent upon, 181—185.
    duty of sheriff, 182.
        form of notice to sheriff, 183, n. (n).
    under process of county court, remedies for rent upon, 184.
    straw, turnips or manure taken under, not to be sold off, 209.
    hay, grass, &c. not to be sold off, contrary to covenants, 209.
    tenant to give notice of covenants to sheriff, 209.
    sheriff to give notice of seizure of produce to landlord, 209.
    goods taken in, cannot generally be distrained, 141.
    growing crops seized under, liable to distress for subsequent rent, 184.
EXECUTION OF LEASES, by deed, 102.
    under powers of leasing, 34.
    by agents, 103.
    effect of non-execution by lessor, 103.
        alterations in lease after execution, 104.
EXECUTORS, leases by, 30.
    of lessor, when they may sue upon covenant broken in his lifetime, 253.
        distrain, 135, 136.
    of lessee, their liability for rent and upon covenants, 254.
        assent of, to specific bequest of lease, 254.

EXPENSES, of lease, 106. *See* COSTS.

EXTRINSIC EVIDENCE, when admissible, 69—71.

FACTORS, goods in hands of, for sale, privileged from distress, 139.

FALLOWS, not exhausted, compensation for, 300.

FALSE DEMONSTRATION, what it is, 74.

FARM,
    meaning of term, 75.
        form of lease of, 328.

FARMING BUILDINGS, meaning of term, 75.

FEME COVERT. *See* MARRIED WOMEN.
    renewal of leases to, 6, 12.
    renewal of leases by, 6, 12.

FENCES,
    liability to repair, where there is no express agreement, 214, 215.
        obligations of tenants for life or years, 214.
                    from year to year or at will, 215.
    ownership of, 215.

INDEX.   349

FERÆ NATURÆ, animals, cannot be distrained, 140.

FIRE, payment of rent after destruction of premises by, 124.
    liability of lessee under covenant to repair, on injury by, 192.
    accidental, liability of tenant for, 190.
    insurance office may lay out insurance money in rebuilding, 222.

FITNESS FOR USE INTENDED,
    no implied contract as to, on lease of unfurnished house, 202.
        of land, 202.

FIXTURES, what articles are, 138—139, 292.
    cannot be distrained, 138.
    belonging to landlord, remedy where taken by sheriff in execution, 184.
    ownership of, 293.
        where there is no express agreement, 293.
            fixtures erected before commencement of tenancy, 293.
                by landlord during tenancy, 293.
                by tenant during tenancy, 293.
            ornamental and useful articles, 294.
            trade fixtures, 294.
            agricultural fixtures, 295.
            within what time removable, 296.
        where there is an express agreement, 297.
            effect of covenant to keep and leave in repair erections and
                improvements, 297.

FOOD, supply of, to animals impounded, 161.

FORCIBLE ENTRY, lawful possession may be acquired by, 306.
    indictment for, 306,

FORFEITURE, of land brought into mortmain, 15.
    by disclaimer, 283.
        acts amounting to, 283.
    on breach of conditions annexed to grants, 283.
    under proviso for re-entry, 284.
        construction of, 89—92.
        by whom lease may be determined under, 284.
        for non-payment of rent, 284.
            demand of rent, 284.
            when writ in ejectment may stand in place of, 285.
    waiver of, 286.
        acts amounting to, 286—287. *See* WAIVER.
        effect of, restricted to breach to which it specially relates, 287.
    relief against, 288.
        for non-payment of rent, 288, 290.
            breach of covenant to insure, 289, 290.
        breaches of covenant for which courts of equity will not relieve, 290.

350 INDEX.

FORMS, warrant of distress, 152, *n*. (z).
 inventory of goods distrained, 164, *n*. (t).
 notice of distress, 165, *n*. (t).
 appraiser's oath, 168, *n*. (q).
 memorandum of appraiser's oath, 168, *n*. (q).
   appraisement, 168, *n*. (r).
 consent of landlord to erection of agricultural buildings, &c., 295, *n*. (f).
 notice by tenant of intention to remove agricultural buildings, &c., 296, *n*. (g).
  to quit given by landlord, 269, *n*. (g).
   tenant, 270, *n*. (g).
  to determine tenancy for optional terms of years, 275, *n*. (c).
  to tenant holding over, to pay double value, 303, *n*. (d).
  to tenant of intention to proceed before justices, 307, *n*. (y).
 of leases, 317—331.
  short statutory, 317.
  statutory form, suitable for small house, 324.
  of house, 325.
   farm, 328.

FORTHWITH, to put premises into repair, construction of covenant, 193.

FOUR-COURSE SYSTEM, meaning of covenant to farm on, 210.

FRAME, entrusted to workman, not distrainable by his landlord, 142.

FRAUD, parol agreements for leases enforceable on ground of, 64.

FRAUDULENT REMOVAL,
 of goods to avoid a distress, landlord's remedy upon, 145—149.
  what constitutes, 148.
  penalty on person assisting in, 147.
  requisites to proceedings under statute, 148.

FURNISHED HOUSE, breach of condition that it is fit for habitation, 202.

FURNISHED LODGINGS, rent of, may be distrained for, 110.

FURNITURE, distrained for rent, where it may be impounded, 159.

GAME, statutory provisions as to, 259.
 construction of demise or reservation of right of shooting, 260.
   form of reservation, 329.
  special agreements relating to, 261.

GOODS, leases of, 2.

GRANT OF REVERSION, remedies of grantees and lessees upon, 252.
 grantee may avail himself of notice to quit given by preceding owner, 271.

GREENHOUSE, when removable by tenant, 293, 295.

GROWING CROPS,
    distress of, 138.
        where to be impounded, 160.
        effect of tender before they are gathered, 166.
        appraisement of, 168.
        when to be sold, 173.
    seized and sold under execution, liable for subsequent rent, 141, 184.

GUARDIANS, leases to, by wards, 44.

HABENDUM, from what time it takes effect, 80.
    certainty as to commencement and duration of lease, 80, 81.
    for years, form and construction of, 79.
    from year to year, form and construction of, 81.
        forms of, 325, 329.
    for life, form and construction of, 81.

HABITATION, condition that house is fit for, what is breach of, 202.

HAY, taken in execution, not to be sold off contrary to covenants, 209.
    construction of agreements relating to, 212.
    distress of, 138.
        where to be impounded, 159.
        sale on condition that purchaser shall consume on premises, 171.

HEDGE, destruction of quickset, waste, 198.
    where none between adjoining fields, obligations of occupiers, 215.
    ownership of, 216.

HOLDING OVER, and payment of rent, effect of, 54.
    pending treaty for new lease, 51.
    by under-tenant, 302.
        co-tenant, 302.
    landlord's remedies against tenant, 302—305.

HONOURS, cannot be granted for years, 2.

HORSES, when distrainable, 143.
    at livery, may be distrained, 140.

HOUSE, unfurnished, no implied contract by lessor that it is fit for habitation, 202.
    what the term may comprehend, 75.
    what may pass as appurtenant to, 76.
        forms of lease of, 324, 325.

HUNT, grant of leave to, does not give grantee liberty of shooting, 261.

HUSBAND, leases by, 10.
HUSBANDLIKE CULTIVATION, what is to be considered as, 207, 211.

ILLEGAL DISTRESS, what is, 150, 154, 155, 175.
   remedies for, 175.
      rescue, 175.
      replevin, 176.
      action of trespass where no rent is due, 178.
      in metropolitan police district, 179.

ILLEGAL OR IMMORAL PURPOSES, rent or damages not recoverable under leases for, 200.

IMPLEMENTS OF TRADE, distress of, 140, 143.

IMPLIED COVENANTS,
   upon the word "demise," 74, 229.
         words "yielding and paying," 83.

IMPOUNDING, charge for, in public pound, 174.
   of distress, 158.
      what constitutes, 158.
      on the premises, 158.
      of furniture, 159.
         corn, straw, or hay, 159.
         growing crops, 160.
         cattle, 160.
            supply of food and water to, 161.
      goods impounded not to be used, 162.
      injury to goods impounded, 162.
      abandonment of distress, 163.
      rescue or poundbreach, 163.

INCOMING TENANT, liability of, to pay for tillages, 301.

INCONSISTENT RELATION, creation of, implied surrender, 281.

INCORPOREAL HEREDITAMENTS,
   lease of, 2.
      how to be made, 69.
      payments reserved upon, by way of rent, 110.

INCUMBENT, leases of glebe by, 16.
   leases to, 21.

INDEFINITE GRANT, effect of, 59.

INDEFINITE LETTING, effect of, 52, 81.

INDEMNITY, covenants of, upon assignment of leases, 250.
   to bailiff on distress, 152.

INFANTS,
    leases by, 2.
        by direction of Court of Chancery, 2.
        of settled estates, 4.
        not in pursuance of statutes, 4.
        confirmation of, 5.
        renewal of, 6.
        disaffirmance of, 4.
    leases to, 5.
        renewal of, 6.
            by person jointly interested with infant, 44.

INJUNCTION, to restrain waste, 200.

INN, goods of guests at, not distrainable, 140.

INSPECTION OF LEASE, by lessee, 106.

INSURANCE,
    construction of general covenant to insure and keep insured, 220.
            covenants to insure in names of specified persons, 221.
        forms of, 321, 326.
    what covenants to insure run with the land, 223, *n*. (d), 247.
    statutory provisions in case of fire, 222.
        lessor to have benefit of insurance not in conformity with covenant, 222.
        insurance money may be laid out in rebuilding, 222.
    relief against forfeiture for breach of covenant to insure, 289.

INTENDED LESSEE, rights of, under agreement for lease, 64.

INTERESSE TERMINI, what it is, 107.
    how and when it may be perfected, 107.
    nature of lessee's interest before entry, 107.*

INTEREST, on rent, effect of agreement to take, 129.
    in land, within sect. 4 of Statute of Frauds, 61.

INTOXICATION, lease made by person in state of, 44.

INVENTORY,
    under distress, 164.
        form of, 164, *n*. (t).

IRREGULAR DISTRESS,
    when distress is irregular, 170, 171, 180.
    action for, 180.
        tenant not to recover if tender of amends is made, 181.
        not maintainable without proof of actual damage, 181.
        measure of damages in, 181.

JOINT TENANTS,
    leases by, 30.
        to whom rent reserved in, is payable, 116.
        effect of severance of reversion, 136.
    distress by, 136.
    notice to quit by one on behalf of others, 271.

JUSTICES,
    proceedings before, for recovery of small tenements, 306.
                                        deserted premises, 310.
                        metropolitan police magistrates, on wrongful distress, 179.

KEYS, demand of by landlord, determines tenancy at will, 263.
    detention of, not necessarily waiver of notice to quit, 273.
    delivery and acceptance of, implied surrender, 279.
        what is evidence of acceptance of, 280.

LADY DAY, custom as to meaning of, 113.

LAND, meaning of term, 75.
    covenants which run with, 246.
    no implied contract on lease of, that it is fit for use intended, 202.

LANDLORD, goods distrained cannot be sold to, 171.
    obligations of, as to repairs, 190.
    notice to, of want of repair, 197.
    entry by, to execute repairs, 197.
    letting premises in dangerous condition, liability for, 191.
    how far bound to disclose to intending lessee condition of premises, 202.

LAND TAX, tenant liable to pay, under reservation of net rent, 84.
    when it may be deducted from rent, 120, 223.
    construction of covenants relating to, 228.

LATENT AMBIGUITY, what it is, 70.

LEASES, of what kinds of property may be made, 1, 2.
    persons capable of making and taking, 2—44.
    how to be made, 67.
        when deed is necessary, 68.
            effect of unsealed lease for more than three years, 68.
    of incorporeal hereditaments, 69.
        how to be made, 69.
    form and construction of, 71—93.
        by correspondence, 72.

INDEX. 355

LEASES – *continued.*
  form and construction of—*continued.*
    ordinary form, 72—93.
      premises, 73.
      date, 73.
      recitals, 73.
      consideration, 73.
      operative words, 74.
      parcels, 74.
      habendum, 79—82. *See* HABENDUM.
      reddendum, 82—84. *See* REDDENDUM.
      covenants, 84—88. *See* COVENANTS.
    proviso for re-entry, 88—92. *See* PROVISO FOR RE-ENTRY.
    power to resume possession of part of premises, 92, 93.
    stamps upon, 93—101. *See* STAMPS.
    matters relating to completion of, 102—108.
      execution, 102. *See* EXECUTION.
      attestation, 103.
      registration, 105.
      custody of lease, 105.
      costs of lease, 106.
      entry of lessee, 106. *See* ENTRY.

LESSEE, cannot rid himself of liability under covenants by assigning lease, 250.
  deemed surety to lessor for assignee, 250, 251.

LESSOR, effect of non-execution of lease by, 103.

LEVEL, meaning of, in mining lease, 71.

LIABILITY,
  of lessee for breaches of covenant, when it commences, 80, 195.
    cannot rid himself of, by assigning lease, 250.
  of landlord for acts of bailiff employed by him to distrain, 153.
  of executors or administrators of lessee, 254.

LICENCE, how distinguished from lease, 47.
  sums reserved by way of rent upon, 111.
  by lord of manor, to lease, 20.
  to assign, 242.
    form of, 242, *n.* (g).
    duty of vendor to procure, 242.
    effect of, restrained to assignment, &c. actually authorized, 243.
  verbal, to quit, not of itself a surrender, 280.
  to take away fixtures, 297.

LIFE,
  leases for, 59, 72.
    different kinds of, 59.

A A 2

LIFE—*continued*.
   leases for—*continued*.
      determinable, 59.
      how made, 72.
      construction of, 82.
      to commence *in futuro*, 81.
      production of persons for whose lives estates are held, 275.
   tenant for, 10, 28.
      of settled estates, leases by, 10, 28.
      leases by, not in pursuance of statute, 28.
      obligations of, as to repairs, 190.
                       fences, 214.
      liability of, for waste, 200.
      claim of representatives of, to emblements, 298.

LIMITATION, STATUTES OF,
   time within which distress for rent-charge may be made, 150.
                        rent may be made, 151.
                        action for rent may be brought, 187, 188.

LIQUIDATION BY ARRANGEMENT, remedy by landlord for rent upon, 187.

LIVERY OF SEISIN, on leases for lives, 72, 81.

LIVE STOCK, leases of, 2, 258.

LOCKED-UP PREMISES, entry upon, by landlord, on expiration of lease, 305.

LODGER, may remove goods before distress, 148.
   sale of his goods, under distress for rent due by tenant, 170.

LODGINGS, rent for furnished, how recoverable, 110.
   length of notice required to determine monthly or weekly tenancy, 265.

LOOMS, entrusted to workmen, not distrainable by their landlords, 142.

LORDS OF MANORS, leases of wastes by, 29.
   licence to lease, 29.

LUNATICS, leases by, 8.
   leases by their committees, 7.
      of their settled estates, 8.
   renewal of leases to them, 8.
            by them, 7.
   assignments of leases to which they are entitled, 240, n. (q).

MACHINERY erected by tenant, when removable by him, 294.
   agricultural, when removable by tenant, 295.

MANURE, construction of agreements relating to, 213.
   taken under execution, not to be sold off, 209.

MARRIED WOMEN,
    leases by, 9.
        when they may demise alone, 9.
        by deed acknowledged, 9.
        not in pursuance of statutes, 11.
        of settled estates, 11.
        of leaseholds, 12.
        renewal of, 12.
        distress for arrears of rent due under, 135.
    leases to, 12.
        renewal of, 6, 12.
        authority of, as agents of their husbands, 115.
        service of notice to quit upon, 271.

MATERIALS entrusted to workman, not distrainable by his landlord, 142.
    sent to manufacturer to be worked up, not distrainable, 139.

MERGER, where it occurs, 277.

MESSUAGE, meaning of term, 75.

METROPOLITAN POLICE DISTRICT, remedy for wrongful distresses in, 179.

MILCH COWS, when impounded, may be milked by person distraining, 162.

MINERALS, construction of exception of, 79.

MINES, leases of, belonging to lunatics, 7.
    construction of covenants in leases of, 122, 206, 233.
    what may be worked, under lease of land, 198.

MISTAKE, effect of payment of rent by, 117.
        deductions from rent permitted by, 122.
        in notice to quit, 269.

MODE OF USING PREMISES,
    where there is no express agreement, 200.
        illegal or immoral purposes, 200.
        fitness of premises for use intended, 201.
        on demise of unfurnished house, 202.
            furnished house, 202.
            land, 202.
    where there is an express agreement, 202.
        construction of contracts relating to exercise of trades, 202, 203.

MONTHLY TENANCY, notice required to determine, 265.

"MORE OR LESS," meaning of term, 77.

MORTGAGEE, leases by, 41.
    leases to, by mortgagor, 44.
    effect of notice by, to tenant under lease made before mortgage, 116, 133.
    distress by, for rent due under lease made by mortgagor before mortgage, 133.
    distress by, for rent due under lease made by mortgagor after mortgage, 133.

MORTGAGOR,
    leases by, before the mortgage, 41.
        to whom rent reserved in, is payable, 116.
    leases by, after the mortgage, 41.
        to whom rent reserved in, is payable, 116.
        distress for rent reserved in, 133.

MORTMAIN ACTS, what leases to corporations are within, 15.

NECESSARIES, where demised premises are, infant lessee liable for rent, 5.

NET RENT, meaning of term, 84.

NOTICE, underlessee deemed to have, of covenants in original lease, 238.
    by mortgagee to tenant of mortgagor, 116, 133.
    by landlord to sheriff upon execution against tenant, 183.
        form of, 183, *n.* (n).
    to landlord, of want of repairs, 197.
    of distress for rent, 164.
        form of, 164, *n.* (t).
        landlord not bound by cause of taking mentioned in, 164.
        effect of want of, 165.
        action for want of, 180.
        how to be served, 165.
    to determine tenancy for optional term of years, 275.
        form of, 275, *n.* (c).
    of tenant's intention to remove agricultural buildings, &c., 296.
        form of, 296, *n.* (g).
    to tenant holding over, to pay double value, 303, *n.* (d).
    of intention to proceed before justices for recovery of possession, 306.
        form of, 307, *n.* (y).

NOTICE TO QUIT,
    length of, where there is no express agreement, 265.
        in quarterly, monthly or weekly tenancy, 265.
    where there is an express agreement, 266.
    period with reference to which notice must be given, 266.
        admissions by tenant, 267.

INDEX. 359

NOTICE TO QUIT—*continued.*
   period with reference to which notice must be given—*continued.*
      where tenant has held over, 267.
         entered under void lease, 268.
           in middle of quarter, 268.
           on different parts of premises at different times, 268.
   how notice must be expressed, 269.
     forms of notice, 269, *n.* (g).
   notice to quit part only of premises leased together, 269.
   by whom, may be given, 270.
   how to be served, 271.
   waiver of, 272. *See* WAIVER.

NUISANCE, liability of landlord, letting premises in such a state as to constitute, 191.

NURSERYMEN may remove trees and hothouses, 295

OATH, *form of appraiser's*, 168, *n.* (q).

OCCUPATION by tenant, effect of, 106—108. *See* ENTRY.

OFFICES, leases of, 2.

OPERATIVE WORDS, in a lease, 74.

OPTION,
   to determine lease, 58, 275.
     by whom exercisable, 275.
     form of notice, 275, *n.* (c).
   to purchase demised premises, effect of, on stamp, 97.
   to take further term, 58.
     when it may be exercised, 59.
     passes to trustee in bankruptcy, 257.

ORNAMENT, articles of, removable by tenant, 294.

OUTGOING TENANT,
   compensation to, for away-going crops, 300.
        tillages, 300.
        straw and manure, 212, 213.

OVERPLUS on sale of goods distrained, 169.

PARCELS, of a lease, 74.
   in agricultural leases, 74.
   legal meaning of terms of description, 75.

PART PERFORMANCE,
   of parol agreement, 62.
     acts which amount to, 63.

360   INDEX.

PAWNBROKER, articles pledged with, not distrainable, 140.

PAYMENT OF RENT, 128.
    to person not entitled to it, 117.
    after destruction of premises by fire, 124.
        flood or enemy, 125.
    where premises are unfit for use or habitation, 125.
    on non-repair by landlord, 125.
    to a third person, by tenant for years, not a forfeiture, 283.
    by bill or note, 128, 132.
    under agreement for lease, or void lease, 53.
    by tenant holding over, 54.

PENAL RENT, no stamp duty chargeable upon, 100.
    construction of reservation of, 118.
    no relief in equity from, 118.
    how long payable, 118.
    distress for, 132.

PENSIONS, assignments of, 2.

PERISHABLE GOODS cannot be distrained, 141.

PERMISSIVE WASTE, what constitutes, 199.

POOR RATE,
    when it may be deducted from rent, 224.
        overseers may agree with owner to pay poor rates, 224, *n*. (h).
        owners may be rated, 224, *n*. (i).

POSSESSION, person letting premises agrees to give, 229.
    tenant's obligation to give, at end of lease, 301.
    when landlord may refuse to accept, 302.
    landlord's remedies for recovering, 302.
        indirect, 302.
            action for double value, 302.
            action or distress for double rent, 304.
        direct, 305.
            entry, 305.
            proceedings before justices, 306.
                for recovery of small tenements, 306.
                      deserted premises, 310.
            proceedings in the county court, 310.
                where tenant holds over after expiration of term, 310.
                where half-year's rent is in arrear and landlord has right to re-enter, 311.
            action of ejectment, 313.

POST, remittance of rent by, 129.
    sending of notice to quit by, 272.

POSTPONEMENT of right to distrain, 150.

POTATOES may be claimed as emblements, 298.

POUND, person distraining liable for injury to animals occasioned by bad condition of, 162.
    charge for impounding in, 174.

POUNDBREACH, remedy for, 163.

POWERS,
    to resume possession of part of premises, 92.
        construction of, 92—93.

POWERS OF LEASING, leases under, 31—34.
    vested in lunatic, how exercised, 7.
    leases by married women in pursuance of, 9.
    relief on defective execution of, 32.

PREMISES, in a lease, 73.

PREVIOUS MODE OF ENJOYMENT, evidence of, to explain lease, 71.

PRODUCE,
    sold by sheriff to be consumed on land, 209.
        not distrainable, 141.
    use and disposal of, by purchaser, 210.

PROMISSORY NOTE, payment of rent by, 128, 132.

PROPERTY, capable of being let, 1.
    in goods distrained, 171.

PROPERTY TAX, when it may be deducted from rent, 119, 223.
    agreements relating to, 225.
        for payment of rent, without deducting, are void, 225.

PROPOSAL for a lease, 44.

PROSTITUTION, leases for purposes of, 201.

PROVISO FOR RE-ENTRY,
    how framed, 88.
        forms of, 323, 328, 331.
    to whom right of re-entry should be reserved, 88.
    construction of, 89—92.
    by whom lease may be determined under, 284.
    for non-payment of rent, 284.
        demand of rent, 284.
    on bankruptcy of lessee, 88.
    on severance of reversion, assignees of each part to be entitled to benefit of, 253.

PURCHASE AGREEMENT, effect of occupation under, 51.

QUARRIES, reservation of, 79, 218.

QUARTERLY TENANCY, what constitutes quarterly reservation of rent, 112.
length of notice required to determine, 265.

QUIET ENJOYMENT,
implied contract for, 229.
on word "demise," 74, 229.
duration of, 229.
how qualified or restrained, 230.
to what wrongful entry limited, 230.
what constitutes eviction, 230.
construction of ordinary covenant for, 232.
in lease of right of shooting and sporting over farm, 232.
stream of water, 232.
construction of general covenant for, 233.
special covenants for, 233.
damages on breach of covenant for, 234.
covenant for, runs with land, 247.
form of covenant for, 324.

QUITTING, terms of, 292.

RABBITS, right of tenant to shoot, 79, 260.
lessee of right of shooting, has no right to bring on to farm, 260.

RATES, by whom payable, 223, 226—228.

RE-ASSIGNMENT, discharges assignee from future liability to lessor, 249.
to whom it may be made, 249.
liabilities of successive assignees upon, 251.

RECEIPTS FOR RENT, evidence of change of tenancy, 281.

RECEIVER, distress by, 134.
notice to quit by, 271.

RECITALS in a lease, 73.

REDDENDUM, form of, 83.

REDUCTION OF RENT, effect of verbal agreement for, 117.

RE-ENTRY, PROVISO FOR, how framed, 88. *See* PROVISO FOR RE-ENTRY.

REGISTRATION OF LEASES, when necessary, 105.

RELATION of landlord and tenant, requisites to, 1.

RE-LETTING, when it deprives landlord of claim to previous rent, 231.

INDEX. 363

RELIEF,
  against forfeiture for nonpayment of rent, 288, 290.
        breach of covenant to insure, 289, 290.
  covenants for breach of which courts of equity will not grant, 291.

REMITTANCE OF RENT, by post, 129.

REMOVAL OF FIXTURES, when to be made, 296.

RENEWAL OF LEASES, to infants or married women, 6.
  by infants or married women, 6.
  of lunatics' property, 7.
  by ecclesiastical corporation, 20.
  surrender for purpose of, valid without surrender of underleases, 282.

RENT,
  reservation of, 83.
    to whom to be reserved, 83.
    mode of reservation, 84.
    net rent, meaning of, 84.
    rent payable in advance, 83.
    certainty as to amount of, 83, 131.
  covenant for payment of, 85.
    runs with the land, 247.
    lessee liable upon, after assigning lease, 250.
  what may be reserved as, 109.
  payments which are not, 110.
    sums reserved on leases of incorporeal hereditaments, 110.
            chattels, 110.
            a mere licence, 111.
            agreement for a lease, 111.
    additional rent for improvements, 111.
    payments over and above the rent, 112.
            reserved on assignments, 112.
              to stranger, 112.
  when payable, 112.
    where there is no express stipulation, 112.
    construction of express stipulations, 112.
    payment before the rent day, 114.
      on morning of rent day, 114.
  where payable, 115.
    where there is no express agreement, 115.
      tenant has covenanted to pay rent, 115.
    on lease by sovereign, 115.
  to whom payable, 115.
    agents, 115.
    under lease made by mortgagor before mortgage, 115.
      effect of notice by mortgagee, 116.

RENT—*continued.*
    to whom payable—*continued.*
        under lease made by mortgagor after mortgage, 116.
            effect of notice by mortgagee, 116.
        upon lease by joint tenants, 116.
            tenants in common, 116.
        assignment of reversion, 117.
    effect of payment to person not entitled, 117.
    amount payable, 117.
        effect of alteration in, 55.
        effect of verbal agreement for reduction, 117.
        increased rent, 118.
        set-off against rent, 118.
        deductions which may be made from rent, 119—122.
    construction of express covenants as to, 122—124.
    payment of rent after destruction of premises, 124.
            where premises are unfit for habitation, 125.
            on non-repair by landlord, 125.
    suspension of, upon eviction by landlord, 126, 231.
    apportionment of, 126.
        in respect of estate, 126.
            time, 127.
    payment of, 128.
        effect of, 129.
            in creating tenancy from year to year, 52, 53, 54.
            as act of part performance, 63.
    within what time recoverable, 151.
    right of landlord to, not barred by nonpayment, 151.
    demand of, before distress, 153.
    not recoverable under leases for illegal or immoral purposes, 200.
    remedies for recovery of, 130—189.
        distress, 131—180.
        on execution against tenant, 181—185.
        on bankruptcy of tenant, 185—187.
        action, 187—188.

RENT-CHARGE, within what time recoverable, 150.

REPAIR,
    liability of tenant as to, where there is no express agreement, 189.
        obligations of tenants at will, 189.
            from year to year, 189.
            for terms of years, 190.
                life, 190.
            underlessee, 238.
            landlord, 190.
    liability of tenant as to, where there is an express agreement, 191.

REPAIR—*continued.*
    construction of general covenant to repair, 191.
                covenant to put into repair, 193.
                keep in repair, 193.
                covenants to repair generally and to repair after notice, 194.
                conditional covenants to repair, 195.
                special agreements relating to repairs, 195.
    when liability of lessee upon covenant commences, 195.
    no relief in equity for forfeiture on breach of, 201.
    measure of damages for breach of covenant to repair, 197.
    when covenants to repair run with land, 247.

REPLEVIN, when applicable, 176.
    substantial damages not recoverable upon, 176.
    proceedings in, 176—178.
    security upon, 178.

RESCUE, remedy for, 163.
    of illegal distress, 175.

RESERVATION,
    how it differs from an exception, 77.
        construction of, 77.
            of right of hunting, shooting, &c., 79.

REVERSION,
    what is sufficient to support a distress, 132.
        tenant from year to year underletting from year to year, 136.
    effect of severance of, on lease by joint-tenants, 136.
                on conditions of re-entry, 253.
    grant of, 252.
        remedies of grantees, 252.
            lessees, 252.
        grantee may avail himself of notice to quit given by preceding owner, 271.
    when surrendered or merged, next vested estate to be deemed reversion, 283.

ROYALTY, payable to owner of brickfield, 110.

SALE UNDER DISTRESS, requisites to, 164.
    when to be made, 169, 172.
    standing corn and growing crops, 173.
    how long landlord may remain on premises for purpose of selling, 172.
    no order required to be observed upon, 170.
    of hay and straw prohibited from being carried off the premises, 170.
    where it may be made, 171.

SALE UNDER DISTRESS—*continued.*
    to whom it may be made, 171.
        to appraisers, 171.
        not to landlord, 171.
    action for not selling for best price, 170, 180.
            selling before the proper time, 173, 180.
    postponement of, 172.
        form of consent to, 172, *n.* (r).
    of cattle impounded, to recover cost of food and water, 162.

SECOND DISTRESS, cannot generally be made, 157, 175.
    when it may be made, 158, 163.

SECOND NOTICE TO QUIT, when waiver of former notice to quit, 273.

SEE, leases of lands assigned as endowment of, 19.

SEIZURE, of goods under distress, how made, 156.
    requisites to, 156.

SEPARATE USE, leases by married women of property settled to, 9.

SERVANT, occupation by, 47, 51.
    service of notice to quit upon, 271.
    of landlord, effect of tenant's becoming, 281.

SERVICE, of notice of distress, 165.
    of notice to quit, 271.
        given by landlord, 271.
            tenant, 272.

SERVICES, personal, reserved as rent, 110.

SET-OFF,
    against rent, 118.
        general rule, 118.
        on action for rent, 119.

SETTLED ESTATES, leases of, 34—41.
    lunatics', leases of, 8.
    leases of, by husbands entitled in right of wives, 10.

SEWERS' RATE, when it may be deducted from rent, 120, 223.
    tenant liable to pay, under reservation of net rent, 84.

SHEEP, when distrainable, 142, 143.

SHERIFF, duty of, on execution against tenant, 182.
    action by landlord against, 183.
    form of notice to, 183, *n.* (n).
    taking fixtures belonging to landlord, restrained by Court of Chancery, 184.

SHERIFF – *continued.*
    not to sell clover or artificial grass growing under standing corn, 208.
    not to sell off straw, turnips or manure in any case, or hay, &c. contrary to covenants, 209.
    may dispose of produce subject to agreement to expend it on land, 209.
    to send notice by post to landlord and his agent, stating that produce has been seized, 209.

SHOP,
    covenant not to use premises as, 205.
    form of, 322.

SIGNATURE, whether essential to leases, 103.

SMALL TENEMENTS, proceedings before justices for recovery of, 306.
    proceedings in county courts for recovery of, 310.

SPECIFIC PERFORMANCE,
    of contract for agreement for lease, 65.
        requisites to, 65.
        where not granted, 66.

SPORTING, construction of reservation of right of, 79, 260.
    construction of covenant for quiet enjoyment in lease of exclusive right of, 232.
        grant of leave to hunt over premises, 261.
        special agreements relating to, 261.

STAMPS, on agreements, 66.
    on leases, 93—101.
        amount of duty, 98, 99.
            how charged on produce, &c. reserved as rent, 99.
            on leases by ecclesiastical corporations, 100.
                Trinity College, Dublin, 100.
        where duty may be denoted by adhesive stamp, 101.
        where two stamps are necessary, 97.
        effect of want of, 93.
        provisions as to stamping instruments after execution, 94.
                executed abroad, 94.
        terms upon which unstamped instruments may be received in evidence, 94.
        on counterparts and duplicates, 102.
        on appraisements, 168.

STATUTES CITED. *See* INDEX OF.

STATUTORY FORM OF LEASE, 317—324.

STRANGER TO THE REVERSION, sums by way of rent reserved to, 112.

STRAW,
    distress of, 138.
        where to be impounded, 169.
        sale of, on condition that purchaser shall consume it on premises, 170.
    taken in execution, not to be sold off, 209.
    construction of agreements relating to, 212.

SUFFERANCE, tenancy by, instances of, 49.
    effect of assent of owner, 50.
    how determined, 262.

SUFFERANCE, tenant by, cannot underlet, 235.

SUNSET, distress made after, illegal, 150, 175.

SURETIES FOR RENT,
    in lease of wife's lands not acknowledged by her, 104.
    how discharged, 273.

SURRENDER, apportionment of rent upon, 126.
    express, 278.
        how to be made, 279.
    implied, 279.
        acts which constitute, 279.
            delivery and acceptance of keys, 279.
            acceptance of new lease, 280.
                by landlord of third person as tenant with consent of prior tenant, 281.
            creation of inconsistent relation, 281.
    operation of, on rights of third persons, 281.
    for purpose of renewal, valid without surrender of underleases, 282.

SUSPENSION OF RENT, on eviction from part of premises, 126.

TAIL, tenants in, leases of settled estates of lunatic, 8.
    leases by, 26.

TAXES,
    liability to pay, where there is no express agreement, 223.
        taxes which fall on landlord, 119, 120, 223.
        statutory provisions as to payment of poor rates, 224.
    agreements relating to property tax, 225.
    payment of tithe rent-charge by landlord or succeeding tenant, 225.
    construction of agreements relating to payment of, 226.

TECHNICAL TERMS, when evidence of, is admissible to explain lease, 70.

TENANCY, creation of, 1.
    different kinds of, 49.

TENANCY—*continued.*
 different kinds of—*continued.*
  by sufferance, 49.
  at will, 50.
  from year to year, 53.
  for years, 57.
  for life, 59.
 contract of, 60.
  agreements for leases, 61.
  leases, 67.
 terms of, 109.
 determination of, 262.

TENANT'S FIXTURES, what articles are, 294.

TENDER, of amends in action for irregular distress, 181.
 of rent, 167.
  what constitutes, 167.
  person distraining entitled to, 151.
  to whom to be made, 166.
  effect of, before seizure under distress, 154, 175.
   after seizure, but before impounding, 166.
   after impounding, 166.
   on distress of growing crops, 166.
  to prevent a forfeiture, 285.

TERMS, of tenancy, 109.
 of quitting, 292.

THEREABOUTS, meaning of, 77, *n.* (a).

THOUSAND, meaning of, by local usage, 71.

TILLAGES, compensation for, 300.
 landlord bound to pay for, where no incoming tenant, 301.

TIMBER, what are timber trees, 217.
 property in, 217.
  as between landlord and tenant, 217.
      third persons, 217.
  windfalls, 218.
 construction of exception of, 78.
      agreements relating to, 218.

TITHE RENT-CHARGE, when it may be deducted from rent, 120, 223.
 left unpaid by outgoing tenant, 225.

TITHES, leases of, 69.

TITLE, lessor's, to be made out on sale of lease, 252.
 implied contract as to, on agreement for lease, 64.

F.   B B

TITLE-DEEDS, cannot be distrained, 139.

TOLLS OF TURNPIKE ROADS, agreements for letting, 69, *n.* (i).

TRADE, contracts in restraint of, when valid, 202.
covenants prohibiting exercise of trade on demised premises, 203
    run with the land, 247.
    relating to trading with particular persons, 205.
fixtures, 294.

TREES, what, are timber, 217.
property in, 217.
    bushes, 218.
    windfalls of trees, 218.
construction of agreements relating to, 218.
planted by tenant, not removable by him, 294.

TRESPASS, ACTION OF, not maintainable until entry, 107.
for illegal distress, 178.

TRINITY COLLEGE, DUBLIN, stamp duty on leases by, 100.

TRUSTEE, leases by, 30.
leases to, by *cestui que trust*, 44.
in bankruptcy may dispose of lease, notwithstanding proviso or covenant against assignment, 241.
what property vests in, 257.
may disclaim onerous lease, 257.

UNDER-LEASE,
right to underlet where there is no express agreement, 235.
    tenant for years or from year to year, 235.
    tenant at will or by sufferance, 235, 264.
construction of express covenants relating to underletting, 236.
how distinguished from an assignment, 236.
surrender of, not necessary on surrender of original lease for purpose of renewal, 282.

UNDER-TENANT, implied agreement by his landlord to protect him from superior landlord's distress, 230.
when he may deduct from rent payments to original landlord, 121.
rights and liabilities of, 237.
    as against original lessor, 237.
        underlessor, 238.
        other under-tenants, 239.
original landlord cannot recover against, by notice to quit in his own name, 271.
effect of holding over by, 302.

UNIVERSITIES, leases by, 22.

INDEX. 371

UNSTAMPED INSTRUMENTS, on what terms received in evidence, 94.

USAGE. *See* CUSTOM.
when evidence of, is admitted to explain lease, 70.

USE, things in, cannot be distrained, 140.

USE AND OCCUPATION, when maintainable, 108, 188.
measure of damages in, 188.
against person in possession under contract of sale, 51.

USUAL COVENANTS, what are, 85.

USUAL FEASTS, meaning of term, 113.

VERBAL DISCLAIMER, what expressions amount to, 274.

VERBAL EVIDENCE, when admissible, 69—71.

VERBAL LEASE, in what cases valid, 68.

VOID,
lease, effect of occupation under, 51.
    payment of rent under, 53.
    acceptance of, not implied surrender, 280.
assignment, not a breach of covenant not to assign, 242.

VOLUNTARY WASTE, what amounts to, 198.

WAIVER,
of notice to quit, 272.
    by second notice to quit, 273.
        acceptance of rent, 273.
        holding over, 273.
    consent of both parties requisite to withdrawal of notice to quit, 273.
of forfeiture, 286.
    acts amounting to, 286.
        acceptance of rent due after forfeiture, 286.
        unqualified demand of rent after forfeiture, 287.
        agreement by landlord to grant new lease after expiration of forfeited lease, 287.
        advice by landlord after forfeiture, to purchase interest of lessee, 287.
        where breach of covenant causing forfeiture is continuous, 287.
of double value, 304.

WALL, ownership of, 216.

WARRANT OF DISTRESS,
    form of, 152, n. (z).
        implied indemnity to bailiff under, 152.
        express indemnity to bailiff, 153.

WASTE,
    voluntary, what constitutes, 198.
        acts of destruction, 198.
        changing nature of demised premises, 199.
    permissive, what constitutes, 199.
    liability for, of tenants for life or years, 200.
                                at will, or from year to year, 200.
    remedy for, 200.
        action at law, 200.
        injunction of court of chancery, 200.
    by tenant at will, determines his tenancy, 264.

WASTES, leases of, by lords of manors, 29.

WATER, meaning of term, 75.

WAY, RIGHT OF, under what words will pass, 76.
    leases of, 69.

WEEKLY TENANCY, length of notice required to determine, 265.

WILL, TENANCY AT, how created expressly, 50.
    when it arises by implication, 50.
        effect of payment of rent, 52.
        reservation of rent upon, 52.
    how determined, 263.
        expressly, 263.
        impliedly, 263.
            by what acts of landlord, 263.
                                tenant, 264.

WILL, TENANT AT,
    obligations of, as to repairs, 189.
                        fences, 215.
    liability of, for waste, 200.
    underleases by, 235.
    claim of, to emblements, 298.

WINDFALLS of timber, to whom they belong, 218.

WINDING-UP, distress after commencement of, 143.

WRIT, in ejectment, when it may stand in place of demand and re-entry, 285.

YEAR TO YEAR, TENANCY FROM, how distinguished from tenancy at
  will, 53.
  how created expressly, 53.
  where it arises by implication, 53, 68.
  how implication may be rebutted, 54.
  when implied tenancy commences, 56.
  when determinable, 265.
  how determinable, 265—274.
    notice to quit, 265—274.
    verbal disclaimer, 274.
  circumstances showing intention to create, 52.
  terms consistent with, 56, 57.

YEAR TO YEAR, TENANT FROM,
  obligations of, as to repairs, 189.
                      fences, 215.
  liability for waste, 200.
  right to underlet, 235.

YEARS, TENANCY FOR, how created, 57.
  what certainty requisite, 58, 80, 81.
  may be made dependent on contingency, 58.

YEARS, TENANT FOR,
  obligations of, as to repairs, 190.
                      fences, 214.
  liability of, for waste, 200.
  right to underlet, 235.

F.   C C

www.ingramcontent.com/pod-product-compliance
Lightning Source LLC
Chambersburg PA
CBHW022119290426
44112CB00008B/735